# MBTI® Step II™ Manual

# MBTI® Step II™ Manual

## Exploring the Next Level of Type with the Myers-Briggs Type Indicator® Form Q

Naomi L. Quenk
Allen L. Hammer
Mark S. Majors

cpp
Mountain View, California

CPP, Inc.
1055 Joaquin Road, 2nd Floor
Mountain View, CA 94043
800-624-1765
www.cpp.com



Printed in the United States of America.
21 20 19 18 17 16 15 14 13 31 30 29 28 27 26 25 24

# Contents

# Tables

## Chapter 1



## Chapter 2



## Chapter 3



## Chapter 4



## Chapter 5



## Chapter 6

## Chapter 7



## Chapter 8



## Chapter 9



## Chapter 10



## Appendix A



## Appendix B



## Appendix C



## Appendix D

# Figures

# Foreword

The *Myers-Briggs Type Indicator*® (MBTI®) instrument is a unique phenomenon in the history of psychological testing. It is the product of the creative genius and dedication of a brilliant mother-and-daughter team applied to the theory of psychological type formulated by Carl Gustav Jung. Katharine Cook Briggs had the vision to recognize the benefits to individuals and groups of understanding and applying Jung's theory. Her daughter, Isabel B. Myers, had the brilliance, sense of mission, and tenacity to create an inventory that could give individuals access to their Jungian preference type and thus to the rich benefits of self-knowledge. The potential of the MBTI instrument as an aid in the enhancement of human relationships is now legendary.

Briggs and Myers worked in almost total isolation for many years in a culture indifferent to, and often scornful of, the ideas of Carl Jung. Gradually, however, curious and open-minded counselors began to discover the MBTI instrument. After trying it and finding it useful to themselves and their clients, they became advocates of the rich understanding it provided into the complexity of human behavior. With its growing popularity, many of these individuals also became aware of the dangers of superficial interpretation and consequent misuse of the instrument. Over the years, a community of users emerged. It is now a worldwide community embracing ongoing learning, sound development, and ethical application of the MBTI instrument and psychological type. Members of the type community range from students who have just become aware of the MBTI instrument and Jungian theory to the most experienced practitioners. The common denominator for all is a commitment to responsible use of the instrument and to continued learning.

Since the beginning, all developmental work on the MBTI instrument has been driven by a consciously formulated mission statement and philosophy. The mission statement contains and continues the vision, mission, and goals of Myers and Briggs: "to enable individuals to grow through an understanding and appreciation of individual differences in healthy personality and to enhance harmony and productivity among diverse groups." Embodied in this philosophy is a combination of tradition and change that reflects the spirit of Jung, Briggs, and Myers. Tradition is represented by the never-ending quest for deeper understanding of emerging ideas. Change continually recognizes the possibilities of new and untried methods, and the additional insights that can be derived from research and new knowledge.

The revision of the Step II™ tool and the accompanying manual provide two graphic illustrations of the mission statement in action. The revision is the next phase in the ongoing work of Isabel Myers and Katharine Briggs. The contributors to this manual represent the next generation following in the footsteps of Katharine Briggs, Isabel Myers, and Mary McCaulley. They are among the new leaders in the community of MBTI practitioners, researchers, and theoreticians.

Members of the core team responsible for the revision of the Step II instrument with the supporting manual and materials are Naomi Quenk, Allen Hammer, Wayne Mitchell, Mark Majors, and Jean Kummerow. As co-guardians of and primary advocates for the work and values of Isabel Myers, we wish to express our deep appreciation for the integrity and excellence of their work. We also wish to acknowledge the contributions of the many other researchers, theoreticians, and practitioners who contributed to the enterprise.

The revision of the Step II tool and the creation of this manual are truly illustrations of the biblical quotation that gave rise to the title of Isabel Myers' book *Gifts Differing* and represent "each giving according to his or her gifts." Out of these "gifts differing" has come a work that maintains the integrity of the mission by expanding the knowledge and usefulness of psychological type and the *Myers-Briggs Type Indicator* instrument.

Katharine Downing Myers
Peter Briggs Myers
April 2001

# Preface

In developing the *Myers-Briggs Type Indicator* (MBTI) personality inventory, Isabel Myers' principal goal was to provide individuals with access to their Jungian type. From the time she embarked on her lifelong enterprise, she anticipated providing people with individualized information about their way of expressing their type. This manual is a realization of Myers' plan to further illuminate the qualities that contribute to each individual's unique personality.

The *MBTI® Step II™ Manual* provides users of the four-page Step II™ Profile and the seventeen-page Step II™ Interpretive Report with information for understanding and interpreting Step II facets (formerly called subscales) within the context of the Jung-Myers theory of psychological type. The Step II profile and report are obtained through computerized scoring of Form Q of the MBTI instrument. The Step II instrument builds on the respondent's understanding of his or her basic four-letter type (referred to as Step I type) by providing results on twenty facets that identify some of the component parts of the four type dichotomies. It identifies a number of the distinctive ways in which a respondent expresses the four pairs of opposites that interact to form his or her dynamic type. The Step II instrument can also be clarifying and affirming for respondents who are puzzled or curious about how they differ from others of their same basic type.

## Relationship Between the MBTI® Step I™ and Step II™ Instruments

Practitioners can most effectively interpret and apply the Step II tool by understanding its relationship to the Step I tool. The Step I tool identifies four-letter type by eliciting a person's preferences on four dichotomies—two opposite pairs of attitudes (Extraversion–Introversion and Judging–Perceiving) and two opposite pairs of mental functions (Sensing–Intuition and Thinking–Feeling). The respondent's Step I type description results from the dynamic interaction of the four preferences. The nature of these interactions is specified in the Jung-Myers theory and is expressed in the concepts of dominant, auxiliary, tertiary, and inferior functions and their respective attitudes of Extraversion or Introversion.

The Step I instrument gives us access to many of the insights and practical applications that emerge from Jung's complex personality theory and Myers' elaboration and extension of that theory. It is unique among personality measures in several ways.

The Step I assessment describes personality as a dynamic system that stems from differences in our ways of perceiving, organizing, and drawing conclusions about our perceptions. Jung postulated four basic mental functions that are used in both the outer and the inner world, each with its own distinctive characteristics. Different personality patterns develop as the result of the varying energy and focus applied to each mental function. The four MBTI dichotomies represent Myers' way of achieving her goal of offering individuals access to the benefits of knowing their Jungian psychological type. Inherent in the resulting four-letter type are the ordering of the preferences, the manner in which the preferences interact with one another, and the probable sequence in which a person's type develops. The four MBTI dichotomies interact in such a way that a personality type is far more than the sum of its four dichotomies. A person's uniqueness is more qualitative than quantitative.

Because the poles of the four MBTI dichotomies are considered equally valid and are used by all of us as we adapt to life, they are described in neutral and positive terms. There is no implication, for example, that it is better to prefer one of the two ways of making judgments, Thinking or Feeling, or one of the two ways of using energy, Extraversion or Introversion.

Each dichotomy of the MBTI personality assessment is complex and multifaceted, encompassing many different aspects or expressions. For example, a preference for

Extraversion or Introversion is expressed in a number of ways, such as sociability, reflectiveness, and preferred level of stimulation. MBTI items do not ask directly about a person's preferences on a complex dichotomy. Instead, Myers conceived of the items as "straws in the wind," pointing to behavior that is more complex than anything described by a set of items. Observing which way the straws are blown enables us to make inferences about the direction of the wind itself, or which pole of a dichotomy an individual prefers, either consciously or unconsciously.

The Step II instrument builds on the multifaceted nature of type as elicited in the Step I instrument. Step I Form M items are embedded in Form Q. Such identification can provide insight into an individual's type development and can aid in whole type identification when a Step I interpretation has not achieved clarity for a respondent. The Step II tool is an elaboration of the Step I tool and is always interpreted within the context of the dynamic whole that is the person's Step I type.

In a 1970 letter to Dr. Mary McCaulley, with whom she collaborated in developing her work on within-type differences and individual type development, Myers explained her rationale for delaying publication of this particular body of work. She stated that "type is the cake and type development is the icing on the cake. We have too much to do *now* to establish applications of the cake to spend time on the icing" (McCaulley, 1997, p. 23). In the more than 30 years since Myers made that statement, the "cake" has become quite well established, and applications of the "icing" represented by the Step II instrument now rest on a very solid foundation.

# Acknowledgments

An unusually large number of people helped bring this manual to fruition. Katharine Myers and Peter Myers helped shape the philosophy and approach to the revision. Their insights into the depth and breadth of Isabel Myers' goals for the MBTI instrument are implicit throughout the text. Jean Kummerow provided a careful critique of the manuscript, which greatly improved its accuracy and applicability. We most gratefully acknowledge the work of Wayne Mitchell. His contributions to the theoretical basis, structure, and descriptions of the Step II facets are especially evident in chapters 2 and 3, and they permeate much of the rest of the text.

Kathy Simon provided incisive and knowledgeable developmental editing of the original manuscript. Her understanding of the complexities of both the Step I instrument and the Step II instrument made our task much easier. Julianne Arnold, Project Manager at CPP, Inc., ably coordinated the many separate but interrelated facets of the project and kept everyone on track. We also appreciate the efforts of Jill Anderson-Wilson, Managing Editor, and Laura Ackerman-Shaw, Director of Publishing Services, who managed the complexities of the project with persistence and good humor. Gloria Forbes, Manager of Manufacturing and Inventory, and Kari Martell, Product Marketing Manager, both lent their expertise to the project.

A host of people in Step II workshops and in other settings volunteered their time and personalities to filling out Form Q, often answering Form K as well. Their willingness to give freely of their time and energy is greatly appreciated. We especially thank the following individuals: Margaret Howell, Sharon Hughley, Bob Jenkins, Fran Kasinof, Caprice Lantz, Peggy LeBlanc, Ernie Lopez, Patrice Lyons, Gail McCaullers, Mamie Morgan, Ann S. Morson, Sue Pressman, Linda Raymond, Jane S. Seigel, James Tulley, Bonnie Barnes Voit, Annette Wiechert, Olga Williams, and Rebecca Wilson.

PART

# The Context for the Step II™ Instrument

# I

The three chapters in part I orient readers to the historical, theoretical, and practical context within which to understand and apply the *Myers-Briggs Type Indicator* (MBTI) Step II instrument.

Chapter 1, "Introduction and Overview," reviews basic Step I type theory and reinforces the reader's understanding of type dynamics, explains the development of the Step II instrument and the changes that have occurred since its earliest (1989) introduction in the form of the Expanded Analysis Report (EAR), clarifies important differences between the Step I Form M and Step II Form Q, and identifies the differences between the 1996 Step II instrument and its current version.

Chapter 2, "Theoretical Issues and Implications of Type Theory for the Step II™ Instrument," focuses on the important theoretical and practical effects of using a type- rather than a trait-based approach to personality, discusses bipolarity and the multifaceted nature of type constructs that form the basis of the Step II tool, and places the MBTI personality inventory within the framework of general versus individualized personality descriptions. An understanding of the critical nature of these issues will help practitioners apply the Step II instrument effectively.

Chapter 3, "Descriptions of the Step II™ Facets," gives the context and rationale behind the ordering of the facets. The detailed descriptions of the poles of each facet will equip practitioners with a firm basis for understanding and explaining facet results to their clients. To aid in understanding and discriminating among the facets in each dichotomy, a final research section provides correlational evidence that shows similarities and differences among the facets.

# Introduction and Overview 1

CHAPTER OVERVIEW



The MBTI Step II instrument is the result of many years of research and observation that began with Isabel Myers' development of the MBTI personality inventory in the 1940s (see Myers & McCaulley, 1985; Myers, McCaulley, Quenk, & Hammer, 1998). The basic versions of the instrument (Form M and the earlier Form G) yield type descriptions distinguishing the sixteen types from one another but offer relatively few clues as to how people of the same type may differ. In adding items that were not scored for four-letter type, Myers' intent was to enable exploration and identification of individuality within each of the sixteen types. She was in the process of developing this aspect of her work more fully at the time of her death in 1980.

## Basic Type Theory and the Step II™ Instrument

Because the Step II instrument must be interpreted within the context of Step I four-letter type, relevant aspects of the type theory that encompasses both are summarized briefly in the following pages. For a more detailed discussion of type theory, see Jung, 1971; Myers, 1995; and Myers et al., 1998.

## The Theory of Psychological Type

A basic tenet of type theory holds that much seemingly random behavior is actually the result of differences in how we perceive the world, how we make sense of our perceptions, where we choose to direct our energy, and how we choose to live in the world. The theory thus posits interactions among four pairs of opposites, or dichotomies, two of which represent attitudes or orientations (Extraversion and Introversion, Judging and Perceiving) and two of which represent functions or processes (Sensing and Intuition, Thinking and Feeling). The poles of each dichotomy are seen as qualitatively distinct opposites that do not vary along a quantitative continuum. Type theory assumes that each person is born with a disposition to develop a preference for one or the other pole of each dichotomy. The exercise of these preferences over time results in the identification of an individual as one of sixteen qualitatively distinct types.

## Multifaceted Nature of the MBTI® Dichotomies

Each of the four dichotomies of the MBTI personality inventory is made up of a number of component parts, or facets, that represent aspects of the complex nature of the dichotomy. These dichotomies are thus termed *multifaceted.* For example, the Extraversion–Introversion dichotomy encompasses such facets as sociability, activity level, and expressiveness. A different measurement approach to Extraversion–Introversion might focus on a single facet, for example, sociability. In such an approach, the items making up that measure would ask only about the respondent's attitudes or behaviors regarding sociability.

The multifaceted nature of type dichotomies was a precondition for the development of the Step II instrument. The items Myers wrote for each dichotomy encompassed the different facets Jung and Myers had identified as aspects of the Extraversion–Introversion (E–I), Sensing–Intuition (S–N), Thinking–Feeling (T–F), and Judging–Perceiving (J–P) dichotomies. This provided the basis for Myers' long-range goal of individualizing type reports.

Building on this feature of Myers' approach, David Saunders, a psychologist and psychometrician who had worked closely with Myers during the MBTI instrument's development, factor-analyzed the combined nonscored and scored items (i.e., those used to determine the overall preferences) of Form F of the instrument. Form F contained many items that were written by Myers with a view toward identifying facets within dichotomies and that were not used to determine the overall preference. Factor analysis is a technique that groups items together based on the homogeneity of their content. Saunders identified 27 such factors, 20 of which represented facets of the four dichotomies. The remaining 7 factors were termed Comfort–Discomfort scales and are included in the *Type Differentiation Indicator* (TDI; Saunders, 1987).

Saunders subsequently formulated the 290-item Form J, which was composed of every item used by Myers in successive forms of the MBTI assessment tool. The 131-item Form K was a subset of the items in Form J and enabled identification of the twenty subscales. Five subscales were identified for each of the four familiar MBTI dichotomies. These facets were available through administration of Form K, the Step II form that preceded Form Q.[1] The revision of the Step II tool that is elicited through Form Q also identifies five subscales for each of the MBTI dichotomies.

In order to provide a Step I context for understanding Step II facet scales, tables 1.1–1.4 each define a Step I dichotomy and provide brief descriptions of the poles of the five Step II facets that make up the dichotomy.

# Type Dynamics and the Step II™ Instrument

In applying the Step II instrument, it is important to bear in mind that, with typology, the whole is greater than the sum of its parts. In other words, a four-letter type does not result from simply adding together a person's four preferences. Rather, a type is composed of interactions among the four preferences that are specified in the Jung-Myers theory. These interactions reflect the dynamic nature of type theory. In type theory, the term *dynamic* refers to the flow of psychological energy between and among the four functions included in a person's type.

## Dynamic Status of Functions

Type theory assigns a different dynamic status to each of the four functions. The dynamics of the sixteen types include the following four functions.

- The *dominant function* is most energized, accessible to the individual's control and direction, and amenable to conscious development. This function tends to be used primarily in the person's preferred attitude of either Extraversion or Introversion. For example, one person's dominant function might be extraverted Intuition while another's might be introverted Thinking.
- A complementary *auxiliary function* balances the dominant function in two ways. First, it provides balance between perception and judgment because it is one of the functions in the other function pair—that is, if the dominant function is one of the perceiving pair (Sensing or Intuition), the auxiliary function will be one of the judging pair (Thinking or Feeling), and vice versa. Second, it provides balance between Extraversion and Introversion in that the auxiliary function tends to operate primarily in the nonpreferred attitude of Extraversion or Introversion. The auxiliary function is seen as somewhat less energized and accessible to control

## Table 1.1 Facets of the Extraversion–Introversion Dichotomy

| **Extraversion (E)** *Directing energy mainly toward the outer world of people and objects* | **Introversion (I)** *Directing energy mainly toward the inner world of experiences and ideas* |
|---|---|
| *Initiating:* Find themselves acting as social facilitators. Good at mingling, small talk, meeting new people, conversing at length with almost anyone, networking, and making connections with others. | *Receiving:* Are more at ease being introduced than initiating introductions; in large groups, are more comfortable letting conversations come to them than in mixing, mingling, and initiating talk with people they don't know well. |
| *Expressive:* Readily show their feelings and make their interests obvious; express typically positive feelings; cheerful, warm, and humorous; usually find it easy to confide in others and describe themselves as easy to know. | *Contained:* Tend to be willing to share thoughts, feelings, interests, and concerns only with those they trust highly. Describe themselves as difficult to know; primary emotional responses are internal; may be difficult for them to confide in others because the more upset they become, the less they allow it to show. |
| *Gregarious:* Enjoy maintaining friendships with a diversity of people having varied interests. Skilled at communicating with different kinds of people in various settings. Maintain a wide and diverse circle of friends and acquaintances. Enjoy meeting new people. | *Intimate:* Maintain a more limited circle of close, trusted friends; tend to have a similarly concentrated range of interests and favorite activities. In group settings, prefer to talk one on one with others they know well; may be uncomfortable making chitchat with people they have just met. |
| *Active:* Favor direct involvement in active environments. Learn best by doing, listening, and questioning. Generally prefer active rather than passive entertainment. | *Reflective:* Obtain personal meaning through visual, intellectual, or mental engagement rather than through physical or verbal exchange with the environment. Learn best in quiet settings permitting extended mental reflection. |
| *Enthusiastic:* Tend to be talkative, hearty, and lively, enjoying the dynamic flow of energy in conversation for its own sake. Like being the center of attention and are adept at making group conversation into an art form. Like hearing and telling stories as a way of sharing who they are and learning about others. | *Quiet:* Appear reserved and quiet, but often have an abundance of rich internal responses to what is going on around them. Can be hard for them to find words to describe this rich interior world; may use understatement as a means of emphasis. |

*Sources:* Myers et al., 1998; Mitchell, Quenk, and Kummerow, 1997. Used with permission.

and direction, and less capable of conscious development, than the dominant function. Yet, it is still more energized, accessible, and capable of development than the tertiary and inferior functions.

- The *tertiary function* is opposite in function to the auxiliary function and is even less energized or amenable to control, direction, and conscious development. An attitude is typically not specified for the tertiary function due to alternative views on this issue. For further information on alternative views, see Myers et al., 1998.
- The *inferior function* is opposite in function and attitude to the dominant function. There is little conscious energy, and it is therefore largely unconscious and minimally subject to control, direction, and development.

**Illustration of Type Dynamics** The rationale and method for determining the dynamics of each type are beyond the scope of this manual. That information is provided in detail elsewhere, in works such as Quenk, 1993; Myers and Kirby, 1994; and Myers et al., 1998. An illustration of the practical implications of type dynamics, however, may provide readers with a basis for exploring the contribution of Step II information to Step I dynamics and development.

For this illustration, we will use an ENFP type. For an ENFP type, the dominant function is extraverted Intuition, the auxiliary function is introverted Feeling, the tertiary function is Thinking, and the inferior function is introverted Sensing. In dynamic energy terms, therefore, an ENFP has a great deal of energy available for processing ideas and insights that are directed toward the outer world and is able to control that energy. Somewhat less energized and available is auxiliary introverted Feeling, which is used to judge the worthiness and meaningfulness of the ideas and insights brought forth by extraverted Intuition. Logical analysis (tertiary Thinking) of the ENFP's inspirations is likely to be ignored in comparison because little energy and interest is available for this kind of judgment. Inferior introverted Sensing, in the form of attention to and concern for facts and details, is largely disregarded by the ENFP. Suppose that a particular ENFP shows a preference for the "Questioning" pole (Thinking pole) rather than the "Accommodating" pole (Feeling pole) of the Thinking–Feeling set of facets. Such a questioning approach in making decisions may indicate a useful development of one facet of this ENFP's tertiary (Thinking) function. Similar hypotheses about type dynamics or development can be

**Table 1.2 Facets of the Sensing–Intuition Dichotomy**

| **Sensing (S)** *Focusing mainly on what can be perceived by the five senses* | **Intuition (N)** *Focusing mainly on perceiving patterns and interrelationships* |
|---|---|
| *Concrete:* Prefer to work with and talk about things that are concrete, tangible, literal, and verifiable by the senses; this applies to perceptions, communication, learning styles, view of the world, preferences for entertainment, and values. Cautious about going beyond the facts. | *Abstract:* Prefer to focus on concepts and on the abstract meanings of ideas and the relationships among them. Comfortable with nonliteral interpretation. |
| *Realistic:* Prefer things to have useful and tangible benefits to themselves and others. Value common sense because it is practical, realistic, and, being field-tested by experience, has been shown to work. Place a high value on personal comfort and family security. | *Imaginative:* Value possibilities over tangibles. Find what might be more interesting than what is. Are resourceful in dealing with new and unusual experiences. Enjoy finding new solutions to any problem. |
| *Practical:* Prefer working with known materials and objects using familiar and practical methods. Interested in physical comfort that can be experienced in the here and now. Prefer building to innovating, are more interested in modest tangible gains than in risky opportunities for much larger gain. | *Conceptual:* Are comfortable with complexity and more intrigued by implied or inferred meanings than by meanings explicitly given, stated, or presented. Value ideas and possibilities over the tangible details of what is immediately visible. Tend to score well on tests. More willing to take risks for large potential gain. |
| *Experiential:* Use experience as the primary criterion for truth and relevance. See no gain in changing methods already proven experientially. For new tasks lacking established procedures, prefer a trial-and-error approach starting with what is already known to be the best approach. | *Theoretical:* Are convinced that the relevance of something goes beyond its relation to tangible things to its potential relation to other concepts and ideas. Less interested in what is already discovered or well known. Prefer to explore the world by seeking new connections among abstract concepts and ideas. Resourceful and insightful in approaching new tasks. |
| *Traditional:* Prefer traditions and conventions because they provide continuity, security, and validation by one's social environment. Uncomfortable with fads and practices running against traditional norms because they lack the validating tests of time, experience, and societal approval. | *Original:* Value originality as means of self-expression and a way of infusing meaning into day-to-day activities; may be clever, inventive, adventurous, and enterprising. Take the initiative to expound their original ideas. Find variety conveys meaning and progress while sameness detracts from meaning. |

*Sources:* Myers et al., 1998; Mitchell, Quenk, and Kummerow, 1997. Used with permission.

made for a wide variety of individual patterns of responding on the Step II facets.

## Dynamic Characteristics of Whole Types

In spite of this hypothesized hierarchy of dynamic energy, however, Jung and Myers specified that every person's typological makeup includes the ability to use each function and each attitude at least some of the time. Step II facets may be used to explore the expression of nonpreferred functions and their associated attitudes. The data presented in chapter 5 (interpreting and verifying) and chapter 8 (validity) also provide evidence for dynamic differentiation among the sixteen types. As a reminder, table 1.5 (p. 9) summarizes the dynamic characteristics of the sixteen types.

## The Dynamic Nature of the Step I™ Instrument

Just as each of the sixteen whole types is more than the sum of its four preferences, each type dichotomy is more than the sum of its facets. There are two reasons for this.

First, there may be additional facets of each dichotomy that have not yet been identified. The number of identifiable facets is limited by the pool of items available. It is possible that a broader pool of items might yield additional facets of one or more of the dichotomies. However, experience with the MBTI revision has demonstrated the difficulty of writing items that accurately separate people into types, so the addition of new items is not a trivial matter.

Second, the number of possible interactions among the twenty facets and between the facets and the four dichotomies is so great and implies such complexity that it is beyond complete comprehension. Even if we were confident of the accuracy of a person's four-letter type and the individual facet results, we would not fully grasp the totality of any individual's typological makeup. Nevertheless, Step II facet information gives us considerably increased insight and a better understanding of a person's individuality within his or her type.

**Dichotomous Nature** The Step I and Step II instruments are integrally related to each other in both their underlying assumptions and their style and format. For example, just as the Step I tool describes the opposite type preferences in neutral or positive terms, so the opposite poles of the twenty facets are described as equally acceptable and valuable. However, the dichotomous nature of a few of the

**Table 1.3 Facets of the Thinking–Feeling Dichotomy**

| Thinking (T)<br>*Basing conclusions on logical analysis with a focus on objectivity and detachment* | Feeling (F)<br>*Basing conclusions on personal/social values with a focus on understanding and harmony* |
|---|---|
| *Logical:* Believe that the world and the people in it are best understood through logic and reason. Rights, fairness, and reasonableness are highly valued standards for relationships, and generally more dependable than feelings. | *Empathetic:* Believe relationships are the source of meaning and truth in life. Truth is personal as well as universal, and is never detached from people. Feelings and relationships are more important than rights. |
| *Reasonable:* Are demonstrably logical in everyday decision making; make effective use of sequential reasoning; confident and clear thinking. | *Compassionate:* Take into consideration the unique and personal individual needs of others; value mercy over fairness. |
| *Questioning:* Believe that challenging and questioning are justified in order to understand, to solve problems, to find a common ground with other people, or to expose the flaws in an opposing viewpoint. | *Accommodating:* Value harmony highly. Believe challenge and confrontation are less effective than seeking to incorporate diverse viewpoints into compromises that will satisfy as many people as possible. |
| *Critical:* Regard criticism as justified as a means for getting at the truth, and expect others to accept it impersonally. Believe criticism helps in setting things right, getting at the truth, improving ideas, situations, or procedures, and avoiding the consequences of flawed plans, decisions, or viewpoints. | *Accepting:* Are kind and tolerant toward others and expect others to respond in the same way. View "win-win" resolutions of problems as possible and worth striving for. |
| *Tough:* After a considered appraisal of situations, possibilities, and people involved, stand firm in their decisions. Believe that to do otherwise would be to reject all of the logic, reason, questioning, and critique that went into the decision that was made. | *Tender:* Use affection and gentleness to achieve their objectives; behind their tenderness lies an awareness that there are two mutually contradictory sides to many issues, making it impossible to reach purely rational resolutions. |

*Sources:* Myers et al., 1998; Mitchell, Quenk, and Kummerow, 1997. Used with permission.

twenty facets is somewhat less well defined than is the case for the four MBTI dichotomies (E–I, S–N, T–F, J–P). This is likely due to the small number of items in each facet scale, since this makes the establishment of a true midpoint problematical. It is also a function of the specificity of some of the facets, which may appear in a form similar to behavioral traits.

**Facet Results** Facet results, as components of each of the four dichotomies, give us insight into an individual's distinctive ways of expressing type. Particular patterns of facet scores within dichotomies may reflect the ways in which less preferred aspects of personality are expressed. The particular components of a dichotomy that may be evidence of such expression of less preferred aspects will vary with each person, perhaps reflecting individual accommodations to life experiences and environmental pressures.

Habitual use of one or another aspect of a dichotomy may be reflected in particular facet scores that occur at or near the pole opposite the underlying preference (out-of-preference response) or in the middle of the range of possible scores (midzone response). Interpreting these variations within Step I type can enrich our understanding of individual type development and differentiation. Hypothetically, the more narrow or context-specific the behavior involved, the more likely it is that out-of-preference and midzone responses will occur. This will be especially true if a person must operate in a context that requires or rewards behavior associated with the facet pole opposite the underlying preference. For example, many people who report an underlying preference for a Perceiving attitude (P) score as Early Starting (the J facet pole) rather than Pressure-Prompted (the P facet pole) on the Early Starting–Pressure-Prompted facet of the J–P block. This facet focuses narrowly on a person's approach to meeting deadlines. The demands of the workplace require and reward employees who begin tasks far enough ahead of time that they do not subject themselves and others to last-minute time pressures.

Step I understanding of type provides knowledge of whole type through the interaction of four type preferences, while Step II facets are appropriately interpreted and applied within the context of Step I understanding. Together, the Step I and Step II instruments provide a powerful, wide-ranging, and affirmative way of helping people recognize and use their individuality.

## Development of the Step II™ Instrument

With the publication of *Manual: MBTI® Expanded Analysis Report* (Saunders, 1989), MBTI practitioners had access to self-reports that contained more-detailed descriptions

**Table 1.4 Facets of the Judging–Perceiving Dichotomy**

| **Judging (J)**<br>***Preferring the decisiveness and closure that result from dealing with the outer world using one of the judging processes (T or F)*** | **Perceiving (P)**<br>***Preferring the flexibility and spontaneity that result from dealing with the outer world using one of the perceiving processes (S or N)*** |
|---|---|
| *Systematic:* Prefer orderliness in many areas of their lives, ranging from the physical environment of work and home, to the planning and scheduling of tasks and leisure activities, to the systematic methods with which they approach all of these things. | *Casual:* Have a high tolerance for surprise; are comfortable taking things as they come and adjusting their activities as necessary; are typically described as leisurely. Do not necessarily value closure in decisions, preferring to keep their options open as long as possible. |
| *Planful:* Prefer to plan and schedule leisure time and activities well in advance. Value such planning because it ensures they will not miss the things that are worth planning for. | *Open-Ended:* Prefer to make decisions on the spur of the moment; value freedom, live in the here and now, and like to "go with the flow." Dislike being tied down by long-range plans; want plans to be flexible. |
| *Early Starting:* Like to allow plenty of time so that an activity can be carried out efficiently, without fuss and bother; accomplish the most by doing one thing at a time and seek to structure their lives in accordance with this rule. May become inefficient under the stress of working right up until the last minute on a deadline. | *Pressure-Prompted:* Work best, most creatively, and with the most energy under the stress of an imminent deadline. Their seeming procrastination is often a gestational period during which they are generating the ideas and inspiration to do their best work. |
| *Scheduled:* Are comfortable with routine; regard tried methods and tested routines as the only reliable, efficient way to get things done; routine provides an important degree of comfort and security. | *Spontaneous:* Work best and with greatest energy when they have constant variety or the freedom to decide what tasks they will do when. Newness and variety are highly valued. The worst fate of all is to end up in a rut at work or home where the routine never changes. |
| *Methodical:* Strongly prefer to organize the materials, tools, people, and sequence of steps that are required to complete complex projects. Good at following sequenced directions and may be uncomfortable if there is no way to tell what needs to be done when. | *Emergent:* Take an informal, ad hoc approach to problem solving; plunge ahead without detailed plans. May not read directions before starting the assembly of kits. Are good at unstructured projects requiring improvisation. |

*Sources:* Myers et al., 1998; Mitchell, Quenk, and Kummerow, 1997. Used with permission.

of the four type dichotomies and the bipolar preferences they encompass. The 131-item Form K was scored for type based on Form G items and scoring. Its twenty facets are described in *Manual: MBTI® Expanded Analysis Report* (Saunders, 1989), the *Interpretive Guide for the MBTI® Expanded Analysis Report* (Kummerow & Quenk, 1992a), and the *Workbook for the MBTI® Expanded Analysis Report* (Kummerow & Quenk, 1992b).

The original EAR was not widely used by type practitioners. However, changes that accompanied the renamed Step II scoring system in 1996, publication of a new and more accessible profile, and the availability of a computerized individual report have dramatically increased both interest and use. Consequently, the vast majority of current users of the Step II tool are unfamiliar with the earlier EAR.

Readers who are interested in characteristics of the earlier version are directed to appendix A for a description of the differences between the 1996 Step II instrument and the EAR. The present manual focuses on differences between the previous Step II tool, published in 1996, and the current (2001) version.

In 1996, as part of an ongoing revision process, the following changes were made: The names and order of presentation of some of the facets were changed (see table A.1, in appendix A; appendix A also includes the rationale for name and order changes); the EAR was renamed the MBTI® Step II™ Expanded Profile (Myers & Briggs, 1996); a 3-page profile replaced the former 1-page profile; and a 24-page individualized report of results was made available in the MBTI® Step II™ Expanded Interpretive Report: Form K (Quenk & Kummerow, 1996).

A user's guide titled *MBTI® Step II™: A Description of the Subscales* was published and then revised (Mitchell, Quenk, & Kummerow, 1997, 1999). The information included in these publications was based on a large accumulation of clinical, experiential, and empirical data and greatly increased our understanding of how the facets help identify an individual's distinctive type.

In 1998, Form M, the current standard form of the MBTI personality inventory, was published, along with the revised *MBTI® Manual* (Myers et al., 1998).

## Statistical Basis for the Step II™ Instrument

Form M is the first MBTI form to use a national sample for scale development and to apply item response theory (IRT) for both selection and scoring of responses. All previous MBTI forms used Myers' prediction ratio method for selection and scoring. Nearly half the items now on Form M are modifications of items that had been written earlier by

**Table 1.5 Dynamic Characteristics of the Sixteen Types**

| Whole Type | Hierarchy of Functions: Dominant | Auxiliary | Tertiary* | Inferior |
|---|---|---|---|---|
| ESTJ | Extraverted Thinking | Introverted Sensing | Intuition | Introverted Feeling |
| ENTJ | Extraverted Thinking | Introverted Intuition | Sensing | Introverted Feeling |
| ISFP | Introverted Feeling | Extraverted Sensing | Intuition | Extraverted Thinking |
| INFP | Introverted Feeling | Extraverted Intuition | Sensing | Extraverted Thinking |
| ISTP | Introverted Thinking | Extraverted Sensing | Intuition | Extraverted Feeling |
| INTP | Introverted Thinking | Extraverted Intuition | Sensing | Extraverted Feeling |
| ESFJ | Extraverted Feeling | Introverted Sensing | Intuition | Introverted Thinking |
| ENFJ | Extraverted Feeling | Introverted Intuition | Sensing | Introverted Thinking |
| ESTP | Extraverted Sensing | Introverted Thinking | Feeling | Introverted Intuition |
| ESFP | Extraverted Sensing | Introverted Feeling | Thinking | Introverted Intuition |
| INTJ | Introverted Intuition | Extraverted Thinking | Feeling | Extraverted Sensing |
| INFJ | Introverted Intuition | Extraverted Feeling | Thinking | Extraverted Sensing |
| ISTJ | Introverted Sensing | Extraverted Thinking | Feeling | Extraverted Intuition |
| ISFJ | Introverted Sensing | Extraverted Feeling | Thinking | Extraverted Intuition |
| ENTP | Extraverted Intuition | Introverted Thinking | Feeling | Introverted Sensing |
| ENFP | Extraverted Intuition | Introverted Feeling | Thinking | Introverted Sensing |

*An attitude (Extraverted or Introverted) is not specified for the tertiary function column, as there are differences of opinion about this issue. See page 30 of the *MBTI® Manual* (Myers et al., 1998) for more information.

Myers or are new to the MBTI instrument. The Step II revision addressed in this manual incorporated all Form M items and thus enabled determination of four-letter type. It also allowed the new Form M items to be placed on their facet scales, enhancing the reliability and validity of the scales.

A second national sample was drawn for development of the current revision of the Step II instrument. (See chapter 6 and appendix B for a description of the national sample.) Although most of the names and essential meanings of the facet scales have been retained in this revision, the items that constitute the facet scales, associated item weights, and descriptions of facet scale meanings emerged from data collected from this national sample. Newly created Form M items were incorporated into the revised facet scales, and existing items were added or deleted from particular facet scales as warranted by data analyses. The result is an instrument with greatly enhanced internal consistency and a wealth of information about the relationship between the facet scales and a variety of dependent variables. This manual provides the basic knowledge necessary to understand, interpret, and apply the revised Step II tool in all appropriate settings.

## Terminology Changes Introduced with Form Q

It should be noted that the term *facet* has generally replaced the previous term *subscale* in this revision of the Step II instrument. As an analogy, just as the facets of a diamond subtly reflect its different qualities, so the facets of each type dichotomy reflect some of the nuances of the underlying construct. This terminology change is consistent with similar language changes that were instituted with the publication of Step I Form M and the revised *MBTI® Manual* (Myers et al., 1998). The term *dichotomy* replaced the term *scale* in referring to E–I, S–N, T–F, and J–P, and in psychometric discussions the term *preference scale* is often used. Similarly, the term *facet scale* is used in psychometric discussions in this manual.

## Research Presentation

Since the publication of Form J and Form K, a rich combination of research and clinical and observational data about the twenty facets has accumulated. Their meaning and expression through attitudes and behaviors were first presented in detail in Kummerow and Quenk's *Interpretive Guide for the MBTI® Expanded Analysis Report* (1992a) and its companion *Workbook for the MBTI® Expanded Analysis Report* (1992b), and more recently in the MBTI® Expanded Interpretive Report Form K (Quenk & Kummerow, 1996) and its current revision as the MBTI® Step II™ Interpretive Report Form Q (Quenk & Kummerow, 2001). The information in these works makes explicit Isabel Myers' foundation for individualized type reports.

Readers should note that relevant information in an earlier user's guide (Mitchell, et al., 1997) has been incorporated into this manual when appropriate. The 2001 manual supplants the 1997 user's guide as well as the earlier manual for the EAR (Saunders, 1989) and its interpretive guide (Kummerow & Quenk, 1992a).

## Comparison of the Step II™ Form Q and Step I™ Form M Instruments

People who are familiar with the Step I tool and new to the Step II tool are sometimes confused by differences between the scale lengths and by the graphical representation of client results. The Step II tool differs in several ways from the standard Form M of the MBTI assessment. Its twenty facet scales result from answers to 144 items, whereas Form M requires 93 items to elicit an individual's preference on each of the four MBTI dichotomies. Form Q includes every one of these 93 items. The additional items in Form Q, in combination with the 93 Form M items, allow for the scoring of scales describing various facets of the MBTI dichotomies.

Form Q and Form M also differ in the derivation of their scales, their graphical representation, and the methods used to appropriately interpret their results. The important similarities and differences between the Step I and Step II tools are summarized below.

### Items Used

- Step I results are based on responses to the 93 items of Form M that yield an individual's four preferences and the clarity of those preferences. Preference clarity is reported as the preference clarity index (pci) or preference clarity category (pcc).
- Step II results are based on responses to the 144 items of Form Q that elicit client preferences on the twenty Step II facet scales. The 93 items of Form M are included in Form Q.

### Scoring Methods and Weighting

- Step I scoring uses item response theory (IRT) to identify a person's preferences on the four familiar MBTI dichotomies, E–I, S–N, T–F, and J–P. For a detailed description of this method, see Myers et al., 1998.
- Step II scoring of the twenty facet scales also uses IRT. A response is assigned a weight based on the amount of information it contributes. The IRT weights and final facet scale transformation result in an eleven-point facet scale score that identifies the clarity of a person's preference for one pole or the other of the particular facet scale.

### Graphic Array of Results

- Step I Form M preferences are arbitrarily set up so that scores to the left of the midpoint are associated with E, S, T, or J preferences. Thus, the graph of Form M results shows E, S, T, and J preferences to the left of the midpoint and I, N, F, and P preferences to the right of the midpoint. Clarity of preference is reported as a pci that ranges from 1 to 30. A midpoint separates the two poles of a preference. Figure 1.1 shows a sample Form M profile for an INTP.
- Step II facet scale results are similarly arrayed with scores to the left of a 0 center point associated with the E, S, T, or J facets of a dichotomy and scores to the right with I, N, F, or P facets. Clarity of preference is reported as a score of 1 through 5 on either side of 0. Although a score of 0 separates the two poles of a facet, for interpretive purposes, the dividing area is termed a *midzone* that encompasses scores of 1 to the left of 0, 0, and 1 to the right of 0. The rationale and meaning of this midzone are explained in chapter 5. Figure 1.2 shows the Step II profile for the INTP whose Step I profile appears in figure 1.1.

### Goal of Scoring Methods

- Step I scoring identifies a respondent as either E *or* I, S *or* N, T *or* F, J *or* P. The four preferences together identify the person's whole type and its associated type dynamics.
- Step II scoring identifies some of a respondent's distinctive expressions of his or her whole type. This often occurs with habitual use of some facets of the less preferred pole of a dichotomy. An individual's facet scale scores may thus be at the same pole as the underlying preference (in-preference), at the pole opposite the underlying preference (out-of-preference), or in the midzone (0 or 1).

For example, a person whose Step I results indicate an underlying preference for Extraversion could have many different facet scale patterns, such as the following: all five E–I facet scales associated with the E pole; three scores at the E pole, one score at the I pole, and one score in the midzone (0 or 1); two scores at the E pole and three scores in the midzone; or three scores at the E pole and two scores at the I pole.

Thus, one client's Step II profile may show scores across the whole range of eleven data points, another client may have scores that are concentrated at the pole that represents the underlying preference, and another client may have scores concentrated around the midzone. Exploring the possible meanings of these arrays with the client is a major focus in profile interpretation.

Occasionally, a person's facet scale results may seem to "contradict" Step I results, as when three, four, or (even more rarely) five of the facet scales are toward one pole but the reported preference is at the opposite pole. This *may* suggest that the client's Step I preference on that dichotomy has not been accurately reported. It could also reflect a living or working situation in which the person is required to use or is rewarded for using the opposite preference, at least as measured by the facets we have available. Step II facet scale information may prove clarifying for such a client.

**The five facet scale scores do not "add up" to a person's Form M preference clarity index.**

It is also important for interpreters to understand the psychometric reason that underlies such a seeming contra-

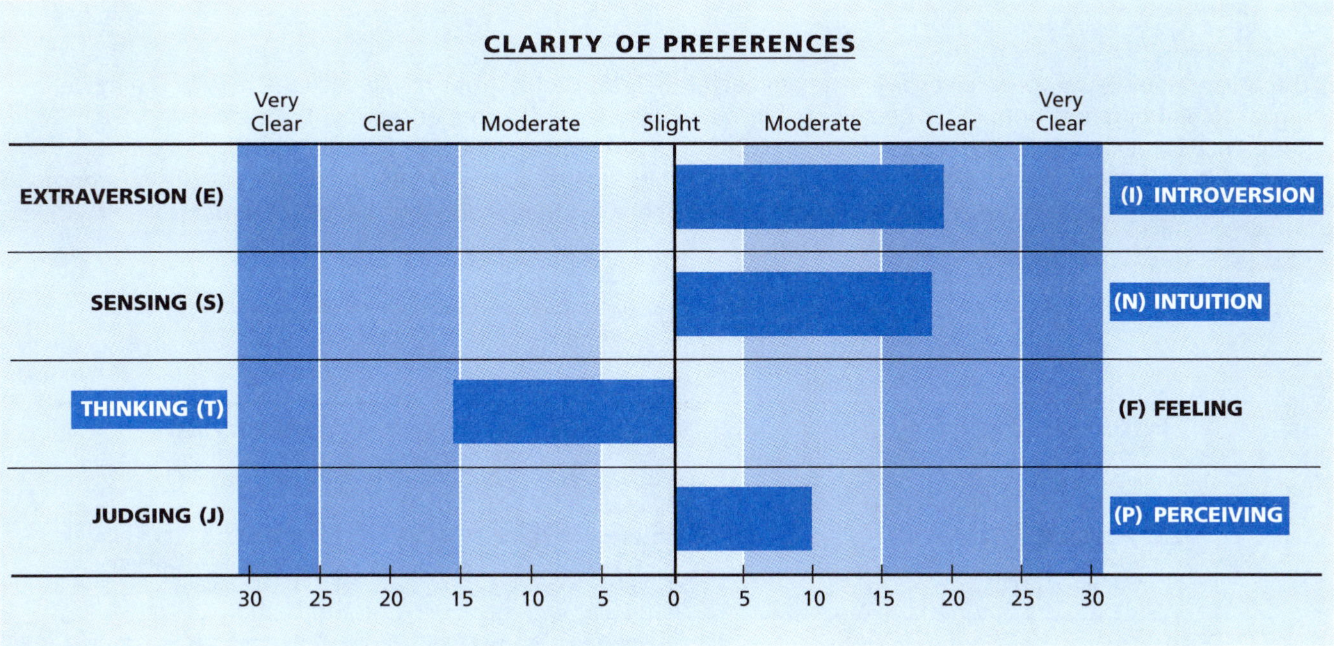


Figure 1.1 Sample Form M Profile for an INTP

*Note:* The profile design shown here is the one that appears on Step II profiles, not the profile design presented when standard Form M has been administered.

diction in type results, namely the following important fact about the two scoring methods: An individual's Step I preference clarity is based on a specially selected set of MBTI items that are assigned weights using IRT, a complex statistical procedure. A Step II facet scale score is based on a different subset of items (also scored using IRT), some of which are not even part of the Step I item pool. IRT scoring therefore assigns very different weights to facet scale items. In each case, the weights are determined by the criterion. In the case of the Step I tool, the criterion is accurate classification into one of two poles of the overall dichotomy. In the case of the facet scales, the criterion is accurate classification at one of two poles of the facet, without reference to the overall preference.

## Comparison of Earlier (1996) and Current Versions of the Instrument

A number of features in the two versions of the instrument are essentially the same, while others are different.

### Similarities

- Both versions of the Step II instrument have twenty facet scales, five for each of the four dichotomies. The twenty facet scales are in the same order.
- Results are available as either a profile (formerly 3 pages in length and now 4 pages) or an interpretive report (formerly 24 pages, now 18 pages). Both profile and report provide a summary page of scoring details for the interpreter's use, as did the 1996 version.

### Differences

- Current facet scales are based on a sample that was balanced by type and drawn from a random sample of the U.S. population; earlier facet scales used a sample of convenience in the form of all cases available for analysis. Although the samples of convenience were very large, the new sample is more representative of the U.S. population.
- Items for the revised facet scales were chosen by a process of exploratory and confirmatory factor analysis followed by final item selection utilizing IRT; the previous facet scales were derived from exploratory factor analysis only.
- Facet scale item content and relative item weightings are slightly to moderately different on most facet scales, and facet descriptions have been modified to accommodate changes in some of the item content.
- Form M rather than Form G four-letter type is reported.
- Scores are now arrayed in relation to a center point of 0, with 5 data points identified in the direction of each pole of the bipolar facets; the earlier version arrayed scores from 0 through 10, with scores near the 0 pole associated with E, S, T, and J preferences and scores near the 10 pole associated with I, N, F, and P preferences.
- There are two name changes: *Active* replaces *Participative* to form the Active–Reflective facet; *Conceptual* replaces

## Your Step II™ Results

The graphs show how you express five facets of each MBTI dichotomy. Your results indicate how you may be similar to and different from other people of your personality type. The longer the bar, the clearer your preference is for that pole of the facet. Scores of 2–5 that are on the same side as your overall preference indicate in-preference results. Scores of 2–5 on the opposite side of your preference indicate out-of-preference results. Scores of 0 and 1 are in the midzone and often mean a situational or muted use of either pole.

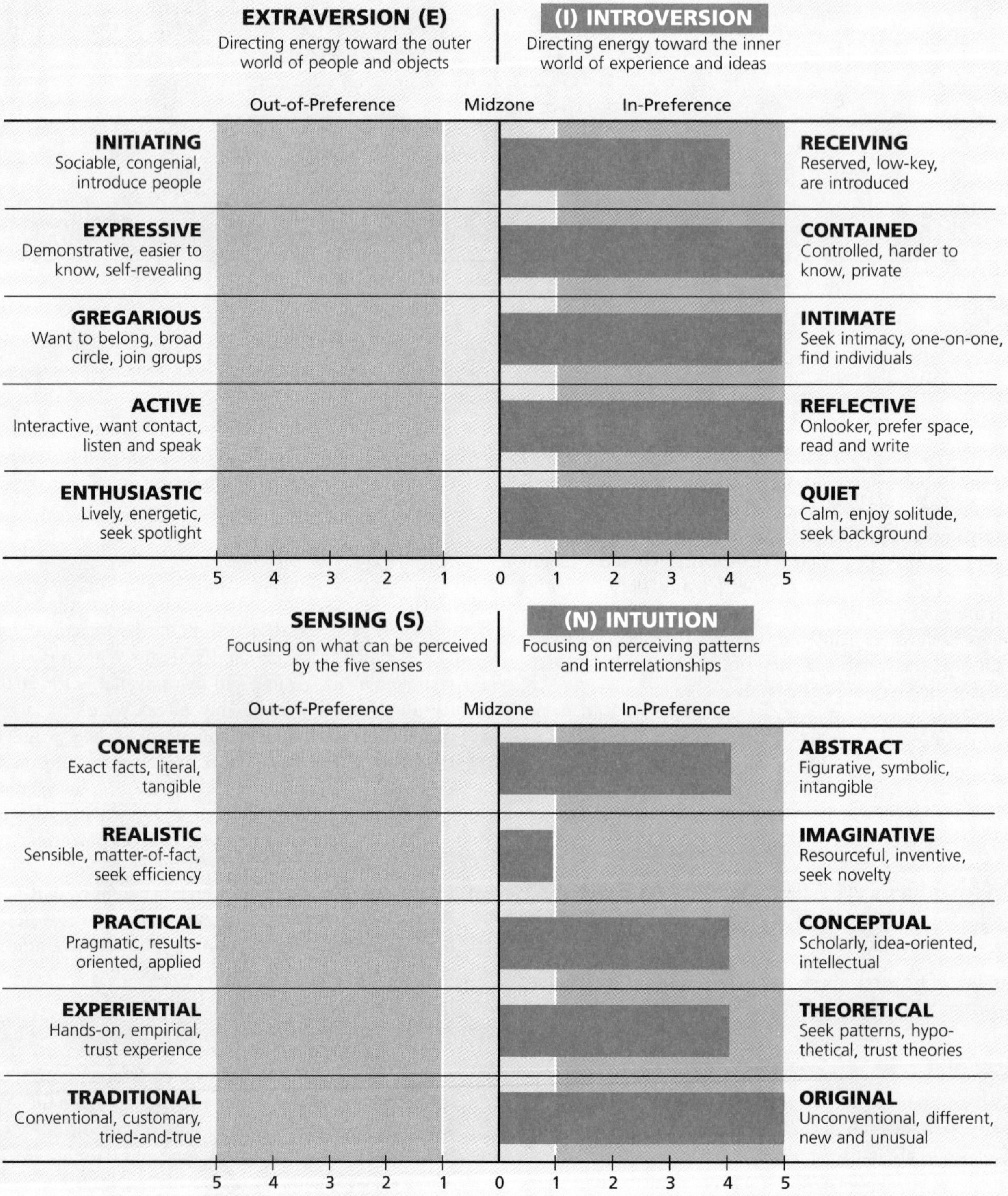


Figure 1.2 Sample Step II™ Profile for an INTP

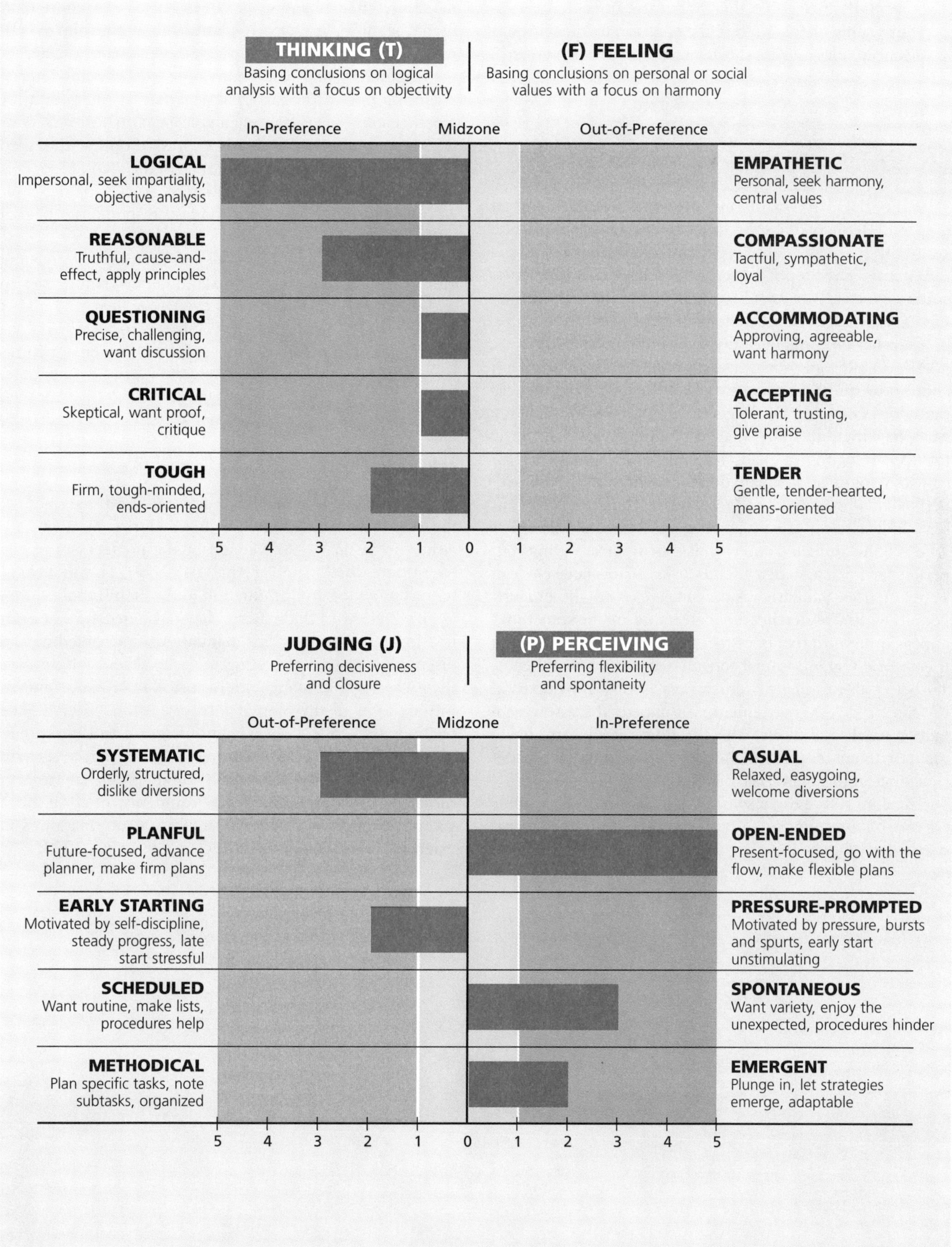


Figure 1.2 Sample Step II™ Profile for an INTP, *continued*

*Inferential* to become the Practical–Conceptual facet. These name changes retain the appropriate meanings of the facet poles and are shorter and simpler descriptors.[2]

## Uses of the Step II™ Instrument

Type theorists have maintained for years that each person is simultaneously like everyone else of the same type, like some others of the same type, and like no others of the same type. The Step II instrument zeroes in on the "like some others of the same type" issue and lets us see just how a respondent can simultaneously be like everyone else of his or her type and like only some others of that type.

The Step II tool provides substantially more information about how the respondent exercises basic type preferences than does Form M. The facets represent some of the many ways in which an individual may express the eight basic type preferences. For example, Step II results make it possible to explore and explain differences between two Extraverts, one who is quiet and reserved in certain settings but has a large circle of friends and acquaintances, and the other who is quite animated and enthusiastic in most settings but prefers having a few close friends rather than a large circle of acquaintances. Similarly, results can give us insight into why people with a preference for Perceiving might sometimes appear quite orderly about meeting deadlines or planning their work. Organizational consultants working with teams are better able to identify differences among individuals of the same type that may enhance or impede the way a team works together, and researchers studying groups are able to identify differences that are not apparent within the broader categories of the eight basic preferences.

The Step II tool can also be of help in exploring possible reasons for a respondent's uncertainty about his or her type, particularly when the clarity of a preference is slight or moderate. It can show us which facets are consistent, inconsistent, or not clearly identifiable within the overall preference. We can then form a hypothesis about whether the respondent simply has not expressed a clear preference regarding *any* of the facets of a particular dichotomy, or whether some facets from each pole are clearly preferred, or whether a preference is clearly expressed only with regard to one particular facet of either pole of the dichotomy. This kind of information about different aspects of the preferences can guide us in clarifying a respondent's overall preference.

Practitioners can find more information about using Step II results to better understand clients' similarities to and differences from others of their type in parts I and II of the *MBTI® Step II™ User's Guide: Practitioner's Tool for Making the Most of Step II™ Interpretations* (Quenk & Kummerow, 2011).

## Conclusion

This manual is designed for practitioners who are new to the Step II instrument and for those who are familiar with either its earlier, 1996, version or the predecessor of the Step II tool, the Expanded Analysis Report. This first chapter has provided an introduction to the Step II tool, as well as an overview of the issues to be considered and the context for understanding this manual. Also presented was an orientation to understanding the Step II tool within type theory as a whole, along with historical information and an introduction to the Step II facet scales and profile. The chapters that follow cover administration and interpretation of the Step II assessment; research relevant to its construction, reliability, and validity; and appropriate uses of the Step II tool in different environments. In addition to several appendices containing supporting information is an extensive glossary of terms, which begins on page 193.

# Theoretical Issues and Implications of Type Theory for the Step II™ Instrument

# 2

CHAPTER OVERVIEW

Type Versus Trait View of Personality

Bipolarity in Jungian Theory

Multifaceted Type Constructs

General Versus Individualized Personality Descriptions

Conclusion

The Jung-Myers theory differs from many other current personality theories in assuming that a large proportion of differences in personality and behavior can be successfully explained and predicted using a personality typology. The typology postulates qualitatively distinct categories of perception, judgment, and energy use that combine in a way that identifies sixteen distinctive types. Because the Step II instrument is properly understood within the context of the Jung-Myers theory of psychological type (see chapter 1 for a more detailed description of type theory), there are several conceptual and measurement concerns that are relevant to understanding, interpreting, and applying the Step II tool.

A central issue, familiar to most *Myers-Briggs Type Indicator* (MBTI) practitioners, is the fact that the MBTI personality inventory is designed to identify qualitatively different *types* and not quantitatively varying *traits*. The theoretical implications of this feature of type theory are explored in this chapter, and its implications for accurate interpretation of both the Step I and Step II instruments are covered in chapter 5. This chapter also presents three other theoretical issues relevant to the Step II tool: the implications of the bipolarity approach to personality, the importance of the concept of multifaceted type constructs and its practical implications for the Step II tool, and the MBTI approach to the issue of general versus individualized personality descriptions. These four interrelated issues together contribute to the elegance of the theory of psychological type.

## Type Versus Trait View of Personality

For those who are new to the field of personality or to the MBTI instrument, the notion of personality types may seem like just a shorthand way of talking about the differences among people. But looking at personalities as types is quite different from seeing them as a series of traits. Therefore, a primary concern in administering, interpreting, and applying the MBTI instrument is the common tendency of both practitioners and clients to misinterpret type categories as trait variables.

### Contrasting the Two Approaches

The type approach is in marked contrast to existing trait theories that attempt to explain and predict differences in personality and behavior by identifying a number of individual personality and behavioral traits. Individual differences among people are then attributed to varying *amounts* of the identified traits.

For many of the commonly measured traits, such as anxiety, dominance, and autonomy, there is either an explicit or an implicit assumption about how much of the trait is desirable. For example, we may assume that too much anxiety can lead to an inability to perform well or may even require a person to take medication in order to function, while at the same time we may associate too little anxiety with low energy and insufficient motivation. A very dominant person may be seen as overbearing and intolerant; one who does not exhibit much of this trait may be considered weak and ineffectual. "Too much" autonomy may describe a rebellious, antisocial person, and "too little" may describe an extreme conformist. For traits such as these, the best or "healthiest" amount to have would apparently be an "average" amount, but for other traits—for example, intelligence—a greater amount is preferable to an average amount.

Because type theory assumes equally legitimate but qualitatively different opposite categories, amounts of a type preference are irrelevant. Scores are primarily a device by which to accomplish the task of sorting individuals into the categories to which they already belong. A person is free and able to use either pole of a dichotomy but generally experiences and expresses a preference for one pole over the other.

One pole of a dichotomy is never defined relative to an amount or degree of the other pole. For example, Thinking is not defined as a deficit in Feeling, nor is Feeling defined as a deficit in Thinking. They are two separate and distinctly different ways of arriving at conclusions.

Table 2.1 summarizes the important ways in which trait-based instruments and the MBTI instrument differ.

### Implications of Studying Types Rather Than Traits

The implications of looking at personalities as types as opposed to a series of traits are significant enough that when we start talking about average scores for people in general (called *norms* by those in the field), we must approach them quite differently than when they pertain to MBTI types.

The Jung-Myers theory regards personality types as distinct wholes that cannot be described by looking at just one of the dichotomies. Further, the theory says that types are not just labels. They are frameworks for developmental processes that unfold over an entire life span and proceed differently for each type. Myers was therefore sensitive to gender and age as influences on individual expression of type.

When we are trying to see what is "normal" or "typical" on the Step II facet scales, we cannot just collect a large number of people and compute average scores. Instead, we must consider the differences that may be caused by type, age, and gender. Taking the average scores of a large sample of adults and reporting the data in a table as the "normal" scores for adults in general would be very misleading. If types are real and not just convenient labels, and if a person's type influences how Step II items are answered, then these results would not tell us anything about specific types. More important, the average scores in the table would be influenced by how many of each type were in our sample. So if the sample had a lot of ESTJs and not very many ISFPs, the average scores in the table would be overweighted by ESTJ responses and underweighted by those of ISFPs. Even if we used a sample that was balanced for all sixteen types, as was done in relevant analyses in the Step II revision, important information would be lost because averages for the population at large would not show us how each type differs from the others. We also would not be able to see differences due to age or gender. Therefore, meaningful comparative data should be arrayed for each type, for each gender, and for different age categories.

**Normative Data for the Step II™ Tool** The national sample that served as the basis for the Step II revision did not contain enough subjects to permit presentation of data in such type-specific gender and age categories. With the accumulation of larger samples for the Step II tool, tables detailing average scores within these categories will become available, providing useful information for individual interpretation and for validating the Jung-Myers theory. At present, however, data are only available for each of the sixteen types, disregarding gender and age, and can be found in appendix B as well as on the Interpreter's Summary page

**Table 2.1 Differences Between Trait-Based Instruments and the MBTI® Instrument**

| Trait Instruments | MBTI® Instrument |
|---|---|
| Assume universal qualities—people vary only in the amount of the trait possessed. | Assumes qualitatively distinct categories—individuals prefer one or the other category. |
| Measure the amount of each trait. | Sorts individuals into one or the other category. |
| Scores are expected to be normally distributed—most scores are in the middle. | Scores are expected to be bimodal—few scores at the midpoint. |
| Scores are variables that show how much of the trait a person has. | Scores are estimates of confidence in the accuracy of the sorting procedure—placement into the category indicated. |
| Interpretive interest is in people at the extremes of the distribution. | Interpretive interest is in people near the midpoint, where accuracy of sorting may be in doubt. |
| Assume that behavior is caused by relevant underlying traits. | Assumes that behavior is an expression of underlying type preferences. |
| Assume that traits are largely independent of each other. | Assumes that the four type preferences interact dynamically to form a whole that is different from the sum of its parts. |
| Traits are usually identified by a single descriptor. | Type dichotomies are identified by their two opposite poles. |
| Very high and/or very low scores on a trait can be negative or diagnostic. | The numerical portion of MBTI results has no negative or diagnostic meaning. |

*Source:* Quenk, 2000a. Reprinted by permission.

of the Step II profile and report. Bear in mind that these comparative data are of limited informational value for individual interpretation, for the reasons described earlier.

## Bipolarity in Jungian Theory

Jungian psychology rests on the assumption that personality develops through the dynamic flow of energy between a number of important sets of opposite qualities—consciousness versus unconsciousness, male versus female, dark versus light, and so on. Jung thus conceived of our personalities as operating in a bipolar fashion, each pole of an element being qualitatively different from its opposite in every way. The opposite categories specified in the Jung-Myers type theory are one very important example of Jung's general theory of bipolarity. It is also the part of his theory that is most practical and accessible in our daily lives.

### Implications for Format and Scoring

The format and scoring of a theory-based instrument such as the MBTI personality inventory must conform to the assumptions and tenets of the theory upon which it is based—in this case, the Jung-Myers theory of psychological type. The forced-choice format of MBTI items is perfectly consistent with the bipolarities of Jungian theory. For all items, respondents are given two answers and must select the one that describes them best. They can always tell the difference between the choices in an item, but respondents occasionally say that they like or dislike both choices equally or that they sometimes do one thing nearly as often as they do the other.

The first issue here is whether a particular item's content matches the theory. Because the theory describes personality in terms of bipolar preferences, the item format models the theory by requiring a choice between two mutually exclusive answers. A second issue is how we identify a preference among behaviors that may all describe a person at one time or another. Jung never said that Introverted types always behave in an introverted way. He was fully aware that people display both introverted and extraverted behaviors at different times and in different situations. However, because both poles of a dichotomy cannot be used simultaneously, a person who consistently chooses one pole rather than the other will eventually develop a detectable preference. Forcing a person to make a choice is one way of determining this preference within the constraints of a self-report assessment instrument.

## Multifaceted Type Constructs

Until recently, theorists and researchers in psychology avoided multifaceted constructs, which were often regarded as the result of poor theories, sloppy thinking, or inept measurement. From the viewpoint of traditional psychometrics, measures of theoretical concepts should focus on one dimension at a time. In this view, scales that tap more than a single concept muddy the waters and do not allow us a clear view of the relationships between concepts. If two or more independent variables are not measured separately, for example, it is hard to determine which one produced the changes seen in a dependent variable. Emphasis on measuring only one attribute at a time is best suited to studying personality *traits*. This approach to measurement has been the hallmark of high-quality research grounded in the assumption that personality is best described as a series of separate, unrelated attributes.

With a typological instrument like the MBTI personality inventory, however, we do not regard personality characteristics as independent of one another.[1] The Jung-Myers theory assumes that the main categories of personality interact in complex ways. The connections among these categories make it *impossible* to describe each type as simply a profile of scores on the four separate preferences identified by the MBTI instrument.

Further, the preferences are complex; they are not pure, narrowly focused, single attributes. They consist of many different qualities that are related to one another, like a musical theme and its variations. Depending on the situation, a person with a Feeling preference, for example, may be sensitive, accommodating, merciful, tactful, sympathetic, understanding, caring, tender, empathetic, or encouraging. Such descriptors are what Carver (1989) has termed *multifaceted constructs*. He describes them as "composed of two or more subordinate concepts, each of which can be distinguished conceptually from the others and measured separately, despite being related to each other both logically and empirically" (p. 577).

For these reasons, type cannot be measured by the traditional psychometric approaches used for trait-based descriptions of personality. It is obvious from a reading of Jung that his concepts of Extraversion and Introversion, for example, could not be measured accurately by a one-dimensional scale (Jung, 1971). They are broad, general concepts that can be expressed in many ways.

Each attitude may be thought of as a set of distinct but related concepts tied together by the fact that they are all variations of the same attitude toward the world. Just as a person's behavior varies in different situations, Introversion and Extraversion are also expressed differently according to context. However, these differences in behavior do not make us think that we are talking to someone else every time a person's behavior changes. Similarly, differences in how Introversion shows itself from one time to another do not make us think that each expression of Introversion requires a new psychological concept.

### Nature of the Item Pool

The multifaceted nature of the item pool is one of the features that distinguishes the MBTI instrument from trait instruments. The items used to assess each attitude (Extraversion or Introversion, Judging or Perceiving) or function (Sensing or Intuition, Thinking or Feeling) do not attempt to get exactly at the attitude or function. Rather, each item asks about different aspects of one attitude or function.

When we work with trait instruments, we are mainly concerned with how accurately the scores reflect the amount of each trait. This results in a set of items that cover a narrow domain and in repetition of items. In contrast, when we use the MBTI instrument, we are mainly interested in sorting people accurately. Because of the multifaceted nature of type constructs, the accuracy of our sorting depends not only on how *many* items are used to assess E–I, S–N, T–F, or J–P, but on how well those items sample the different facets that are relevant within each dichotomy.

The Step II instrument allows us to look in detail at several facets of each bipolar preference. Because the Step II tool has more items than the Step I tool, it can amplify facets that may be tapped by only one or two items on Form M, thus increasing the amount of information available for verifying an individual's type. In some cases, we are better able to determine the reasons for the person's uncertainty about a given preference or for his or her report of some type-discrepant behaviors.

### Variation of Items in the Item Pool

The MBTI instrument uses forced-choice categorical responses and items that describe a variety of behaviors in many different situations, thereby offering the respondent the opportunity to reveal his or her preference across many different aspects of an attitude or function and in a variety of contexts. For example, when we look at the number of times a person has chosen the extraverted option over the introverted one, we know how many ways of being an Extravert that person has reported as typical. The MBTI item pool does not include every possible aspect of each of the attitudes or functions, but it includes a sufficient variety to help us identify a respondent's type.

Because it includes more items than Form M, the Step II instrument does a much better job of showing us the different ways in which a person may report being Extraverted, or using Sensing, or making Feeling judgments. By reporting results on the five facets belonging to each of the primary bipolar dichotomies, the Step II tool provides us with a richly textured, individualized description of how a particular respondent expresses his or her type. Such descriptions are perhaps much closer to the multifaceted constructs Jung used in describing his psychological types.

### Use of Factor Analysis

Variation in the items is consistent with the complex, multidimensional descriptions of the preferences in both Jung and Myers. A problem arises, however, as soon as we select a pool of items broad enough to cover what we think we mean by, for example, "Judging" and "Perceiving." We find that our technique for identifying a J–P dichotomy (normally, factor analysis of the items) now shows that we have several scales instead of just one. So how do we tell whether all these scales belong to J–P?

A second-order factor analysis, which factor-analyzes the scales we have identified in order to create another factor, is a standard way of answering this question. If we find one factor consisting entirely of J–P type scales, we feel safe in saying that these scales have captured at least some aspects of the multifaceted J–P concept. This process was used in the development of the Step II instrument. In the first factor analysis of items, some twenty factors (termed *subscales* or *facet scales*) were found. A second-order factor analysis was then done to determine whether these scales were "loose ends" or whether they represented different aspects of the MBTI instrument's main dichotomies.

As it turned out, E–I, S–N, T–F, and J–P were each found to have five distinct facets that were reflected in separate subscales. In short, the Step II tool provides an excellent example of measuring the kind of multifaceted constructs described by Carver (1989). See chapter 6 for tables showing the correlations among the current facet scales and between the facets and theta scores for the main preferences. The data in these tables illustrate statistically the kinds of relationships Carver discussed.

One strong caution is in order, however. Users who are familiar with Jung and the MBTI assessment tool are fully aware that type preferences consist of many facets, but no one knows with confidence exactly how many facets exist. Jung gave us such rich descriptions of the types that the facets he enunuciated could not all be included in the Step II assessment without making it too long.

For example, although there are many different aspects of Thinking—such as criticality, logicality, trenchancy, incisiveness, detachment, impersonality, firmness, inquisitiveness, and reasonableness, among others—Form Q contains only five facet scales reflective of Thinking because these five scales were found to contain several items that tap similar qualities. Factor analysis identifies facets by finding items that are correlated; single items that do not correlate well with other items are dropped, even if they might measure important aspects of the larger multifaceted construct. We take this approach because all items have some "noise," or measurement error, and we can dilute, or reduce, this error by using facet scales containing several items that address the same characteristic. In other words, it is better to limit ourselves to fewer facet scales containing smaller errors than to try to measure more facets by using a larger number of items of doubtful accuracy.

### Consistency or Clarity of Preferences

With the MBTI personality inventory, an individual's type is identified by weighting and summing answers to items that measure preference on each bipolar dichotomy. Because many items are used to identify a given preference and because these items are designed to cover many facets of the overall preference, we can look at the person's choices over a broad sample of situations and behaviors. By using a multifaceted item pool, we get a better picture of how consistently the person uses each function or attitude in a variety of situations. Our count of the behaviors sampled, however, does not quantify their relative importance in the person's daily life. It only tells us how consistently the respondent has chosen the behaviors sampled by our items. However, we infer that our best available estimate of the importance of the sampled behaviors is the consistency with which they are used, which is reported as the preference clarity index (pci) or preference clarity category (pcc) provided in Form M results.

The pci and pcc do *not* represent traits or amounts of one-dimensional characteristics. The numerical ranges associated with the "slight," "moderate," "clear," and "very clear" pci and pcc categories, however, may look similar to the numbers displayed with trait-based instruments, especially to naive users. The goal of using the concepts of preference clarity index and preference clarity category for Form M, rather than the preference score reported for previous MBTI forms, is to discourage a trait-based interpretation of MBTI dichotomies. Avoiding such a misconception is critical because the meaning of these numbers is entirely different than in trait instruments, as can be readily seen in table 2.1.

## General Versus Individualized Personality Descriptions

Another long-standing subject of debate in personality literature is known as the nomothetic versus ideothetic (or ideographic) approach to personality measurement. The extensive literature on this topic cannot be summarized here, but its vast array of titles attests to its importance in the field.

Briefly, the nomothetic approach seeks to discover *general* laws or principles of personality that can be used to predict behavior. Since personality is a characteristic of individuals, the aim is to predict behavior from a knowledge of personality variables.

The goal of the ideothetic approach is also to predict behavior, but the focus is on discovering and measuring the *individual* differences that will help us do so. Proponents often argue that normative approaches to personality cannot predict individual behavior and that such prediction requires paying more attention to individual differences.

There are advantages and disadvantages to both approaches. Nomothetic approaches have been successful at identifying general characteristics of personality that apply to a wide variety of people but are less helpful in predicting behavior in specified situations. Ideothetic approaches provide a rich description of individual differences but do not contribute as much to the development of personality measures that may help in comparing different people.

## The MBTI® Approach

Coming from a typological rather than a trait orientation, the MBTI personality inventory approaches this problem differently. It seeks to measure types rather than traits, so the instrument's description of personality begins at a much more specific level than do trait descriptions.

Because the MBTI instrument describes people in terms of types that are defined by particular relationships among its four dichotomies, it can add details about a person's behavior that are not provided by scores on the four separate dichotomies only (as is true of trait descriptions). Thus, with its identification of types at the Step I level of scoring, the MBTI instrument has already taken a step toward an ideothetic description of personality while remaining anchored to a foundation of generalized characteristics (that is, the E–I, S–N, T–F, and J–P preferences).

When we use the Step II instrument, we move to a still more specific level and begin to look at individual variations within the types. With Step II facets, the number of variations we can describe goes up enormously. It turns out that relatively few of the logically possible Step II patterns turn up very often. The more common ones allow us to generalize about the structure of personality while describing individual differences. (See the discussion of out-of-preference facets in chapter 5 and tables 5.3 through 5.5, on pages 63 through 65.) As a second-level scoring of the MBTI instrument, the Step II tool thus brings us even closer to the goal of developing personalized (ideothetic) descriptions of personality combined with a solid foundation of general (nomothetic) principles.

# Conclusion

This chapter lays the groundwork for understanding the remaining chapters in the manual. It builds on the Step I context described in the previous chapter so that Step II results can be appropriately understood and interpreted to clients. Practitioners who would benefit by reviewing and enhancing their understanding of the Jung-Myers Step I theory are encouraged to read the theory chapters (chapters 3 and 4) and the construction and validity chapters (chapters 7 and 9, respectively) in the *MBTI® Manual* (Myers et al., 1998).

# Descriptions of the Step II™ Facets

# 3

CHAPTER OVERVIEW



This chapter presents detailed, in-depth descriptions of the twenty facets that make up the essence of the Step II instrument. In focusing on the qualities associated with the poles of each facet, the facets' bipolar nature becomes evident. Readers will note that, consistent with the definitions of the poles of the four *Myers-Briggs Type Indicator* (MBTI) dichotomies, each facet pole is described as qualitatively different from its opposite, and each is presented as legitimate and valuable in its own right. The last section of the chapter provides selected research results that will help practitioners focus on similarities and differences among the facet scales within each block of facets. These data were collected concurrently from the national sample used to create Form Q.

**A Note to Readers:** This chapter is an updated version of the work of Wayne D. Mitchell, whose ongoing research with the earlier Step II subscales formed the basis for the current revision and the present Step II manual.

## Context for Viewing Facet Descriptions

In one sense, it might seem contradictory to claim that the MBTI personality inventory measures whole types and then proceed to describe the separate facets of the Step II tool. In looking at single Step II facets, we are, in effect, focusing a microscope on certain aspects of the main type dichotomies. This magnified view can be valuable because it enables us to examine simpler parts of the types in detail. But we must remember that in real life, all the facets described here are displayed by people who are whole types and not just Introverted or Thinking types, or other fragments of full types.

The facet descriptions in this chapter may be used as benchmarks when comparing people whose other type preferences are known. In general, a respondent's type preferences and whole type should be used as a context within which to more fully interpret his or her facet scale results. Specifically, the following four considerations should be kept in mind when reading the descriptions.

- First, the descriptions of the separate facets of the Step II tool do not take into account interactions among type preferences. For example, the description of the Intimate pole of the Gregarious–Intimate facet is generalized across all Introverted types. It does not consider how the Intimacy of an Introvert might vary depending on whether the other preferences are for Sensing or Intuition, Thinking or Feeling, or Judging or Perceiving. Nor does the description of the Gregarious pole consider how the expression of that pole by an Introvert with an out-of-preference score (see chapter 5 for a discussion of in-preference and out-of-preference facet scores) might differ from the expression of a Gregarious Extravert whose score is consistent with his or her Extraverted preference.

  These other factors, which affect a particular person's expression of each of the facets, may explain how two people who prefer Thinking, for example, would use their logic differently, or the different ways in which two Sensing types might display their concreteness. But because we are discussing the facets rather than the main preferences, these differences will not be as great as those between Thinking and Feeling types, or between Sensing and Intuitive types, or between any other pair of bipolar opposites. In short, by looking at specific facets, we have moved down a level from the broad generalities of the main type preferences.
- Second, there are individual variations in type, age, gender, and developmental history that may influence how a particular person expresses a preference for the facets measured by the Step II instrument. As noted in the preceding chapter, only type-specific variations in facet scale scores are presently described for the Step II tool. Chapters 5 and 7 contain information about age and gender differences.
- Third, facet descriptions in this chapter refer to the poles of the facets, so the descriptions are thrown into sharper relief compared to the way people scoring in the midzone might be described. People scoring in the midzone may look somewhat like a mixture of both poles. This is not equally true for all facets, however. A few facets are less bipolar than others (e.g., Early Starting–Pressure-Prompted), both conceptually and empirically, and many of the facets do not have enough items to allow us to identify a distinct midpoint as we can for the four main dichotomies of the MBTI instrument. Such facets may be distributed more normally (see chapter 6 for examples).
- Fourth, it is vital to remember that since types are more than the sum of their parts, they possess features that go beyond the four main bipolar dichotomies. Certain facets that have a narrow focus and more normal-looking distributions may possibly be measuring some of the extra-bipolar attributes of type.

In spite of the considerations mentioned above, exploring the facet scales in detail adds considerably to our understanding of the depth and richness of type. Predictions of external variables from the facet scales (as presented in chapter 8) provide both theoretical and interpretive specificity to type constructs that are not possible for predictions from the four type dichotomies alone.

## Ordering of the Facets

In general, the facets are ordered by one or both of two criteria: the conceptual and/or statistical breadth and generality of the facet, and the natural sequence in which the facets of the functions or attitudes would be used and would relate to one another. For the functions (S–N and T–F), both criteria apply. The facet that is listed first fulfills the criterion of breadth and generality from a conceptual point of view, and the order of the facets within these functions approximates the natural sequence in which the facets would be used.

In using the perceiving function (S–N), for example, the Concrete–Abstract facet captures the broad perceiving orientation to either Sensing or Intuition. This facet scale also shows the highest correlation with Form M Sensing–Intuition, although differences among correlations of the facets with S–N are small. The percentage of out-of-preference scores on this facet is very low as well. The next three facets, Realistic–Imaginative, Practical–Conceptual, and Experiential–Theoretical, have more to do with how we begin to make meaning out of our initial Concrete or Abstract perceptions. Finally, the Traditional–Original facet describes how we assemble our initial perceptions and meanings to influence what we see and look for in the environment.

With the judging function (T–F), the first step is to establish whether to apply a Logical or an Empathetic criterion. This judgment can then be enacted by being Reasonable or Compassionate. These two facet scales also correlate most highly with the Form M Thinking–Feeling preference. Both show the highest percentages of in-preference scores for respondents and the fewest out-of-preference scores. When people have differences of opinion and viewpoint, they employ a Questioning or an Accommodating approach and then follow up by being Critical or Accepting of conclusions. Finally, once a decision has been made, it will be implemented or defended with either a Tough or a Tender style.

The ordering of the E–I and J–P facets rests primarily on the breadth/generality criterion—whether the facet is broad and general or focused and specific. Among the E–I facets, for example, several indicators suggest that the Initiating–Receiving facet reflects a fundamental difference in energy flow. It correlates most highly with Form M Extraversion–Introversion, has the highest percentage of respondents answering in accord with their underlying E or I preference, and has the lowest percentage of respondents scoring both midzone and out-of-preference compared to the other E–I facets. The remaining E–I facets focus on more specific contexts or styles in which this energy flow takes place.

For the J–P facets, Systematic–Casual seems to describe a fundamental orientation toward dealing with the environment, although its correlation with the Form M J–P scale and its percentages of in-preference, midzone, and out-of-preference scores do not provide clear statistical evidence for its position of primacy among the five facet scales. (See chapter 5 for in-preference, midzone, and out-of-preference comparisons and chapter 6 for relevant correlational data.) From a conceptual point of view, however, the remaining J–P facets seem to describe instances in which the general Systematic–Casual orientation is played out in more specific ways. It seems likely that the behaviors associated with these facets can be learned more readily or may be influenced by environmental demands. For relevant evidence for such a view, see the discussion of test-retest reliabilities of the J–P facet scales in chapter 7.

# Text and Content of Facet Descriptions

The facet descriptions depict the poles of the facets rather than their midzones. Because the facet scales have at most nine items, it was not possible to accurately identify precise midpoints. The difficulty in identifying midpoints made it even harder to describe people who score in the midzones of the facet scales. However, the emphasis on the poles of the facet scales is consistent with the familiar descriptions of the MBTI instrument's bipolar dichotomies. With the facets, we can look at type at a microlevel as well as at the level of the larger dichotomies, thus capturing some of the unique features that make types more than the sums of their parts.

The following facet descriptions are based on the item content of the facet scales. There are undoubtedly other characteristics associated with these facets that have not been directly measured by the facet scales. Such characteristics may be discovered in research with the Step II instrument or in working with clients who provide additional examples and elaboration of the behaviors measured by the facets. A great deal of research evidence showing the relationship of the facets to other measures is reported in several chapters in this manual.

## Comparison with Step II™ Interpretive Report Descriptions

The Step II™ Interpretive Report draws on a wealth of experience with clients in various settings. It is based on feedback from the self-descriptions of many respondents and the patterns that have emerged in discussing their profiles. Consequently, the Interpretive Report goes beyond the descriptions here. It does this in the following ways.

- It takes into account the respondent's type preferences in making interpretations of his or her facet results.
- It incorporates consistently reported behavior patterns that are strongly tied to certain score patterns but transcend the item content of the facets. For example, it describes subtle differences between in-preference and out-of-preference expressions of a facet.
- It describes characteristics of people who have scores in the midzones of the facets.

Thus, the Step II report does not duplicate the descriptions presented here but rather provides additional information tailored to each respondent's individual profile.

## Reading the Descriptions

Some of the facet descriptions may seem quite similar on first reading. But keep in mind that each facet, along with four others, belongs to one basic attitude or function. Within each dichotomy, all the facets are moderately correlated with the underlying preference (E–I, S–N, T–F, or J–P), depending on the facet block under consideration. All the facets within a dichotomy are also correlated with one another. Table 6.5, on page 104, presents these correlations and provides a good picture of the overlap among facets within each dichotomy. For example, the E–I facets correlate from .69 (Gregarious–Intimate) to .88 (Initiating–Receiving) with the E–I scale, and the S–N facets range from .76 (Traditional–Original) to .87 (Concrete–Abstract) with the S–N scale. Based on such data, there is and should be some overlap in the content of some facet scales, so the descriptions must be read carefully.

Table 3.1 provides a succinct overview of facet content and may be used as a guide to the differences and similarities among the facets in each dichotomy.

Another way to get a better picture of the content of each facet is to try the following procedure.

- First, focus on one dichotomy at a time by reading all the descriptions for its facets one after the other. This will give you a general idea of the ground that is being covered.
- Next, read through the same descriptions again, this time keeping in mind what is common while noting the subtle differences. For example, the J–P facets are all concerned with an individual's approach to organizing. However, one facet focuses on organization as applied to leisure time, while another focuses on the sequencing of smaller tasks that are necessary to complete a larger project, and yet a third emphasizes the way a person prepares to meet a deadline. Similar differences are found among facets from the other dichotomies as well.

## The Extraversion–Introversion Facets

The five facets of the Extraversion–Introversion dichotomy are Initiating–Receiving, Expressive–Contained, Gregarious–Intimate, Active–Reflective, and Enthusiastic–Quiet. See table 3.2, on page 40, for correlational data related to the facets of this dichotomy.

**Table 3.1 Content Outline of the Facets**

| E–I Facet Scales | Descriptions |
|---|---|
| Initiating–Receiving | Core facet of E–I dichotomy; broad and general focus; describes our basic orientation to communicating and connecting with others. |
| Expressive–Contained | Focuses on communication of our emotional state, including feelings, interests, and experiences. |
| Gregarious–Intimate | Focuses on the breadth and depth of our connections to others. |
| Active–Reflective | Focuses on how we engage with our general environment for entertainment, socializing, and learning. |
| Enthusiastic–Quiet | Focuses on the level and kind of energy we use in our exchanges with others, rather than the content of the exchanges. |
| **S–N Facet Scales** | **Descriptions** |
| Concrete–Abstract | Core facet of S–N dichotomy; broad focus on how we generally perceive the world and the kinds of things to which we direct our attention. |
| Realistic–Imaginative | Describes how we develop something new through dealing with the tasks and problems of daily living and working. |
| Practical–Conceptual | Deals with the products or outcomes of our perceptions, rather than the process of perception itself. |
| Experiential–Theoretical | Emphasizes the process by which we derive knowledge or meaning from our perceptions. |
| Traditional–Original | Emphasizes a social-context background that gives meaning to our perceptions. |
| **T–F Facet Scales** | **Descriptions** |
| Logical–Empathetic | Core facet of T–F dichotomy; emphasizes criteria used to make decisions. |
| Reasonable–Compassionate | Emphasizes the standards we use to maintain relationships when making Thinking or Feeling judgments. |
| Questioning–Accommodating | Focuses on how we deal with differences of opinion. |
| Critical–Accepting | Describes what we do after our initial judgments have been made. |
| Tough–Tender | Focuses on the impact of our judgments and how we proceed once our judgments have been made. |
| **J–P Facet Scales** | **Descriptions** |
| Systematic–Casual | Core facet of J–P dichotomy; focuses on how we organize our physical environments, including the flow of events, activities, tasks, and projects. |
| Planful–Open-Ended | Emphasizes how we arrange our leisure time activities, including both daily and future plans. |
| Early Starting–Pressure-Prompted | Fairly narrow focus; emphasizes how we manage time with regard to deadlines. |
| Scheduled–Spontaneous | Centers on the degree of structure in one's daily activities. |
| Methodical–Emergent | Narrowly focused; centers on how we sequence the smaller tasks required to finish larger projects; time and scheduling are not considerations. |

## Initiating–Receiving

This core facet of the E–I dichotomy is broad and general and describes a person's basic orientation to communicating and connecting with others.

Initiating People at this pole get pleasure from mingling with others in large or small gatherings. They enjoy connecting and helping people in a group make connections with others. They are particularly adept at and enjoy the light conversation characteristic of receptions, meeting breaks, and formal and informal parties. Connecting with people they already know, even if only briefly, is also an essential part of the process. At large social gatherings, they are usually quite comfortable introducing themselves to people they may have heard about but do not yet know. In doing so, they are adroit at finding some common ground from which to get to know the other person.

Initiating people are able to keep a conversation going. They can talk to almost anyone indefinitely and have the socially relevant information that is useful in unstructured settings. They enjoy mixing, so they tend to seek others out. They may even feel somewhat stifled if they can't easily circulate and make contact with a lot of people in informal group settings. They will readily move on to new connections in a conversation as they are good at starting up a dialogue. However, they keep a continuous lookout for new people with whom to make contact. Once Initiating people see someone they have not yet had a chance to connect with, they will often wrap up their present conversation and move on to the new person. Initiating people also help facilitate interaction among others. They enjoy "getting things going" in a social situation and often have the kind of information that helps them make such connections.

Receiving People at this pole are much more comfortable letting conversations come to them than initiating contact. This is particularly so in a group and with people they don't know. At social gatherings they are much more likely to be introduced to new people than to introduce their friends or acquaintances to one another. They are more comfortable talking to people they know than making new connections. Part of their Receiving approach stems from the effort it takes to keep a conversation going with someone with whom they seem to have little in common. In addition, their Receiving approach makes it unlikely that they will have enough common ground for a lengthy conversation with someone they don't know. However, Receiving people are often introduced by an Initiating friend to someone who values their unique job, expertise, personal background, leisure activity, or travel experience. When this happens, the Receiving person is quite able to talk at length with a new acquaintance because the discussion centers on a topic that he or she knows in depth and enjoys sharing. Unlike Initiating people, Receiving people may feel uncomfortable and adrift in informal group settings if they are not anchored by a known person or topic. As a result, they may literally corner someone they know and spend as much time as possible in conversation with that person.

## Expressive–Contained

This facet's focus is on communicating one's emotional state, feelings, interests, and experiences.

Expressive People at this pole are quite ready and willing to share their feelings, thoughts, personal history, interests, and opinions with others. Indeed, they feel that not doing so would be dishonest and possibly damaging to the health of their relationships. They prefer open and honest communication and are forthright about expressing their feelings. In a meeting or group setting in which an uncomfortable but unacknowledged feeling is circulating, an Expressive person is often the one to bring that feeling into the open. The whole group is then able to deal with it. Expressive people seek two-way and open conversations about feeling states. If a relationship lacks this essential characteristic, they may experience it as not complete or genuine, and usually will say so. They are therefore easy to get to know since it does not take long for them to make their feelings and views known. Their openness also includes whatever aspects of themselves are relevant to the conversation, situation, or relationship at hand. At its best, this facet is Extraversion in its most sincere and genuine form. It is not compromised by self-conscious hesitations, second thoughts, or a wish to impress others. In addition to expressing themselves to others, Expressive people need the feedback others give them. This two-way interaction helps them process their own thoughts, feelings, or issues. People at the Expressive pole often discover how they feel or what they think in discussion with others. Others can thus acquire a very close knowledge of the Expressive person's thought processes.

Contained People at this pole are selective about what and with whom they share information about themselves. This includes, among other things, feelings, thoughts, personal history, interests, and opinions. They tend to reveal their interests most readily when a conversation happens to hit on a favored topic and share their personal history when comfort has been established with another person and such sharing becomes relevant to the conversation. It is often difficult for others to know about Contained people's thoughts and feelings since they tend to be sparing with both words and body language. When they are under stress or upset, Contained people may be less able to talk to others about their distress than they normally would be. The greater their distress, the harder it is for them to find either the words or the energy to communicate their inner state. They believe that their turmoil is known and can be understood only by them, so others' input would not be helpful. They do not think that others would want to know what is going on with them, or they may fear that discussing themselves will be an interruption or an imposition. It therefore takes considerably longer to get to know Contained people than it does their Expressive counterparts. A sufficient level of trust must exist before they feel free to share truly personal matters. Even when personal affairs are not the issue, Contained people still may not be given to a high level of self-disclosure. This is not because they are guarded, mistrustful, worried, or self-conscious about themselves. Rather, they need to process their experiences internally and at length before they will be ready or even able to share them. Processing an issue through talking to others is usually a very poor way for Contained people to discover their own thoughts and feelings. Talking can even hinder self-discovery because others' input may interfere with their own assessments. External sharing can begin and others' views can be helpful only after the internal processing has been completed.

## Gregarious–Intimate

The focus of this facet is on the breadth and depth of one's connections to others.

**Gregarious** People at this pole enjoy friendships and associations with a variety of people. The number of relationships and their heterogeneity are both important in their social life. Such relationships are typically enjoyed in group settings, where group interaction is likely, rather than in one-on-one dialogue. Variety in relationships is highly valued because of the diverse interactions involved and the wide range of activities made possible. Being popular and known by a wide circle of people provides Gregarious individuals with the meaningful foundation needed to develop their personal identity. It is from the broad expanse of such networks and the popularity they offer that a sense of personhood occurs. Gregarious people also value the freshness and adventure of making new friends and the chance to connect with others who have larger social networks. They like opportunities to expand their circle of friends and acquaintances through meeting new people. They also see their friendship networks as a way of opening doors to new and bigger horizons of experience. If they want or need to change jobs, they have a readily available network of people with whom they can connect, and they are able to make the most of their contacts. Being cut off from this network is stressful in two ways: It prevents them from knowing the latest news about the many people with whom they interact, and it leaves a void in their sense of self. This void cannot be filled even by frequent contact with their closer friends. Through contacts with many different people, people at this pole develop the social dexterity to respond to diverse expectations without compromising their own identities. They are able to juggle several different people-oriented tasks at once without compromising their performance of any of them. Maintaining connections with a variety of people also gives them a heightened sensitivity to the subtleties of communication. They are apt to pick up on nuances of meaning that may be overlooked by people with fewer social contacts. In large-group settings they are aware of the flow of the group's mood or sentiment. However, they may not always be sensitive to the opinions or emotional states of more reserved group members. In smaller groups, where they have more time and opportunity to connect with most people, they can be quite attuned to involving quieter people who may have unique viewpoints or needs.

Finally, Gregarious people can respond rapidly in social contexts that involve a series of quick exchanges with others. They are comfortable with the lively give-and-take of social mingling that occurs in large groups. In group meetings where they know most of the people, their contributions may carry more weight than those of their Intimate counterparts. One reason is the broad awareness of group sentiments that they acquire by touching base with many people. In doing so, they get a good sense of what views, proposals, or compromises may be acceptable to the majority of group members.

**Intimate** People at this pole are most at ease in social exchanges with others whom they know well. They find social mingling and quick chitchat with a large number of people unappealing, if not something to be avoided. They prefer lengthy one-on-one conversations with few interruptions. For them, conversation cannot occur in a group. Rather, it involves a back-and-forth exchange with one person where together they spiral deeper into a topic. They don't like people changing the subject or intruding other topics into the discussion. Their preference for deep, intimate exchange may lead them to avoid large group situations where they don't know anyone. When they are in a large group, they try to find others who prefer one-on-one exchanges. In a large, freely mingling group, they may spend an entire evening talking to one or a few friends with whom a private, exclusive, and well-known connection can be maintained.

People at the Intimate pole greatly prefer a limited range of friendships. They feel comfortable sharing the more personal aspects of their lives with very few people. A Gregarious person might share such details with a much broader circle. For the Intimate person, both the information itself and the sharing of it are reserved for only certain people. For this reason, the Intimate person's friendships entail a significant amount of trust, tend to develop slowly, and require a fair amount of time to maintain. The time commitment is great enough, in fact, that Intimate people feel they simply do not have the time or energy to maintain a large number of true friendships.

Intimate people also tend to be involved in a more selective set of interests and activities than are their Gregarious counterparts. They enjoy concentrating their energy on specific interests that they can explore in depth over fairly long periods of time. They dislike being involved in so many activities that they are unable to give each of them the extended attention they feel is needed, appropriate, and satisfying. Cursory involvement may make the work meaningless or make them feel uncomfortable about not being able to do a better job.

For people at this pole, the intimacy involved in sharing secluded parts of oneself with a trusted friend is much more highly valued than is popularity. The shared parts of the Intimate person constitute the real "who I am." An Intimate person who lacks deep friendships and the opportunity they offer to share on an intimate level may feel unaffirmed as a person. Having a few deep friendships is as important to the Intimate person as being popular and having a wide social circle is to the Gregarious person. However, it may be more difficult for the one seeking intimacy to satisfy this need. In group discussions, the views and comments of Intimate people may involve a fairly in-depth consideration of both the topic and their associations to it. Consequently, when the exchange involves a rapid series of remarks by different people, the Intimate person's lengthier processing may delay his or her comments and observations. As a result, a valuable contribution may remain unspoken because of the dynamics of a large group.

In social contexts, people at the Intimate pole seek out experiences they believe they are more likely to enjoy. They prefer environments with intimate interactions, and they may not value opportunities for networking. Their comfort, interests, and satisfaction lie in intimate connections with others. They want to focus on the substance of their own and their friends' inner lives. In focusing at that level, they may be more adept at picking up nuances of meaning from intimate friends than they are at recognizing the nuances of group dynamics.

## Active–Reflective

The focus of this facet is on how a person engages with his or her general environment for entertainment, socializing, and learning.

**Active** People at this pole like to be actively engaged with their environment, especially when this means energetic face-to-face interactions with others. They prefer active involvement over passive viewing and find parties more entertaining than watching a performance. They like to be actively and socially engaged rather than detached and removed from the action. Active people may lean toward pursuits that permit them to actively engage with the world. They may also prefer work and activities where they can contribute by speaking rather than writing. They are comfortable meeting strangers and often take the lead and do much of the talking in social interactions. They also tend to learn better by doing, listening, and questioning than by independent study or reading, and they like to communicate by speaking to people face-to-face. Participation is the means by which they come to know themselves, the world, and how self and world are dynamically connected.

**Reflective** People at this pole seek out and enjoy entertainment that evokes visual, intellectual, or mental responses. They prefer this over participation in an activity and, in fact, such evocation may actually be the way they participate. They enjoy the interaction of their own mental responses with creative, artistic, intellectual, or cultural works. They participate just as fully as Active people, but with different kinds of activities that can be enjoyed internally rather than externally. For Reflective people, the meaning of things arises from their active mental engagement with them. Physical or verbal interaction with the environment is often unnecessary. Consequently, they tend to learn best from written material that they can read on their own. In this way, their learning can be structured by the (possibly lengthy) mental associations they make to the material. A group process that interrupts their internal dialogue is not an effective way for Reflective people to learn or an enjoyable way for them to use leisure time. They communicate with others most comfortably through writing and reading. Meeting and interacting with strangers can be uncomfortable and they are likely to let others keep a conversation going in social situations.

## Enthusiastic–Quiet

This facet focuses on the level and kind of energy one brings to exchanges with others, rather than on the *content* of what is exchanged.

**Enthusiastic** People at this pole are talkative, hearty, and lively. They enjoy conversation for its own sake. They like the give-and-take of conversation and emit and receive energy through talking to others. Verbal exchange is a stimulant; it activates a reservoir of social energy that bubbles forth with high octane and good spirit. As a result, they especially enjoy discussions in group settings; the lively input from several people helps create a conversational event bordering on a spontaneous social art form. Their enthusiasm for connecting in a direct and immediate way also carries over to one-on-one conversation. The basic enjoyment comes from a love of communicating with others.

Enthusiastic people tend to be among the first to know what is going on among their network of friends and acquaintances. This is because they are attracted to settings where people are mingling at a high level of energy. They readily pick up and remember information about people they may not know personally but who are the subject of current conversation. Enthusiastic people seek out group settings where collective energy is high and upbeat. They are attracted to places and events with lots of action and to other people who like the same level of energy. This does not necessarily mean they like raucous parties. Rather, people at this pole enjoy gatherings where the joy of just being with others can flow freely and find expression in whatever form happens to evolve at the time.

Enthusiastic people tend to like being the center of attention and, in their enthusiasm, may overstate or embellish their accounts of events. For Enthusiastic people, the main purpose of an entertaining conversation is not to communicate matters of fact. Rather, it is to create a social, interactional happening that is engaging, lively, and simply fun. Stories are often a primary medium for this kind of exchange. Through stories, they can share the most entertaining sides of their personal histories as well as emotional states in the present moment. While they are not the only instrument by which Enthusiastic people create amusement, stories are a particularly engaging means by which they can entertain themselves and others.

**Quiet** People at this pole usually have a calm bearing. They are reserved and quiet, even in group settings where their Enthusiastic counterparts are creating lively and animated interactions. The quiet and reserve of people at this pole are a function of energy level; their response to group and social exchanges is simply at a lower level of energy. The stimulation from interacting with others neither energizes nor animates them. In fact, it may drain the energy they have available for interacting with the world. This does not mean they are uninterested or uninteresting. Rather, their level of social output and response is subdued. One effect of their reserve is that the subtleties and meanings of their responses may easily be overlooked or misunderstood. Others may catch their meaning only if they are willing and able to attend carefully to the low-key style of Quiet people.

There is evidence suggesting that this kind of quietude has a physiological basis. It is likely that Quiet people have a highly active internal response to social stimuli. They are not underresponding, although it might look that way to an observer. Studies of brain wave patterns have shown that Introverts exhibit much greater levels of arousal to external stimuli than do Extraverts. This difference is what we may be seeing in Quiet people. Their internal responses are so active and riveting that they minimize the energy available for making animated reactions that the outside world can see. Whether this phenomenon is specific to the Enthusiastic–Quiet facet as opposed to a generalized feature of an underlying preference for Extraversion or Introversion must await further brain wave studies.

One consequence of being energized internally is that Quiet people may sometimes be more succinct and reveal less than they intended, especially to people who don't know them well. This is not a deliberate effort to economize words, to keep others in the dark, or to maintain a high level of privacy. They say less than they may mean because of the overwhelming richness of the inner experience they are trying to convey. Quiet people may not be able to fully describe their interior world because its parts are so highly interconnected (for Intuitive types) or so rich in detail (for Sensing types). They find it hard to put their awareness and understanding of their inner, personal world into words. They may thus understate things in order to minimize the cascade of inner images that a stronger statement would create. Finally, Quiet people may be the last on a grapevine to hear what is going on. This is partly because they interact with fewer people and thus have less access to the exchange of information. Being one of the last to hear, however, is not the same as not knowing. Quiet people generally do have connections with others who will keep them informed.

## The Sensing–Intuition Facets

The five facets of the Sensing–Intuition dichotomy are Concrete–Abstract, Realistic–Imaginative, Practical–Conceptual, Experiential–Theoretical, and Traditional–Original. See table 3.3, on page 41, for correlational data related to the facets of this dichotomy.

### Concrete–Abstract

This core facet of the S–N dichotomy has a broad focus on how we generally perceive the world and the kinds of things to which we direct our attention.

**Concrete** People at this pole are grounded in the tangible aspects of their world. They like factual information and favor things that are tangible and concrete over those that are intangible and abstract. They use their concrete orientation for communicating with others, in their style of learning, and in forming their views of how the world works. Their Concrete approach also shows in their choice of daily activities as well as in their preferences for entertainment and leisure pursuits.

Concrete people are apt to use literal and specific words and to employ images that convey the fine details of sensory impressions. They understand best when others communicate with them in a similar style. Their most trusted referents are words and descriptions pointing to things that are tangible and real to the senses. For them, the world primarily consists of things that can be perceived by the senses and verified experientially. Such verification must be based on some physical, sensory process that is directly experienced by themselves or others. Verification is thus central to a Concrete view of the world. Concrete people tend to rank things according to how verifiable or real they are. They are likely to dismiss abstract concepts because they seem less believable, important, and relevant, not simply because they are intangible.

Concrete people tend to make little distinction between things that are abstract and those that are fanciful. Both have lower credibility, meaning, and value than sensate things. Abstractions are not physically verifiable and do not provide information about tangible things or their relationships. They therefore seem less valuable, useful, or true. Concrete people value specific instructions about how to fix a carburetor, wire a house, or bake a cake much more than the principles of combustion or the theories of electric currents or chemical bonding. Fanciful things are not appealing to Concrete people because they are unreal, or simply boring and a waste of time. A Concrete approach attaches a value hierarchy to intangible things. This does not involve a Thinking or Feeling judgment; rather, it is a function of how grounded something is in the tangible world. Once its "tangibility value" has been determined, Thinking or Feeling judgments can be brought to bear.

**Abstract** For people at this pole, real and important meanings lie in ideas and abstractions. The tangible world merely provides the associations from which meaning is created. Physical reality does not have meaning in and of itself, and may be regarded at times as irrelevant, annoying, distracting, or misleading. Concrete reality is primarily a stimulus for directing attention to the more interesting realm of intangibles. Meanings arise from the relationships of "things" to one another, and from their power to generate additional ideas or associations. Abstract people find it appealing to consider the number and variety of possibilities that emerge when one abstracts the meaning of things.

For the Abstract person, ideas are brought to life and given reality by their meanings and associations. A "fact" may be just an isolated occurrence and therefore may have no inherent meaning; it is what the fact *represents* that is primary. Ideas that cannot be connected to other notions are not as real. They do not have the value, interest, or excitement of ideas with many interconnections. The reality of the person at this pole is made up of ideas, abstractions, symbols, and figurative images. Physical objects or events that appear to contradict an abstraction or idea are likely to be regarded as exceptions, flukes, or simply obstacles to be overcome and worked around. Tangible evidence mainly serves to redirect the pattern of associations the Abstract person tries to make among ideas. The Abstract person will not necessarily abandon his or her ideas because of contrary material facts. Such physical evidence will only later stimulate modifications of ideas, abstractions, and generalizations.

People at this pole tend to communicate using words, expressions, and descriptions that evoke associations. This is because the tangible world is less important than the world of symbols and ideas. Even when referring to specific objects or events, meaning is not limited to what is tangible. Instead, the gist of what is being communicated lies in the abstract associations that can be made to the word. Thus language is primarily a means of implying something rather than specifying it. Using language to describe the details of one's environment is only a secondary consideration.

## Realistic–Imaginative

This facet describes how we develop something new through dealing with the tasks and problems of daily living and working.

**Realistic** People at this pole focus on things that are pragmatic, where one can make a useful difference. They therefore emphasize objects, activities, ways of doing things, and kinds of knowledge. Realistic tasks may involve everything from the routines of daily living to those required to build a boat or construct a space shuttle. A central goal is efficiency in use of time, energy, and money, especially in serving a useful and tangible purpose. Realistic people attach a value to practical things that has nothing to do with Thinking or Feeling judgments. Valuing of things stems from the greater attention, credibility, and time that the Realistic person gives to them. Things having little or no tangible impact on the detailed steps involved in a task or activity are considered to be of little value.

Realistic people value "things" in and of themselves as well as the uses to which these things can be put. They therefore tend to get along better and enjoy being with others who also appreciate tangible objects and goals. Such relationships allow Realistic people to benefit from factual knowledge and experience in areas beyond their own expertise. A shared Realistic outlook also provides a means of verifying, sharing, and reaffirming who one is, what life is about, and what is important. The shared worldview of Realistic people leads to a shared sense of humor. The humor of Realistic people differs from that of Imaginative people.

Realistic people like to have a generalized sense of how things work in the tangible world. With repeated experience and practice, their hands-on knowledge of the material world becomes the "common sense" that is so highly valued by Realistic people. Such common sense adds a worthwhile stability and efficiency to daily life. It also helps them feel, quite literally, grounded in the world. It prevents having to deal with the inevitable complications that result when common sense is lacking. The Realistic person therefore attends more to sensible, matter-of-fact things, solutions to problems, and people than to those that might be considered fascinating or imaginative. For Realistic people, things that are merely fascinating or imaginative are apt to offer little utility because they refer to things that are removed from tangible reality.

**Imaginative** For people at this pole, tangible things are not nearly as important as the possibilities they suggest. Matters of fact are valuable mainly for the associations and images they bring to mind. Images are real and important; the material things from which they derive are only secondary. In fact, once a chain of associations and images has been inspired by something tangible, the initial object or fact may be forgotten. The Imaginative person will then take great delight in stringing together a succession of creative images. This kind of creative process itself may be valued as much as any of the ideas that are generated by it. For example, Imaginative people may fill journals or sketchbooks with creative output that is never published or shown to another person. When the process has run its course, the Imaginative person may move on to something entirely different or focus on the reality of whatever idea seems most "promising." There is unlikely to be any practical, step-by-step procedure for getting something done.

Imaginative people value creativity for its own sake; the very newness of an idea is itself appealing. They can mentally play with an idea, exploring a new and previously unknown territory of possibilities. The originality of Imaginative people is frequently inspired by the need for a solution to a practical problem, to which they can respond by trying to transcend what they see as the limits imposed by specific details. They question "tried-and-true" procedures and implicit assumptions about things, operations, objectives, and people. Because they work on the problem at a level that is mentally removed from its tangible details, their solution may not be workable in its original form. However, with a refocus on concrete reality and a little refining, it may turn out to be an ingenious solution.

In business settings, people at this pole are attracted to strategic planning. They may envision new markets, services, and products and construct mental images of a company's future and of how it should recreate itself in order to get there. In other settings, they may become aware of a problem or need and envision a new program to meet it. Their vision will consist primarily of mental images that develop into a tangible form.

## Practical–Conceptual

This facet deals with the product or outcome of one's perceptions, rather than with the process of perception itself.

**Practical** People at this pole are attracted to others who display practicality and common sense. For Practical people, ideas are valued and useful only when they can be applied to practical, down-to-earth problems. Practical people prefer putting things together from known objects and materials, using familiar and practiced methods. Their creativity is derived from experience. It is grounded in a thorough understanding of the materials used and how these materials are formed and fit together. Any new developments they create will evolve from step-by-step changes, with each stage being fully tested before any modifications are made. People at the Practical pole tend to be builders rather than innovators. They prefer the solid over the nebulous, value certainty over vagueness, and would rather deal with substances than with the purely symbolic. They are more oriented to the details of daily living and their work than to trends and events that may occur in the future. New ideas are accepted if their immediate application can be seen or if they offer tangible improvement over current practices.

**Conceptual** People at this pole look for meanings in what they see around them. Tangible things are primarily reflections of a reality greater than the world of the five senses. Their focus is therefore on inferences they can draw at a conceptual level rather than on what is immediately present. They are not content, however, just to make inferences. Inferences give birth to ideas, and ideas are what excite them. They may be interested in documenting or tracing the development of an idea or concept. They particularly enjoy making connections and finding relationships among a variety of ideas. They value abstract intellectual discourse and are attracted to the exceptional rather than the mundane. They enjoy the stimulation of people with quick and insightful minds with whom they can have a lively exchange of ideas. They value intellectual and scholarly pursuits over practical and active endeavors.

When people at this pole make or build something, it arises out of their mental images. These images include what they are trying to do as well as the meaning their creation has for them. The step-by-step process of putting something together is not nearly as satisfying as the symbolic meaning that they may give something when it is finished. Conceptual people are oriented toward the future because insights and images lying beyond what is immediately tangible are foremost. Their interest is not in specific practical accomplishments, but in the ideas and meanings behind their efforts. They are more interested in the concept of a new thing than in the thing itself.

## Experiential–Theoretical

This facet emphasizes the process by which one makes knowledge or meaning out of one's perceptions.

**Experiential** For people at this pole, something must be validated by experience to be worthy of more than their brief attention. Experiential people are wary of theory, preferring instead the certainty of their own active participation in the world. They want instructions to include specific action steps that are based on practical experience. Experience is the primary criterion for truth and relevance. An Experiential person finds it difficult to talk about truth apart from the trial and error of experience. Truth and relevance are inseparable for these people. A primary pleasure comes from expertly applying their experience. This provides the opportunity to become immersed in an active, tangible expression of both truth and relevance. The resulting product yields a singular kind of personal fulfillment because it embodies both of these qualities. Experiential people have little incentive for changing methods that have been proven to work repeatedly. Trying to improve techniques that already work is a waste of time that could be spent more productively in accomplishing the task at hand. For the Experiential person, producing something is much more satisfying than attempting an unknown approach. However, if there are no established procedures for a new task, the Experiential person will adeptly use a trial-and-error approach to find out what does work. The trials will begin with what the person already knows from similar situations. Such knowledge tells him or her how well the old methods work and where they need to be adapted.

**Theoretical** People at this pole generally operate at a level or two removed from the immediately tangible. They search for patterns in what they see and discern meanings in those patterns. Their understanding and knowledge of the world are contained in an abstract series of principles, explanations, and theories. These are derived from understandings, sympathies, and values, depending on whether their judging function is Thinking or Feeling. Theoretical people like to explore things by looking for new connections among the concepts they use to understand the world. These new associations create fresh meanings that promote further explorations. The generation of ideas takes on a life of its own and becomes something sought for its own sake. Theoretical people are therefore ready to try new ideas or ways of doing things just to get this mental process started. A task or work that offers no new ideas or approaches to try becomes boring. Theoretical people like to weave concepts together to form a coherent set of principles or explanations that help us understand or predict something in the world.

Theoretical people learn better if they are given theories and concepts in addition to any relevant factual information. They primarily understand things at that level. Facts are apt to have little meaning by themselves and are likely to be forgotten unless they can be tied to a theory or put into some larger context. Immediate and tangible relationships between things are far less compelling to them. While Theoretical people can certainly recognize beauty in their physical environment, they find the beauty in concepts and theories to be even more awe-inspiring.

## Traditional–Original

This facet emphasizes social context as the background that gives meaning to our perceptions.

**Traditional** People at this pole prefer doing things in established ways that are shared by most other people. It is appealing to them to rely on the security that comes from fitting in with a community or group. They like the feeling of belonging to or being part of something larger than themselves. This preference involves one's entire lifestyle, not merely specific tasks. It includes style of dress, choice of charities, type of housing, and recreational and leisure activities. Traditional people find the conventional appealing in many respects. Convention offers ways of doing things that are continually validated by the social environment. When they see others living in similar ways, Traditional people are assured that their manner of living is valued and correct. They receive immediate confirmation that their way of living is "on target" by checking it against their social surroundings. As a result, they are uncomfortable going against the grain of custom, culture, and traditional norms. Tradition is associated with what is good.

For the Traditional person, fads are suspect because they don't have the validating test of time and experience. Fads also lack the societal breadth and depth that occur when traditional styles and customs are followed. Following a fad is not an effective way of achieving the stable and comfortable relationship to one's environment that comes from acting in accord with the traditional styles and customs of one's group. Another avenue to such stability is to follow family traditions, which affirms one's role and relationships among one's kin. Such traditions provide self-definition and give meaning to one's own and one's family members' lives. Traditional people greatly respect tradition and change their ways only reluctantly. For change to be acceptable, it must be grounded in what was done before and must proceed gradually. For Traditional people, deliberate changes made just for the sake of change are meaningless at best. At worst they may destroy cherished meanings that are the foundation of social, organizational, and family life. Traditions are ways of honoring or appreciating what is right and good. Traditional people admire those who can serve as solid role models for behavior and are interested in passing down their traditions to the next generation. They are often perplexed when the next generation is unappreciative of treasured traditions.

**Original** For people at this pole, repetition and sameness in important areas of life are almost a trigger for innovation. Original people do not disrespect traditions; rather, they find that doing things exactly the same way time after time diminishes the meaning in an event. They may prefer to retain the basic theme of something but apply variations on the theme. For the Original person, it is the variations that convey meaning, rather than the theme itself. Exact repetition of a traditional way of doing something would make the activity as dull as a musical score that simply repeated the same theme over and over using the same notes.

Changes in established ways of doing things also give people at this pole opportunities for self-expression. Their originality may be displayed in their approach to tasks or activities, or in their choice of dress, leisure activities, or lifestyle. They can find inspiration to put their best effort into their work by inventing different ways of doing something. Having to do it the way someone else has done it may make their effort dead and meaningless. If the job simply does not allow for anything unique, the Original person will not be able to connect with the work and will become unmotivated. However, Original people do not need to be original in every part of their lives. In many instances, they tend to concentrate their originality in circumscribed areas that are especially meaningful to them. They admire people who stand out because of their willingness to be different. For Original people, eccentricity is a virtue.

## The Thinking–Feeling Facets

The five facets of the Thinking–Feeling dichotomy are Logical–Empathetic, Reasonable–Compassionate, Questioning–Accommodating, Critical–Accepting, and Tough–Tender. See table 3.4, on page 42, for correlational data related to the facets of this dichotomy.

### Logical–Empathetic

This core facet of the T–F dichotomy emphasizes the criteria we tend to use to reach a judgment.

**Logical** People at this pole understand the world best if it makes logical sense. Objects, events, and statements must be analyzed using reason. If they are internally consistent and logical, they are accepted as true. If not, the issue in question must be either untrue or not understandable. It should therefore be rejected because illogical statements are not worthy of time and attention.

Logical people start with a set of assumptions or facts and use specific rules to make deductions. They assume that universal rules permit such logical deductions. Therefore, when they don't understand something, they try to find out what the prevailing premises or assumptions are. Even when the other person is unaware of his or her implicit assumptions, the Logical person must discover the relevant premises in order to understand and proceed.

A person at this pole receives a great deal of confirmation that reason is a direct means to accuracy and understanding. This is because many things can be understood logically. Logical people may therefore find it hard to accept contradictory explanations that don't follow the laws of logic. Their worldview is internally consistent and they expect everything to function in that same consistent way. Even though Logical people may at times be inconsistent in their views of themselves, other people, and the world, such inconsistencies are not bothersome if they do not directly contradict a Logical person's scheme for understanding things.

When there are several competing viewpoints on a matter, Logical people are likely to be persuaded only by arguments that make logical sense. Facts must support conclusions and must be capable of fitting into the relevant logical scheme. Facts about another person's emotional state may be just as relevant as "objective" facts. However, they too must fit into a consistent analytical framework. Any inconsistencies in another person's chain of reasoning weakens the credibility of the other person, the other perspective, or both. This is especially true when the inconsistency is central to the person's argument. A person at this pole can strongly disagree with another and still have respect for that individual. This is because logic is a personally detached process. The Logical person respects the other person's ability as a thinker, not his or her viewpoint, because the person is separate from the viewpoint. Being able to think clearly and consistently is a highly valued general ability. Repeated signs of illogic, inconsistency, and contradiction in another's statements can easily lead to diminished respect.

People at this pole tend to apply generalized and impersonal principles to a broad range of relationships. They value rights, fairness, and reasonableness as standards for making decisions in personal and contractual relationships. They apply these standards for deciding about others, and they expect others to judge them the same way. They view rights and reasonableness as good tools for relationships because they can be consistently, fairly, and logically applied. Everyone involved then knows what to expect from the others.

**Empathetic** People at this pole see the world as operating within a rational framework of relationships that link people and things to one another. They view detached logic as only one way (and a limited way) of understanding the world. For Empathetic people, relationships, life experience, and personal meanings are what is important. Interactions within these areas are transformative. Thus life and the world are best understood as a drama with characters, themes, and plots. Just as the characters in a novel have distinct motivations and personalities that affect the unfolding of the story, so do real-life personalities affect the twists and turns of an evolving drama. For Empathetic people, truth is not separate from people and their lives. It therefore makes no sense to apply logically consistent principles irrespective of the people involved. Understanding of the world comes from the mutual sharing of experiences, so understanding can occur through knowing someone else's experience and not just one's own experiences.

Empathetic people put logic and reason into their conceptions of how life may be experienced and understood, just as Logical people put empathetic concerns into their logical schemas as a way of understanding them. The use of logic is just another human characteristic among many others. What is known through logic simply takes its place among many other human experiences, modes of understanding, and ways of living. These are all valuable and even necessary for grasping the meaning in life.

Empathetic Intuitive people have an implicit notion that every person's life is a miniature variation on timeless, universal themes. Sharing a common humanity with others is a central aspect of caring for and staying connected to another person. For Empathetic Sensing people, the central focus is on the ups and downs of people they know or their own significant relationships. Empathy and meaning are grounded in the shared experience of personal histories. However, regardless of their Sensing or Intuitive preference, people at the Empathetic pole value other people for their basic humanness as well as for their worth as unique persons.

Truth for Empathetic people is both personal and universal, a view that is easily understood by Empathetic people but difficult for Logical people to accept. Similarly, Logical people may find it difficult to convince Empathetic people of the universality and absoluteness of detached logical truth. The inconsistencies in values of the Empathetic person primarily involve relationship issues. Compartmentalizing may be one way of handling these inconsistencies, as in having separate, circumscribed contacts with friends who don't like each other. The Empathetic person may handle differences in more intimate relationships by accepting them as part of the other's uniqueness as a person. This works best when the differences do not involve key values.

People at this pole pay more attention to the feelings than to the rights of other people. Someone who uses power in the name of "rights" demonstrates heartless self-interest, especially if another person is hurt by this. For the Empathetic person, impacts on people and personal feelings are of far higher value than any rights or standards of fairness that ignore the individuals involved.

## Reasonable–Compassionate

This facet emphasizes the standards we use to maintain relationships when we make Thinking or Feeling judgments.

**Reasonable** People at this pole tend to see their relationships as primarily task-focused. This includes factoring human needs into one's problem-solving logic, since each person brings his or her needs into situations. Reasonable people, especially men, often demonstrate caring for others by analyzing and solving problems. They may analyze both the immediate situation and the long-range consequences of proposed solutions. They do not believe that sympathizing is a helpful approach to problem solving and decision making. While they may feel sympathy, they demonstrate their care for others by fixing or modifying things. This may involve adjusting an employee's work schedule to deal with a family crisis, making exceptions when circumstances arise, or doing something special in recognition of someone's extra effort.

Being Reasonable means being consistent. When exceptions are made for individuals, they must also be made for others having similar problems. If this does not happen, the making of exceptions is the same as playing favorites. There should be no favorites before the law. For reasonable people, mercy may be equivalent to letting sympathy for one individual overrule principles of fairness.

Reasonable people find it difficult to work for someone who is not consistent. Rewards and punishments from such a person would be divorced from task performance and therefore illegitimate. Reasonable people try to resolve disagreements so that positive or negative consequences are equitably distributed. The fairness in such solutions and the effort it takes to arrive at them are expressions of caring. For the Reasonable person, both giving and receiving fair treatment are ways in which everyone's worthiness is acknowledged. This is far more important than attending to one's own or others' feelings or emotional states, since equity of treatment is independent of oneself or the particular other people involved. Their view is that attending to the feelings won't really solve anything; it is more helpful to attend to the behavior or help the person see the consequences.

**Compassionate** People at this pole see the world as personalized and interconnected rather than impersonal and detached. They therefore pay attention to the unique needs that other people bring to situations. Recognizing each person's uniqueness is more important than policies, procedures, and rules. Laws, rules, and agreements help define the boundaries of relationships, but they are not their essence. People relate to each other through their shared experience as human beings. Each person has hopes, hurts, dreams, and discouragements that are similar to one's own. They must be treated with recognition of that fact, not merely with fairness. Compassionate people also care for and about other people in a personalized way. For them, mercy is not spinelessness or an excuse to put sympathy ahead of law. Rather, mercy is the basis on which judgments of another person should be made. It takes into account unique (and possibly mitigating) circumstances or characteristics of the person, and thus values the person over abstract principles. For the Compassionate person, fairness is not defined as treating everyone the same. Rather, it is judging each person in terms of his or her unique character and circumstances. Failing to take into account another's uniqueness when making a judgment hurts the other person as well as oneself. That "no man is an island" (in the poem by John Donne) is one reason that the hurt goes both ways for Compassionate people.

Compassionate judgment is active rather than passive. This quality is shared with the Feeling poles of several of the other T–F facets, specifically the Accepting and Tender facet poles. Both failure to recognize the need for compassion and failure to act compassionately hurt the other person because both failures yield the same outcome.

Finally, Compassionate people respond best in relationships if they are treated sympathetically and compassionately. They highly value being recognized as individuals who are connected to others in a network of friendships. Such recognition validates their uniqueness and the importance of their relationships. Sympathy, pleasantness, and compassion will give rise to devotion and loyalty in them, whereas fairness or mere consistency are unlikely to have such an outcome.

## Questioning–Accommodating

This facet focuses on how people deal with differences in point of view as they attempt to arrive at a judgment. It is the part of the judgment-forming process that is involved when the judgments must be shared with others.

**Questioning** People at this pole seek detached, impersonal truth. There are three typical motivations involved. The first is to find reasons that makes logical sense; when questions, statements, events, or observations don't fit together logically, Questioning people ask direct questions. They want what others say to be logically consistent with what they already know. Their Questioning approach is not a personal attack or disregard for other people. Rather, it is an attempt to get at objective truth. Questioning people may be somewhat distrustful of others who want them to agree to something before all their questions have been adequately answered. They tend to approach all statements with some degree of skepticism.

Questioning is also a way to solve problems. A Questioning person who prefers Intuition may question established practices, beliefs, information, principles, designs, or even facts. A Questioning person who prefers Sensing may similarly question solutions, changes, predictions, or the likely success of proposed problem solutions. Questioning people believe that there is a logical order to everything. If something is not working, it must be because assumptions about how its parts should go together are wrong. Questioning such assumptions may very well lead to a solution.

A third approach to questioning is in dealing with other people. Questioning people may raise questions or objections when they are asked to accept or conform to things that don't make logical sense. They question in order to find a common ground of understanding from which they and the other party can proceed. Truth is independent of personalities for Questioning people. Therefore, their questioning is not intended to disparage another viewpoint or person. If someone cannot satisfactorily answer their questions, however, Questioning people may take offense. Forcing a Questioning person to accept an important decision that has not been thoroughly examined is experienced as an affront to his or her intelligence. Such devaluing of truth is not likely to go unchallenged, and the Questioning person may use sarcasm to communicate his or her disdain. The hurt such a tactic may cause another person is felt to be justified by the offense to truth that has occurred.

**Accommodating** For people at this pole, reality is socially defined. Accommodating people are much more concerned with how truth is understood, valued, and used by others than with an assumed "objective" truth. Their primary focus is on their own and others' experience and understanding of the world. If a person's understanding is incorrect, he or she can be gently corrected, but never disparaged. Direct questioning of someone's statements can be construed as a personal attack. Once that happens, the opportunities for growing a relationship or establishing consensus are diminished. If their questioning might threaten a relationship or their membership in a group, it is better to trust the statements and motives of others.

People at the Accommodating pole may value harmony so highly that they are simply unwilling to question another viewpoint. If differences of opinion occur, they will try very hard to encourage a decision that satisfies everyone. If they are unsuccessful, they will feel somewhat dissatisfied with themselves. Accommodating people also work to ensure that harmony prevails at family gatherings. They will be greatly distressed if other family members are unable or unwilling to make concessions that will keep the peace.

For people at the Accommodating pole, the most important truths are validated by group consensus or by personal relationships. Truth is not separate from people, and groups cannot function well if different perspectives are not accommodated. Agreement and harmony are not merely signs of a good relationship; they are the mortar that keeps it together. Accommodating people avoid hurting other people's feelings and expect the same consideration from others. Disagreements in intimate relationships are particularly distressing; people at this pole often avoid such disagreements and confrontations by letting matters pass unchallenged. It seems better to preserve the relationship by being agreeable than to risk the relationship itself.

## Critical–Accepting

This facet describes what we do after our initial judgment has been made.

**Critical** People at this pole are interested in correcting what is incorrect and setting things right. They want to get at the truth in order to improve things, situations, or procedures. Their overriding motivation is to make things better; to do this, critiquing is necessary to determine an issue's relative merits. Then a way to make things better can be devised. For the Critical person, not to critically evaluate is irresponsible. Because truth is more important than others' feelings, Critical people may not exercise tact in communicating their judgments. They tend to see being honest with themselves and others as kinder in the long run than being untruthful. They usually point out what is wrong before noticing or commenting on what is right. That is because achieving accuracy is a major concern. They believe that there is no point in mentioning things that are all right because it wastes time and will make no improvement. On the other hand, telling someone what they did wrong may help them avoid getting hurt again.

Truth is so valuable to Critical people that they find it distasteful and dishonest when others try to smooth over disagreements or disagree so mildly that their objections are not registered. They do not value merely getting people to agree because that might compromise the truth and make things worse. Hurting someone's feelings is a small price to pay for needed corrections and improvements. Critical people hold that people can recover from hurt feelings, but the consequences of a wrong judgment or decision can hurt many people in the long run.

People at this pole tend to put others' feelings, viewpoints, and emotional needs into broader contexts than their Accepting counterparts. They are not oblivious to the human factor, but they do not want to lower their standards or forget what they see as truth. They hold themselves and others to very high standards. To suppress the natural competitiveness that accompanies their high standards would be dishonest. For Critical people, collaborating with others or complimenting them simply with a goal of creating harmony compromises their beliefs or values and is disrespectful. However, when absolutely necessary, they can consciously decide to put up with others' shortcomings and tolerate less-than-optimal standards, performance, or outcomes.

**Accepting** For people at this pole, truth is quite different. Accepting people want to affirm a truth that focuses on the value and worth of other people's ideas and viewpoints. "Objective" judgments about the truth are less important than the truth about other people and their relationships. For an Accepting person, the environment is primarily human and social. Passing critical judgment on someone's ideas or contributions may harm the person and also destroy the relationship, whereas being open to and accepting of others' views validates the person and enhances the relationship. Factual or nonpersonal issues are only of passing concern in comparison.

Building up relationships and people is as important to the Accepting person as is avoiding harm. Accepting people, therefore, do not merely tolerate lapses and "deficiencies" in others, they overlook them. Harmony is as essential to human sustenance as sunlight is to living creatures. Even though disharmony may sometimes be unavoidable, it must eventually give way to agreement between people. Acceptance brightens human relations and also nourishes them so they can achieve their full potential.

Acceptance for the person at this pole is a very active response that gives others the space and freedom to be themselves or to be right about an issue. Accepting someone in this way is not weakness, failure to recognize truth, a lack of sound judgment, or a mere passive reaction. Active affirmation of others is so important that it is often maintained despite potential risks to the Accepting person. Risks may range, for example, from financial loss from accepting a spouse's decision to pursue a dream, to personal disappointment at seeing a child fail when given the freedom to test his or her wings. Accepting people tend to first notice and comment on what is right or well done, and offer correction only secondarily. This helps in accepting and affirming others; they are likely to take a collaborative approach, at times putting their own desires or ambitions aside in favor of those of others.

## Tough–Tender

This facet focuses on the impact of our judgment and how we carry out a decision once a judgment has been made.

**Tough** People at this pole stand firm in the judgments they have made. This stems from exercising other facets of their decision making in their assessment. For the Tough person, a thorough, well-considered evaluation must result in the best decision that can be made. Compromise is not appropriate under these circumstances, even if it would avoid hurt feelings or outcomes that might hurt some people. A judgment that was honestly and thoroughly processed must stand, regardless of one's own or anyone else's personal opinion. Anyone who used the same information and the same judging process would arrive at the same conclusion. It does not matter to Tough people whether those conclusions are popular or welcome. The rightness of a conclusion is independent of both the person making the decision and other people.

Tough people distrust considerations based on feelings, personal attachments, or a desire to maintain warmth and harmony. Judgments based on such criteria play havoc with their trusted decision-making process. Personal considerations should be weighed along with all nonpersonal factors in making a decision. But once a judgment is reached, there is no justification for changing it simply because it is unpopular or may have negative personal impact. In fact, the value of a detached Thinking assessment is that unassailable logical truth can be achieved regardless of personal attachments. Compromising the truth is repugnant for Tough people, even if they themselves experience a negative outcome. They want to "stand firm" behind a decision that they believe in.

**Tender** For people at this pole, the effects one's decision may have on others far outweighs any logical process by which one reaches the decision. Tender judgments focus on the impacts of a decision on people. Kindness, caring, and consideration of others are primary concerns in both making a decision and implementing it. Tender people bring warmth and concern for others to decision making because the well-being of people is integral to their decision-making process. Having arrived at a Feeling decision, the Tender person may be just as convinced of the rightness of a conclusion as is the Tough person. However, his or her tenderness, warmth, and gentleness will be used to communicate the decision to others. If that decision is unpopular or hurtful to some of the people involved, the approach of the Tender person includes caring concern for those people. For Tender people, there is no absolutely correct truth apart from the way things affect people. They therefore insist that others be treated with kindness and consideration. People at this pole also respond best when they are treated with the same gentleness and warmth they so willingly give to others.

## The Judging–Perceiving Facets

The five facets of the Judging–Perceiving dichotomy are Systematic–Casual, Planful–Open-Ended, Early Starting–Pressure-Prompted, Scheduled–Spontaneous, and Methodical–Emergent. See table 3.5, on page 43, for correlational data related to the facets of this dichotomy.

### Systematic–Casual

This core facet of the J–P dichotomy focuses on how we organize our physical environment, including the flow of events, activities, tasks, and projects.

**Systematic** People at this pole have a variety of ways of achieving orderliness in their lives. They have a methodical and deliberate approach to doing both small, brief tasks and large, long-term ones; they have a need to schedule tasks and activities efficiently; and they want to be punctual in beginning and ending things on time. They use structures, methods, and deliberate systematic approaches to use their time efficiently, meet deadlines, and predict how long activities will take. Their approach permits them to have reserves of energy and time that would otherwise be wasted. This gives them the freedom to enjoy doing things for which they would not otherwise have time. They manage their leisure time and activities in the same systematic, well-ordered way, and for the same reason—it allows them to make the most of their leisure time and enjoy it more.

People at this pole maintain that if they were not systematic, too many things could go awry, wasting time, effort, and resources. Inefficiency and waste are unacceptable to them. They try to keep their homes and offices free of clutter and disarray. Clutter disrupts their ability to concentrate. Chaotic environments, be they at work or at home, interfere with their ability to get things done. Systematic people prefer to spend a few hours organizing things at the outset, and a few minutes a day to keep them that way, to avoid wasting time looking for misplaced files, memos, or tools. They consider it crucial to control their time, physical environment, and approach to work. They are quite uncomfortable if they do not have that control because that will lead to disorder that will have disastrous consequences. However, they can readily yield personal control to someone else who is also Systematic, once they know that the other person will maintain the necessary orderly structures.

The need for order and system extends beyond the physical environment for Systematic people. They also seek closure. Leaving decisions hanging is the same as having a messy desk or leaving tools scattered all over. When a task or decision is left unfinished, its incompleteness creates tension. Such tension depletes energy that could be better used for acting on the decision or tending to other matters.

**Casual** People at this pole prefer a more spontaneous approach for accomplishing things. For them, system and order are burdens and impediments to working effectively, especially when being orderly inhibits their immediate response to what interests them. Casual people dislike the effort it takes to be systematic and may find such efforts to be quite difficult. They are most comfortable with an easygoing approach to schedules, deadlines, decision making, their physical environment, how they spend time, and how they perform tasks. This casualness entails an openness to seeing and experiencing things in new and fresh ways. At times, others may mistake this for laziness. When there is too much order and predictability, Casual people miss the excitement, energy, and variety that spontaneity brings. They actively seek variety and newness and avoid constraining structures and systems. A loose, unstructured approach allows them to see, experience, or respond to opportunities they might otherwise miss. Casual people bring the greatest energy and enthusiasm to their work when, for example, an unexpected task is dropped in their lap. They do not mind being interrupted and asked to do something else in the middle of the day. Such interruptions create the kind of variety that keeps work from becoming patterned and boring. They like surprises that keep their days from being too predictable and repetitive.

Casual people are at their best when they are free to act on impulse, work on whatever tasks happen to strike their fancy, or respond to whatever requests or events come their way. Although they are certainly able to work systematically when necessary, variety and newness are intrinsically very satisfying to Casual people. They may therefore be at their best in work settings where procedures are not well established, and in nonroutine types of jobs and activities. They are likely to thrive and perform well on projects requiring rapid development of goals and methods.

People at this pole are comfortable postponing decisions, and often prefer to do so. They may postpone making an important decision until they are satisfied that they have considered it from all angles. For minor decisions, they may simply prefer to let a period of time pass before they make their final decision. When it is time to decide, they make a decision based on all the information that has been brought to their attention. They are able to make a decision before they are ready if circumstances require this, but they may change it if new information becomes available later. On the other hand, when they have reached a decision after thoroughly weighing the issues involved, they may be quite reluctant to change it later. This is because they have invested so much effort in making the decision the first time.

## Planful–Open-Ended

This facet emphasizes how we arrange our leisure time or social activities. Both daily and future plans are involved.

**Planful** People at this pole like a definite schedule for their leisure time, one that specifies what day and what time they will do something. Such advance scheduling ensures that everything planned will actually happen. This requires knowing what you want to do ahead of time so a schedule can be devised. Planful people tend to structure many areas of their lives in orderly, planned ways. They like to plan in advance how they will spend each day, including vacation time and recreational activities. They prefer to know the dates and times of parties, dinners, and other social affairs in advance. They can then be certain that they will not miss something by scheduling another activity at the same time. This planfulness also means that they will likely not be available to accept invitations or attend social events on short notice, since their time will already be scheduled.

Their planfulness also extends to future events and goals. Such long-range planning ensures, for example, that they will meet their important financial and educational objectives. Planful people are not comfortable leaving such important areas of life to chance occurrences in the future over which they will have no control. They are therefore likely to devote time and energy to gathering the information needed to accomplish such long-range planning.

**Open-Ended** People at this pole prefer their leisure time to be unscheduled so they can take advantage of unexpected opportunities that may arise. Planning free time in advance virtually guarantees that something else will come up that is more interesting, important, or rare. In such situations, Open-Ended people may cancel preset plans rather than miss out on a more appealing activity. Their approach to leisure time involves the vibrancy and enthusiasm that results from interacting with an ongoing flow of events. Their liking for variety and improvisation in their use of such time is as meaningful as the specific activities in which they participate.

For Open-Ended people, variety and having the freedom to choose among the events that present themselves are what is most important. They do not necessarily feel they have missed something by choosing one thing over another on the spur of the moment. They may regret having to bypass a particular activity, but this is usually balanced by being able to choose something that matches the mood of the moment. This matching of oneself to the flow of life events and activities cannot occur if the activities and events are planned far in advance. It is only possible with an Open-Ended approach.

## Early Starting–Pressure-Prompted

The fairly narrow focus of this facet is on how we manage time with regard to deadlines.

**Early Starting** People at this pole much prefer to cope with deadlines by starting a task far enough in advance to allow plenty of time to finish. They tend to become quite stressed when they find themselves working until the last minute on projects that have deadlines. The stress caused by time pressure often spills over into relationships outside of the task they are trying to complete because their tension becomes general and persists until the task is done. This is often noticeable to the other people around them.

Early Starting people prefer to know their assignments well in advance. They can then begin their work early and not be pressured to get it done at the last minute. They do their best work when they can avoid last-minute rushes. Unexpected tasks or events that use up the time they had reserved for a scheduled project will be quite distressing for them. Severe time pressure can become so stressful for Early Starting people that they may find it hard to concentrate on what they are doing. They will then use their available time inefficiently.

Early Starting people feel like failures when they miss a deadline or were so rushed that they were not able to do their best work. Finishing just in time may be somewhat disconcerting, particularly if they have not had a chance to check their work thoroughly. Having time to spare after a task is completed is especially satisfying to them and they explicitly include such time for checking or reviewing in their plan.

**Pressure-Prompted** People at this pole do their best work when they are under sufficient time pressure that meeting the deadline is a challenge. They find it hard to work well without the time pressure of a deadline. In fact, others observing them may have grave doubts that they will complete the job on time. Pressure-Prompted people find the adrenaline rush of trying to meet a tight schedule almost enjoyable. They may put off working on a project until the deadline is close enough that they will have to make a significant effort to finish it in time. This can be mistaken for procrastination, but it is actually not an avoidance of doing the task. While they appear to be doing nothing and letting valuable time slip by, they are actually working inside their heads. During this "inactive" time these people are doing something very similar to what a steam engine does when it stands idly building up a head of steam. Pressure-Prompted people need a "gestation" period to stimulate the energy they need to tackle the project. If they are working on several projects, this gestation may even occur while they rush to finish other tasks whose deadlines are imminent.

The Pressure-Prompted approach to work involves more than just enjoying the energy aroused by time pressure. People at this pole feel that they actually do their best work under the stress of a severe time constraint. They have more ideas, work more efficiently, and think more clearly under those conditions. Depending on what kind of work they are doing, they may not know how long it will take them to finish. However, their awareness of the time available helps them determine what to include in the finished product and what to discard. Time pressure is thus an important part of their work style and they can use this to structure their finished product. If Pressure-Prompted people meet a deadline with time to spare, they are likely to feel that they began too soon and wasted time that could have been spent on something else. In fact, their enthusiasm may also fade near the end of a project if they finish too early. Such waning of enthusiasm may be a short-lived problem, however, as Pressure-Prompted people usually have several other imminent deadlines to which they can turn their attention.

## Scheduled–Spontaneous

This facet centers on the degree of structure in one's daily activities.

**Scheduled** People at this pole are comfortable with routine because it enables them to function efficiently. The appeal of routine is that time and energy are not wasted and things can be done "correctly." Routine promotes concentration and ensures continuity in work, so that it all flows together smoothly, efficiently, and as flawlessly as possible. Scheduled people enjoy fitting themselves into a routine that allows them to blend their own abilities and energy with those of other people. This ensures a predictable and productive flow of tasks and activities. They like structuring their daily activities in a known sequence because it prevents the energy waste that could occur if they had to suddenly shift gears. Scheduling their time allows them to look forward to all parts of their day, whether they are restful, satisfying, personally meaningful, or exciting. For scheduled people, routine itself is restful and comfortable in that one is not caught by surprise.

For the Scheduled person, routine also includes broad spans of time, in addition to morning rituals of rising, dressing, and getting ready for work. Weekly, seasonal, and yearly patterns of work, leisure, and family time are involved. The repetition used for some daily and longer-term routines is itself meaningful, providing a kind of anchor by which friendships and family relations are maintained.

Scheduled people are able to function without a fixed pattern of daily activities, for no one's days are all the same. However, they are apt to feel uncomfortable without a structure by which their days and weeks can be organized. If such a structure is missing, they may seek ways of recapturing at least parts of their previous routines to restore order and avoid distressing confusion.

**Spontaneous** People at this pole are energized by the prospect of variety in their daily work. The very thought of following the same routine day after day feels cramped and confining. They can work within a routine when it is necessary but find it painful to do so. They work best and with greatest energy when their work presents them with constant variety, and they will likely find as many ways as possible to introduce it into their work. Otherwise, they will become bored. They like the freedom to decide what tasks they will do and when. If they have this freedom, they may begin their workday by tackling whatever task strikes their fancy first, moving on to the others as they feel inclined, regardless of any deadlines attached to tasks.

Spontaneous people may also be bored by the thought of longer-term routines. Annual family vacations, holiday and birthday celebrations, and other recurring events may leave them cold. They may suggest some variations in ways of celebrating seasonal holidays just to keep them fresh. If there is too much routine in too many areas of their lives, people at this pole can break the monotony by exploring new activities. They may take courses at local colleges, join clubs, do volunteer work, or otherwise spend leisure time doing things they have never tried before. Variety and the freedom to respond on the spur of the moment are essential for their mental health. Being stuck in a rut from which there is no obvious escape is one of the worst things that can happen to them.

## Methodical–Emergent

This facet is narrowly focused on how we sequence the smaller tasks that need to be done in order to finish larger projects. Time and scheduling are not considerations here.

**Methodical** For people at this pole, getting ready to tackle a large project begins with organizing themselves and whatever materials, tools, or other people they will need. They may make lists of what they need to do and make notes about the specific steps required and the order in which they will do them. They make sure they have the necessary materials available or arrange to acquire them when they are needed. They may even arrange their materials in the order in which they will be used. They therefore will be unlikely to have trouble finding what they need when they need it. If help from others in doing something is necessary, Methodical people will contact those people well in advance. They may also call to remind these helpers shortly before they are needed.

Methodical people believe that approaching tasks in this way saves time. It also minimizes mistakes and reduces costs. These efficiencies produce faster and better work, as well as personal satisfaction. Methodical people enjoy organizing their work, tools, and materials. Doing so frees them to concentrate on doing a good job. If they have to work on a task with someone who is not Methodical, they may find the resulting inefficiencies frustrating. They may do as much advance organization as possible to minimize such frustration and accomplish the task efficiently.

Methodical people are likely to read through the complete set of directions that come with a project before starting to work on it. That way they know what tools and tasks are required and what sequence they should follow. By doing this, they may get a good enough grasp of the project that they can complete it correctly with only minor detours. Methodical people like to set subgoals or milestones to help them assess whether they are on track.

Methodical teachers and trainers function best by making well-ordered lesson plans that build the students' knowledge sequentially. This ensures that important objectives are covered adequately. They also organize their lesson plans around explicit learning objectives. The lesson's parts must fit together well so that students will be best able to grasp new material.

**Emergent** People at this pole tend to treat projects as explorations or discoveries and take delight in finding out what to do and how to do it as they go along. They do not usually start a large task by beginning with the first step. In fact, they may not complete any of the steps in a particular order, unless this is absolutely necessary. When they do make an outline or a list of required tasks in tackling a large project, it is apt to be very general. The list may include the tasks to be done, but it will not necessarily reflect the order in which they need to be or will be done. Taking time to organize tools, materials, and people before beginning is not satisfying, interesting, or efficient for Emergent people. They prefer a looser, less structured approach to preparing for and carrying out tasks. They are eager to tackle parts of a task that interest them first, and they proceed to the other steps the same way. When a strict sequence of steps is required to complete the task correctly, they may discover this sequence by trial and error. As a last resort, they may read directions. Their exploratory approach means that they most likely will look for tools only when they get to a stage that requires them. At that point, they may have difficulty finding them; the tools may have been left with another project, or not yet returned to their usual place.

If they read directions at all, people at this pole almost never read them completely through before beginning a project. That would take the exploratory spirit out of the whole endeavor. They may glance at any diagrams shown, begin looking for parts that match those in the picture, and proceed from that point. If a part is missing or mislabeled, they will likely discover this only after they have already partially assembled the piece.

With the exploratory approach of Emergent people, the completion of one task leads to starting another. This trail of associations from one task to another can be best described as playing the whole thing by ear. At the end, the Emergent person will have an overall picture of how all the pieces fit together. This approach is particularly suited to new situations or projects where the specific tasks involved are not known, or where improvisation is needed. By tackling the core piece first, Emergent people spend most of their time and energy on what is most important. They then don't need to spend as much energy on the "frills."

Teachers and trainers at the Emergent pole prefer an adaptable approach to lesson plans. Their plans are likely to be general rather than detailed and to leave much room for improvisation. They may introduce new material that was not in their outline or digress and explore a particular topic in greater depth than they originally had planned. They are likely to explore new areas that were not in the plan at all if class interest warrants this. They will still cover the major learning objectives, but their sequence arises dynamically out of their unique interaction with a particular class on a particular day.

## Research Data Supporting the Facets

Research data included in this section are limited to correlational relationships with the *California Psychological Inventory*™ (CPI™) scales, the *Adjective Check List* (ACL) scales, and specific adjectives that respondents indicated as describing themselves. Brief definitions of CPI scales and ACL scales can be found in appendix C. Only scales correlated for both males and females are included. Data showing gender differences in research relationships for selected variables appears in chapter 5.

Please also note that each facet block is considered as a unit distinct from the other three facet blocks. Thus, for example, some CPI scales may be correlated with facets within the Extraversion–Introversion block as well as with some in the Sensing–Intuition block. Each table presents only common and unique relationships *within each facet block.*

In addition, within each facet block, the word *commonalities* refers only to relationships that are shared by all five facets or are shared by four of the five facets, and the term *distinctive qualities* refers only to relationships that are unique to one of the five facets in a block or are shared with just one other facet in that block.

To aid in differentiating between qualities that are common to all or most facets within a dichotomy and qualities that distinguish individual facets, table 3.2 (the E–I facet block), table 3.3 (the S–N facet block), table 3.4 (the T–F facet block), and table 3.5 (the J–P facet block) contain the following information:

- Correlational commonalities found in statistical analyses of concurrently collected data from the national sample used for the development of the MBTI Step II revision
- Correlational data describing features that appear to distinguish the facets from one another

Readers should bear in mind that correlational data reported here help validate the meaning of the facets and add richness to our general understanding. However, these research results should not necessarily be taken as applying to all individuals or to any particular individual who has taken the MBTI Step II assessment. The statements included are based on correlations of .20 or higher, which means that a great deal of variability in facet relationships can be attributed to factors other than any one correlated variable. Tables showing correlation coefficients of Step II facets with other variables appear in chapters 5 and 8.

## Conclusion

Practitioners who are new to the MBTI Step II instrument will likely notice the depth, breadth, and detail in this chapter. They may also feel somewhat overwhelmed by the amount of information and subtleties of meaning reflected in the five facets within each facet block. As with any instrument that acknowledges the complexity of human personality, the practitioner's comfort with the Step II instrument requires experience in using it with clients. By providing feedback to clients about Step II facet scales, practitioners will increase their understanding and skill with surprising speed. Keeping this chapter available when working with clients is highly recommended.

**Table 3.2 Correlational Data for the Extraversion–Introversion Facets**

**Similarities Among Facets**

- In CPI relationships, all five of the facet poles associated with Extraversion are correlated with *Dominance, Sociability, Social Presence, Self-acceptance, Independence, Leadership Potential,* and *Vector 1*. All but the Gregarious facet pole are correlated with *Empathy, Intellectual Efficiency,* and *Creative Temperament.*
- In ACL scale relationships, all five Extraversion facet poles are correlated with the *Exhibition* and *Free Child* scales, all but Expressive are related to the *Heterosexuality* scale, and all but Active are related to the *Free Child* scale.
- People having all five Extraversion facet poles describe themselves as *cheerful, jolly, sociable, talkative,* and *outgoing.*
- No ACL scales and no CPI scales were correlated in common for all five of the facet poles belonging to Introversion. However, people with all five facet poles described themselves as *withdrawn,* and all facet poles but Reflective described themselves as *shy, silent,* and *quiet.*

**Research Correlates for the Initiating–Receiving Facet**

- On the CPI instrument, Initiating and Expressive share a relationship to *Achievement via Independence* and *Work Orientation.*
- No ACL scale relationships were unique for either facet pole.
- Initiating people uniquely described themselves as *confident, energetic,* and *spontaneous;* they shared the adjectives *enthusiastic* and *humorous* with Enthusiastic people and *outgoing* with Gregarious people. Receiving people described themselves as *timid.*

**Research Correlates for the Expressive–Contained Facet**

- On the CPI instrument, Expressive was uniquely correlated with *Psychological-mindedness* and shared with Initiating a relationship to *Achievement via Independence* and *Work Orientation.*
- No ACL scales were unique to either Expressive or Contained.
- Contained people uniquely described themselves as *complicated, aloof,* and *irritable.*

**Research Correlates for the Gregarious–Intimate Facet**

- No CPI scales were unique to either Gregarious or Intimate respondents.
- Gregarious people shared an association with Active people on the *Self-confidence* and *Nurturing Parent* scales of the ACL.
- No individual adjectives were unique to either pole.

**Research Correlates for the Active–Reflective Facet**

- On the CPI instrument, the Active facet pole is uniquely associated with the *Femininity/Masculinity* scale and shares with the Enthusiastic facet pole a correlation with the *Narcissism* scale. There were no correlates on CPI scales for the Reflective pole.
- Active shares the ACL scale *Nurturing Parent* with the Gregarious facet pole. There were no correlates with ACL scales for the Reflective pole.
- Active people uniquely described themselves as *playful* and share *outspoken* with Initiating people. Reflective people uniquely described themselves as *moody, tense, inhibited,* and *interests narrow.*

## Table 3.3 Correlational Data for the Sensing–Intuition Facets

### Similarities Among Facets

- In CPI relationships, all five Intuition facet poles are correlated with *Capacity for Status, Social Presence, Self-acceptance, Empathy, Achievement via Independence, Vector 1,* and *Creative Temperament.* All but the Imaginative facet pole are correlated with *Dominance* and *Independence*, and all but the Original facet pole with *Sociability* and *Intellectual Efficiency*. There were no commonly correlated CPI scales for the Sensing poles of this facet block.
- On ACL scale relationships, all five Intuition facet poles are correlated with the *Creative Personality* scale, all but Imaginative with the *Ideal Self* scale, all but Conceptual with the *Free Child* scale, and all but Abstract with number of *Favorable* adjectives checked.
- People with all five Intuition facet poles described themselves as *artistic, insightful, unconventional,* and *introspective*. All but Theoretical people described themselves as *inventive*. There were no commonly checked adjectives for the Sensing poles of this facet block.

### Research Correlates for the Concrete–Abstract Facet

- No CPI scales were unique for either the Concrete or the Abstract pole of this facet.
- On ACL scales, Abstract shared A-2 with Theoretical.
- Abstract people uniquely described themselves as *charming* and, along with Imaginative people, as *adventurous, dreamy,* and *interests wide*. *Individualistic* was shared with Theoretical and *rebellious* with Original.

### Research Correlates for the Realistic–Imaginative Facet

- No CPI scales were unique for either the Realistic or the Imaginative pole of this facet.
- On ACL scales, Imaginative people shared a correlation with Original people on the *Change* scale.
- Imaginative people uniquely described themselves as *enthusiastic* and, along with Abstract people, as *adventurous* and *interests wide*.

### Research Correlates for the Practical–Conceptual Facet

- On the CPI instrument, the Conceptual pole is uniquely correlated with the *Leadership Potential* scale.
- On ACL scales, the A-4 scale is unique to Conceptual.
- Conceptual people, along with Theoretical people, describe themselves as *reflective*.

### Research Correlates for the Experiential–Theoretical Facet

- No CPI relationships were found for either pole of this facet.
- On ACL scales, the Experiential pole was uniquely correlated with the *Self-control* scale.
- Theoretical people uniquely described themselves as *uninhibited*. Along with Abstract people, they described themselves as *individualistic* and shared *reflective* with Conceptual people.

### Research Correlates for the Traditional–Original Facet

- On the CPI instrument, the *Self-control* scale is uniquely correlated with the Traditional facet pole, and the *Narcissism* scale is unique for the Original facet pole.
- On ACL scales, the *Deference* scale is uniquely related to the Traditional facet pole. Along with the Imaginative pole, the Original pole is correlated with the *Change* scale.
- Original people uniquely described themselves as *daring, enterprising,* and *progressive*.

## Table 3.4 Correlational Data for the Thinking–Feeling Facets

### Similarities Among Facets

- No CPI or ACL scales were common to either T or F facet poles. Nor were any shared by four of the five facet poles.
- No individual adjectives were checked for all or four of the five facet poles.

### Research Correlates for the Logical–Empathetic Facet

- No CPI scale was uniquely associated with the Logical pole.
- The ACL scale *Heterosexuality* was uniquely related to Empathetic, and the *Nurturance* scale was shared with the Tender pole.
- Empathetic people uniquely described themselves as *sentimental* and *sympathetic*.

### Research Correlates for the Reasonable–Compassionate Facet

- On the CPI instrument, the Reasonable pole is uniquely correlated with the *Independence* scale, while the Compassionate pole is uniquely related to the *Femininity/Masculinity* scale.
- The Reasonable pole is uniquely related to the ACL *Adult Scale*.
- No adjectives were held in common for either pole.

### Research Correlates for the Questioning–Accommodating Facet

- On the CPI instrument, Questioning people are uniquely correlated with the *Creative Temperament* and *Narcissism* scales. Accommodating people share with Accepting people a relationship to the *Self-control, Good Impression,* and *Amicability* scales.
- On the ACL scales, Questioning is uniquely correlated with the *Dominance, Exhibition, Autonomy, Change, Creative Personality,* and *Free Child* scales. It shares a relationship to the *Aggression* scale with the Critical pole of Critical–Accepting.
- Questioning people uniquely described themselves as *sarcastic*.

### Research Correlates for the Critical–Accepting Facet

- On the CPI instrument, the Critical pole shares with the Questioning pole a correlation with the *Narcissism* scale. The Accepting pole is uniquely correlated with the *Tolerance* scale and shares the *Self-control, Good Impression,* and *Amicability* scales with the Accommodating pole of Questioning–Accommodating.
- On ACL scales, the Critical pole shares an *Aggression* scale correlation with the Questioning pole.
- No adjectives were held in common for either the Critical or the Accepting pole of this facet.

### Research Correlates for the Tough–Tender Facet

- On CPI scales, the Tender pole shares a correlation to the *Femininity/Masculinity* scale with the Compassionate pole of the Reasonable–Compassionate facet.
- No ACL scales were unique to either the Tough or the Tender pole.
- Tender people uniquely described themselves as *trusting*.

## Table 3.5 Correlational Data for the Judging–Perceiving Facets

### Similarities Among Facets

- On CPI scales, all Judging facet poles were correlated with *Vector 2.* All except Early Starting were correlated with the *Achievement via Conformity* scale. All Perceiving facet poles were correlated with the *Flexibility* scale.
- On ACL scales, all Judging facet poles except Planful were correlated with the *Order* scale.
- No individual adjectives were held in common across all facet poles.

### Research Correlates for the Systematic–Casual Facet

- On the CPI instrument, the Systematic pole is uniquely correlated with the *Socialization* scale.
- On the ACL, Systematic was uniquely correlated with the *Endurance* and *Self-control* scales. The Casual pole was uniquely correlated with the *Change* scale.
- Systematic people uniquely described themselves as *methodical* and *organized,* while Casual people uniquely described themselves as *impulsive*.

### Research Correlates for the Planful–Open-Ended Facet

- There were no correlations that met the criteria for inclusion for either pole, probably because none of the available measures was designed to tap this aspect of leisure activity.

### Research Correlates for the Early Starting–Pressure-Prompted Facet

- There were no research correlates that met the criteria for inclusion for either pole of this facet.

### Research Correlates for the Scheduled–Spontaneous Facet

- On the CPI instrument, the Scheduled pole is uniquely correlated with the *Socialization* and *Amicability* scales and shares the *Responsibility* scale with the Methodical pole of the Methodical–Emergent facet.
- No other correlates that met the criteria were found.

### Research Correlates for the Methodical–Emergent Facet

- On the CPI instrument, the Methodical pole is uniquely correlated with the *Leadership Potential* scale and shares its correlation with the *Responsibility* scale with the Scheduled pole of the Scheduled–Spontaneous facet.
- No other correlates that met the criteria were found.

PART

# Administration and Interpretation

# II

The two chapters in part II form the basis for effective application of the *Myers-Briggs Type Indicator* Step II instrument in any setting.

Although it is the briefest chapter in this manual, chapter 4, "Administering and Scoring the Step II™ Instrument," provides the groundwork needed to ensure accurate and candid results from clients. The chapter includes a review of materials available, suggestions for orienting clients to the Step II tool and dealing with different levels of type awareness, and the various scoring options.

Chapter 5, "Interpreting and Verifying Step II™ Results," is considerably longer than chapter 4. It describes the Step II profile and report and explains in-preference, out-of-preference, and midzone scores and how to interpret and verify them with clients. It also covers the polarity index and its interpretation, as well as the uses and limitations of type-specific score ranges. The chapter offers a detailed procedure for interpreting Step II results to both individuals and groups, and readers are sensitized to the possible influences of age and gender on Step II results. A final section summarizes important Step II information for each of the sixteen types, enabling practitioners to interpret Step II results within the context of dynamic type.

Practitioners may also want to read part III of the *MBTI® Step II™ User's Guide* (Quenk & Kummerow, 2011) for more information about administering and interpreting the Step II assessment.

# Administering and Scoring the Step II™ Instrument

4

CHAPTER OVERVIEW



Many issues and concerns that apply to the administration of the Step I instrument also apply to the Step II assessment. Practitioners who wish to review the relevant Step I information can find it in chapter 5 of Myers et al., 1998. Administration issues related to particular application areas can be found in chapters 10–14 of that volume. This chapter covers the administration and scoring of Form Q.

A major difference between the Step II and Step I instruments is that the Step II tool requires computer scoring to obtain results on the twenty facet scales, while the Step I tool provides the additional options of template scoring and self-scoring to obtain results on the four preferences.

## Step II™ Purchase, Administration, and Use Requirements

The Step II instrument is classified as a level-B tool, which means there are purchase and use requirements. The purchaser must meet one of the following criteria:

- Hold a degree from an accredited college or university and have satisfactorily completed a course in psychological tests and measurement
- Be employed with an academic institution and use the Step II instrument under the supervision of a person at the institution who has the appropriate degree and training

CPP, Inc., publisher of the *Myers-Briggs Type Indicator* (MBTI) personality inventory, offers a certification program that will qualify those with college degrees who have not taken the course in tests and measurement. The program, which is also recommended for purchasers who satisfy the educational requirements, covers the basics of measurement and includes a wealth of information about the MBTI instrument, including the Step I and Step II tools, that is essential for its appropriate administration and interpretation. Purchasers who attended a program prior to January 1, 2009, and wish to use the Step II tool are encouraged to seek training in its interpretation through workshops conducted by several type-training organizations. Further information about certification programs and Step II training may be obtained from CPP, Inc.

Regardless of formal qualifications, appropriate use of the Step II instrument requires a good working knowledge of the basic concepts of type theory as a dynamic approach to understanding personality. This knowledge is available in detail in the most recent edition of the *MBTI® Manual* (Myers et al., 1998).

## Appropriate Populations for Administration

The MBTI Step II instrument is most appropriate for adults and students ages 14 and over who read at a seventh-grade level. However, the same cautions that apply to Form M regarding respondent age and the accuracy of type results also apply to the Step II tool. Step II results can be considered reasonably accurate for students and adults who read at the recommended level, but the tool has not been used with enough younger respondents to confirm that the facet descriptions are correct for them. In addition, Step II facets deal with behaviors that are narrower and more specific than those described by the four MBTI dichotomies and can vary considerably in relation to a respondent's underlying preference, even if the respondent is an adult. Without extensive validation with younger age groups, we do not know how well these facets describe them. Therefore, anyone administering and interpreting the Step II instrument to young people should proceed with caution, since the facets were constructed using an adult population ages eighteen and older. For example, few young people have had enough experience with handling projects to know whether their preference is for being Methodical or Emergent. The same may be true for other narrow areas of preference associated with other facets.

Respondents with vision problems may have difficulty locating the circles on the answer sheet that correspond to the appropriate questions in the question booklet. They may inadvertently skip a line on the answer sheet, and from that point on their answers will be scored incorrectly. Frustration with the answer sheet may lead some respondents to stop before they finish. There are several ways to accommodate the special needs of visually impaired respondents, but some require written permission from the publisher. If the group to be assessed includes many people with vision problems, the practitioner should contact the publisher for advice and/or permission to administer or score the questions in a different format.

The Step II assessment has been translated into several languages. Contact CPP, Inc., for existing and pending translations of the various forms of the MBTI instrument.

## Materials and Options for Administration

Practitioners must make several decisions regarding the Step II materials they intend to use for an individual client or client group. Their choice of options depends on the intended uses of Step II results and the overall context within which the type information is to be used.

### Assessment Materials

The Step II assessment (Form Q of the MBTI instrument) consists of a booklet containing 144 forced-choice items and several different prepaid answer sheets for computer scoring. Answer sheet selection will depend on the administrator's choice of scoring option, as described below. Question booklets are reusable, whereas answer sheets are not.

The Step II tool requires the use of computers because of the complexity of the scoring system, which uses varying item weights to score the twenty facets. Template scoring for the Step II facets is not available. However, practitioners can use Form M templates to obtain each client's Step I four-letter type prior to scoring Step II answer sheets by computer. This procedure is useful when clients have not taken Form M or received an interpretation of their Step I type prior to administration of Form Q. Further information on this option can be found in the administration guidelines below.

It is important to select the Step II form that will produce the desired output—either a four-page profile or an eighteen-page report that includes the profile in a somewhat different format. All options require purchase of Step II (Form Q) item booklets, which are reusable. The four-page profile and the seventeen-page report require their own answer sheets, as shown in table 4.1.

### SkillsOne® Internet Delivery of the Step II™ Instrument

The CPP Web administration site is available under license from the publisher for electronic administration of the Step

**Table 4.1 Answer Sheet Options for Step II™ Administration**

| Option Used | Answer Sheet Requirements |
|---|---|
| **4-page Profile** | MBTI® Step II™ Form Q Profile answer sheet (prepaid) |
| **17-page Report** | MBTI® Step II™ Form Q Interpretive Report answer sheet (prepaid) |

II tool. This system allows the practitioner to provide a Step II interpretation to clients in remote areas. The site has been designed to maintain confidentiality of results.

To begin administration of the Step II assessment, the professional provides the client with a password. The professional is automatically informed via e-mail after the client has taken Form Q and can then download the client's responses to his or her personal computer to produce either the Step II profile or the Step II report. The professional must then use standard Step I and Step II verification procedures to verify the client's type and results on the Step II facets. Other assessments such as the MBTI Step I, CPI, *Strong Interest Inventory*®, and FIRO-B® instruments are also available via this delivery system. Contact the publisher for further information about this option for scoring the Step II assessment.

### Administration Time and Mental Set Requirements

Regardless of the administration option selected, respondents take an average of 25 to 35 minutes to complete Form Q. Respondents with vision problems or those who speak English as a second language may need more time. There is no time limit for taking the Step II assessment. However, as is recommended for the Step I assessment, respondents should be encouraged to work rapidly and make spontaneous choices, rather than study the items at length or strive for consistency in their responses.

### Omissions Policy

Respondents should be encouraged to answer all questions unless they find it impossible to choose between two options. As with the Step I assessment, forcing respondents to choose when a choice would be the same as a guess does not provide evidence of a preference. However, because some Step II facets are composed of as few as five items, too many omissions can affect the accuracy of a respondent's results on a particular facet. A Form Q answer sheet will not be scored if more than five omissions occur over the 144 items. Scoring a profile with this many or more omissions would likely affect the accuracy of the facet scale results.

## Introducing the Step II™ Instrument

In gaining client cooperation for administration of the Step II instrument, one or more of the following brief statements is recommended, depending on the knowledge level and interest of the client:

- The Step II instrument provides information about how an individual expresses five different aspects (or parts) of each of his or her type's four dichotomies (or opposite preference categories).
- The Step II instrument provides information about a person's individuality within his or her type—it explains some of the ways in which people who have verified the same type are different from one another.
- Step II information can help resolve doubts for people who are unsure of one or more of their preferences.
- Remember to answer the Step II questions according to what you prefer and are most comfortable doing, not what you can do when it is required of you.

Because the Step II assessment is appropriately administered and interpreted within the context of the Step I assessment, it is an advantage when respondents have had a Step I whole type interpretation before being presented with the meaning of Step II facets. Practitioners may use one of two administration options, but the Step II tool is introduced in the same manner regardless of the method chosen.

### When the Client Knows His or Her Type

If the client has previously answered standard Form M (or its predecessor, Form G) and was provided with an appropriate interpretation of four-letter type by a qualified professional, Form Q is administered to the client so that the twenty facets can be interpreted. A few cautions are appropriate in this situation.

- Make sure that the previous administrator provided the client with an opportunity to verify his or her type and that the client's basic type knowledge is adequate. If in doubt, review the preferences and help the client identify his or her Step I type. Note, however, that some clients take the Step II assessment in order to obtain clarification about one or more preferences. In such a case, moving quickly to facet results is advisable.
- It is quite likely that a client's understanding does not include an adequate conception of type as a dynamic system. If a client thinks of the four preferences as equivalent to traits that vary in a quantitative fashion, he or she will almost certainly misunderstand and misuse the facet results. A brief review of type dynamics before the Step II interpretation will eliminate that possibility. (For a brief method of explaining the dynamic nature of type, see Myers et al., 1998, pp. 119–20.)

## When the Client Is New to Type

When the client has not answered Form M or Form G and has had little or no exposure to type, Form Q is administered to the client so that both the four-letter type and the twenty facets can be interpreted. The following procedure is recommended.

Use standard Step I guidelines for introducing the MBTI personality inventory. Explain that this form of the instrument (Form Q) also provides detailed information about a respondent's distinctive ways of expressing his or her type, and that you will use both kinds of type information to help the client verify his or her type.

Please note that if you are using a mail-in scoring option, you may wish to use Form M scoring templates *before* mailing in the answer sheets for Step II scoring. Your Step I interpretation can then occur before you have the Step II profile or report available.

## Scoring the Step II™ Instrument

Scores on each of the twenty facets are arrayed around a center point of 0, with 5 points on either side. The Step II profile is arranged so that scores to the left of 0 indicate a preference for facet components associated with Extraversion, Sensing, Thinking, and Judging. Scores to the right of 0 indicate a preference for facet components associated with Introversion, Intuition, Feeling, and Perceiving. This range of scores is typically divided into three categories:

- Scores of 2, 3, 4, or 5 to the left of 0 (associated with E, S, T, or J components)
- Scores of 2, 3, 4, or 5 to the right of 0 (associated with I, N, F, or P components)
- A score of 0 or of 1 to either the left or the right of 0, which defines a midzone that is not clearly associated with either preference pole

The Step II profile and report identify scores with this system, which also provides the basis for interpreting the pattern of a client's results as in-preference (consistent with the underlying Form M preference reported), out-of-preference (opposite the underlying Form M preference reported), or midzone (not associated with either pole of the dichotomy under consideration). The implications of these patterns of scores are discussed in chapter 5.

## Conclusion

In administering the MBTI Step II assessment, it is safest to assume that respondents are unaware of the differences between the MBTI personality inventory and other instruments they may have taken earlier. If they have already received MBTI Step I results, they need to know that the Step I and Step II tools use different scoring systems and that their scores will be interpreted differently. It is therefore best to remind them of the following points:

- The MBTI Step I and Step II instruments are indicators, not tests.
- There are no right or wrong answers, no better or worse types, and no better or worse facet patterns.
- Taking the MBTI Step I and Step II assessments is voluntary, and results depend on the respondent's candid responses.
- Respondents are the final arbiters of the accuracy of Step I and Step II results and will have an opportunity to verify the results of both forms of the MBTI personality inventory.
- Neither the Step I nor the Step II instrument measures intelligence, competence, career success, or psychological health or illness.
- Although the Step I and Step II tools are related in important ways, the scores on the Step II assessment do not add up to the scores on the Step I assessment and must be interpreted differently.

# Interpreting and Verifying Step II™ Results

5

CHAPTER OVERVIEW



Step II results, like Step I results, are meant to be given directly to respondents. Consistent with the *Myers-Briggs Type Indicator* (MBTI) interpretation model, respondents are given the opportunity to verify the accuracy of their reported results in collaboration with a qualified professional. The goal of this chapter is to provide practitioners with the information they need to verify results and interpret the Step II instrument in a variety of circumstances with clients whose levels of knowledge, understanding, interest, and motivation will differ considerably. This chapter covers verification procedures and provides detailed information that will enhance the interpretation process, including suggestions for helping clients clarify their dynamic four-letter type.

## General Interpretation Issues

Clients take the Step II assessment for a variety of reasons. Many people who have taken the Step I assessment hope to gain some insight into their individuality through the Step II assessment. Others want information that will help them clarify their underlying preferences on the Step I assessment, and still others hope that the individual differences revealed by the Step II assessment will prove useful in areas such as personal and career counseling, team relationships, and leadership. Some people are asked to take Form Q for work-related purposes and may be minimally motivated or largely unaware of its potential usefulness. It is also quite possible that filling out Form Q may be a person's first introduction to psychological type concepts, which means that interpreting and verifying Step I results along with interpreting Step II results are also part of the practitioner's task. Regardless of respondent motivation or its absence, however, experience indicates that clients overwhelmingly appreciate and use Step II information that has been effectively provided to them.

Step II results are even more likely than Step I results to be misinterpreted, overinterpreted, or too readily accepted as "true" by clients. Adding to this likelihood are the number of facets to be reviewed, the narrowly defined content focus of many facets, and the complex relationship of the facets to underlying preferences, type dynamics, and whole type. Interpreters must therefore use skill in explaining the purposes of the the Step II instrument, describing its content, and guiding clients in evaluating their reported results. Because Step II results must be interpreted within the context of the Step I tool, practitioners should also be attentive to their clients' varying levels of Step I knowledge and make every effort to establish adequate Step I understanding as a solid basis for a Step II interpretation.

### Evidence Regarding Client Verification of Step II™ Results

The Step I instrument has been the subject of a number of studies that compare reported and client-verified type, although the comparability of study designs, samples used, and verification methods is somewhat problematical (see Myers et al., 1998, for studies of Step I reported and best-fit type). Systematically collected data comparing reported and verified Step II results are not yet available, although such information would be highly desirable. At this time, anecdotal evidence from practitioners is the only estimate of client assessments of the accuracy of their results. A survey of six practitioners who have been regularly administering the Step II assessment (Form K version) for more than five years indicated that clients generally agree with their facet placements. Disagreements tend to involve shifts from a midzone to one or the other pole of a facet, or shifts to a midzone from a facet score that was associated with one or the other pole. It is rare for a client to judge that he or she is more accurately described by the pole opposite a reported result. This finding is borne out by the test-retest data reported in chapter 7. Overall, client disagreement on facet scale placement ranges from none to two out of the twenty facet scales.

Practitioners also report that clients find their out-of-preference results especially meaningful in helping them resolve doubt or confusion about their type. Clarification may occur with respect to one or another underlying preference and may also include understanding the dynamics of their type. Similar consistent observations have been forthcoming from attendees of professional workshops that provide training in the use of the Step II instrument.

### Verification of Client Step I™ Knowledge

Step I practitioners often find themselves with clients or several members of a client group who have already taken the MBTI personality inventory. In these cases, it is essential to clarify client understanding of the instrument, particularly with regard to its typological and dynamic nature. Without this step, practitioners risk client misinterpretation of the applications or advanced training they are preparing to introduce. When using the Step II tool, it is equally if not more important to verify the accuracy of client knowledge of the Step I tool.

**Naive users of the MBTI instrument and their clients often mistake the four MBTI dichotomies for four unidimensional independent traits. The potential for viewing the twenty Step II facets as independent traits is even greater.**

There are two reasons for the greater risk of misinterpreting the Step II facets. First, there are so many of them, and second, many of the facets (for example, Gregarious–Intimate) appear similar to common behavioral traits. Technically qualified users of the Step II instrument (those who meet purchase requirements but have neither read the manual nor received Step II training) can easily infer such a trait perspective. They are unlikely to think of each facet as describing opposite "miniature worldviews" (as revealed in the descriptions of the facets in chapter 3 and supported by the validity data in chapter 8) that encompass much more than the simple behaviors reflected in the item content of the facet. Interpreters are encouraged to use language that will convey Step II meaning appropriately, thereby avoiding inaccurate inferences by clients. Table 5.1 lists common interpretation errors that occur with both Step I and Step II results when users misrepresent type categories as trait variables.

## Interpretation Materials Available

Practitioners can use either a four-page profile or an eighteen-page report when providing feedback to clients. The information in the four-page profile is included in the eighteen pages of the report. In the following discussion, *the profile* refers to the four-page profile and *the report* refers to the lengthier report.

### The Profile

There are two parts to the profile: the client profile and the Interpreter's Summary.

**Table 5.1 Interpretation Errors Resulting from Treating Type Categories as Trait Variables in the Step I™ and Step II™ Instruments**

| Step I™ Error | Step II™ Error |
|---|---|
| Reading positive or negative meaning into numerical preference clarity indexes by assuming that more clarity, less clarity, or moderate clarity is better or worse. | Assuming that Step II scores have positive or negative meaning—i.e., that scores at the poles of facet scales are better than scores in the midzone, or vice versa. |
| Assuming that people with very clear preferences have more of the function or attitude than people with preferences that are less clear. | Assuming that people who score at a facet pole have more of that pole and less or none of the opposite pole and/or that people in the midzone have either an equal amount or a deficit of both poles. |
| Believing that greater preference clarity implies greater skill or maturity of use of a preference. | Believing that people who score at the poles have greater skill or maturity of use of that pole—or that people who score in the midzone are equally skilled at using both poles. |
| Inferring that one or the other preference pole of a dichotomy is better or healthier than the other. | Inferring that one or the other pole of a facet scale is better or healthier than the other. This error is even more potent in Step II because there are obvious societal biases favoring some facet poles over their opposites (e.g., Early Starting–Pressure-Prompted). |
| Assessing people from the standpoint of a single norm of psychological health or competence rather than considering what is usual and expected for their type. | Assessing psychological health and competence from the standpoint of societal biases that value one facet pole over its opposite. |

**Client Profile** The first three pages are devoted to the client profile, which provides a very brief description of Step I Form M results and a graph showing preference clarity indexes on the four dichotomies. Step II results are introduced by a concise explanation of how to interpret the graphs, which show the respondent's results on the five facets of each dichotomy. Three descriptive words or phrases appear under each facet pole. Scores are shown as bars that vary in length according to numerical scores. Areas with contrasting shading (or different colors for the color-printed version) identify score ranges that are in-preference, out-of-preference, or in the midzone. Figure 5.1 shows the first three pages of a sample four-page client profile.

**Interpreter's Summary** This is the fourth page of the profile. It provides information that may be useful during the interpretation session, including an indication of the average range of scores for people of the respondent's reported type, the polarity index (discussed later in this chapter and in chapter 7), information on item omissions, and brief definitions of terms. The Interpreter's Summary is also designed for ease of use by researchers. Interpreters may share the details of this summary with clients at their discretion. Bear in mind, however, that clients can easily misunderstand or misinterpret numerical data, especially those associated with type concepts. It is therefore important to ensure that clients understand the information in the Interpreter's Summary. Figure 5.2 shows a sample Interpreter's Summary that completes the client profile in figure 5.1.

## The Report

The report includes the following information:

- A brief explanation of psychological type and the four dichotomies
- A graph of the respondent's reported Form M type and a corresponding type description
- An explanation of the Step II facets and instructions on how to understand the graphs of facet results
- Four pages of detailed information on the client's facet preferences for each dichotomy (one page per dichotomy), containing the graph of results on that set of facets and a set of statements that describe the facet pole or midzone result reported. These statements combine the consistent self-reports of many clients and workshop participants with the item-based descriptions in chapter 3. Clients can look at graphs of their results to find the three descriptive words associated with the nonpreferred facet pole, or with both poles, in the case of midzone results. Figure 5.3, on page 59, shows a sample report page for the E–I dichotomy.
- Individualized facet scale information in the areas of communication, decision making, change management, and conflict management. (See chapter 10 for a description of report content in these areas.)
- Information about type dynamics and the natural sequential development of the respondent's type

# LAURA QUINCY

## REPORTED TYPE: **ENFJ**

AUGUST 8, 2008

This profile gives you information about your personality type based on your answers to the MBTI Form Q instrument. It first indicates your Step I results—your reported four-letter type. Next it shows your Step II results—your expression of five facets of each of the four type dichotomies.

## Your Step I™ Results

ENFJs tend to be sociable, diplomatic, empathetic, responsive, and responsible. They feel concern for what others think or want and try to handle things with due regard for the other person's feelings. They enjoy being in groups and enjoy helping others develop their potential.

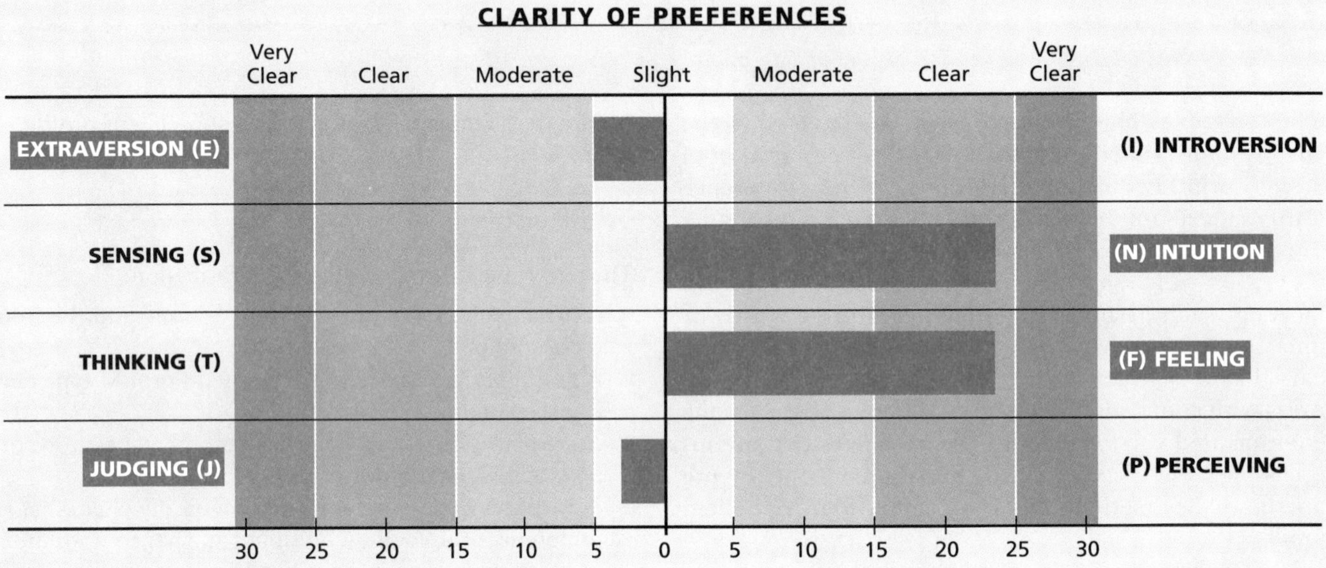


The length of the bars on the graph above shows how consistently you chose one preference pole over the other. The longer the bar, the more often your answers indicated that pole, and the more likely it is that the instrument has accurately reflected your preference.

Figure 5.1 Pages 1, 2, and 3 of Sample Profile

## Your Step II™ Results

The graphs show how you express five facets of each MBTI dichotomy. Your results indicate how you may be similar to and different from other people of your personality type. The longer the bar, the clearer your preference is for that pole of the facet. Scores of 2–5 that are on the same side as your overall preference indicate in-preference results. Scores of 2–5 on the opposite side of your preference indicate out-of-preference results. Scores of 0 and 1 are in the midzone and often mean a situational or muted use of either pole.

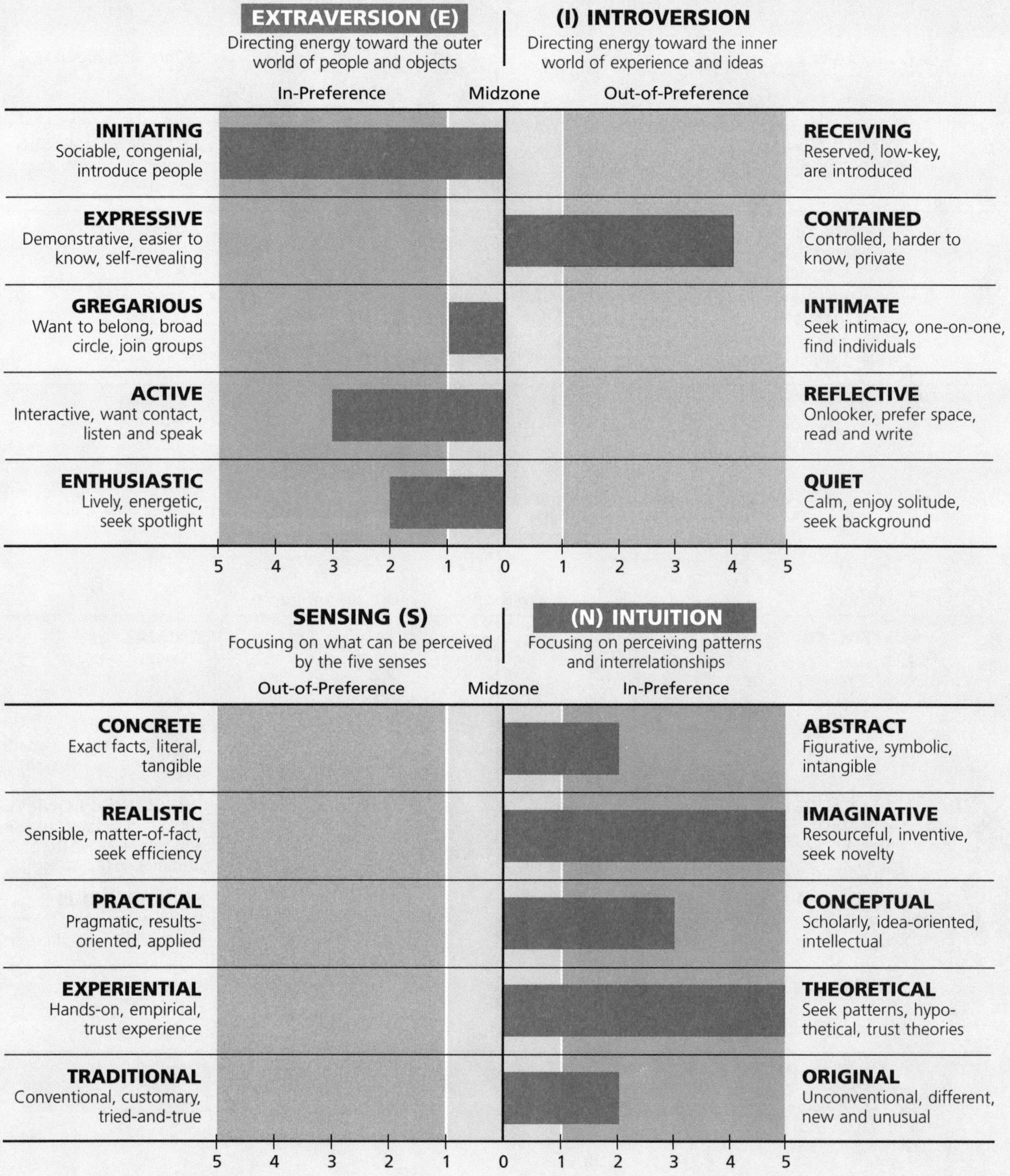


Figure 5.1 Pages 1, 2, and 3 of Sample Profile, *continued*

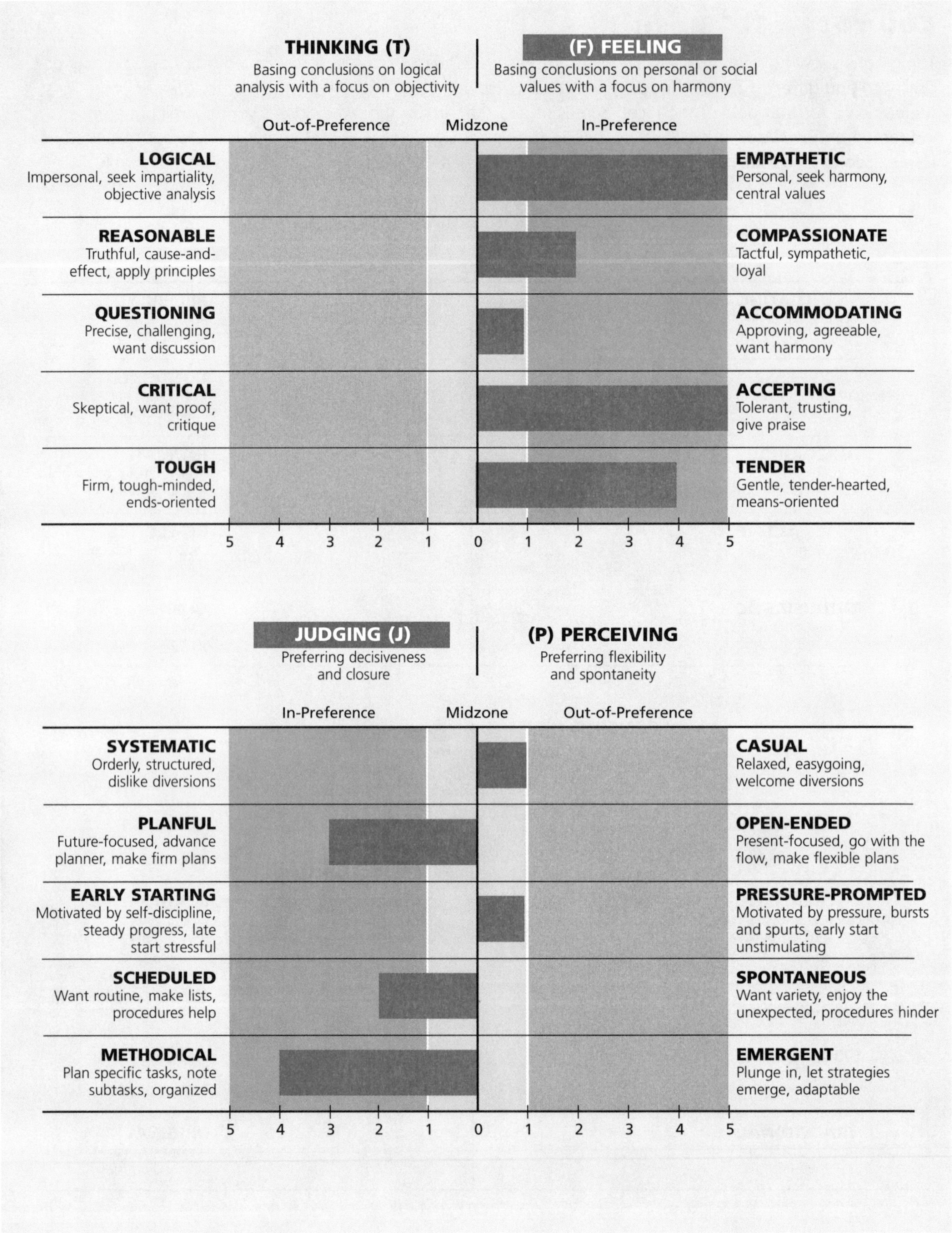


Figure 5.1 Pages 1, 2, and 3 of Sample Profile, *continued*

## Interpreter's Summary

### PREFERENCE CLARITY INDEXES FOR REPORTED TYPE: ENFJ

| Extraversion: Slight (5) | Intuition: Clear (23) | Feeling: Clear (23) | Judging: Slight (3) |
|---|---|---|---|

### FACET SCORES AND THE AVERAGE RANGE OF SCORES FOR OTHER ENFJs

The bars on the graphs below show the average range of scores that occurred for the ENFJs in the national sample. The bars show scores that are −1 to +1 standard deviation from the mean. The vertical line in each bar shows ENFJs' mean score. The bold numbers show the respondent's scores.

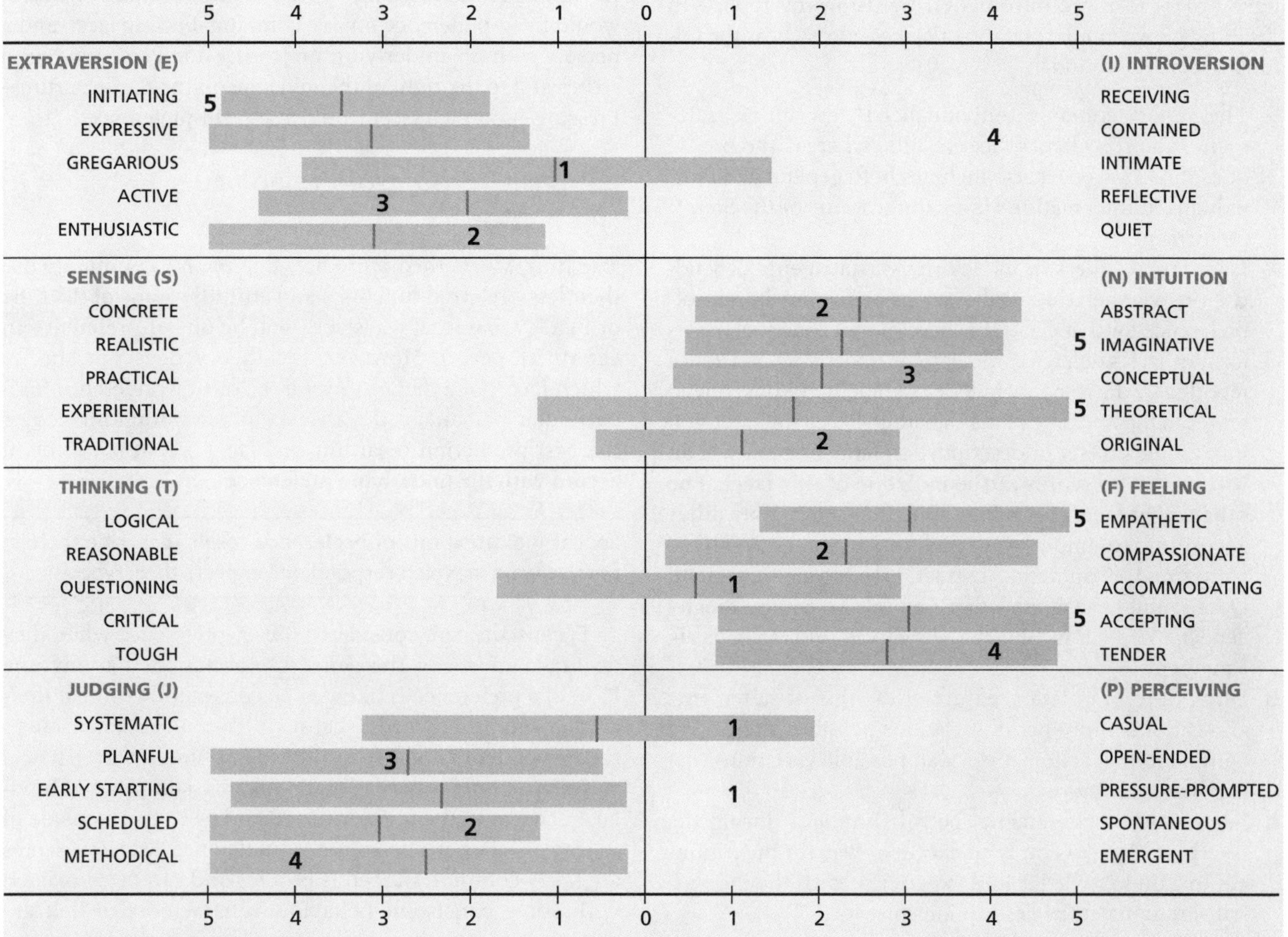


### POLARITY INDEX: 66

The polarity index, which ranges from 0 to 100, shows the consistency of a respondent's facet scores within a profile. Most adults score between 50 and 65, although higher indexes are common. An index that is below 45 means that the respondent has many scores in or near the midzone. This may be due to mature situational use of the facet, answering the questions randomly, lack of self-knowledge, or ambivalence about use of a facet. Some such profiles may be invalid.

**Number of Omitted Responses: 0**

Figure 5.2 Sample Interpreter's Summary

- An individualized type designation that integrates distinctive features of the respondent's Step II results with his or her whole type. For example, a respondent might be described as an "Accommodating, Scheduled ISTP." Laura Quincy (figures 5.1 and 5.2) would be called a "Contained ENFJ."
- A client summary page showing the respondent's brief type description, graph of facet results on all twenty facets, and individualized type designation
- The Interpreter's Summary, as described above

Naturally, the greater length of the report compared to that of the profile means that both practitioner and client have access to more information by using the report. In deciding between interpretation devices, please bear the following points in mind.

- The report contains individualized descriptive statements about a client's facet results, whereas the profile does not. The report also includes both general and individualized information about applications of the Step II instrument.
- Each report differs in its descriptive statements depending on whether the results are in-preference or out-of-preference for that client. In addition, midzone statements for nine facets differ according to the underlying preference reported by the respondent. For example, an Extravert who scores in the midzone of the Initiating–Receiving facet will find a different set of descriptive statements than will an Introvert who scores in the midzone of this facet. The other eight facets for which midzone statements differ according to underlying preference are Expressive–Contained, Concrete–Abstract, Traditional–Original, Questioning–Accommodating, Critical–Accepting, Tough–Tender, Early Starting–Pressure-Prompted, and Methodical–Emergent.
- Due to the proprietary nature of the sets of statements and the sheer number of variations possible, there is no compilation of statements for all possible variations that occur across reports.
- Reviewing the statements both before and during the interpretation session is an excellent way for practitioners to gain knowledge and experience with the individual variations in the descriptions provided.

## Interpretation of Facet Scores

As previously described, facet scores are arrayed as eleven data points consisting of scores of 1–5 to the left and 1–5 to the right of a 0 center point. As is traditional in arraying MBTI data, scores to the left of the central point indicate E, S, T, or J poles of a facet, while scores to the right show facet poles associated with I, N, F, or P. Within any of the four dichotomies, an individual's facet scores can be on the same side as the underlying preference as reported by Form M (in-preference scores), on the opposite side to the underlying preference (out-of-preference scores), or in the midzone. Although the 0 point separates facet scores associated with E, S T, or J from those associated with I, N, F, or P, a broader midzone range of scores is used for purposes of interpretation.

### In-Preference Scores

Facet scores are considered in-preference when they conform to the respondent's underlying preference. For example, a person with a Sensing preference whose facet score of 5 lies to the left of the midzone on the Concrete–Abstract facet is in-preference on this facet, a Thinking type with a score of 3 to the left of the midzone on the Logical–Empathetic facet would be in-preference on the Thinking–Feeling facet, and a person with an underlying preference for Perceiving who scores at 2 to the right of the midzone on the Early Starting–Pressure-Prompted facet would also be in-preference.

### Rationale for Out-of-Preference and Midzone Scores

The Jung-Myers theory predicts that people commonly use their less preferred functions and attitudes some of the time or in a few habitual ways (i.e., will be out-of-preference in certain respects). However, the theory does not specify which facets of a dichotomy will be out-of-preference for a particular person. In the absence of such foreknowledge, the best prediction regarding any facet is that it will be in accord with the underlying preference.

**Scores indicating out-of-preference results describe the distinctive ways in which respondents express their type.**

Facet scores are considered out-of-preference when they do not conform to the general expectation that any one facet of a preference is likely to be consistent with that preference—in other words, that it will be on the same side as the respondent's underlying attitude or function preference.

Because type theory is based on an assumption of bipolarity, scores in the midzone (at 0 and at 1 on either side of 0), can also be considered out-of-preference. Midzone scores are fairly common in Step II profiles and can be associated with some consistent behavioral characteristics that are summarized later in this chapter. However, the interpretation of midzone scores on any facet requires caution for two reasons. First, items on the facets ask about specific behaviors in particular circumstances that, while related to the underlying dichotomy, may not be *central* to it, and second, unlike with the descriptions of the poles of the facets, there is no psychometric basis for descriptions of midzone scores.

### Out-of-Preference Scores

A score that falls at the pole opposite the respondent's underlying preference is out-of-preference. As a general rule, scores of 2–5 to the right of the midzone for E, S, T, and J

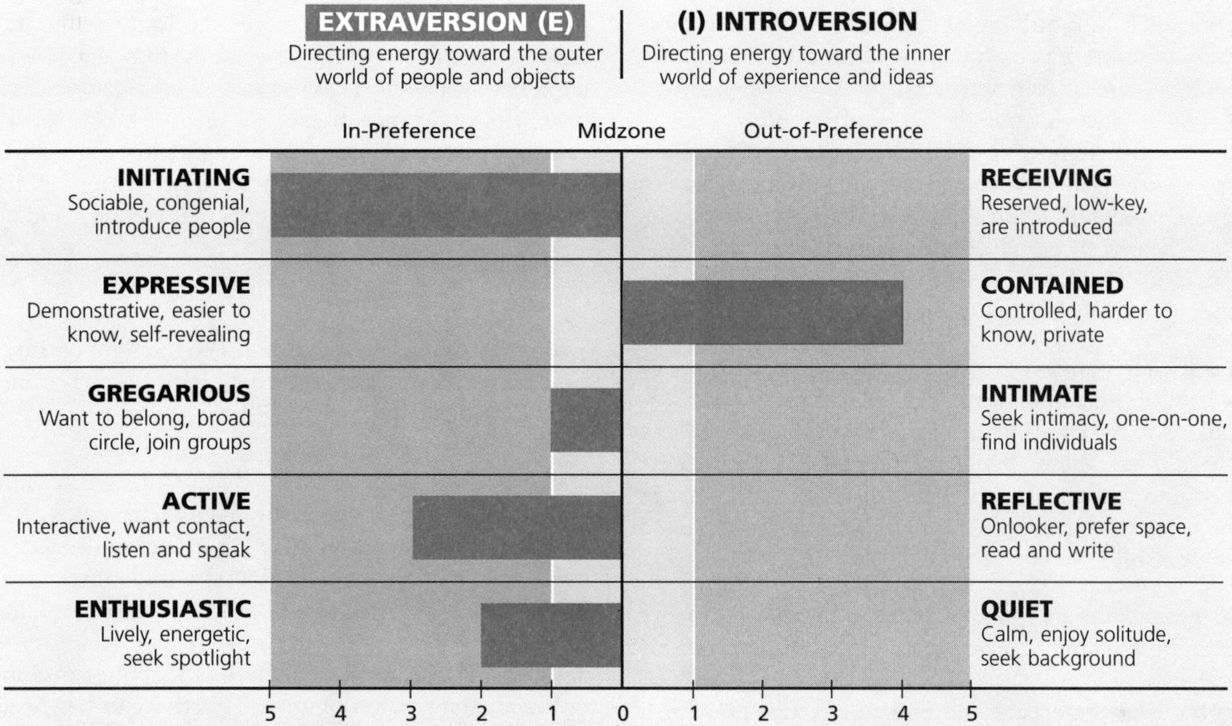


**Initiating** (in-preference)

- Are assertively outgoing in social situations, planning and directing gatherings.
- Act as a social facilitator, arranging the situation to get what you feel is best.
- Carry out social obligations with finesse, introducing people to each other with ease.
- Enjoy linking people whose interests are similar.
- Genuinely want people to interact.

**Contained** (out-of-preference)

- Have a private, vulnerable part that is very hard to share, even with people close to you.
- Use your extraverted manner to avoid talking about anything too personal.
- May feel awkward talking about private matters.
- Don't talk much, unless you feel your contributions will really add something.

**Gregarious–Intimate** (midzone)

- Like large-group activities or one-on-one conversations at different times.
- Find that your degree of comfort with strangers depends on the situation.
- Appear outgoing at times and reserved at other times.
- May not want many intense intimate relationships.
- Are moderately comfortable relating to casual acquaintances.

**Active** (in-preference)

- Prefer active participation rather than passive observation.
- Learn better by doing, hearing, and asking questions than by reading and writing.
- Like to communicate in person, either face-to-face or voice-to-voice.
- Would rather talk than write about a topic.

**Enthusiastic** (in-preference)

- Like being where the action is.
- Often seek to be the center of attention.
- Show wit and humor when you talk with others.
- Feel that life is meant to be exciting.
- Catch others up in your enthusiasms.
- Get bored without activity, so you make it happen and often engage others in the activity.

Figure 5.3 Sample Report Page for Facets of the E–I Dichotomy underlying preferences and scores of 2–5 to the left of the midzone for I, N, F, or P preferences are considered out-of-preference.[1] Thus, a person with a preference for Intuition who has a score of Concrete 2 on the Concrete–Abstract facet of the S–N block would be out-of-preference.

An out-of-preference result that is verified by the client may provide evidence about that individual's type dynamics or type development. Similarly, verified midzone results may also be evidence of dynamically appropriate use of the tertiary or inferior function. The practitioner might ask one or more of the following questions:

- Has the client always functioned in accord with his or her out-of-preference or midzone score?
- Can he or she identify life experiences or circumstances that may have stimulated development of this approach?
- How and when is the opposite (in-preference) pole of the facet (or both poles, for a midzone result) used comfortably?

Many respondents are aware of nuances of their personality functioning and enjoy giving examples of their motivations and behaviors.

Both out-of-preference and midzone results are worth discussing with clients as evidence of distinctiveness within their type. For example, a 45-year-old ENTJ manager may adaptively express her inferior introverted Feeling function by being Accommodating rather than Questioning. When asked about it, she may respond that she learned to use this approach as a way of accomplishing important goals. Her Accommodating approach is now habitual in many situations, and it is comfortable and satisfying. Or an INTP whose auxiliary function is extraverted Intuition may have a score of 3 on the Practical side of the Practical–Conceptual facet of the S–N block. He expresses a love of underlying concepts but also a desire to see his ideas result in practical improvements in his areas of interest. This could be a way of expressing his tertiary Sensing function. An ENTP systems programmer may explain his midzone score on the Methodical–Emergent facet as behavior he consciously learned for his job. Although he has made good use of a Methodical approach over the years, he is aware of the effort it requires and knows it is not his natural one.

## Out-of-Preference Results That Do Not Meet the Specified Criteria

Sometimes one score that is numerically in the midzone (0 or 1) "appears" to be out-of-preference relative to clear scores on the other three or four facets in that block. However, because the score is in the midzone, the computer program that generates the Step II report does not identify the result as out-of-preference. Nevertheless, such results may be worthy of exploration as possibly out-of-preference for a particular client, especially if that client feels he or she is not well described by the midzone interpretation. Figure 5.4 shows such a pattern on the E–I dichotomy for a person with an E preference. Four of the five scores are clearly on the "E" side, making the fifth score of "1" toward the Contained side of the Expressive–Contained facet worthy of consideration as possibly out-of-preference. In fact, the client who obtained these scores found them quite meaningful in relation to both childhood and adolescent issues and her current difficulties in sharing her innermost concerns with her husband.

## Midzone Scores

Scores of 1 to the left of 0, 0, and 1 to the right of 0 are midzone scores. Midzone scores may indicate one or more of the following qualities.

### Habitual Consideration of Both Poles of a Facet

A person might report comfort in using both poles of a facet and feel equally satisfied with either pole. An ENFJ homemaker might explain that she finds it necessary to use both poles of several S–N facets because the behaviors described by both poles are valuable and necessary in her daily life. For example, she may talk about developing a rather abstract vision of a family activity in her head and then planning how to work it out given the practical constraints of her immediate situation (Concrete–Abstract facet). She may also note that although the activity was a new one, it incorporated some of the familiar routines her family enjoys (Traditional–Original facet).

### Ambivalence About Use of a Facet

A person may be equally drawn toward and away from the two opposite poles of a facet, finding that neither is consistently appealing or totally satisfying as an approach. For example, an ISTP may want to remain receptive to possibilities when solving problems at work (Spontaneous) yet also appreciate the advantages of sticking to a schedule in order to implement problem solutions (Scheduled). This individual may have developed a way of accommodating the type dynamics of an ISTP, combining the energy of the auxiliary extraverted Sensing function, which wants to stay open to experience, and the introverted Thinking energy of the dominant function, which is exerting pressure for an efficient, effective solution.

### Habitual Situational Use of a Facet

Some respondents who score in the midzone describe their use of one or the other pole of a facet as a function of the particular circumstances in which they find themselves. Sometimes the choices may be clearly connected to work versus home; at other times and for other people, the distinctions may not be as clear-cut. For example, an ENTP may describe his "tough" approach to colleagues at work and his "tender" way of relating to his children, or an INFJ may explain her midzone score on Methodical–Emergent as a function of whether she is working and managing her household or on vacation.

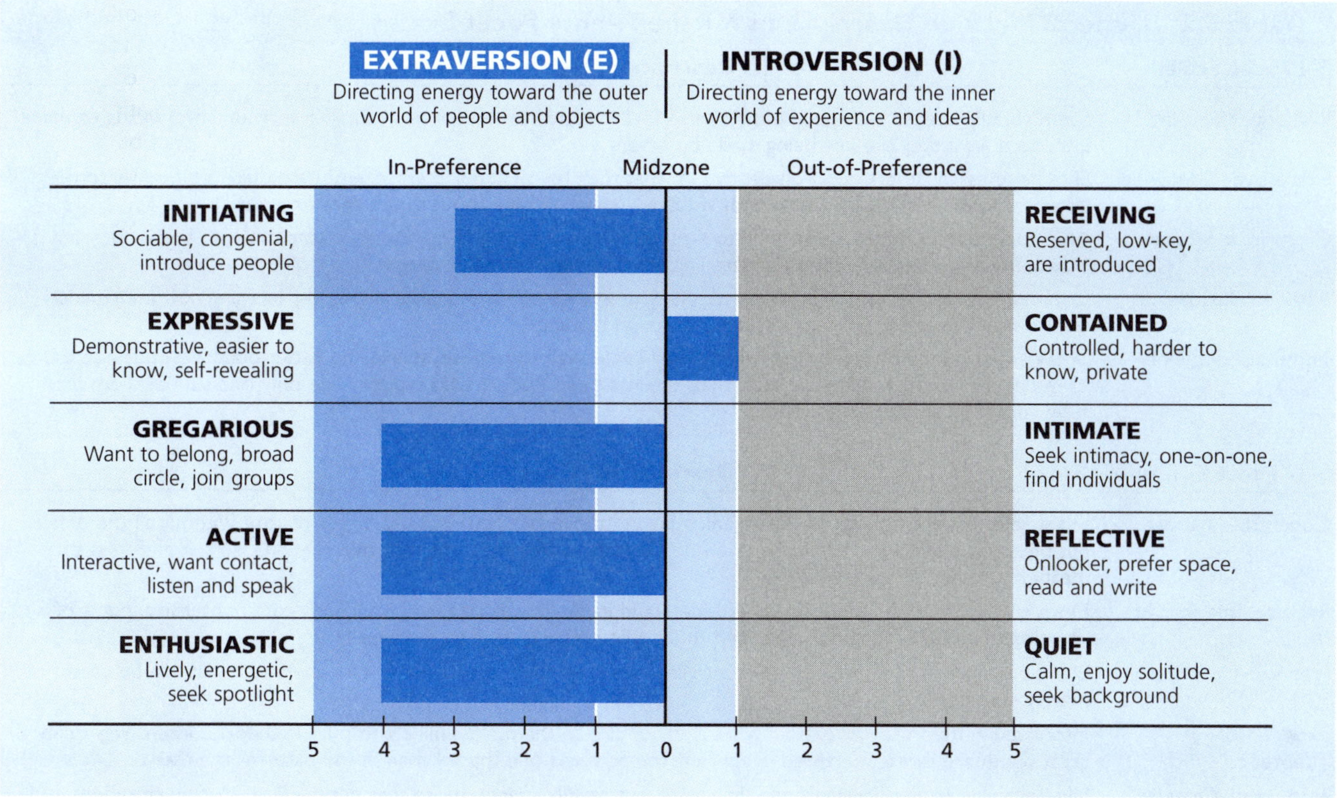


Figure 5.4 Example of Out-of-Preference Results That Do Not Meet Criteria

When interpreting midzone scores to a client, it is best to carefully elicit the particular experience and understanding of that facet by using the verification and interpretation procedures described later in this chapter. Inquiry may reveal that a client feels better being described by one or the other pole of the facet, or that he or she has a unique way of using the facet due to individual experience and circumstances. However, if the client verifies a midzone expression of a facet, this presents an opportunity to explore its meaning by considering one or more of the preceding possibilities.

Table 5.2 presents some of the general ways of interpreting midzone scores for the twenty facets. In using the information in this table with clients, bear in mind that the descriptions provided here do not take underlying preference into account as do many of the midzone descriptions in the Interpretive Report. It is therefore best to elicit clients' spontaneous comments about their experience of the facet as a way of understanding their individuality.

## Interpretation Value of Facet Scores

Determining whether a particular score is in-preference, out-of-preference, or midzone provides the basis for recognizing and understanding individual differences within people of the same type. In giving feedback to a client, the most important verification issue is the accuracy with which the scores reflect the respondent's placement at either pole or in the midzone. If a client disagrees with results on a facet, interpretation will be affected. For example, a client may judge a facet that was reported as midzone as actually out-of-preference or in-preference. In such an instance, statements in the report will be incorrect for that facet, so the practitioner must provide appropriate interpretive information that corresponds to the client's verified placement.[2]

Table 5.3 shows the percentages and rank order of in-preference, midzone, and out-of-preference scores for the twenty Step II facets. Interpreters may find this table useful because it shows which facets are more and less likely to yield scores in these three categories. There are wide variations in the frequency with which facets are likely to be out-of-preference. Questioning–Accommodating leads with 27% of the national sample being out-of-preference, followed by Early Starting–Pressure-Prompted at 24.4%. The T–F facet Reasonable–Compassionate and the J–P facet Scheduled–Spontaneous appear least likely to elicit out-of-preference responses. However, a comparison of the percentages and relative ranking of facet scales within the four dichotomies indicates that, overall, E–I and S–N are less subject to out-of-preference responses, while T–F and J–P are more likely to include such responses. This

## Table 5.2 General Midzone Descriptions for the Twenty Facet Scales

| E–I Facet Scales | Descriptions |
|---|---|
| Initiating–Receiving | Seem socially at ease with people they know well; initiate conversations in familiar surroundings; willing to make introductions if they are not being made by others. |
| Expressive–Contained | Show interest in others but are selective in what they reveal about themselves; share quite a bit of personal information with friends and little with strangers; speak readily about topics they know well. |
| Gregarious–Intimate | Are moderately comfortable relating to strangers, depending on circumstances; comfort with being outgoing is situational; prefer to have deep, intimate relationships with very few people. |
| Active–Reflective | Communicate in person about personal issues, in writing about technical issues; like learning new information face-to-face; prefer to update information through reading. |
| Enthusiastic–Quiet | Show enthusiasm with topics and people they know well, otherwise, stay in the background; desire for action or calm depends on how active or calm their day has been; people who typically see only one side of them may have very different images of them. |

| S–N Facet Scales | Descriptions |
|---|---|
| Concrete–Abstract | Want selected facts as well as the meaning behind those facts; can see the bigger picture without all the details but believe the big picture must be grounded in facts; under pressure, may overrely on one fact and miss the meaning. |
| Realistic–Imaginative | Move quickly to apply a new idea and understand its limitations; stay in touch with commonsense aspects of situations; dislike "far-fetched" ideas and those that take too long to discover. |
| Practical–Conceptual | Blend pragmatism and curiosity; enjoy juggling ideas and their applications; want their best ideas to be used, not merely considered. |
| Experiential–Theoretical | Interested in theories that explain what is important to them; are unlikely to pursue theories intensively or in great depth; are more interested in applying the patterns of a theory than in the patterns themselves. |
| Traditional–Original | Like following established methods that work, but readily change those that don't; value selected traditions and consistency in certain family activities; enjoy novelty that doesn't conflict with selected traditional values. |

| T–F Facet Scales | Descriptions |
|---|---|
| Logical–Empathetic | Believe an ideal decision should consider both logical consequences and feeling values and appear neither overly logical nor overly concerned about others' feelings; may experience some tension in deciding between an analytical and a personal approach. |
| Reasonable–Compassionate | Make decisions based on concern for others as well as the logic of the situation; may vacillate in decision making if they feel that using objective criteria will hurt someone important to them; others may sometimes see them as ambivalent. |
| Questioning–Accommodating | Ask questions only when necessary and then in a mild and tactful way; are neither noticeably confrontational nor overly conciliatory; may become confrontational and direct when an important value or principle is threatened. |
| Critical–Accepting | Critique ideas and actions readily, taking little for granted; see flaws quickly and clarify what is wrong in situations; may critique silently or aloud, depending on the circumstances. |
| Tough–Tender | Prefer being conciliatory at first but will be tough when needed; are comfortable pushing others to necessary action; are devoted and loyal to those close to them. |

| J–P Facet Scales | Descriptions |
|---|---|
| Systematic–Casual | Like general plans with some contingencies; inhibited by too much detail; don't mind interruptions if no plan is in place but dislike them once a project is under way. |
| Planful–Open-Ended | Exhibit varying degrees of planning in everyday life, depending on the activity; often plan for big social events but not little ones; may feel uneasy without at least some long-range plans. |
| Early Starting–Pressure-Prompted | Have difficulty beginning a task too far in advance of the deadline; need some pressure to get started; work best when the deadline is close enough to create some pressure. |
| Scheduled–Spontaneous | Welcome a moderate amount of routine, which provides them with both predictability and freedom to respond to the unexpected; see schedules as helpful at work but confining at home, or vice versa. |
| Methodical–Emergent | Comfortable without a plan in familiar situations; don't need to have all the steps in place before starting a task; are seen as generally flexible. |

*Note:* The descriptions provided here are based on behavioral reports and observations sampled from the more detailed midzone descriptions that appear in the Step II report.

**Table 5.3 In-Preference, Midzone, and Out-of-Preference Percentages and Rankings for the Twenty Facet Scales**

| | In-Preference | | Midzone (–1 to +1) | | Out-of-Preference | |
|---|---|---|---|---|---|---|
| **Step II™ Facet Scale** | **%** | **Rank** | **%** | **Rank** | **%** | **Rank** |
| *E–I Facet Scales* | | | | | | |
| Initiating–Receiving | 76.6 | 3 | 17.9 | 18 | 5.4 | 15 |
| Expressive–Contained | 62.2 | 13 | 30.0 | 7 | 7.8 | 11 |
| Gregarious–Intimate | 57.5 | 17 | 30.6 | 6 | 12.0 | 5 |
| Active–Reflective | 58.8 | 15 | 31.9 | 3 | 9.3 | 9 |
| Enthusiastic–Quiet | 65.2 | 7 | 24.7 | 14 | 10.1 | 7 |
| *S–N Facet Scales* | | | | | | |
| Concrete–Abstract | 65.9 | 6 | 28.9 | 8 | 5.2 | 17 |
| Realistic–Imaginative | 68.1 | 5 | 27.1 | 11 | 4.8 | 18 |
| Practical–Conceptual | 62.0 | 14 | 28.5 | 9 | 9.4 | 8 |
| Experiential–Theoretical | 77.4 | 2 | 15.3 | 19 | 7.3 | 13 |
| Traditional–Original | 63.9 | 10 | 28.2 | 10 | 7.8 | 12 |
| *T–F Facet Scales* | | | | | | |
| Logical–Empathetic | 68.3 | 4 | 26.4 | 13 | 5.3 | 16 |
| Reasonable–Compassionate | 64.9 | 9 | 31.6 | 4 | 3.4 | 20 |
| Questioning–Accommodating | 46.4 | 20 | 26.6 | 12 | 27.0 | 1 |
| Critical–Accepting | 57.7 | 16 | 24.4 | 15 | 18.1 | 3 |
| Tough–Tender | 62.6 | 12 | 32.1 | 2 | 5.4 | 14 |
| *J–P Facet Scales* | | | | | | |
| Systematic–Casual | 56.9 | 18 | 34.9 | 1 | 8.2 | 10 |
| Planful–Open-Ended | 80.7 | 1 | 8.4 | 20 | 10.9 | 6 |
| Early Starting–Pressure-Prompted | 53.3 | 19 | 22.3 | 16 | 24.4 | 2 |
| Scheduled–Spontaneous | 65.1 | 8 | 31.4 | 5 | 3.5 | 19 |
| Methodical–Emergent | 63.8 | 11 | 18.2 | 17 | 18.0 | 4 |

*Source:* National sample.

may be evidence that E–I and S–N are less malleable or more "hardwired" than T–F and J–P and/or that social desirability and survival needs, especially in the workplace, encourage development and use of aspects of T–F and J–P that are less preferred.

The data shown in table 5.3 provide general information about the comparative "popularity" of different ways of responding on the facet scales. However, this table does not tell us, for example, whether Introverted types are more or less likely than Extraverted types to be out-of-preference, and which of the 40 ways of being out-of-preference is most prevalent. Comparisons such as these can provide insights into a client's individuality during the interpretation process. A client may find it useful to know that his out-of-preference result on a facet scale is relatively frequent for people with his preference or that such a result is unusual. Table 5.4 provides this information.

## Midzone Patterns

Having one or two midzone scores within a facet block is quite common and can be enlightening for the client. However, a pattern of many midzone scores within a dichotomy can present additional issues for exploration and interpretation. The criteria for identifying such a midzone pattern in the facet scores within a block are the following:

- At least four of the five facets have midzone scores (1 to the left of 0, 0, or 1 to the right of 0).
- Scores on the fifth facet (if only four meet the first criterion) are neither 4 nor 5.

When these criteria are met, it may indicate a generalized response to the underlying dichotomy itself. The individual might not have developed a clear or practiced preference for either pole, which may be reflected in a lack of familiarity with or ease in using any of the facets of the dichotomy. Alternatively, perhaps the person's expression of a preference on that dichotomy is not elicited in the Step II assessment. Bear in mind that the Step II tool measures only the five *known and measurable* facets of a dichotomy available through Form Q. A particular individual's primary expression of a dichotomy may be through one or more hypothetical, nonmeasured facets.[3] In any case, the

**Table 5.4 The 40 Out-of-Preference Patterns**

| E–I Out-of-Preference | % | S–N Out-of-Preference | % |
|---|---|---|---|
| Initiating Introvert | 8.7 | Concrete Intuitive type | 3.4 |
| Receiving Extravert | 1.2 | Abstract Sensing type | 5.9 |
| Expressive Introvert | 9.8 | Realistic Intuitive type | 4.2 |
| Contained Extravert | 5.2 | Imaginative Sensing type | 5.0 |
| Gregarious Introvert | 11.7 | Practical Intuitive type | 5.2 |
| Intimate Extravert | 12.4 | Conceptual Sensing type | 11.0 |
| Active Introvert | 11.4 | Experiential Intuitive type | 12.1 |
| Reflective Extravert | 6.5 | Theoretical Sensing type | 5.5 |
| Enthusiastic Introvert | 12.5 | Traditional Intuitive type | 10.5 |
| Quiet Extravert | 7.0 | Original Sensing type | 6.8 |
| **Average % for Introverted types** | **10.82** | **Average % for Intuitive types** | **7.08** |
| **Average % for Extraverted types** | **6.46** | **Average % for Sensing types** | **6.84** |

| T–F Out-of Preference | % | J–P Out-of-Preference | % |
|---|---|---|---|
| Logical Feeling type | 6.7 | Systematic Perceiving type | 12.0 |
| Empathetic Thinking type | 3.1 | Casual Judging type | 4.9 |
| Reasonable Feeling type | 4.3 | Planful Perceiving type | 8.7 |
| Compassionate Thinking type | 1.9 | Open-Ended Judging type | 12.8 |
| Questioning Feeling type | 23.3 | Early Starting Perceiving type | 42.2 |
| Accommodating Thinking type | 33.3 | Pressure-Prompted Judging type | 8.7 |
| Critical Feeling type | 13.3 | Scheduled Perceiving type | 6.5 |
| Accepting Thinking type | 26.0 | Spontaneous Judging type | 0.8 |
| Tough Feeling type | 4.8 | Methodical Perceiving type | 26.2 |
| Tender Thinking type | 6.3 | Emergent Judging type | 10.8 |
| **Average % for Feeling types** | **10.48** | **Average % for Perceiving types** | **19.12** |
| **Average % for Thinking types** | **14.12** | **Average % for Judging types** | **7.60** |

*Source:* National sample.

respondent may certainly benefit from exploring the possible meanings and effects of these and any other hypotheses he or she may offer. In a counseling setting, such a discussion may provide an opportunity for deeper clinical understanding and insight.

Midzone patterns as defined here did not occur with great frequency in the national sample. The highest percentage of midzone patterns (4.57%) was found for Introverted types on the E–I facet block (for Extraverted types, it was 1.57%), and the lowest (0.19%) was for Judging types on the J–P facet block (1.92% for Perceiving types). Midzone patterns appeared more often (3.27%) for Sensing types on the S–N block, compared to 2.41% for Intuitive types, and the rate of occurrence for Thinking types was 1.72% on the T–F block, compared to 3.58% for Feeling types. The higher percentages of midzone patterns for Introverted, Feeling, and Perceiving types may be related to social pressure toward Extraversion, Thinking, and Judging. Interpretation of midzone patterns should consider this factor in exploring the meaning of these patterns with clients.

Table 5.5 summarizes these data and also shows the percentage of midzone patterns by type for each of the four dichotomies. Although the percentages are small overall, note that the highest are reported for INTPs on E–I (7%), for ISFPs on S–N (6.1%), for ENFPs on T–F (6.7%), and for ENTPs on J–P (4%).

**Table 5.5 Percentage of Midzone Patterns by Type**

| | E–I% | S–N% | T–F% | J–P% |
|---|---|---|---|---|
| **ESTJ** | 2.1 | 3.3 | 3.1 | 0.0 |
| **ENTJ** | 0.0 | 3.4 | 3.4 | 0.0 |
| **ISTP** | 2.7 | 0.0 | 1.4 | 1.4 |
| **INTP** | 7.0 | 2.3 | 2.3 | 0.0 |
| **ESFJ** | 2.8 | 3.5 | 3.5 | 0.0 |
| **ENFJ** | 0.0 | 2.6 | 5.12 | 0.0 |
| **ISFP** | 4.1 | 6.1 | 1.4 | 1.4 |
| **INFP** | 1.1 | 2.2 | 2.3 | 1.1 |
| **ESTP** | 0.0 | 3.8 | 3.7 | 3.7 |
| **ESFP** | 3.7 | 3.7 | 3.8 | 2.8 |
| **ISTJ** | 5.3 | 1.1 | 2.2 | 0.5 |
| **ISFJ** | 5.2 | 4.7 | 3.2 | 1.0 |
| **ENTP** | 4.0 | 0.0 | 0.0 | 4.0 |
| **ENFP** | 0.0 | 2.9 | 6.7 | 1.0 |
| **INTJ** | 5.3 | 0.0 | 0.0 | 0.0 |
| **INFJ** | 5.9 | 5.9 | 2.9 | 0.1 |

*Note:* Mean for Extraverts on E–I = 1.57, for Introverts = 4.57; mean for Sensing types on S–N = 3.27, for Intuitive types = 2.41; mean for Thinking types on T–F = 1.72, for Feeling types = 3.58; mean for Judging types on J–P = 0.187, for Perceiving types = 1.92

*Source:* National sample.

## Profile Patterns That Appear to Be Contradictory

Interpreters and clients are sometimes puzzled when they see a pattern of results in a facet block that seems to contradict the client's underlying Form M preference, that is, where three or even four facet scores are on the opposite side of the person's overall preference on the dichotomy. In understanding and interpreting such results, keep the following information in mind.

- The shaded midzone area on the profile is the appropriate criterion that separates the two poles of any facet. As described in chapter 6, it is quite rare for three or more facet scores to occur on the side opposite the underlying preference. When this does happen, it most often occurs within the T–F facet block, because this dichotomy has the lowest item overlap between Form M scoring of T–F and Form Q scoring of the facets. And when it occurs within the T–F block, it is most likely to be seen on the Questioning–Accommodating and Critical–Accepting facets, two facets that reveal many out-of-preference results. (See chapter 6 for further information about this interesting phenomenon.)
- Form M preferences are determined by using 93 items, scored with a complex system based on item response theory (IRT) that is unrelated to the scoring of the facets of that dichotomy. The additional 51 items included in Form Q are not available on Form M. These 51 items are used, along with Form M items, on the twenty facet scales.
- A pattern that looks contradictory, when accompanied by a slight preference clarity index (pci) on the Form M results for a dichotomy, may indicate one of the following:
  - Respondent's belief that his or her facet scales are accurate but the best-fit preference has not been accurately reported on Form M
  - A valid pattern of out-of-preference results on that dichotomy
  - Accurate Form M results but inaccurate facet scale results

Figure 5.5 and figure 5.6 illustrate two examples of the opposite effects with the Questioning–Accommodating and Critical–Accepting facets. The client in figure 5.5 reported ISFJ on Form M scoring but has two very clear scores toward the T side on these two facets and two other scores in the midzone. The ISTJ in figure 5.6 has the opposite pattern of scores, toward Accommodating and Accepting, and, more slightly, toward Tender. These results can occur because there are fewer Form M items that overlap with the items for these two facet scales (see table 6.5, on p. 104). However, until an interpretation is made and verified for these two people, it is not possible to determine simply by visual means which of the three possibilities listed above best describes them. What is known is that

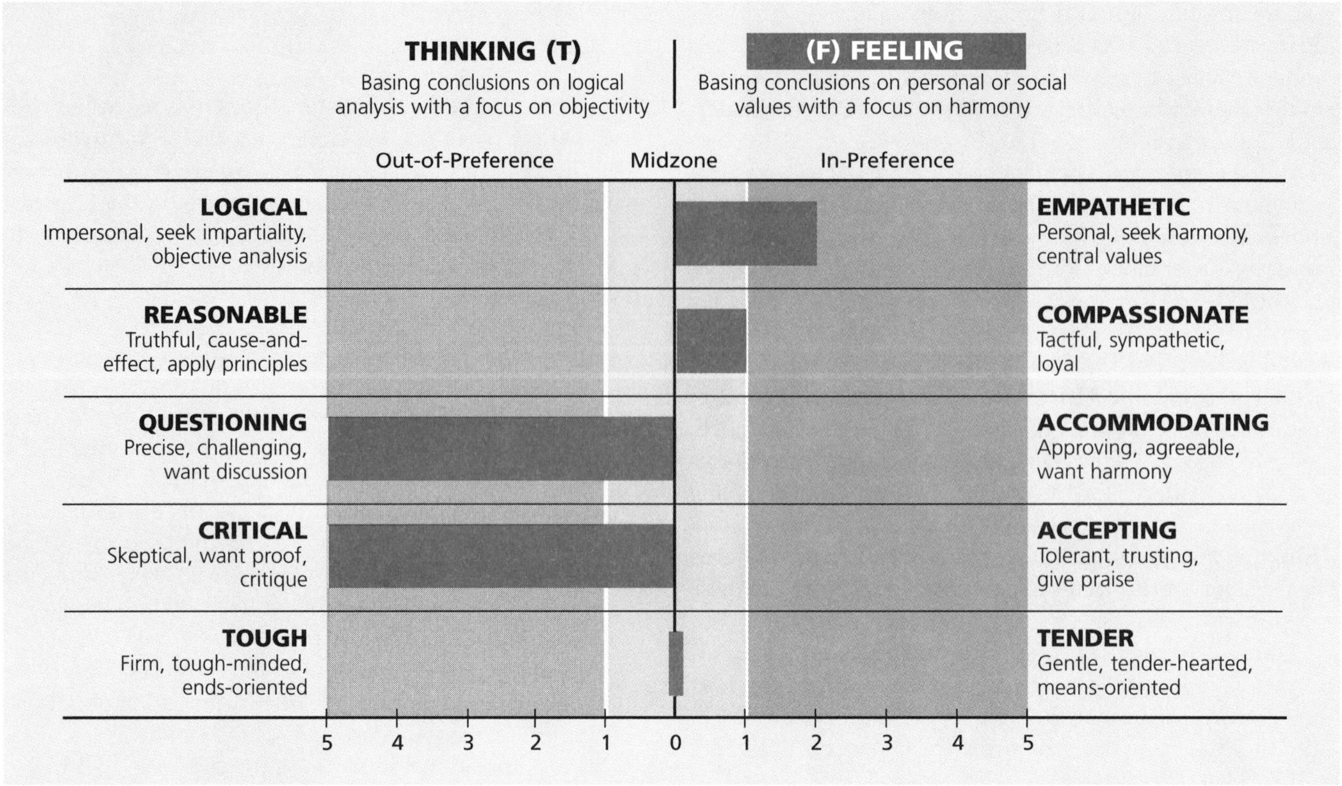


Figure 5.5 ISFJ with Two Clear Scores on the T Side

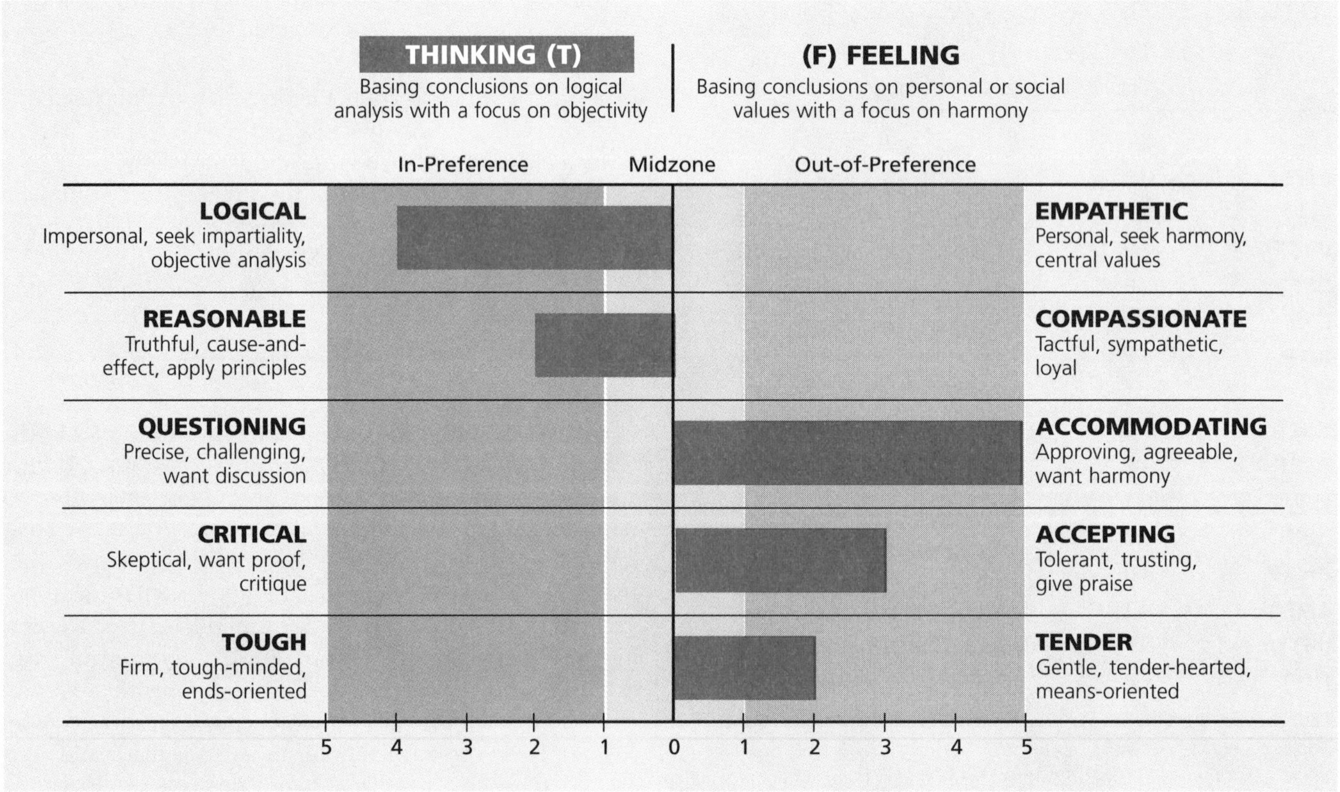


Figure 5.6 ISTJ with Two Clear Scores on the F Side

the results on both Form M and the Questioning–Accommodating and Critical–Accepting facet scales reflect how the clients responded to the questions.

When interpreting unusual profiles or those that appear to contradict Step I information, it is important to be aware of the psychometric factors that are often involved, although, as stated above, these cannot explain the meaning of the results until the respondent has had a chance to verify the results. In addition, factors such as type development and situational pressure may influence an individual's profile. But regardless of whether a client's profile looks straightforward, unusual, intriguing, or puzzling, every client can benefit from a thorough interpretation, and every interpreter can gain increased understanding about the nuances of psychological type.

## Review of Step I™ and Step II™ Terminology Changes

As described in earlier chapters, both Step I (Form M) and Step II (Form Q) instruments introduce some changes in terminology. These modifications are summarized here because appropriate terminology is important in interpreting the MBTI personality inventory.

**Every profile, whether straightforward or unusual, provides an opportunity to gain insight into the client's experience and expression of psychological type and offers a more detailed view of his or her distinctiveness within one of the sixteen types.**

The term *preference clarity index* (pci) is used in place of the MBTI Step I *preference score* in order to discourage the interpretation of broad type preferences as quantitative traits. Preference clarity indexes range from 1 to 30 on all four dichotomies, whereas the previous preference scores varied in their ranges. Changes in other Step I terms were made for the same reason. In the interests of consistency between the Step I and Step II assessments, similar terminological changes for the Step II tool are introduced in this revision, such as *facet scale* rather than *subscale*. Terminology changes for both assessments appear in table 5.6. Using the revised terminology with clients is a helpful way of minimizing misinterpretation of the numerical data that appear on profiles.

## The Polarity Index

Chapter 7 presents information on the reliability of the Step II instrument as reflected in its internal consistency (the consistency with which respondents answer different parts of the instrument) and the stability of their results over time (test-retest reliability). The Interpreter's Summary of the Step II report includes an additional measure of consistency in the form of the polarity index, which is a way of looking at the reliability of a single individual's scores. For an example, see figure 5.7. The polarity index was designed by Saunders (1987) to describe how consistently a person has scored toward the poles of the facets. It thus gives us information on an individual level that traditional reliability statistics cannot provide.

The polarity index ranges from 0 to 100 (see chapter 7 for a description). One of Saunders' initial goals in including such a measure was to provide a way of estimating whether a profile was valid, or composed from candid answers. The operating assumption derived from type theory is that people

**Table 5.6 Terminology Changes for the Step I™ and Step II™ Instruments**

| Step I™ Instrument | | Step II™ Instrument | |
|---|---|---|---|
| Previous Term | Current Term | Previous Term | Current Term |
| Scale; dimension | Dichotomy | Subscale | Facet |
| Scale (psychometric use) | Preference scale | Subscale | Facet scale (psychometric use) |
| Preference score | Preference clarity index | Subscale score | Facet scale score* |
| Opposite preference | Preference pole | Subscale pole | Facet pole; facet preference |
| | | Norm | Average range of scores |

*Although the term *preference clarity index* replaces *preference score*, using the term *facet clarity index* in place of *subscale score* is not appropriate because of the small number of items in the scales.

# Interpreter's Summary

## PREFERENCE CLARITY INDEXES FOR REPORTED TYPE: ENTP

| Extraversion: Slight (2) | Intuition: Slight (2) | Thinking: Slight (5) | Perceiving: Slight (5) |
|---|---|---|---|

## FACET SCORES AND THE AVERAGE RANGE OF SCORES FOR OTHER ENTPs

The bars on the graphs below show the average range of scores that occurred for the ENTPs in the national sample. The bars show scores that are –1 to +1 standard deviation from the mean. The vertical line in each bar shows ENTPs' mean score. The bold numbers show the respondent's scores.

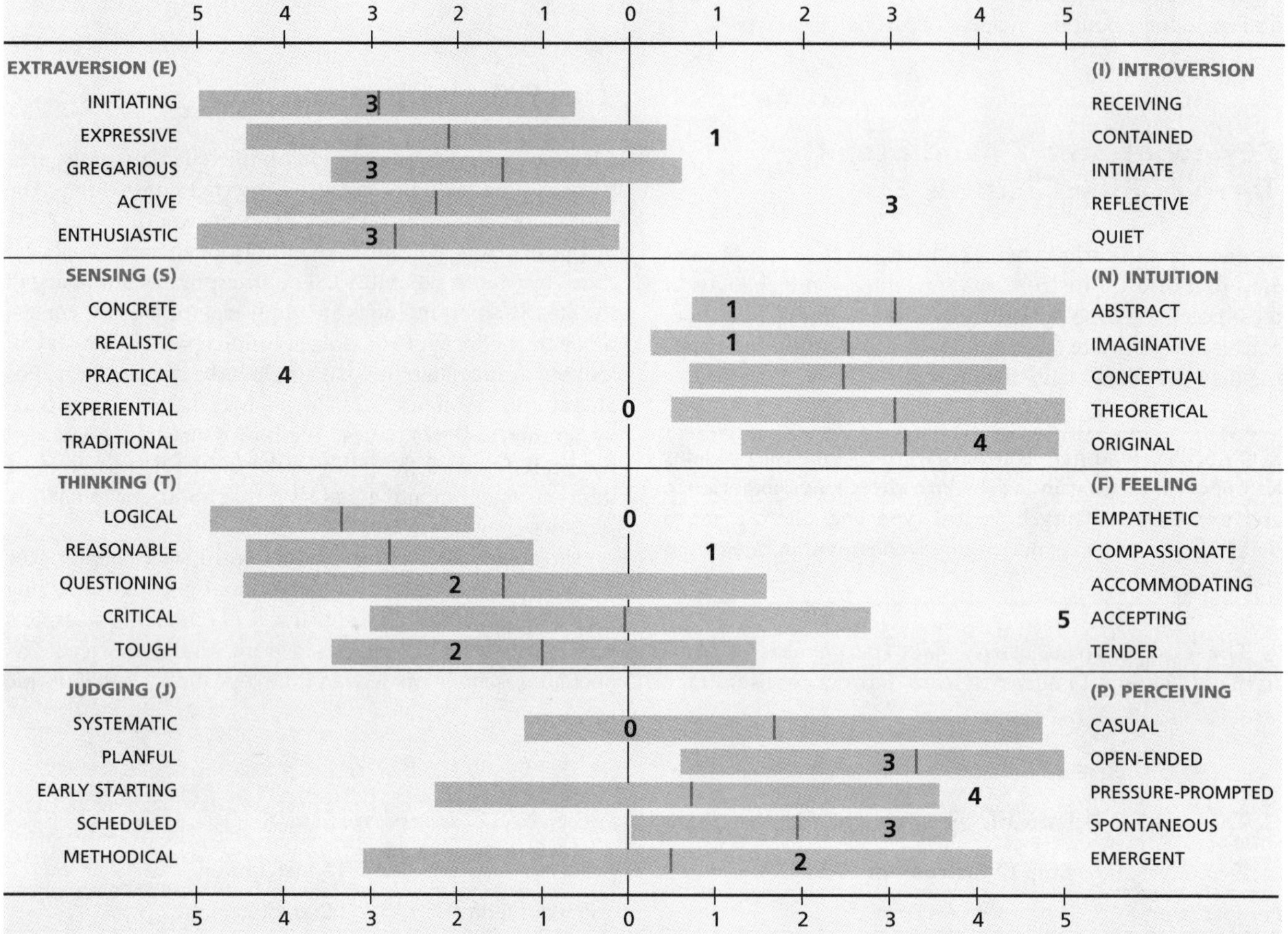


### POLARITY INDEX: 53

The polarity index, which ranges from 0 to 100, shows the consistency of a respondent's facet scores within a profile. Most adults score between 50 and 65, although higher indexes are common. An index that is below 45 means that the respondent has many scores in or near the midzone. This may be due to mature situational use of the facet, answering the questions randomly, lack of self-knowledge, or ambivalence about use of a facet. Some such profiles may be invalid.

**Number of Omitted Responses: 2**

Figure 5.7 Sample Interpreter's Summary with Polarity Index Highlighted are likely to respond with a preference for one or the other pole of a facet instead of with a great many scores in the midzone. Individual variations in the polarity index allow us to form hypotheses that can be significant in individual interpretations. Important basic information about the polarity index can be summarized as follows:

- An index of 100 occurs when scores on all facets are at the poles, that is, are all at 5.
- An index of 0 occurs when all facet scores are 0.
- Most adults obtain a polarity index that lies between 50 and 65, although higher indexes are common.
- Random responses yield an average index of about 30.
- Low polarities (< 45) *may* indicate an invalid profile.
- Polarity indexes above 80 are not unusual.

## The Meaning of High Indexes

A person with a high index (70 or above) is very clear in preferring one or the other pole of each facet, regardless of whether a particular score is in-preference or out-of-preference. The numerical value of the index, however, does not tell us whether the person has clear preferences for all facet components associated with all four of his or her type preferences. One INTJ, for example, may clearly favor all the I, N, T, and J poles of the facets (and correspondingly may have clear or very clear preference clarity indexes on all four Step I Form M preferences). This situation is shown in figure 5.8. Another INTJ may have several facets with scores of 4 or 5 that clearly correspond to her preferences along with others that occur at the poles opposite her preferences. For an example, see figure 5.9. Thus, the polarity index alone tells us that these two INTJs are very clear in their facet preferences, but it does not describe the particular array of those preferences. However, the patterns for both of these INTJs are incentive for exploring their individuality.

### High Polarity Indexes with All or Most Scores In-Preference

With such a profile, we might merely infer that the Step II instrument verifies the client's clear preferences in all the dichotomies that make up his or her type and provides no information about the person's distinctive expression of type. Nevertheless, reviewing the profile with the client provides an opportunity to explore the client's unique ways of using his or her type for the following reasons.

- First, the Jung-Myers theory specifies that people use all the functions and attitudes at least some of the time and that this is necessary for adaptation. Given this general working assumption, inquiry into how and when the client calls upon the less preferred personality attributes is appropriate.
- Second, the Step II instrument does not necessarily encompass all the possible facets of each dichotomy. Respondents whose Step II results are mostly or entirely consistent with their underlying preferences may be using opposite preference poles in ways that are not detectable by the Step II instrument.

It is certainly possible that a person may be so firmly committed to his or her type as to be one-sided—unable or unwilling to use opposite approaches when necessary. However, there is no evidence to support such a conclusion, using only the preference clarity indexes of Form M or the facet scores of Form Q. Rather, facet scores that are very consistent with a person's overall type are an interesting variation on the theme of individuality and worthy of further exploration.

For example, a Step I interpreter might ask someone with a clear preference for Sensing to give an example of when and how he or she uses Intuition. This interpretive technique demonstrates that the client does in fact use some less preferred personality characteristics and that a preference for Sensing does not proscribe the use of Intuition.

A similar approach can be even more fruitful in interpreting Step II results. It may be easier for a client to come up with examples of using the opposite poles of the five facets of a dichotomy because the facet focus is more specific than the generalized focus of the whole dichotomy. Such a discussion may also reveal distinctive features of the client's type dynamics and development, which can provide important insights for both client and practitioner.

### High Polarity Index with Both In-Preference and Out-of-Preference Results

Such a profile is not unusual and, when the scores are verified by the client, often elicits a good many insights regarding individual dynamics and development. The technique of asking clients for examples of using both the preferred facet poles and their opposite, nonpreferred poles can be quite interesting, especially when the preferred pole is out-of-preference and the nonpreferred pole is in-preference. For example, an Enthusiastic (facet score of 5) INFJ musician may remark that when it comes to his passion for music, he is lively and energetic and likes to be at the center of things, whereas in most other circumstances, he is content to stay quietly in the background and reserve his energy for his music. He appears to have developed a habitual way of using the Enthusiastic facet of his nonpreferred Extraversion attitude as a way of fulfilling his goals as a musician. Similarly, Melanie, the INTJ in figure 5.9, verified that her out-of-preference result as a "Pressure-Prompted" Judging type fit perfectly with her style of working. She liked being highly organized, planful, and methodical in her work, but had always worked in situations that involved last-minute crises and therefore working under pressure. She said she had become so used to working in this way that she had become quite comfortable with this approach to deadlines and actually enjoyed the excitement involved.

# LILLY SMITH

## REPORTED TYPE: **INTJ**

AUGUST 8, 2008

This profile gives you information about your personality type based on your answers to the MBTI Form Q instrument. It first indicates your Step I results—your reported four-letter type. Next it shows your Step II results—your expression of five facets of each of the four type dichotomies.

## Your Step I™ Results

INTJs tend to be independent-minded, theoretical, and original. They have great drive for their own ideas and purposes. They are skeptical, critical, determined, and sometimes stubborn. In areas of expertise, they will develop systems to organize and carry through a project with or without help.

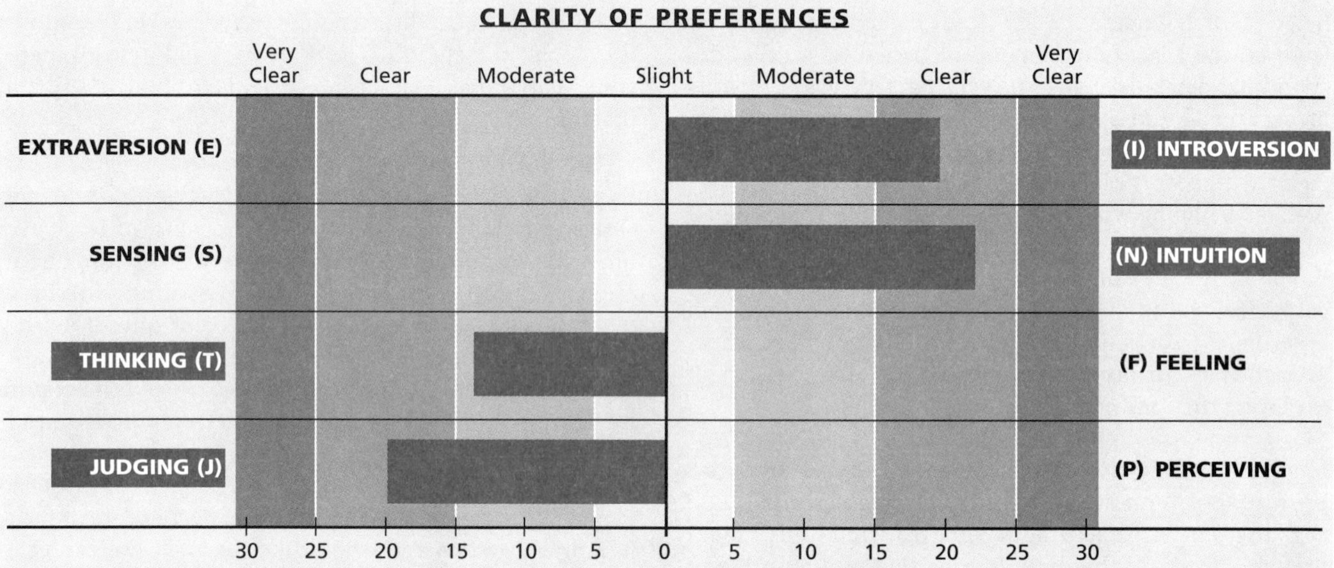


The length of the bars on the graph above shows how consistently you chose one preference pole over the other. The longer the bar, the more often your answers indicated that pole, and the more likely it is that the instrument has accurately reflected your preference.

Figure 5.8 INTJ with All In-Preference Scores

## Your Step II™ Results

The graphs show how you express five facets of each MBTI dichotomy. Your results indicate how you may be similar to and different from other people of your personality type. The longer the bar, the clearer your preference is for that pole of the facet. Scores of 2–5 that are on the same side as your overall preference indicate in-preference results. Scores of 2–5 on the opposite side of your preference indicate out-of-preference results. Scores of 0 and 1 are in the midzone and often mean a situational or muted use of either pole.

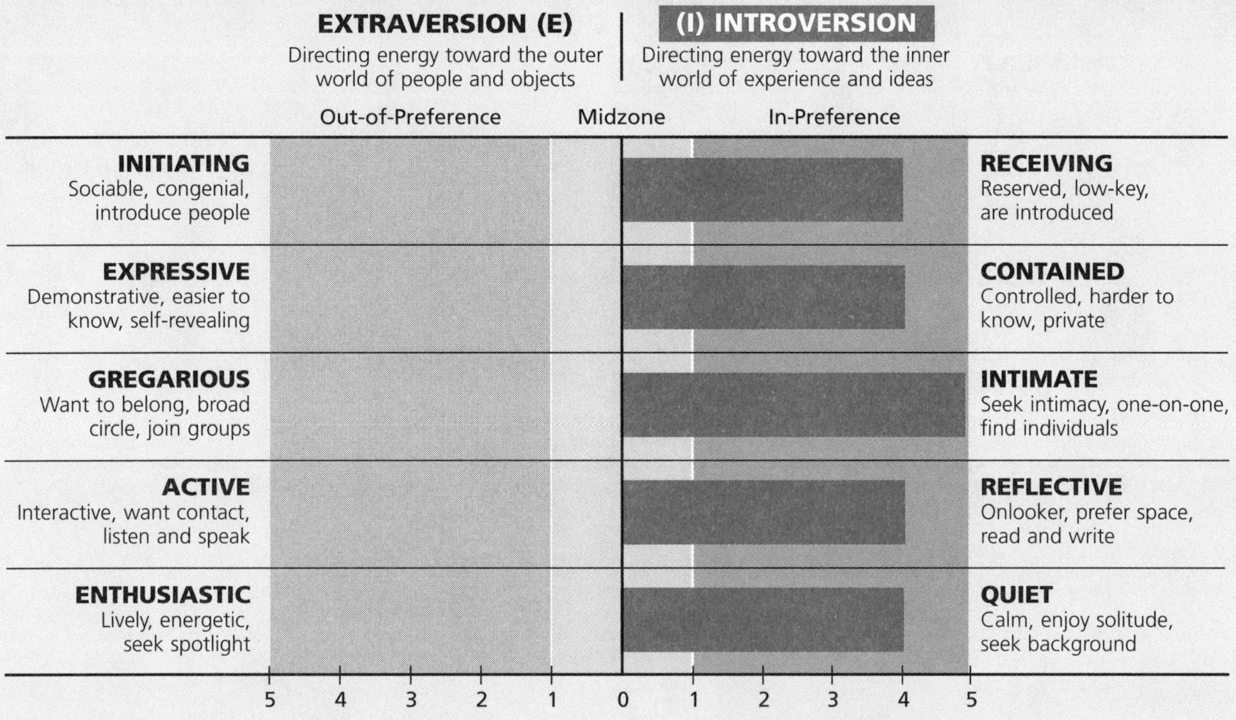


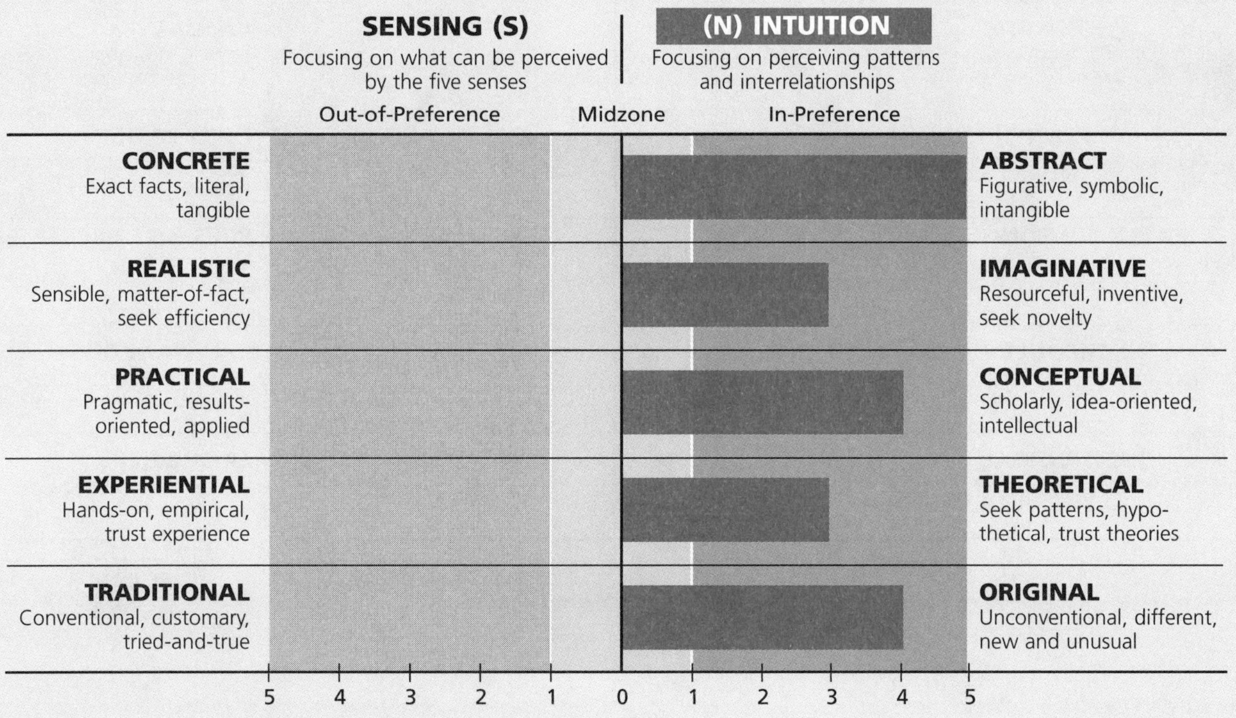


Figure 5.8 INTJ with All In-Preference Scores, *continued*

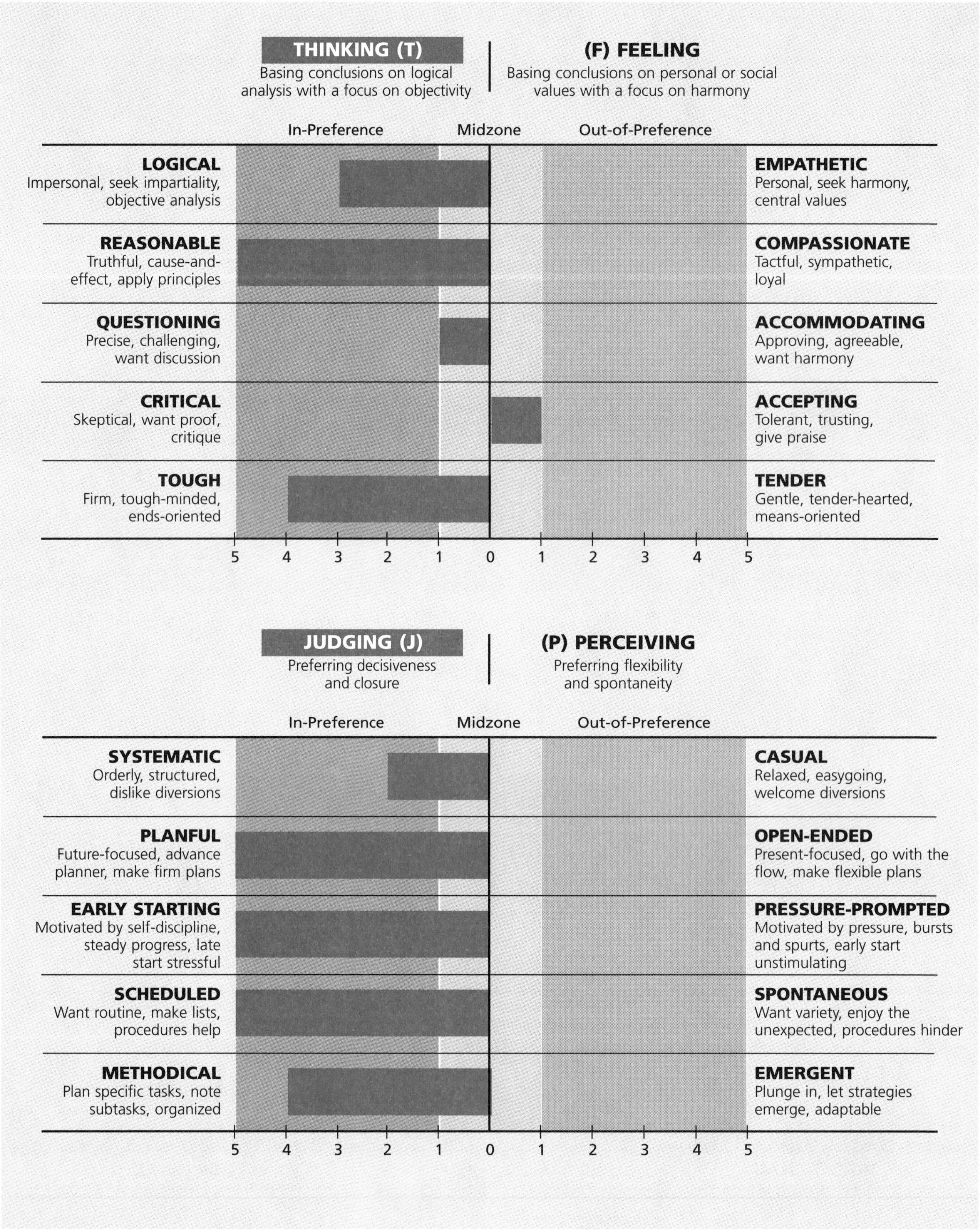


Figure 5.8 INTJ with All In-Preference Scores, *continued*

# MELANIE JONES

## REPORTED TYPE: **INTJ**

AUGUST 8, 2008

This profile gives you information about your personality type based on your answers to the MBTI Form Q instrument. It first indicates your Step I results—your reported four-letter type. Next it shows your Step II results—your expression of five facets of each of the four type dichotomies.

## Your Step I™ Results

INTJs tend to be independent-minded, theoretical, and original. They have great drive for their own ideas and purposes. They are skeptical, critical, determined, and sometimes stubborn. In areas of expertise, they will develop systems to organize and carry through a project with or without help.

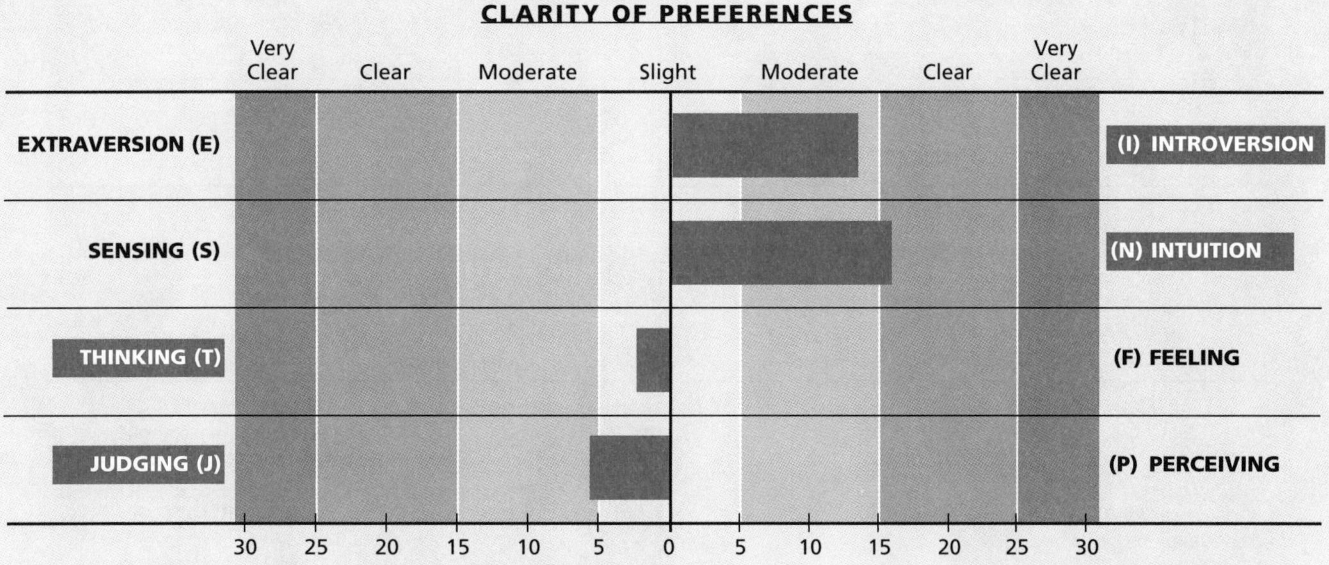


The length of the bars on the graph above shows how consistently you chose one preference pole over the other. The longer the bar, the more often your answers indicated that pole, and the more likely it is that the instrument has accurately reflected your preference.

Figure 5.9 INTJ with In- and Out-of-Preference Scores

## Your Step II™ Results

The graphs show how you express five facets of each MBTI dichotomy. Your results indicate how you may be similar to and different from other people of your personality type. The longer the bar, the clearer your preference is for that pole of the facet. Scores of 2–5 that are on the same side as your overall preference indicate in-preference results. Scores of 2–5 on the opposite side of your preference indicate out-of-preference results. Scores of 0 and 1 are in the midzone and often mean a situational or muted use of either pole.

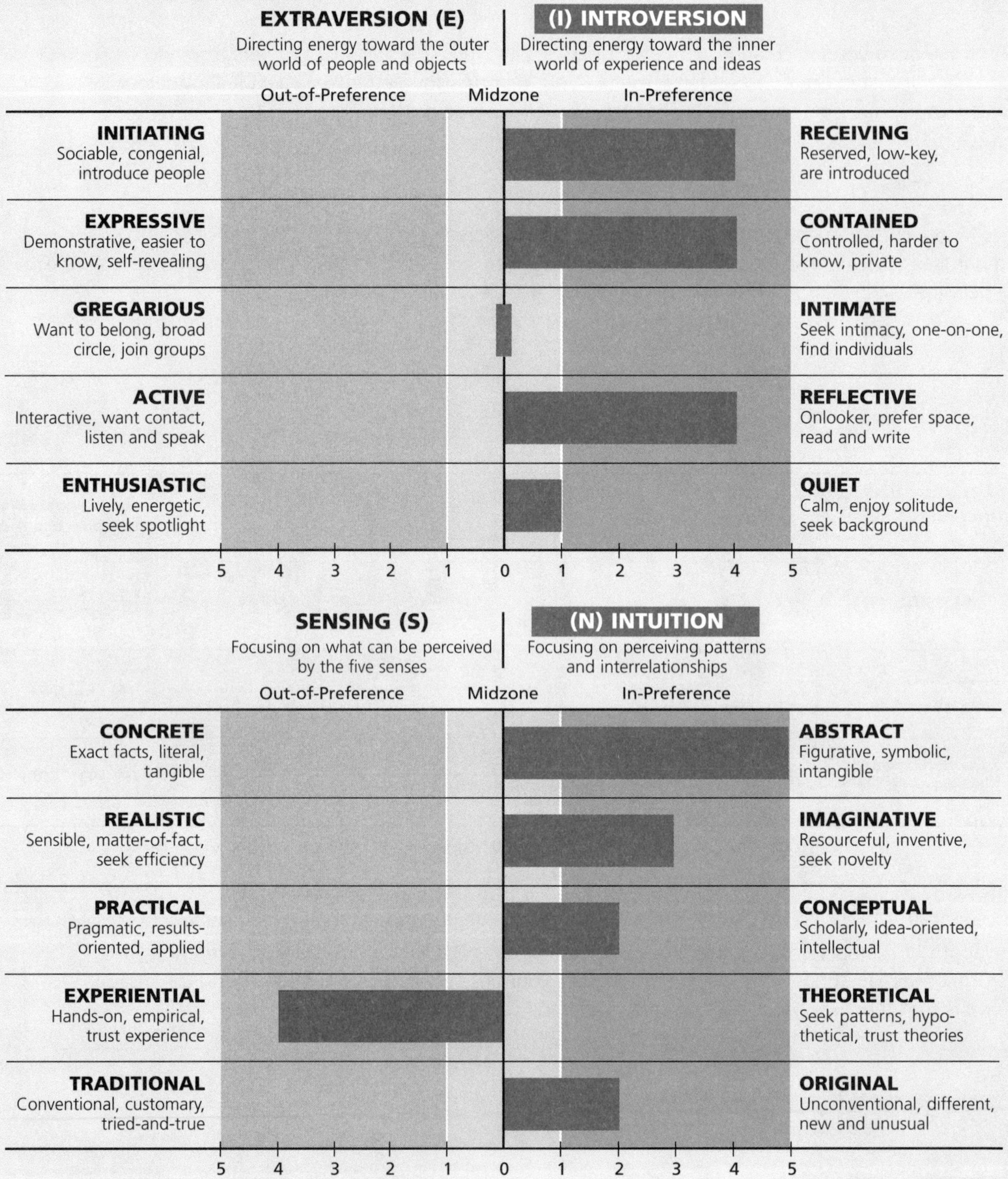


Figure 5.9 INTJ with In- and Out-of-Preference Scores, *continued*

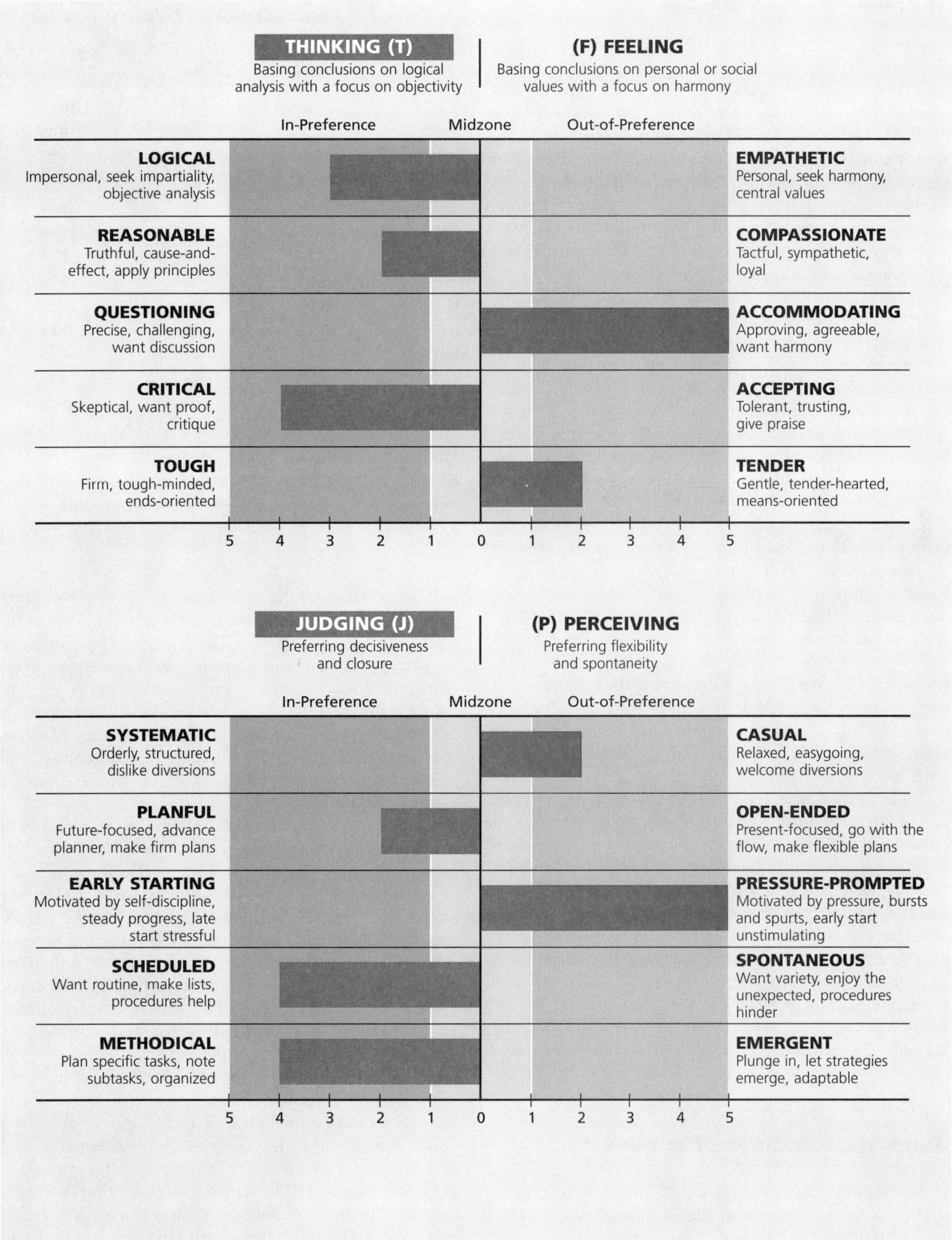


Figure 5.9 INTJ with In- and Out-of-Preference Scores, *continued*

## The Meaning of Low Indexes

Low indexes (45 or below) may be the result of reasons that are likely to emerge during the standard interpretation session. For example, respondents might not have formed clear preferences for the facet components and will have difficulty verifying a best-fit type, or they may habitually function in a manner consistent with many midzone scores yet readily verify a best-fit type. Clients may also be unwilling to reveal themselves, perhaps due to mistrust of the testing situation. In some cases, respondents answer falsely or arbitrarily, or answer sheets are unintentionally mismarked due to language, reading, or vocabulary problems.

Clients themselves may offer clues to the origins of a low polarity index. For example, a client may be puzzled by the first few facet scale results and remark that the results do not fit him or her at all. In that case, perhaps a mechanical error occurred and the profile is wrong. Or a client may express doubt or resentment about being compelled to participate, which would warrant an inquiry from the practitioner as to whether the respondent was pressured into the test situation or misinformed about the purpose of the Step II instrument. Note that providing adequate information to clients before they take the assessment (as described in chapter 4) will reduce occurrences of this circumstance.

Interpreters should be cautious in assessing the possible meaning of low polarity indexes. As with all aspects of type interpretation, the respondent's judgment regarding the accuracy and personal meaning of results is critical. Practitioners have reported a fair number of instances in which clients have verified low polarities as reflecting their approach in using a number of facets in several dichotomies, although occasionally respondents with low polarities are unable to verify any type and do not find the typological approach particularly meaningful.

Table 5.7 lists mean polarity indexes presented in rank order from highest to lowest and the corresponding standard deviations (*SD*) for each type. While there is some variation in these indexes by age, gender, and educational attainment (see chapter 7), the differences are not large enough to suggest that our interpretation of an individual client's polarity index must accommodate such trends. However, in using the table to interpet a specific client's polarity index, take note of the standard deviations. For most types, there is a fair range of variability in the polarity index. The standard deviations provide a guide as to how far from the mean an index may fall and still be within the average range for a given type.

**Table 5.7 Rank Order of Polarity Indexes by Type**

| Type | Mean | *N* | *SD* |
|---|---|---|---|
| ISTJ | 68.38 | 183 | 10.31 |
| ENTJ | 68.27 | 29 | 8.05 |
| ENFP | 67.33 | 105 | 9.71 |
| ESTJ | 67.14 | 97 | 9.26 |
| ENTP | 66.60 | 25 | 8.94 |
| ENFJ | 65.97 | 38 | 7.44 |
| INTJ | 65.36 | 19 | 8.14 |
| ESFJ | 65.30 | 143 | 8.33 |
| ISFJ | 64.69 | 191 | 9.59 |
| INFP | 63.65 | 88 | 9.54 |
| INTP | 62.09 | 43 | 11.91 |
| ESTP | 61.85 | 54 | 9.79 |
| INFJ | 60.73 | 34 | 9.78 |
| ISTP | 60.50 | 73 | 9.32 |
| ESFP | 59.25 | 108 | 8.08 |
| ISFP | 59.02 | 148 | 8.99 |

*Source:* National sample.

## Type-Specific Score Ranges

Differences in Step II results among the sixteen types—such as variations in average polarity indexes and percentages of in-preference and out-of-preference scores—can provide information about type dynamics and offer interpretational clues for individual clients. We may also compare types to one another and understand individual differences among members of the same type by looking at the average range of scores on each facet that is typical for that type. Traditionally known as *norms* in standard trait instruments, these averages specify the mean or average score for a type on each facet and show the range of scores that are plus and minus 1 standard deviation above and below that mean (about 68% of the sample, assuming a normal distribution).

In the Form K version of the Step II instrument and in the Expanded Analysis Report (EAR), the term *norm* was used to identify these ranges of scores. However, in order to discourage a trait interpretation of this variable, the ranges are currently designated as *type-specific ranges*. Type-specific ranges are shown on the Interpreter's Summary (for an example, see figure 5.2 or 5.7) and allow comparison of a respondent's scores on each facet to the average range of scores for all persons of that type in the national sample. The length of the bar shown on the profile for each facet indicates the range of scores that fall between 1 standard deviation above and below the mean score. The mean itself is shown as a vertical line. For any facet, therefore, about 68% of the people of that type obtain scores within the range shown. Participants who obtain scores above or below the average range are reporting either a greater or lesser preference for that facet pole compared to others of their type. Facet scores that fall outside the standard deviation for a type are often, but not always, out-of-preference scores.

**Type-specific ranges provide practitioners and clients with one kind of context within which to interpret scores.**

## Uses of Type-Specific Score Ranges

Type-specific score ranges enable insight into dynamic differences among the types in general while offering clues to an individual's type functioning. In particular, when a client's basic four-letter type is in question, comparing the norms for two or more types can be suggestive.

For example, if a client finds that both ESTJ and ISTJ descriptions are equally appropriate, comparing his or her scores to the average ranges for both these types might suggest reconsideration of the type that more closely approximates the respondent's scores. However, bear in mind that these averages do not allow for age, gender, or any other variable. Therefore, such a score comparison must be employed judiciously, so as not to "convince" the client to verify his or her type based on statistical evidence alone. As always, a variety of verification approaches should be used. Appendix D provides the means, standard deviations, and average score ranges for each of the sixteen types.

# Procedure for Interpreting a Step II™ Profile

The foregoing sections form the basis for conducting a Step II interpretation. This section covers logistic information as well as suggested methods of eliciting information from clients. The last section of the chapter summarizes important Step II information for each of the sixteen types.

## Time and Timing of Interpretation

Allow at least twice as much time for an individual Step II interpretation as would be customary for a Step I interpretation. When interpreting to groups, a half day is desirable, and longer if an application of the Step II instrument is included in the feedback process. Ideally, a follow-up session should be planned for individuals and for groups. The Step II tool presents a great deal of information, and clients usually need time to consider its relevance to their lives.

Many clients benefit from a period of time during which they can absorb and explore the meaning of their Step I results. Interpreting both Step II and Step I results in the same session may therefore not be useful. However, with some clients, introducing Step II results early in the process of verifying Step I type can be effective in helping them arrive at a best-fit type. Interpreters should decide what procedure to use on the basis of individual circumstances and client needs.

## Feedback Process

The following seven steps are recommended for the feedback process.

**Step 1:** Conduct a standard verification/interpretation session if clients have not already had one. Give those who are new to the MBTI personality inventory enough time to absorb this information. Review and confirm understanding of critical characteristics of the MBTI instrument for clients who have had a previous interpretation.

**Step 2:** Explain the basis and purposes of the Step II instrument. Ask clients about their particular interests and goals in regard to the instrument.

**Step 3:** Explain and show how Step II information is arrayed using a sample profile. This is preferable to displaying a client's profile, which may result in distraction caused by viewing personal results before understanding has been achieved.

**Step 4:** Before showing a client profile, explain the procedure you will use to verify results. Unlike in Step I verification, it is not customary to have clients self-assess their results on each facet scale before reviewing their profiles. The interrelation of the facet scales to one another and to their underlying dichotomies makes this task too difficult for clients and is impractical when interpretation time is limited.

A good approach is to describe the essence of each facet, give some information or relevant examples, look at the score with the client (or have the client look at the client profile while you look at the Interpreter's Summary), and then ask the client to assess whether the score placement fits and represents an accurate description. Although this procedure may risk facile agreement from some clients, practitioners do not report it as a problem.

- For facet scale scores that are in-preference (or for selected in-preference scores that are of particular interest or relevance to a client), ask the client to give examples of using the preferred and nonpreferred poles, as described earlier in the discussion on interpreting polarity indexes.
- For out-of-preference scores, ask the client to give examples of using facets in an out-of-preference manner as well as in a manner consistent with the underlying preference. Explore issues that pertain to type dynamics and development in the context of the client's distinctive expression of his or her type. The earlier discussion of polarity index interpretation described an approach to this kind of exploration.
- For midzone scores, have the client give examples of typical behavior in regard to the facets in question. You might also ask for an account of the client's thoughts or actions when forced to choose between the behaviors described by the poles of those facets. This may shed light on whether the person's scores result from inability to decide which behavior to use, comfort with using both, or the influence of circumstances, relationships, or personal preferences that pull in opposing directions.

**Step 5:** After verifying each facet, review and reinforce the relevance of the client's whole type, even if the client already has a firm grasp on this concept. If there were doubts, clarity may have been achieved during the verification process. If not, explore possible type dynamics evidence (Myers & Kirby, 1994), including the typical expression of the client's inferior function (Quenk, 1993, 2000).

**Step 6:** If the report has been generated for the client, he or she should not try to read all of it during the interpretation session. Instead, point out particular areas that are relevant to the client's reasons for taking the Step II assessment and ask the client to read the report in private after the session is completed. Suggest an opportunity for comment and follow-up.

**Step 7:** Schedule a follow-up session if possible, either as a single meeting or as part of a continuing consultative process.

### Recommended Support Materials

Even experienced interpreters of Step II results find it helpful to have available some materials that are briefer than the descriptions in chapter 3, although sharing all or parts of those lengthy descriptions with a client can be useful in an interpretation session. If the report is available, the client can be asked to read selected statements in the report. If only the profile is used, practitioners may also provide information from table 3.1, on page 24 (content outlines of the facets), the brief descriptions of facet scale poles that appear in tables 1.1–1.4, on pages 5–8, and the descriptions of midzones that appear in table 5.2, on page 62. Interpreters will find that clients often provide pertinent examples of the meaning of the facets, which will enrich subsequent interpretation sessions.

## Additional Interpretational Considerations

Individual client needs and the nature of client-practitioner interaction will inevitably present distinctive interpretation issues. In addition, the following areas can influence results and therefore should be taken into consideration in interpreting to clients.

### Influence of Gender on Step II™ Results

Although Jung did not incorporate gender differences into his theory, Myers discovered their presence in responses to items on the T–F dichotomy with all forms prior to Form M. Items that elicited different answers from men and women were removed from Form M (see Myers et al., 1998, for a discussion). We cannot tell whether the differences Myers found arose due to cultural or biological factors. But regardless of their source, real gender differences in the expression of type can be readily observed and are a natural outgrowth of the different socialization experiences and expectations of the two genders. For example, women who verify INTP as their type tend to appear more "sociable" than male INTPs.

Support for assertions regarding differing gender-based expressions of the same type can be seen in the different patterns of correlations with Step II facet scales. For example, table 5.8 contrasts Step II facet scales that are highly correlated for men and women with a selection of *Adjective Check List* (ACL) scales (see table C.2, on p. 182, for brief definitions of ACL scales). Looking at this table, we can see, for example, that the Dominance scale for males is correlated with the Step II facet poles Initiating, Expressive, Enthusiastic, Original, and Questioning. Females share all but Original with males and, in addition, are characterized by six more facet qualities: Gregarious, Active, Logical, Reasonable, Critical, and Tough. Similarly provocative comparisons occur for many other ACL scales.

Being aware of the operation of these gender differences should sensitize interpreters to possible distinctions in the way male and female clients experience themselves typologically. Insights forthcoming from these kinds of considerations can be particularly useful in the workplace as a way of differentiating between personality differences and social expectations.

### Influence of Age on Step II™ Results

Jung did not regard types as static. He believed a developmental process takes place over the adult life span. This individuation, as he called it, happens in distinctive ways for each type. While the specific details of this part of Jungian theory are beyond the scope of this manual, the main point is that Jung saw developmental changes occurring for each type with age. He did not assign responsibility to chronological age itself, nor did he think these changes are inevitable. The polarity index data reported in chapter 7 give some support to Jung's developmental notions. However, not everyone completes the individuation process, and people of the same type do not complete it in exactly the same way or at the same rate. Nevertheless, over their lifetimes, people of each type face common developmental problems that are different from those of other types.

This implies that people of the same type who differ in age may express their type somewhat differently. Because individuation is not inevitable and does not happen according to a fixed schedule, there are no age brackets we can use to identify a person's stage of individuation. But, based on what we know from other research on adult development, we can make educated guesses about the age groups that are likely to express type differently. Individuation is an integral part of Jung's theory of types, so it is important to consider the variations in type that may appear with age.

When we are interpreting an individual's Step II results, the average scores for all ESFPs, for example, may

**Table 5.8 Step II™ Facet Scales Highly Correlated with *Adjective Check List* (ACL) Scales for Males and Females**

| Males | Females | Males | Females | Males | Females |
|---|---|---|---|---|---|
| **Achievement** | | **Dominance** | | **Endurance** | |
| Initiating | Initiating | Initiating[a] | Initiating[b] | Original | Tough |
| Enthusiastic | Enthusiastic | Expressive | Expressive[a] | Systematic | Systematic[b] |
| Abstract | Conceptual | Enthusiastic[a] | Gregarious[a] | | Planful[a] |
| Imaginative | Theoretical[a] | Original | Active[a] | | Early Starting |
| Theoretical | Original | Questioning[a] | Enthusiastic[b] | | Scheduled[b] |
| Original[a] | Questioning | | Logical | | Methodical |
| Methodical | Tough | | Reasonable | | |
| | Systematic | | Questioning | | |
| | Planful | | Critical[a] | | |
| | Scheduled | | Tough[a] | | |
| **Order** | | **Intraception** | | **Nurturance** | |
| Initiating | Conceptual | Abstract | Conceptual[a] | Expressive | Initiating |
| Gregarious | Systematic[b] | Conceptual | Theoretical | Gregarious | Expressive[a] |
| Systematic | Planful | Theoretical | Systematic | Empathetic | Active[a] |
| Early Starting | Early Starting[a] | Original | | Accommodating | Empathetic |
| Scheduled | Scheduled[a] | Accepting | | Accepting | Compassionate[b] |
| Methodical | Methodical[a] | | | Tender[a] | Tender[a] |
| **Affiliation** | | **Heterosexuality** | | **Exhibition** | |
| Enthusiastic | Initiating | Initiating | Initiating[a] | Initiating[b] | Initiating[c] |
| Abstract | Expressive | Gregarious[a] | Expressive[a] | Expressive[a] | Expressive[b] |
| Conceptual | Gregarious | Active[a] | Gregarious[a] | Gregarious | Gregarious[b] |
| Accepting | Active[a] | Enthusiastic[a] | Active[c] | Active[a] | Active[b] |
| Tender | Enthusiastic | Empathetic | Enthusiastic[b] | Enthusiastic[c] | Enthusiastic[d] |
| | Empathetic | Compassionate | Empathetic | Original | Questioning |
| | Compassionate | Tender | | Questioning[a] | Critical[a] |
| | | | | | Tough |
| **Autonomy** | | **Aggression** | | **Change** | |
| Imaginative | Initiating | Enthusiastic | Initiating | Abstract[a] | Initiating |
| Theoretical | Enthusiastic | Questioning | Logical | Imaginative[b] | Expressive[a] |
| Original[b] | Reasonable[a] | Critical | Reasonable[a] | Conceptual | Gregarious[a] |
| Questioning[c] | Questioning | | Questioning[a] | Theoretical[b] | Active[a] |
| | Critical[a] | | Critical[a] | Original[a] | Enthusiastic[b] |
| | Tough[a] | | Tough[a] | Questioning | Abstract[a] |
| | | | | Casual[a] | Imaginative[b] |
| | | | | Open-Ended | Theoretical[a] |
| | | | | Spontaneous | Original[a] |
| | | | | | Questioning[a] |
| | | | | | Critical |
| | | | | | Casual[a] |
| | | | | | Pressure-Prompted |
| **Succorance** | | **Abasement** | | **Deference** | |
| Traditional | Receiving | Quiet | Receiving[a] | Realistic | Receiving |
| Empathetic | Quiet | Traditional | Intimate | Experiential | Quiet[a] |
| Compassionate[a] | Empathetic[a] | Compassionate | Reflective | Traditional[b] | Traditional |
| Tender[a] | Compassionate[a] | Accommodating[a] | Quiet[b] | Compassionate | Empathetic |
| Planful | Accepting | Tender | Empathetic[a] | Accommodating[b] | Compassionate[a] |
| Scheduled[a] | Tender[b] | Scheduled | Compassionate[a] | Tender | Accommodating[a] |
| | | | Accommodating | Scheduled | Accepting[a] |
| | | | Accepting | | Tender[a] |
| | | | Tender[b] | | |

*Notes:* All scales listed were significant at a minimum level of <.01. Scales with no superscript had a correlation coefficient of .20–.29; [a] correlation coefficient = .30–.39; [b] correlation coefficient = .40–.49; [c] correlation coefficient = .50–.59; [d] correlation coefficient = .60+.

*Source:* National sample.

**Table 5.8 Step II™ Facet Scales Highly Correlated with *Adjective Check List* (ACL) Scales for Males and Females** *continued*

| Males | Females | Males | Females | Males | Females |
|---|---|---|---|---|---|
| **Counseling Readiness** | | **Self-Control** | | **Self-Confidence** | |
| Receiving[a] | Reflective | Receiving | Receiving[b] | Initiating[a] | Initiating[b] |
| Contained | Theoretical | Quiet[b] | Contained[a] | Expressive | Expressive[a] |
| Intimate | Reasonable[a] | Realistic | Intimate[a] | Gregarious | Gregarious[a] |
| Reflective | Questioning | Experiential | Reflective[a] | Active | Active[b] |
| Quiet[b] | Tough | Accommodating[b] | Quiet[c] | Enthusiastic[b] | Enthusiastic[b] |
| Realistic | Systematic | Systematic[a] | Experiential | Abstract | Abstract |
| Experiential | | | Traditional | Imaginative | |
| Traditional[a] | | | Systematic | Conceptual | |
| Accommodating[a] | | | | Theoretical | |
| | | | | Original[a] | |
| | | | | Questioning | |
| **Personal Adjustment** | | **Ideal Self** | | **Creative Personality** | |
| Abstract | Initiating | Gregarious | Initiating | Abstract[b] | Enthusiastic |
| Conceptual | Expressive | Abstract[a] | Expressive | Imaginative[b] | Abstract[b] |
| Accepting[a] | Gregarious[a] | Imaginative[a] | Active | Conceptual[a] | Imaginative[a] |
| Tender[a] | Active[a] | Conceptual[a] | Abstract | Theoretical[b] | Conceptual[b] |
| | Enthusiastic | Theoretical[a] | Imaginative | Original[c] | Theoretical[b] |
| | | Accepting | Conceptual[a] | Questioning[a] | Original[c] |
| | | | Theoretical[a] | Accepting | Reasonable |
| | | | Original[a] | | Questioning |
| | | | Methodical | | Critical |
| | | | | | Tough |

not tell us what is typical for an ESFP at age 65. The sample size available in this revision preclude analysis by age grouping and whole type. However, the trends for eight age groups varying from 15–25 up through 75–94 for the sample as a whole suggest that although there were no consistent trends for any of the E–I facets, with increasing age, people move toward Concrete, Realistic, Practical, Experiential, and Traditional in the S–N block; toward Empathetic, Accommodating, Compassionate, and Accepting in the T–F block (no trend was evident for Tough–Tender); and toward Systematic, Planful, Early Starting, Scheduled, and Methodical in the J–P block. However, bear in mind that the data involved came from the entire national sample, not a balanced sample that removes the bias of over- and underrepresentation of different types. Insufficient sample size precludes the observation of trends in the balanced sample.

## Interpreting Step II™ Results in the Context of Step I™ Information About the Sixteen Types

Interpretation of Step II results has the following two major goals:

- To help a client clarify four-letter type and understand the dynamics that contribute to the distinctiveness of each type
- To give a client insight into his or her unique expression of type as revealed in Step II results

The Step II instrument provides an opportunity to explore type dynamics and developmental issues by considering information for each of the sixteen types. We can look for trends that may reflect generalized expressions of the less preferred poles as a function of each type's unique dynamics. For individual interpretation, it can also be helpful to summarize Step II information for each type, because Step II results are always interpreted within the context of the Step I tool.

For example, table 5.9 shows the facet scales within each dichotomy that display the highest mean scores for each type. The table illustrates some similarities and differences in emphasis between dynamically similar types. Note that all the types preferring Perceiving except ENFP show Open-Ended as their leading J–P facet; ENFPs distinctively lead with Casual. All the people who prefer Judging lead with the Scheduled pole of the Scheduled–Spontaneous facet, with the exception of the two dominant introverted Intuitive types. INFJs lead with Planned, and INTJs with Systematic. ESTPs and ESFPs (dominant extraverted Sensing types) have the same leading facet

**Table 5.9 Facet Scales with the Highest Mean for Each Type in Each Dichotomy**

| | ISTJ | ISFJ | INFJ | INTJ |
|---|---|---|---|---|
| E–I | Quiet | Receiving | Receiving | Quiet |
| S–N | Experiential | Experiential | Conceptual | Theoretical |
| T–F | Logical | Tender | Tender | Logical |
| J–P | Scheduled | Scheduled | Planned | Systematic |
| | **ISTP** | **ISFP** | **INFP** | **INTP** |
| E–I | Receiving | Receiving | Receiving | Contained |
| S–N | Experiential | Experiential | Abstract | Original |
| T–F | Reasonable | Compassionate | Empathetic | Logical |
| J–P | Open-Ended | Open-Ended | Open-Ended | Open-Ended |
| | **ESTP** | **ESFP** | **ENFP** | **ENTP** |
| E–I | Initiating | Initiating | Initiating | Initiating |
| S–N | Experiential | Experiential | Imaginative | Original |
| T–F | Tough | Empathetic | Accepting/Empathetic | Logical |
| J–P | Open-Ended | Open-Ended | Casual | Open-Ended |
| | **ESTJ** | **ESFJ** | **ENFJ** | **ENTJ** |
| E–I | Initiating | Initiating | Initiating | Initiating |
| S–N | Experiential | Experiential | Abstract | Theoretical |
| T–F | Logical | Accepting | Accepting/Empathetic | Logical |
| J–P | Scheduled | Scheduled | Scheduled | Scheduled |

*Source:* National sample.

except for the one for their auxiliary function (T or F): ESTPs lead with Tough, and ESFPs with Empathetic. INTJs and INFJs (dominant introverted Intuitive types) show no overlap in their leading facets.

The observations we make from this and other arrays of Step II results add to our understanding and expand our sensitivity to interpretation issues. Although no single way of looking at the data can be considered definitive, evidence gleaned from a variety of analyses enhances our interpretation efforts.

The tables ranking Step II variables that appeared earlier in this chapter (tables 5.3 and 5.7) enable us to compare one type to another across the sixteen types. In contrast, tables 5.10–5.25 summarize data for each type so that an interpreter will have easy access to information about the probable type (or alternative types) of the client at hand. The tables show the sample size for each type, the mean polarity index, the average number of out-of-preference responses overall for the type, and the percentage of out-of-preference results on each facet scale.

In addition, the tables provide provocative insights into the dynamic qualities of each type. For ease of comparison, the tables are ordered between each of the two dominant types, starting with dominant extraverted Thinking. The brief comments below are limited to differences between the two types that share their dominant functions. However, readers will find many other intriguing comparisons relevant to type-specific data in tables 5.10–5.25.

## Dominant Extraverted Thinking Types

Both types have very high mean polarity indexes compared to other types. The most notable difference for these two types is that three times as many ESTJs show an Accommodating out-of-preference result than do ENTJs. Perhaps ESTJs see the opinions of others as facts, which they must accommodate. Somewhat more ENTJs show Pressure-Prompted and Accepting.

## Dominant Introverted Thinking Types

Much like dominant extraverted Thinking types, ISTPs show three times as many Accommodating out-of-preference results as do INTPs. ISTPs are also more likely to be Early Starting. ISTPs average nearly three scales that are out-of-preference compared to about two for the INTPs.

## Dominant Extraverted Feeling Types

More than twice as many ENFJs as ESFJs have a Questioning out-of-preference result, although this facet yields most of the out-of-preferences scales in the T–F block. The array for T–F is more evenly distributed for the ESFJs. ENFJs are three times more likely to show out-of-preference results

## 5.10 Summary of Data for ESTJ

**Percent Out-of-Preference**

| E–I | % | S–N | % | T–F | % | J–P | % |
|---|---|---|---|---|---|---|---|
| Receiving | 0 | Abstract | 3 | Empathetic | 2 | Casual | 1 |
| Contained | 8 | Imaginative | 1 | Compassionate | 0 | Open-Ended | 11 |
| Intimate | 11 | Conceptual | 8 | Accommodating | 43 | Pressure-Prompted | 5 |
| Reflective | 11 | Theoretical | 3 | Accepting | 31 | Spontaneous | 0 |
| Quiet | 6 | Original | 5 | Tender | 7 | Emergent | 8 |

*N* = 97
Average number out-of-preference = 1.66
Mean polarity index = 67.14

*Source:* National sample.

## Table 5.11 Summary of Data for ENTJ

**Percent Out-of-Preference**

| E–I | % | S–N | % | T–F | % | J–P | % |
|---|---|---|---|---|---|---|---|
| Receiving | 0 | Concrete | 3 | Empathetic | 3 | Casual | 3 |
| Contained | 10 | Realistic | 14 | Compassionate | 3 | Open-Ended | 10 |
| Intimate | 24 | Practical | 7 | Accommodating | 14 | Pressure-Prompted | 17 |
| Reflective | 7 | Experiential | 0 | Accepting | 45 | Spontaneous | 0 |
| Quiet | 3 | Traditional | 10 | Tender | 3 | Emergent | 7 |

*N* = 29
Average number out-of-preference = 1.86
Mean polarity index = 68.27

*Source:* National sample.

## Table 5.12 Summary of Data for ISTP

**Percent Out-of-Preference**

| E–I | % | S–N | % | T–F | % | J–P | % |
|---|---|---|---|---|---|---|---|
| Initiating | 5 | Abstract | 7 | Empathetic | 7 | Systematic | 23 |
| Expressive | 12 | Imaginative | 1 | Compassionate | 1 | Planful | 11 |
| Gregarious | 18 | Conceptual | 11 | Accommodating | 45 | Early Starting | 41 |
| Active | 12 | Theoretical | 8 | Accepting | 20 | Scheduled | 12 |
| Enthusiastic | 12 | Original | 11 | Tender | 5 | Methodical | 29 |

*N* = 73
Average number out-of-preference = 2.95
Mean polarity index = 60.51

*Source:* National sample.

## Table 5.13 Summary of Data for INTP

**Percent Out-of-Preference**

| E–I | % | S–N | % | T–F | % | J–P | % |
|---|---|---|---|---|---|---|---|
| Initiating | 12 | Concrete | 5 | Empathetic | 5 | Systematic | 23 |
| Expressive | 7 | Realistic | 9 | Compassionate | 2 | Planful | 2 |
| Gregarious | 5 | Practical | 5 | Accommodating | 14 | Early Starting | 28 |
| Active | 5 | Experiential | 7 | Accepting | 25 | Scheduled | 5 |
| Enthusiastic | 12 | Traditional | 9 | Tender | 9 | Methodical | 23 |

*N* = 43
Average number out-of-preference = 2.12
Mean polarity index = 62.09

*Source:* National sample.

**Table 5.14 Summary of Data for ESFJ**

| Percent Out-of-Preference | | | | | | | |
|---|---|---|---|---|---|---|---|
| E–I | % | S–N | % | T–F | % | J–P | % |
| Receiving | 1 | Abstract | 8 | Logical | 10 | Casual | 7 |
| Contained | 1 | Imaginative | 9 | Reasonable | 3 | Open-Ended | 12 |
| Intimate | 8 | Conceptual | 9 | Questioning | 12 | Pressure-Prompted | 7 |
| Reflective | 5 | Theoretical | 3 | Critical | 14 | Spontaneous | 0 |
| Quiet | 10 | Original | 3 | Tough | 5 | Emergent | 10 |

*N* = 143
Average number out-of-preference = 1.38
Mean polarity index = 65.30
*Source:* National sample.

**Table 5.15 Summary of Data for ENFJ**

| Percent Out-of-Preference | | | | | | | |
|---|---|---|---|---|---|---|---|
| E–I | % | S–N | % | T–F | % | J–P | % |
| Receiving | 0 | Concrete | 3 | Logical | 0 | Casual | 24 |
| Contained | 0 | Realistic | 0 | Reasonable | 0 | Open-Ended | 13 |
| Intimate | 13 | Practical | 0 | Questioning | 29 | Pressure-Prompted | 5 |
| Reflective | 10 | Experiential | 18 | Critical | 5 | Spontaneous | 0 |
| Quiet | 5 | Traditional | 5 | Tough | 0 | Emergent | 13 |

*N* = 38
Average number out-of-preference = 1.45
Mean polarity index = 65.97
*Source:* National sample.

**Table 5.16 Summary of Data for ISFP**

| Percent Out-of-Preference | | | | | | | |
|---|---|---|---|---|---|---|---|
| E–I | % | S–N | % | T–F | % | J–P | % |
| Initiating | 9 | Abstract | 11 | Logical | 4 | Systematic | 12 |
| Expressive | 5 | Imaginative | 5 | Reasonable | 5 | Planful | 7 |
| Gregarious | 13 | Conceptual | 7 | Questioning | 17 | Early Starting | 59 |
| Active | 9 | Theoretical | 7 | Critical | 18 | Scheduled | 6 |
| Enthusiastic | 15 | Original | 7 | Tough | 9 | Methodical | 25 |

*N* = 148
Average number out-of-preference = 2.52
Mean polarity index = 59.03
*Source:* National sample.

**Table 5.17 Summary of Data for INFP**

| Percent Out-of-Preference | | | | | | | |
|---|---|---|---|---|---|---|---|
| E–I | % | S–N | % | T–F | % | J–P | % |
| Initiating | 11 | Concrete | 5 | Logical | 5 | Systematic | 1 |
| Expressive | 11 | Realistic | 2 | Reasonable | 6 | Planful | 8 |
| Gregarious | 6 | Practical | 7 | Questioning | 39 | Early Starting | 42 |
| Active | 16 | Experiential | 17 | Critical | 9 | Scheduled | 2 |
| Enthusiastic | 25 | Traditional | 14 | Tough | 5 | Methodical | 28 |

*N* = 88
Average number out-of-preference = 2.58
Mean polarity index = 63.66
*Source:* National sample.

## Table 5.18 Summary of Data for ESTP

Percent Out-of-Preference

| E–I | % | S–N | % | T–F | % | J–P | % |
|---|---|---|---|---|---|---|---|
| Receiving | 5 | Abstract | 4 | Empathetic | 2 | Systematic | 20 |
| Contained | 13 | Imaginative | 5 | Compassionate | 0 | Planful | 9 |
| Intimate | 5 | Conceptual | 8 | Accommodating | 28 | Early Starting | 41 |
| Reflective | 0 | Theoretical | 11 | Accepting | 20 | Scheduled | 5 |
| Quiet | 5 | Original | 15 | Tender | 4 | Methodical | 17 |

*N* = 54
Average number out-of-preference = 2.39
Mean polarity index = 61.85

*Source:* National sample.

## Table 5.19 Summary of Data for ESFP

Percent Out-of-Preference

| E–I | % | S–N | % | T–F | % | J–P | % |
|---|---|---|---|---|---|---|---|
| Receiving | 2 | Abstract | 7 | Logical | 3 | Systematic | 11 |
| Contained | 5 | Imaginative | 11 | Reasonable | 5 | Planful | 11 |
| Intimate | 20 | Conceptual | 17 | Questioning | 26 | Early Starting | 44 |
| Reflective | 5 | Theoretical | 8 | Critical | 12 | Scheduled | 7 |
| Quiet | 6 | Original | 13 | Tough | 6 | Methodical | 31 |

*N* = 108
Average number out-of-preference = 2.53
Mean polarity index = 59.25

*Source:* National sample.

## Table 5.20 Summary of Data for ISTJ

Percent Out-of-Preference

| E–I | % | S–N | % | T–F | % | J–P | % |
|---|---|---|---|---|---|---|---|
| Initiating | 9 | Abstract | 4 | Empathetic | 2 | Casual | 0 |
| Expressive | 8 | Imaginative | 2 | Compassionate | 3 | Open-Ended | 12 |
| Gregarious | 11 | Conceptual | 9 | Accommodating | 37 | Pressure-Prompted | 11 |
| Active | 11 | Theoretical | 4 | Accepting | 23 | Spontaneous | 0 |
| Enthusiastic | 6 | Original | 5 | Tender | 5 | Emergent | 11 |

*N* = 183
Average number out-of-preference = 1.75
Mean polarity index = 68.38

*Source:* National sample.

## Table 5.21 Summary of Data for ISFJ

Percent Out-of-Preference

| E–I | % | S–N | % | T–F | % | J–P | % |
|---|---|---|---|---|---|---|---|
| Initiating | 19 | Abstract | 6 | Logical | 12 | Casual | 5 |
| Expressive | 15 | Imaginative | 5 | Reasonable | 4 | Open-Ended | 14 |
| Gregarious | 14 | Conceptual | 13 | Questioning | 15 | Pressure-Prompted | 9 |
| Active | 12 | Theoretical | 4 | Critical | 15 | Spontaneous | 1 |
| Enthusiastic | 10 | Original | 4 | Tough | 4 | Emergent | 13 |

*N* = 191
Average number out-of-preference = 1.82
Mean polarity index = 64.70

*Source:* National sample.

## Table 5.22 Summary of Data for ENTP

Percent Out-of-Preference

| E–I | % | S–N | % | T–F | % | J–P | % |
|---|---|---|---|---|---|---|---|
| Receiving | 0 | Concrete | 4 | Empathetic | 4 | Systematic | 16 |
| Contained | 8 | Realistic | 4 | Compassionate | 0 | Planful | 8 |
| Intimate | 8 | Practical | 4 | Accommodating | 12 | Early Starting | 32 |
| Reflective | 4 | Experiential | 8 | Accepting | 24 | Scheduled | 4 |
| Quiet | 16 | Traditional | 4 | Tender | 20 | Methodical | 32 |

*N* = 25
Average number out-of-preference = 2.08
Mean polarity index = 66.60
*Source:* National sample.

## Table 5.23 Summary of Data for ENFP

Percent Out-of-Preference

| E–I | % | S–N | % | T–F | % | J–P | % |
|---|---|---|---|---|---|---|---|
| Receiving | 1 | Concrete | 0 | Logical | 5 | Systematic | 4 |
| Contained | 5 | Realistic | 1 | Reasonable | 5 | Planful | 9 |
| Intimate | 12 | Practical | 8 | Questioning | 43 | Early Starting | 28 |
| Reflective | 8 | Experiential | 10 | Critical | 9 | Scheduled | 8 |
| Quiet | 4 | Traditional | 5 | Tough | 1 | Methodical | 25 |

*N* = 105
Average number out-of-preference = 1.89
Mean polarity index = 67.33
*Source:* National sample.

## Table 5.24 Summary of Data for INTJ

Percent Out-of-Preference

| E–I | % | S–N | % | T–F | % | J–P | % |
|---|---|---|---|---|---|---|---|
| Initiating | 26 | Concrete | 16 | Empathetic | 0 | Casual | 0 |
| Expressive | 0 | Realistic | 16 | Compassionate | 5 | Open-Ended | 42 |
| Gregarious | 0 | Practical | 0 | Accommodating | 16 | Pressure-Prompted | 16 |
| Active | 5 | Experiential | 16 | Accepting | 42 | Spontaneous | 5 |
| Enthusiastic | 0 | Traditional | 21 | Tender | 0 | Emergent | 5 |

*N* = 19
Average number out-of-preference = 2.32
Mean polarity index = 65.37
*Source:* National sample.

## Table 5.25 Summary of Data for INFJ

Percent Out-of-Preference

| E–I | % | S–N | % | T–F | % | J–P | % |
|---|---|---|---|---|---|---|---|
| Initiating | 9 | Concrete | 3 | Logical | 6 | Casual | 15 |
| Expressive | 12 | Realistic | 3 | Reasonable | 3 | Open-Ended | 6 |
| Gregarious | 12 | Practical | 0 | Questioning | 21 | Pressure-Prompted | 3 |
| Active | 15 | Experiential | 15 | Critical | 18 | Spontaneous | 6 |
| Enthusiastic | 23 | Traditional | 26 | Tough | 3 | Emergent | 9 |

*N* = 34
Average number out-of-preference = 2.06
Mean polarity index = 60.73
*Source:* National sample.

with Casual, and no one in either sample showed a Spontaneous preference. Both types have a low average of out-of-preference facets overall.

## Dominant Introverted Feeling Types

The two dominant introverted Feeling types, INFP and ISFP, are different in their polarity indexes (INFPs are higher), and twice as many INFPs score toward Questioning. ISFPs have even more Early Starting group members than do INFPs. Perhaps the auxiliary preference for Intuition encourages INFPs to do more inquiring, and auxiliary Sensing encourages ISFPs to meet the deadlines they have accepted as facts. The two types appear similar in most other comparisons.

## Dominant Extraverted Sensing Types

The mean polarity index is higher for ESTPs, and four times as many ESFPs show an Intimate out-of-preference result compared to ESTPs, perhaps due to the influence of their overall Feeling preference. There are about as many Accommodating ESTPs as there are Questioning ESFPs. ESTPs show more Systematic out-of-preference results, and ESFPs more Methodical individuals.

## Dominant Introverted Sensing Types

The mean polarity index for ISTJs is quite a bit higher than it is for ISFJs. ISFJs overall have more out-of-preference facets in the E–I block but are similar to ISTJs in this regard on the S–N and J–P blocks. There are many more ISTJs who are out-of-preference on their auxiliary function T–F facets, Questioning–Accommodating and Critical–Accepting, than there are ISFJs who are out-of-preference on these two facets of their auxiliary function.

## Dominant Extraverted Intuitive Types

There are many Questioning ENFPs but correspondingly few Accommodating ENTPs, and (given the overall distribution) more Accepting ENTPs than Critical ENFPs. It is interesting that more ENTPs show an out-of-preference result on Enthusiastic–Quiet. Both have fairly high polarity indexes overall.

## Dominant Introverted Intuitive Types

The polarity index for INTJs is much higher than it is for INFJs, but note the small sample sizes for both types. Almost three times as many INTJs describe themselves as Initiating, but quite a few more INFJs than INTJs are out-of-preference on the other four E–I facets. There appear to be more Concrete and Realistic INTJs than INFJs. There are also many Accepting INTJs and fewer Accommodating ones, somewhat fewer Questioning INFJs compared to other Feeling types, and somewhat more Critical out-of-preference people.

The most striking contrast, however, is the high percentage (42%) of Open-Ended INTJs compared to INFJs (6%), and, to a lesser extent, there is a similar difference for Pressure-Prompted. If these differences hold up with larger samples of INTJs and INFJs, they are likely due to the different auxiliary functions involved. The INTJ results may reflect the desire of the auxiliary Thinking function to pursue truth in an unfettered manner; INFJs may have an equally clear desire to maintain harmony by planning in advance and starting projects early.

# Conclusion

This chapter, in conjunction with the individual practitioner's interpretation experience, will provide clients with a range of insights into their individuality. It gives clients information about similarities to those of their own type as well as similarities in facet results to other types. It is clearly advisable to allow a good deal of time for exploring this second step in type understanding during interpretation sessions. However, if time is limited, it is best to ensure that clients appreciate the Step II instrument as a way of enhancing their Step I understanding. A realistic goal is to supply clients with enough knowledge and recommended resources to stimulate their continued interest in typology and the MBTI personality inventory.

PART

# Research III

Part III presents the research that led to the revised Step II instrument and the evidence attesting to its reliability and validity. This information not only provides statistical legitimacy for the Step II tool but also represents practical information practitioners may use to enhance their understanding and interpretation of client profiles.

Chapter 6, "Construction and Properties of the Step II™ Facet Scales," details the procedure followed in the revision. It includes a description of the goals for the revision, the initial item selection process, collection of data from a national sample, and the final selection of items. The scoring method and definition of out-of-preference scores are also described. The properties of the final set of items are then presented, including the facet scale means and standard deviations, both for the total sample and by age and gender. The scale intercorrelations are also documented, as are the correlations between the original and revised scales.

Chapter 7, "Reliability," presents pertinent data for the facet scales. This includes internal consistency as well as the test-retest reliability of continuous scores and scoring categories. Appropriate ways of interpreting reliability estimates for this kind of instrument are discussed, and the statistical basis for the polarity index and its supporting data are described.

Chapter 8, "Validity," presents validating evidence for the Step II facet scales. In addition to describing a confirmatory factor analysis of the facet scales, this chapter contains a wealth of data showing the relation of the revised Step II facet scales to several other measures. Included are correlations with the *California Psychological Inventory* (CPI), *Adjective Check List* (ACL), *Fundamental Interpersonal Relationship Orientation–Behavior*™ (FIRO-B®), and *Eysenck Personality Inventory* instruments, a variety of behavioral descriptors, and many work-related variables, leadership measures, and measures of stress, coping, and relationship satisfaction. Studies that aim to test type theory using the Step II scales are also discussed. After practitioners familiarize themselves with the fascinating information in this chapter, they will be equipped to satisfy their clients' curiosity regarding the scope and application of the Step II instrument.

# Construction and Properties of the Step II™ Facet Scales

# 6

CHAPTER OVERVIEW



The purpose of this chapter is to describe the development of the revised Step II facet scales and the new scoring system. The twenty facets are not intended to provide complete domain coverage of each of the four dichotomies described by Jung and Myers. The *Myers-Briggs Type Indicator* (MBTI) preference domains are rich and multifaceted. The twenty facet scales provide information about individual differences within type, but type is more than the sum of the Step II facet scales; indeed, it is more than the sum of the four preference scales. Together, however, the four overall preference dichotomies that constitute the Step I instrument and the twenty facet scales that result from Step II scoring provide a complex and individualized portrait of a person's preferences and how these preferences are manifested in different situations and contexts.

The Step II facet scales were created and revised within this theoretical context. In this chapter, item selection procedures are described, along with the analyses and results that led to the new scoring system. The overall process of revision proceeded according to the following steps:

1. Determine the goals for the revision.
2. Select an initial item pool.
3. Prepare a research form.

4. Collect data from a national sample.
5. Select the final items.
6. Determine the optimal scoring procedure.
7. Define out-of-preference scores.
8. Describe the properties of the revised scales.
9. Examine correlational data for the revised scales.
10. Analyze apparent inconsistencies between Step I and Step II results.
11. Compare the original and revised scales.
12. Evaluate the resulting scales for reliability and validity.

The first eleven of these steps are described in the sections below. Once the final items were selected and the scoring method determined, the Step II facet scales were submitted to reliability and validity analyses. The results of these analyses are found in the next two chapters.

## Goals for the Revision

The overall goal of the Step II revision was to produce an accurate representation of individual differences within type. The development of the initial Step II facet scales occurred in 1989 with the publication of the MBTI® Expanded Analysis Report (Saunders, 1989). In 1996, the scale descriptions were updated and a comprehensive new report, the MBTI® Step II™ Expanded Interpretive Report (Quenk & Kummerow, 1996), was created that incorporated additional norms and interpretive information from a sample of more than 16,000 cases (Mitchell et al., 1997). After the publication of the new Step II material, the MBTI Step I instrument was revised as Form M, which became the new standard form for identifying an individual's four preferences (Myers et al., 1998).

Given this history, a revision of the Step II tool was planned to address the following seven goals.

*Goal #1:* Use Form M items and scoring as the method for arriving at the Step I type that provides the foundation for Step II results. Since the Step II instrument represents an attempt to identify individual differences within type, the results are always interpreted in the context of the person's four-letter type. The original Step II reports used Form G items and scoring to determine type; the advent of Form M, with its very different scoring procedures and somewhat altered item pool, made it necessary to bring the procedures of the earlier Step II reports into alignment.

*Goal #2:* Investigate new methods for item selection and scoring of the facet scales. Form M of the MBTI instrument demonstrated the value of newer psychometric methods, specifically item response theory (IRT), for both item selection and scoring. It was therefore desirable to determine whether these methodological advances were also appropriate for the development of Step II facet scales. If so, deriving Step I and Step II results from the same method would be an added advantage.

*Goal #3:* Investigate new methods for reporting scale scores. Employing new methods of scoring meant that new reporting methods could also be explored. The original Step II scale scores, ranging from 0 to 10, sometimes gave the appearance of being closer to measures of traits than to measures (or facets) of type.

*Goal #4:* Item selection and scoring decisions should be based on both a representative national sample and a balanced type sample drawn from the national sample. The original Step II facet scales and item weights were developed using fairly small samples. Although new type-specific norms and interpretive information were later obtained from a very large sample of more than 16,000 persons, item selection and scoring decisions based on a much broader and more representative sample would insure against undue sampling error.

*Goal #5:* Increase the internal consistency reliability of Step II facet scales. Partly due to the fact that a number of the original scales contained only a few items, but perhaps also due to item selection procedures, some of the original scales had fairly low internal consistency reliabilities. In order to determine whether these reliabilities could be increased with the addition of new items, the 1998 additions to Form M were included on the Step II facet scales.

*Goal #6:* Keep the number of items on the new form as small as possible. Form K, which was used to derive the original Step II facet scales, contained 131 items. Based on the popularity of the Step II method, users clearly perceived this length as acceptable, given what they received in return. The length-to-value trade-off was a practical consideration in the development of a new form.

*Goal #7:* To the extent possible, retain the meaning of the Step II facet scales as described in Mitchell, Quenk, and Kummerow (1997). Again, the popularity of the Step II tool demonstrated its value to users, who viewed facet scale interpretation as a great help to their clients. Significant changes in meaning, particularly through the addition of new items, would create confusion among already satisfied users and possibly reduce the value of the instrument.

The first five goals listed above were viewed as opportunities to improve the accuracy and usability of the Step II facet scales and interpretive reports. Only the first goal—incorporating Form M scoring into the Step II report and profile—was assured. The other four goals involved large-scale data collection and intensive analytical effort with no guarantee of success.

The last two goals, those dealing with the number of items and the meaning of the scales, were viewed as practical constraints and were therefore included in the criteria for measuring progress on the other goals. Scale content and meaning thus received higher priority than measurement statistics. For example, it is possible to increase the reliability of a scale (Goal #5) by simply adding more items. However, if in doing so, the meaning of the scale was significantly altered, then the latter goal (Goal #7) took priority, and the change was not made.

## Research Form and Initial Item Pool

The new research form included 268 MBTI items. This initial item pool was created from the following sources:

- All 131 items from Form K. Thus, all the items used to score the original Step II facet scales were included.
- All 93 items from Form M (Step I) of the MBTI assessment, if these items were not already included in the Form K item pool.
- A number of items from Form J of the MBTI instrument that had been previously identified by Wayne Mitchell as potential contributors to the measurement of the Step II facet scales.
- A number of items from Form J of the MBTI instrument that had been used by Isabel Briggs Myers in her very early work on individual differences within type.

Additional measures were also included in the data-gathering phase to collect demographic information both about respondents and about numerous other scales that could be used for validation purposes. These additional measures were the *Adjective Check List* (Gough & Heilbrun, 1983), the *California Psychological Inventory* instrument (Gough & Bradley, 1996), and 33 lifestyle questions.

To avoid overburdening respondents, the sample was split in half. All respondents completed the Step II items, the demographic questions, and the lifestyle questions. However, half the sample, drawn at random, received the *Adjective Check List,* and the other half the *California Psychological Inventory* instrument.

## Data Collection Using a National Sample

Data were collected by an independent professional survey firm using a sampling procedure that employed random-digit dialing of telephone numbers in the United States. If there was no answer on the first call, the firm tried again at least three times in order to improve the odds that the sample would be representative. Calls were made at different times of the day and on weekends. When the phone was answered, a representative of the survey firm explained the nature of the project and requested participation. Neither the MBTI personality inventory nor the name of the publisher was mentioned. Those who agreed to participate were asked a series of questions to determine whether their demographic profiles were still needed to fill gaps in the sample. The goal was to achieve a sample that approximated U.S. census demographics as closely as possible. Anyone who indicated a willingness to participate received a research packet in the mail.

Completed Step II research forms were returned by 1,380 individuals. The final sample was made up of 57% women and 43% men. The mean age of the sample was 50.3 years (*SD* = 16.8). The ethnic distribution, from those who indicated their ethnic groups, was 90% Caucasian, 5% African American, and 5% "other." See table 7.5, on page 116, for the educational distribution of the sample.

For the purposes of certain analyses, a balanced-by-type sample of 450 individuals was randomly extracted from the total national sample. The original goal in drawing such a sample was to obtain an equal number of each represented type, thereby removing structural dominance by types with naturally occurring large-sample representation. However, due to the distribution of types in the national sample, it was not possible to achieve completely equal sample sizes for all sixteen types and still maintain an overall sample large enough to provide a solid foundation for the analyses. The smallest samples were 19 for INTJs and 25 for ENTPs; sample size for all other types was 29.

## Final Item Selection Using Item Response Theory

Using the data from the national sample, a series of initial confirmatory factor analyses (CFA) was performed on three alternative sets of Step II facet scales and items that mirrored the various item sources on the research form. Thus, one set consisted of Form K items scored on the original Step II facet scales. Another was a set of scales and items that had been identified by Wayne Mitchell in preliminary analyses for the Step II revision. The third was the incomplete set of scales and items derived from Myers' unpublished early work.

Scales and their structures were considered for the revised Step II instrument through an iterative process of item selection and CFA evaluation. Unlike exploratory factor-analytic procedures, confirmatory approaches require specifying the loading of the items on the scales in advance. Results are then evaluated in terms of how well they fit the model. The evaluation team used the CFA results to test hypotheses about the theoretical structure of Step II facet scales and produced a 160-item interim version with twenty revised scales. There were alternative forms of some of the scales and a number of items that needed further evaluation.

The effort then moved from structural evaluation to item-level evaluation. Because IRT was so helpful in selecting items for the revision of the MBTI Step I (Form M) instrument, it was used to evaluate each of the 160 potential items in the Step II item pool. The balanced-by-type sample of 450 individuals that had been randomly drawn from the national sample was used for the IRT analyses.

## Applying Item Response Theory to the Step II™ Instrument

The principles followed in applying IRT to Step II item selection and scoring are the same as those used with the Step I tool. Therefore, a full explanation of IRT will not be provided here. Readers interested in a more in-depth understanding of this topic should consult the following sources: chapter 7 of the *MBTI® Manual* (Myers et al., 1998), Harvey (1996), Harvey and Thomas (1996), and Harvey and Hammer (1999).

As the name implies, item response theory is concerned with the relationship between item responses and the underlying construct that presumably produces those responses. Unlike classical test theory, IRT focuses on the item level instead of the scale or test level. Construction and evaluation of tests based on IRT, therefore, scrutinize the relationship between a person's "true score" on the psychological characteristic (or dimension) in question and the likelihood of a particular response to an individual test item. For example, consider an item on the Concrete–Abstract facet scale: IRT asks how likely it is that a person with a "true" preference for Abstract will choose the response keyed in the Abstract direction.

One of the great advantages of IRT models is that they allow both linear and nonlinear relations to exist between the underlying psychological characteristic and the observed item response. This is important for MBTI items, including those intended to measure the facets, because a nonlinear relationship between the items and the facets they measure is both theoretically desirable and empirically accurate.

First, the theory. The relationship between the response and the construct can be graphically described using what is called an *item characteristic curve* (ICC) in IRT. The horizontal axis of an ICC for a particular item shows the varying levels of the psychological characteristic the item is designed to measure. The vertical axis shows the expected rate of item endorsement, or the percentage of people who respond to the item in the keyed direction (PKR; ranges from 0 to 100%), at each of level of the psychological characteristic. The scores measuring the psychological characteristic on the horizontal axis are called *theta* in IRT terminology and are denoted as $\theta$. Theta corresponds roughly to a nonlinear rescaling of the "true score" of classical test theory (Drasgow & Hulin, 1990). In IRT, the theta scale is arbitrary in nature; by convention, it is typically expressed with 0 defining the midpoint and scores below the midpoint being negative and those above being positive. (As described below, however, thetas were converted to an eleven-point integer scale with no negatives, thus avoiding the pejorative connotation when reporting scores.) The direction of the keyed response—that is, which pole of the facet is defined as the keyed direction—is also entirely arbitrary for the purposes of IRT. However, for the sake of consistency with previous MBTI conventions, the I, N, F, and P poles of the facet scales are defined as the keyed direction.

Figure 6.1 shows hypothetical ICCs for two items designed to measure preferences on the Initiating–Receiving facet scale. In both cases, scores on the far left of the scale represent people with very clear preferences for Initiating, and scores on the far right represent people with very clear preferences for Receiving. So, as theta increases from left to right, we would expect higher levels of endorsement in the predicted, or keyed, direction, which is the Receiving pole. In other words, we would expect people with a clear preference for Receiving to demonstrate the Receiving response to this item much more often than would a person with a clear preference for Initiating.

For example, consider the hypothetical item denoted by the solid line in figure 6.1 and assume that the solid line is the ICC for the following item from the Initiating–Receiving facet scale: "In a large group, do you more often (A) introduce others or (B) get introduced?" Since the Receiving response is designated as the keyed response, all individuals who chose (B) would be scored as endorsing the item, and those who chose the Initiating response (A) would be scored as not endorsing the item in the keyed direction. Thus, for any given theta, it is possible to determine the percentage of individuals with that score on the Initiating–Receiving scale who could be expected to mark the Receiving response. To do this, first locate the theta of interest on the horizontal axis. Then find the location on the ICC (the solid line in this case) that is directly above it and read across to the vertical axis to find the percentage. Thus, if we were interested in those who share a theta score of +2.0 toward Receiving, we can determine that approximately 75% of them would respond in the keyed direction, by choosing (B), or "get introduced." The remainder of the people, about one quarter, would select the Initiating response (A), "introduce others."

IRT models designed for dichotomously scored items, such as those on the MBTI instrument, describe each item's characteristics or performance using up to three parameters. These parameters define the way in which a person's placement on theta is related to the observed likelihood that he or she will endorse the item in the keyed direction. They also determine the shape of each item characteristic curve. As with Step I scoring, the three-parameter model seemed to provide the most information and the best fit with the data. We will discuss this more extensively later,

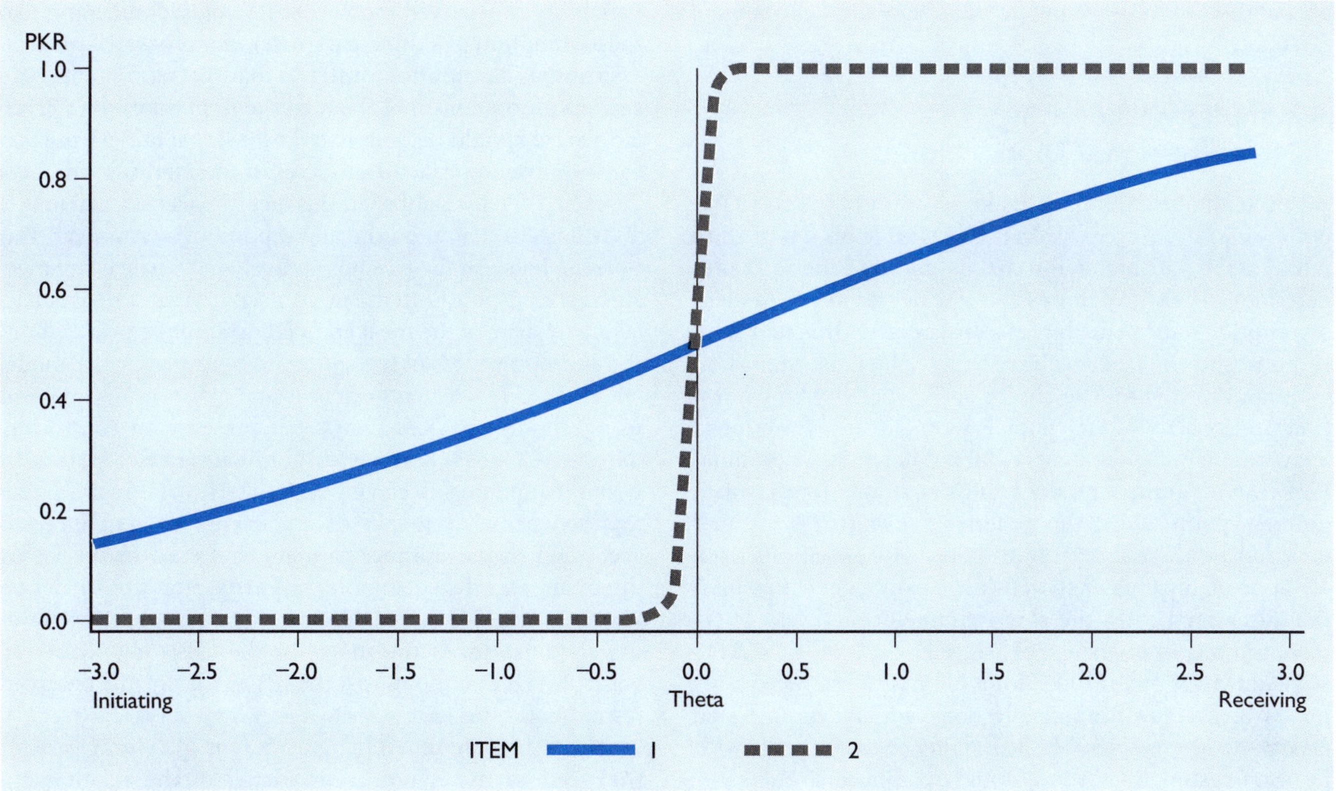


Figure 6.1 Item Characteristic Curves for Two Hypothetical Items from the Initiating–Receiving Facet Scale

*Source:* Adapted from Myers et al., 1998. Used with permission.

but first it is necessary to understand these parameters in more detail.

The *a* parameter describes an item's degree of discrimination. Higher discrimination parameters are associated with items that produce more information regarding a person's preference toward one pole or the other of a facet scale. In figure 6.1, the item producing the dashed ICC has a much higher *a* parameter than the item producing the solid line. The steeper the curve at the theta that is most relevant to the purposes of the measurement, the more information produced and the greater the likelihood that the person will respond to the item in the keyed direction. For a perfectly flat line, *a* would equal 0, which indicates *no* information; for such an item, no matter which theta you examined, the likelihood of a response in the keyed direction would be the same.

The *b*, or difficulty, parameter in IRT quantifies the left-right location of the ICC on the theta scale. For facet items, the main function of the *b* parameter is to tell us where on the theta scale the item produces the maximum amount of information regarding the person's preference on the facet. An item with a high *b* parameter on the Initiating–Receiving facet scale would be one with the greatest slope toward the Receiving pole rather than one centered above the midpoint of the scale. Imagine moving the dashed line in figure 6.1 to the right so that the almost vertical portion of the line is over the theta at 2.0. This item would provide information about people who have a clear preference for Receiving versus those who have a *very* clear preference for Receiving. It would provide little information about a true preference for either Initiating or Receiving because the probability of responding in the keyed direction (Receiving) is the same for all people whose theta is less than 2.0. In other words, it would group together all people with a preference for the Initiating pole, all people who score in the midzone of the Initiating–Receiving pole, and all those whose preference is toward Receiving but with a theta of less than 2.0. Those with a very clear preference toward Receiving would be in the other group. For the purposes of selecting items for the facet scales, we would prefer items whose ICCs center around the midpoint of the scale.

Finally, the *c*, or lower asymptote, parameter defines the baseline for item-endorsement rates expected from individuals who score very far toward the left pole of the facet scale. The *c* parameter can be used with MBTI items to indicate the degree of social desirability of the item responses. In MBTI terms, an item with a high *c* parameter would mean that even people who have a very clear preference toward the left pole of the facet scale have some probability of responding to the item in the opposite direction.

## Assumptions Underlying the Item Response Theory Model

All psychometric methods make assumptions, and IRT is not exempt in this regard. As is true with items designed to measure the four preference dichotomies, it is important to determine, to the extent possible, the degree to which these assumptions are plausible or consistent with actual item responses to the facet scales. Some of the most important assumptions involve the choice of IRT model. Many questions related to model choice were already introduced above: namely, Do the items exhibit differential discrimination (the *a* parameter), does this discrimination occur at different points along the preference scale (the *b* parameter), and are there at least some items with asymptotes that are appreciably greater than 0 (the *c* parameter)? Research that attempted to fit the three-parameter model to MBTI dichotomous item responses (see chapter 7 of the *MBTI® Manual* [Myers et al., 1998] for a summary) produced affirmative answers to all three questions, which demonstrated clearly that considerable variability was present with respect to estimates of the *a*, *b*, and *c* parameters. This same variability is observed for facet scale items, confirming that the assumption of a three-parameter model is warranted.

Another assumption of IRT is that the set of items on a scale is unidimensional. That is, the item pools for a given facet scale should be dominated by a single underlying factor. Confirmatory factor analyses of the Step II item pools described above established this fact for facet scale items.

IRT is also based on the assumption of a nonlinear relationship between the psychological characteristic being measured and responses to the items used to measure that characteristic. One of the most compelling arguments in favor of the appropriateness of using the three-parameter IRT model with the facet scale items can be found in the results obtained using empirical ICCs. Figure 6.2 presents an empirically derived ICC for a strongly discriminating facet scale item from the Initiating–Receiving scale. The squares in this figure represent actual average rates of item endorsement, grouped according to the number of items endorsed in the keyed direction (i.e., the square on the farthest right of the figure represents the average of those people who gave the Receiving response to all the items on the Initiating–Receiving scale). The figure shows that the IRT model fits the observed responses for this facet scale to a very high degree.

The results presented in figure 6.2 make a strong case for the need to use a nonlinear model of the relationship

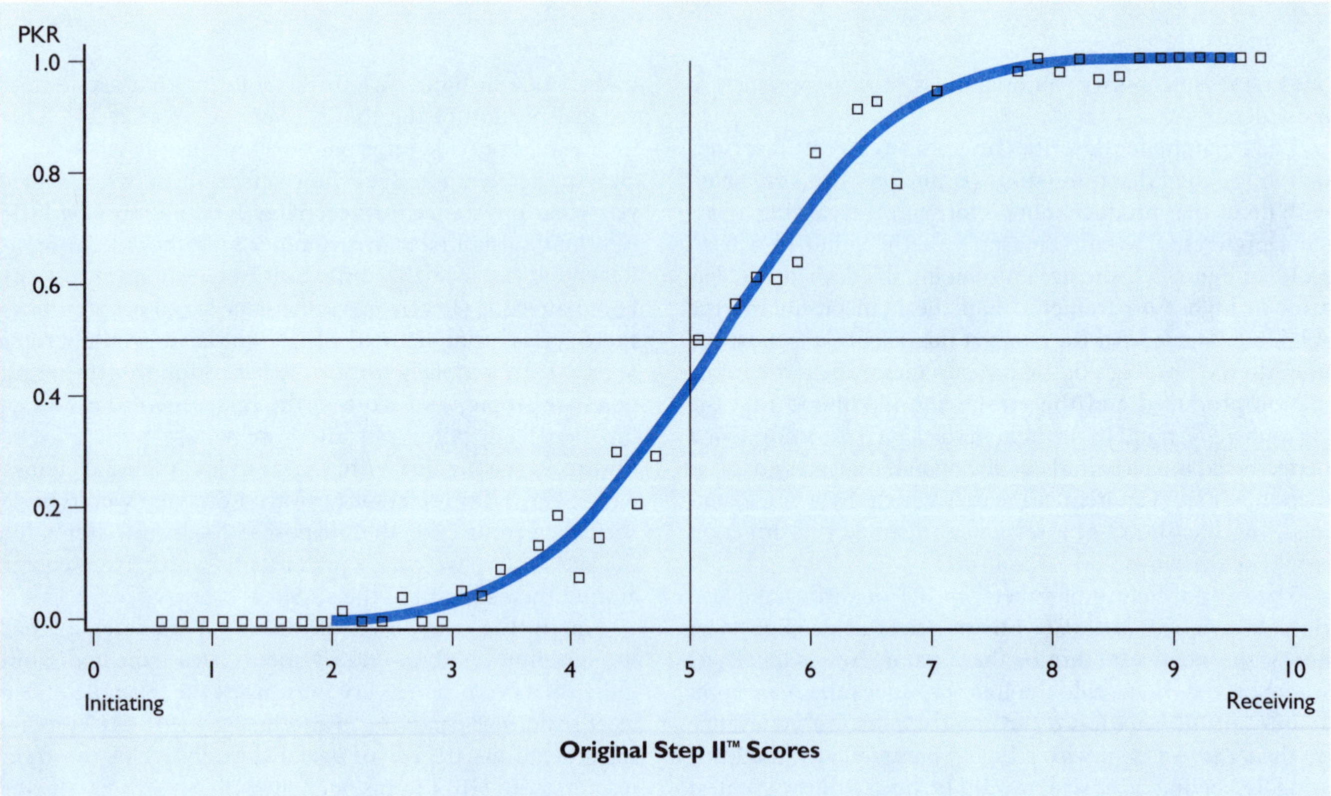


Figure 6.2 Empirical Item Characteristic Curve for an Item on the Initiating–Receiving Facet Scale

*Source:* Adapted from Myers et al., 1998. Used with permission.

between the underlying preference for one pole of a facet scale and the observed likelihood of endorsing an item in the keyed direction. There is a very definite S-shaped relationship, with this item providing a large amount of information in the intermediate range of the facet scale and less information (i.e., a flatter slope) toward either pole. Other items will of course have different curves, some more S-shaped, some less so.

The most extreme case of a nonlinear function for a facet scale item would be an ICC that took the shape of a perfect step function centered exactly over the midpoint of the scale; this would be a case of maximum information and maximum separation between people of opposite preferences on the facet scale. The dashed line in figure 6.1 comes very close to depicting an example. If this were an item from the Initiating–Receiving facet scale, such an ICC would indicate that *all* those with a preference for the Receiving pole would choose the Receiving response and none of those with a preference for the Initiating pole would choose that response, and vice versa. While some items do approach this limit, there are a number of reasons why it is neither required nor expected that all items display this form.

To begin with, the facet scales, by definition, are more narrow than the scales measuring the preference dichotomies. Some represent the exercise of that preference in a special or restricted domain. To the extent that the environment both calls forth and rewards the behaviors related to this domain, and to the extent that the person is conscious of his or her behaviors in relation to the environment, people can learn the behaviors associated with the poles of some facet scales.

For example, a person with a preference for Pressure-Prompted may enter a work environment where behaviors associated with the Early Starting pole are required and/or strongly rewarded. This person may indeed learn how to approach tasks by getting an early start and allowing time to review the project before the deadline. Because of this experience, and especially if the person has been rewarded for this behavior with promotions, compensation, or additional challenging assignments, he or she may choose a few more Early Starting responses than would otherwise have been the case. In such a case, all the items on this scale may not conform to a nice step function centered on the 0 point of the scale. This hypothesis for the Early Starting–Pressure-Prompted scale is supported by distribution statistics for the scales reported in tables 6.1 and 6.2, in the "Analysis of the Properties of Step II™ Facet Scales" section of this chapter.

The second reason not to expect the perfect step function on all facet scale items is that responses toward one pole of a facet scale are not equally popular for all types holding the dichotomous preference indicated by that facet. For example, ENTPs have the highest score toward the Original (N) pole of the Traditional–Original scale, with a mean of 3.16. The Intuitive type with the lowest mean on that scale is INFJ, with a significantly lower mean of 0.32. While the INFJs still score toward the Original pole, they are more inclined on average to respond to some of the items on this scale in the Traditional direction. One hypothesis for this result is that the INFJs have extraverted Feeling as their auxiliary function.

For these reasons, desirable items for MBTI scales would be those that showed the general S shape or pattern but varied somewhat from the pure step function. That even the best of the MBTI items—whether they measure the dichotomies or the poles of a facet scale, or both—do not conform to the ideal demonstrates the theoretical proposition that, for various reasons, including developmental or situational factors, a person has some chance of responding to an item in a direction opposite his or her preference.

## Item Selection Criteria

The primary criterion in selecting items was the meaning of the facet scale. To the extent possible, we sought to retain the meaning of the Step II facet scales as described by Mitchell et al. (1997). These scales had shown promising empirical and clinical validity. Applications in areas as different as psychotherapy, team building, and leadership confirmed the usefulness of these scales. Given the performance of the scales, making significant changes to their meaning was seen as neither necessary nor desirable.

Another requirement, made possible through the use of IRT, was to select items that maximized the amount of information around the midpoint of each facet scale. As with Step I Form M items, this meant items whose theoretically ideal shape approximated a step function. In the IRT analysis, this meant that the shape of the latent distributions was not assumed to be normal continuous but was estimated empirically. Selecting items for the Step II facet scales by using IRT meant that type theory's assumption of dichotomous preferences was applied to the facets of the preferences (i.e., the twenty facet scales), just as it had been to the selection of items for the four overall dichotomous preferences. The item selection procedures for the Step I and Step II instruments were thus consistent, which had not previously been the case.

The effect of adding or subtracting an item on the internal consistency of the scale was another factor in the selection of items. The goal, of course, was to increase the reliability of the scales over that of the original Step II facet scales. However, this goal was subordinate to overall scale meaning. In some instances, there were several items that increased the alpha of a scale by about the same small amount. Since such items were statistically equivalent, there was no objective basis on which to choose among them, and items with content that best matched those already in the scale were selected. It is also possible to increase the alpha coefficient of a scale by adding similar items. But since one of the criteria for the revision was to keep the overall number of items as close as possible to the 131 of Form K, this strategy was not implemented.

Applying these criteria in an iterative fashion resulted in the selection of 144 items for Form Q, the final form of the Step II instrument. Of these 144 items, 142 are used to score the twenty facet scales. The remaining Form M items are included on Form Q, however, because the Step II results include the Form M type as well as the scores on the facet scales.

## Determination of Scoring Method

Since IRT was used to select items for both the Form Q facet scales and the Form M dichotomous preference scales, and because it had proved effective as a scoring method for Form M, IRT was also applied to score the twenty Step II facet scales. BiLog-MG (V1.1C; Zimowski, Muraki, Mislevy, & Bock, 1997) was used to estimate theta—the best estimate of a person's score on a given scale, taking into account all information about the item (i.e., previously estimated item parameters) as well as the person's responses to it. As with the four Step I preference scales, theta scores are positive when the preference on one of the twenty Step II facet scales is in the direction of the I, N, F, and P poles of the dichotomy and negative when in the direction of the E, S, T, and J poles.

A fundamental quantity in all the scoring equations is the expected probability that people with a score of theta would endorse item *i* in the keyed direction (i.e., choosing responses associated with the I, N, F, or P pole of the facet scales), which is a joint function of the IRT scoring parameters *a, b,* and *c*, plus theta and a scaling constant.

Once an estimate of theta has been established, the estimation is refined using a Bayesian expected a posteriori (EAP) scoring approach. The advantage of the Bayesian EAP scoring method is its smaller average measurement error across all possible response patterns. This means that the results will be equally accurate regardless of which pole of the facet is indicated by the individual's responses. In addition, the EAP scoring method allows us to base the item weights (and resulting scores) on the existing distribution in the sample population; there is no need to assume a normal distribution. Because the majority of Step II scales revealed a clear bipolar distribution, the scoring method more accurately assigns the individual to one pole or the other and not toward a common mean about the midpoint (where theta equals 0). In fact, the frequency of scores about the midpoint of theta was typically very low.

The thetas for each of the facet scales were converted into a common metric so as to facilitate interpretation, as was done with the Step I instrument. The metric on the original Step II facet scales was an eleven-point scale ranging from 0 to 10. The metric for the revised Step II facet scales is also eleven points, but the scores now range from –5 to 0 to 5. The Step II profile and reports utilize a metric that takes the form of a two-part score: a numerical score (0–5) and a direction (the pole of the dichotomy indicated by a respondent's scores). For example, on the original Step II assessment, a person who answered all the items on the Expressive–Contained scale by choosing those keyed in the Contained direction would receive a score of 10. If this person also responded to all the items on the Expressive–Contained scale of the revised Step II tool by choosing the same responses—that is, all responses keyed toward the Contained pole of this scale—he or she would receive a score of Contained 5.

## Out-of-Preference Scores Defined

As described in chapter 5, facet scale scores are considered out-of-preference when they do not conform to the expectation that the facets of a preference will likely be consistent with the overall preference. Once the new scoring method had been finalized, it was necessary to determine which scores would be considered out-of-preference. On the original version of the Step II tool, out-of-preference scales were called *out-of-pattern* (they were changed to *out-of-preference* in the revised edition of *MBTI® Step II™: A Description of the Subscales* [Mitchell et al., 1997]) and were defined as scores that occur at the pole opposite that of the person's Form G preference. Out-of-preference scores were carefully defined so as to avoid a situation in which a score is classified as out-of-preference based on responses to just one or two items. To be considered truly or meaningfully different (opposite) from the person's overall Step I preference, the score on the Step II scale had to be pointing clearly in the opposite direction.

The effects of each definition were analyzed by examining the frequency of out-of-preference scales and comparing it to the frequency of occurrences in the original Step II instrument, which had already been subjected to years of clinical observation. A number of potential cutoff points for out-of-preference scores were tested. Different cutoffs were also applied to dozens of new cases by administering the original and the revised versions of the Step II tool and comparing the results. Based on this procedure, out-of-preference scores for the revised the Step II tool were determined to be –5, –4, –3, and –2 when they appear with I, N, F, or P Step I results, and 5, 4, 3, and 2 in conjunction with E, S, T, or J Step I results. Note that although the metric is different, these scores cut off the same portions of the scales as did the scores in the original version. However, since the frequency of out-of-preference scores has decreased with the new cutoffs, we can conclude that measurement is now more precise. For the frequencies of out-of-preference scores for the revised Step II facet scales see table 5.3, on page 63. Chapter 5 also provides a model for interpreting these scores.

The revised Step II instrument differs in important ways from the original: There are more items on every scale, all scales have higher reliabilities, and distributions of scores are more bimodal. Together, these factors suggest that there is less error, or noise, associated with scores on the Step II facet scales.

## Analysis of the Properties of Step II™ Facet Scales

This section describes the properties of the revised Step II facet scales. The means, standard deviations, and distribution statistics for each of the twenty scales from the total national sample are presented. The national sample was then broken down by gender and age group, and these means and standard deviations are displayed and discussed.

### Means and Standard Deviations in the National Sample

The means and standard deviations of the Step II facet scales in the national sample are shown in table 6.1 and are displayed in figure 6.3. For the most part, the means center around the midpoint of each scale. There are six scales with means greater than 1 point from the 0 point in either direction (with the pole closest to the mean in

**Table 6.1 Means and Standard Deviations of the Facet Scales by Total Sample and by Gender**

| | Total Sample ($N$ = 1,378) | | Females ($n$ = 778) | | Males ($n$ = 587) | | Test for Difference Between F and M | |
|---|---|---|---|---|---|---|---|---|
| **Step II™ Facet Scale** | *M* | *SD* | *M* | *SD* | *M* | *SD* | *F* | *Sig.* |
| *E–I Facet Scales* | | | | | | | | |
| Initiating–Receiving | –0.11 | 3.46 | –0.27 | 3.48 | 0.15 | 3.43 | 4.88 | 0.03 |
| Expressive–Contained | –0.02 | 3.07 | –0.24 | 3.07 | 0.32 | 3.01 | 11.17 | 0.00 |
| Gregarious–Intimate | 0.28 | 2.99 | 0.38 | 3.02 | 0.15 | 2.94 | 1.98 | 0.16 |
| Active–Reflective | –0.17 | 2.92 | –0.12 | 2.98 | –0.20 | 2.85 | 0.27 | 0.61 |
| Enthusiastic–Quiet | 0.12 | 3.24 | –0.05 | 3.27 | 0.38 | 3.20 | 5.84 | 0.02 |
| *S–N Facet Scales* | | | | | | | | |
| Concrete–Abstract | –0.78 | 2.94 | –0.60 | 2.91 | –1.01 | 2.97 | 6.55 | 0.01 |
| Realistic–Imaginative | –1.07 | 3.06 | –0.95 | 3.05 | –1.22 | 3.08 | 2.60 | 0.11 |
| Practical–Conceptual | –0.84 | 2.89 | –0.58 | 2.91 | –1.18 | 2.85 | 14.54 | 0.00 |
| Experiential–Theoretical | –1.60 | 3.37 | –1.64 | 3.27 | –1.54 | 3.52 | 0.30 | 0.58 |
| Traditional–Original | –1.06 | 2.87 | –1.22 | 2.85 | –0.83 | 2.89 | 6.22 | 0.01 |
| *T–F Facet Scales* | | | | | | | | |
| Logical–Empathetic | 0.28 | 3.02 | 1.21 | 2.78 | –0.95 | 2.89 | 195.93 | 0.00 |
| Reasonable–Compassionate | 0.29 | 2.88 | 1.22 | 2.57 | –0.95 | 2.81 | 221.23 | 0.00 |
| Questioning–Accommodating | 0.46 | 2.79 | 1.18 | 2.88 | 0.36 | 3.07 | 25.92 | 0.00 |
| Critical–Accepting | 1.11 | 3.21 | 2.04 | 3.01 | –0.13 | 3.05 | 172.00 | 0.00 |
| Tough–Tender | 0.62 | 3.06 | 1.44 | 2.77 | –0.49 | 3.09 | 146.88 | 0.00 |
| *J–P Facet Scales* | | | | | | | | |
| Systematic–Casual | –0.51 | 3.08 | –0.25 | 2.99 | –0.85 | 3.17 | 12.60 | 0.00 |
| Planful–Open-Ended | –0.14 | 3.93 | –0.28 | 3.95 | 0.05 | 3.90 | 2.45 | 0.12 |
| Early Starting–Pressure-Prompted | –1.62 | 3.04 | –1.79 | 3.06 | –1.41 | 2.99 | 5.51 | 0.02 |
| Scheduled–Spontaneous | –1.21 | 3.14 | –1.22 | 3.11 | –1.20 | 3.18 | 0.02 | 0.89 |
| Methodical–Emergent | –0.95 | 3.42 | –0.96 | 3.42 | –0.95 | 3.43 | 0.01 | 0.93 |

*Note:* Total $N$ exceeds the sum of men and women because thirteen people did not indicate their gender.
*Source:* National sample.

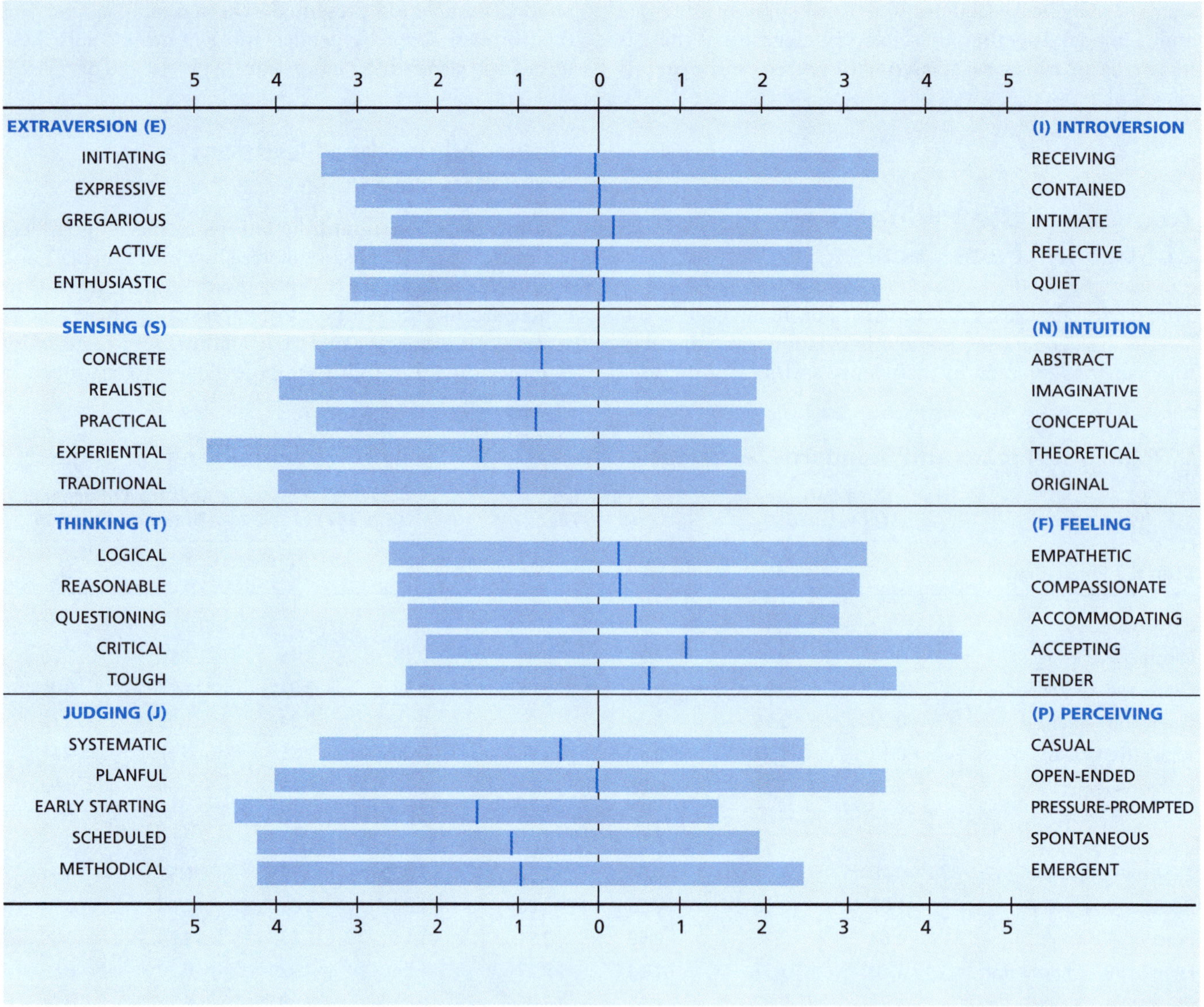


Figure 6.3 Means ± 1 Standard Deviation for the Step II™ Facet Scales

bold): **Early Starting**–Pressure-Prompted, **Experiential**–Theoretical, **Scheduled**–Spontaneous, Critical–**Accepting**, **Realistic**–Imaginative, and **Traditional**–Original. The fact that these means are toward the S, F, and J poles of their respective facet scales in the national sample is consistent with the distribution of overall Step I preferences toward these same poles in two earlier national samples (Myers et al., 1998; Hammer & Mitchell, 1996). There are more people with S, F, and J preferences in the population. The overall distribution on E–I is about equal, which is also reflected in the fact that the E–I facet scales centered around the midpoint.

## Frequency Distributions

As noted above, Step II facet scales were selected from items that functioned to clearly separate people who chose one pole of a scale from those who chose the opposite pole. The use of IRT for item selection and scoring affected the distribution of scores across the Step II facet scales. In the original Step II instrument, the frequency distributions for many scales were rectangular, normal, or saw-toothed. The latter distribution was caused mainly by the necessity of applying weights differentially to a small number of items in order to force all scales onto a common eleven-point metric.

The distributions of the revised Step II facet scales were examined using indexes of skewness and kurtosis. Skewness measures the extent to which a distribution is symmetrical. A normal distribution has a skewness of 0. A skewness index greater than 1 or less than –1 indicates a distribution of responses that is asymmetrical—that is, most of the scores are either very low or very high. Kurtosis measures the degree of peak of the distribution. In the kurtosis measure used for this analysis, a normal curve has a kurtosis of 0. Deviations from 0 represent either flatter or more peaked distributions. A kurtosis that approaches –1 indicates distributions that are flat in the middle and grouped at both ends (bipolar).

Table 6.2 contains the skewness and kurtosis statistics for the revised Step II facet scales. Most of the scales are clearly bipolar, as indicated by a kurtosis value approaching –1 and little or no skew. Only the Early Starting–Pressure-Prompted scale is significantly skewed. Most individuals score toward the Early Starting pole of this scale, which may be a function of the social desirability of Early Starting responses or perhaps of type development, meaning that people learn to begin projects early in order to survive or function well in organizations. In contrast, the Planful–Open-Ended scale is an example of a bipolar scale, with low skewness and high negative kurtosis. The distributions of the Early Starting–Pressure-Prompted and the Planful–Open-Ended scales are shown for visual comparison in figure 6.4.

**Table 6.2 Distribution Shape Statistics**

| Step II™ Facet Scale | Skewness | Kurtosis |
|---|---|---|
| *E–I Facet Scales* | | |
| Initiating–Receiving | 0.387 | –1.189 |
| Expressive–Contained | 0.108 | –1.078 |
| Gregarious–Intimate | 0.019 | –1.060 |
| Active–Reflective | 0.358 | –0.549 |
| Enthusiastic–Quiet | 0.321 | –0.968 |
| *S–N Facet Scales* | | |
| Concrete–Abstract | 0.035 | –0.988 |
| Realistic–Imaginative | 0.157 | –1.118 |
| Practical–Conceptual | 0.033 | –1.041 |
| Experiential–Theoretical | 0.347 | –1.244 |
| Traditional–Original | 0.311 | –0.945 |
| *T–F Facet Scales* | | |
| Logical–Empathetic | 0.178 | –1.120 |
| Reasonable–Compassionate | 0.106 | –0.968 |
| Questioning–Accommodating | 0.071 | –0.643 |
| Critical–Accepting | –0.435 | –0.665 |
| Tough–Tender | –0.278 | –0.927 |
| *J–P Facet Scales* | | |
| Systematic–Casual | 0.240 | –0.828 |
| Planful–Open-Ended | 0.133 | –1.409 |
| Early Starting–Pressure-Prompted | 1.099 | 0.089 |
| Scheduled–Spontaneous | 0.498 | –0.703 |
| Methodical–Emergent | 0.767 | –0.779 |

*Source:* National sample.

## Gender Differences

The means and standard deviations are shown separately for men and women in the national sample in table 6.1. The last two columns of this table also show the *F* test for the difference between the means for men and women and the significance of this test. The means are displayed as a visual representation in figure 6.5.

A number of meaningful differences were observed. Within the E–I facet block, the mean scores for women are in the direction of Initiating, Expressive, and Enthusiastic, while the mean scores for men are toward the opposite poles of these scales. Within the S–N block, men and women both have mean scores toward the Concrete and Practical poles, although the women do not score as far toward the ends of the scale in each case. Men and women also exhibit means toward the Traditional pole, with the women scoring significantly more toward Traditional than the men. Within the T–F block, mean scores for women are toward Empathetic, Compassionate, Accepting, and Tender, while men's average scores are toward the opposite poles of these scales. Both men's and women's scores are toward Accommodating, although women's are significantly more so, and within the J–P block, both men and women score toward the Systematic pole, but women significantly less so than men. Men and women both score toward Early Starting, although women show a more pronounced preference.

## Age Differences

Means on the Step II facet scales for eight age groupings are shown in table 6.3. The last two columns of the table show the *F* statistic and its significance for each scale. Although there are some interesting anomalies, the general trend on scales showing a significant difference across groups is that older age groups score more toward Quiet, Concrete, Realistic, Practical, Experiential, Traditional, Accommodating, Accepting, Systematic, Early Starting, and Scheduled.

# Correlational Data for Step II™ Facet Scales

To further aid in understanding the revised Step II facet scales, a number of analyses were performed, which involved correlating the Step II scales with one another and with the Step I (Form M) preference scales.

## Scale Intercorrelations

Correlations among the Step II facet scales are shown in table 6.4. Facet scales within each dichotomy consistently correlate higher (usually substantially higher) with the other scales of the same dichotomy than they do with scales

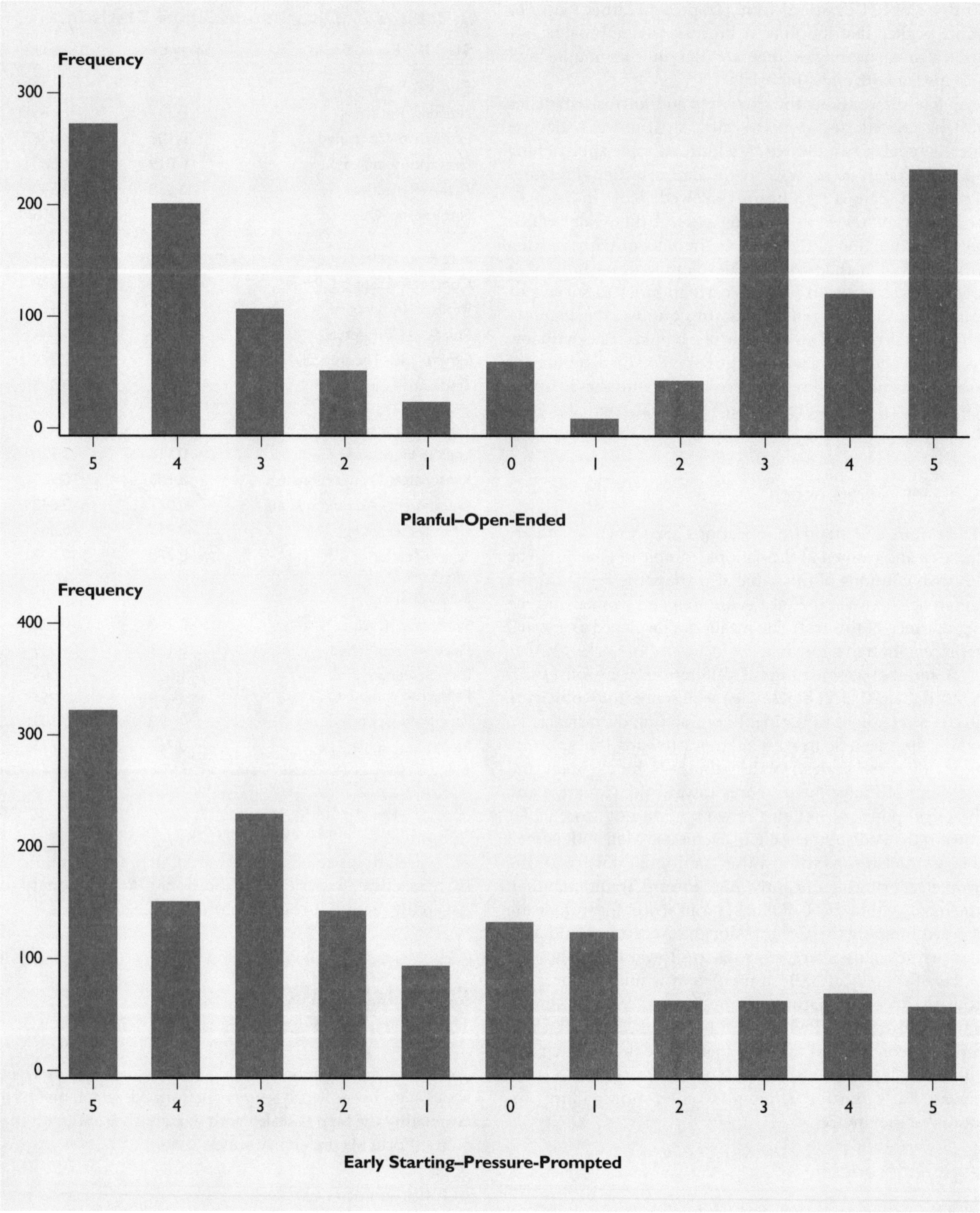


Figure 6.4 Distribution of Two Facet Scales

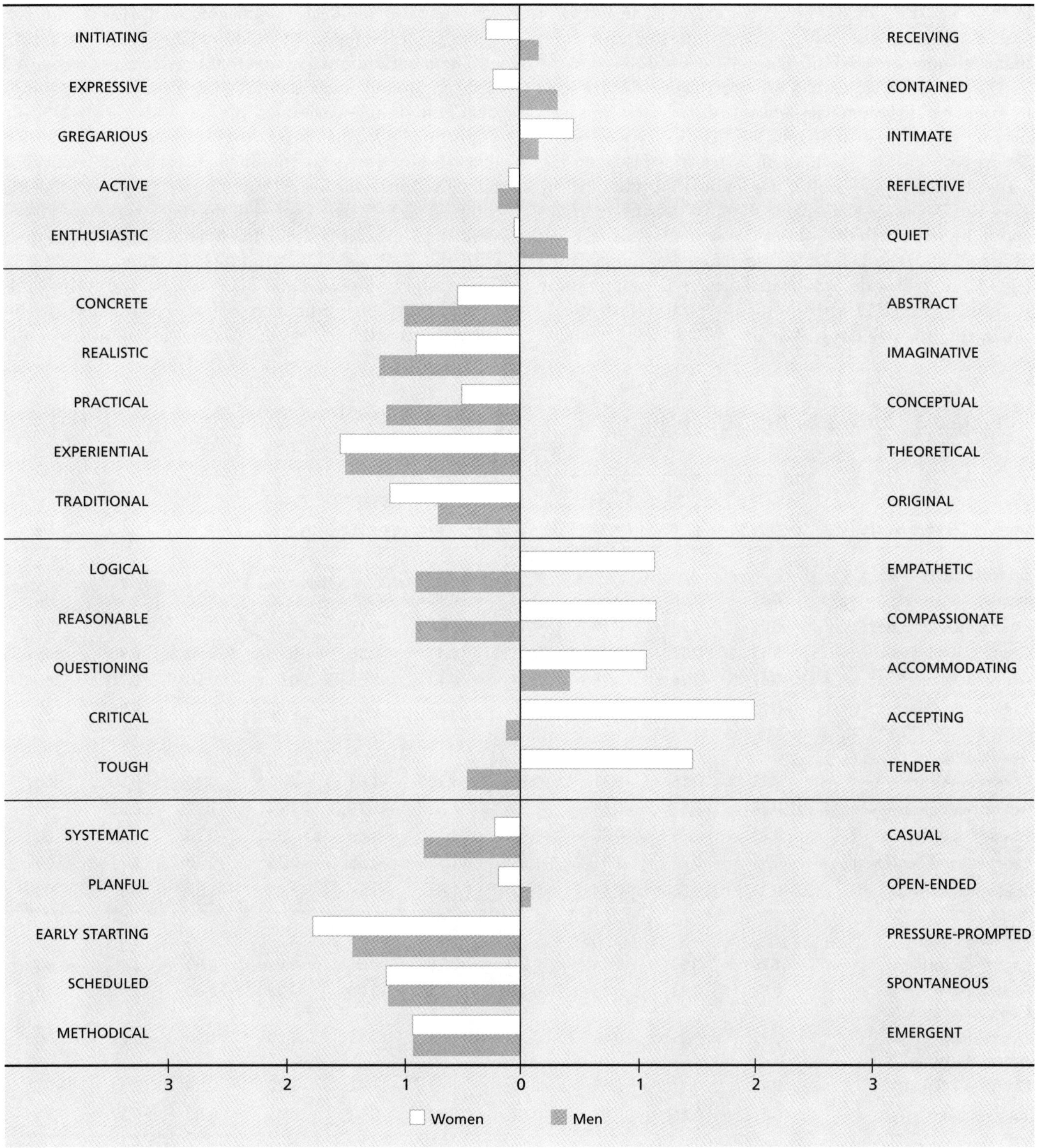


Figure 6.5 Mean Scores of Women and Men in the National Sample

in the other three dichotomies. For example, an E–I facet scale correlates higher with the other four E–I facet scales than with any of the S–N, T–F, or J–P facet scales.

There are a few facet scales whose correlations with a scale from another dichotomy are similar to their correlations with their *lowest* within-dichotomy scales. The T–F scale Tough–Tender correlates at .32 with both Systematic–Casual on the J–P scale and the T–F scale Questioning–Accommodating. Also, the T–F scale Reasonable–Compassionate correlates about the same with the J–P scale Systematic–Casual (.29) as it does with the T–F scale Questioning–Accommodating (.31). The J–P scale Systematic–Casual correlates only slightly higher (.35) with another J–P scale, Methodical–Emergent, than it does with the S–N scales Concrete–Abstract (.30) and Realistic–Imaginative (.31) and the T–F scales Logical–Empathetic (.33) and Tough–Tender (.32).

There are only two scales that correlate higher with a scale in another dichotomy. The T–F scale Questioning–Accommodating correlates higher with the S–N scale Traditional–Original (–.33) than it does with any of the other T–F scales. A questioning approach to differences of opinion seems to be related to finding original ways of doing things. The T–F scale Logical–Empathetic correlates higher with the J–P scale Systematic–Casual (.33) than it does with the T–F scale Questioning–Accommodating (.27). The reason is not clear, and the two scales are entirely different in content. Furthermore, validity coefficients based on correlations with the *Adjective Check List* and the *California*

**Table 6.3 Means by Age Group**

| | Age Group | | | | | | | | | |
|---|---|---|---|---|---|---|---|---|---|---|
| **Step II™ Facet Scale** | 18–24 (N = 76 ) | 25–34 (N = 202) | 35–44 (N = 291) | 45–54 (N = 280) | 55–64 (N = 194) | 65–74 (N = 208) | 75–84 (N = 83) | 85–93 (N = 10) | *F* | *Sig.* |
| *E–I Facet Scales* | | | | | | | | | | |
| Initiating–Receiving | –0.05 | 0.08 | 0.20 | –0.44 | –0.12 | –0.09 | 0.00 | –0.70 | 0.97 | .46 |
| Expressive–Contained | 0.01 | –0.24 | 0.10 | 0.04 | –0.06 | –0.19 | 0.87 | 0.30 | 1.40 | .19 |
| Gregarious–Intimate | 0.45 | 0.53 | 0.33 | 0.24 | 0.44 | –0.08 | –0.14 | 0.40 | 0.98 | .45 |
| Active–Reflective | –0.61 | –0.26 | –0.25 | –0.24 | 0.12 | 0.05 | –0.01 | –0.50 | 0.71 | .68 |
| Enthusiastic–Quiet | –0.70 | –0.51 | –0.24 | 0.15 | 0.73 | 0.67 | 0.88 | 0.50 | 4.26 | .00 |
| *S–N Facet Scales* | | | | | | | | | | |
| Concrete–Abstract | 0.28 | –0.15 | –0.31 | –0.70 | –1.20 | –1.62 | –2.11 | –0.20 | 8.50 | .00 |
| Realistic–Imaginative | 0.26 | –0.37 | –0.64 | –1.03 | –1.53 | –1.79 | –2.64 | –1.30 | 8.93 | .00 |
| Practical–Conceptual | 0.12 | –0.38 | –0.50 | –0.94 | –1.15 | –1.45 | –1.58 | –0.20 | 4.56 | .00 |
| Experiential–Theoretical | –0.43 | –0.97 | –1.41 | –1.53 | –1.95 | –2.35 | –2.55 | –0.70 | 4.71 | .00 |
| Traditional–Original | –0.33 | –0.66 | –0.54 | –0.69 | –1.63 | –1.98 | –2.08 | –1.80 | 8.34 | .00 |
| *T–F Facet Scales* | | | | | | | | | | |
| Logical–Empathetic | 1.28 | 0.63 | 0.14 | 0.21 | 0.28 | 0.01 | –0.01 | –0.80 | 1.96 | .05 |
| Reasonable–Compassionate | 0.88 | 0.43 | 0.48 | 0.21 | 0.02 | –0.04 | 0.28 | 0.00 | 1.42 | .18 |
| Questioning–Accommodating | 0.39 | 0.35 | 0.46 | 0.70 | 1.22 | 1.45 | 1.39 | 1.80 | 3.62 | .00 |
| Critical–Accepting | 0.42 | 0.72 | 0.98 | 1.10 | 1.41 | 1.42 | 1.20 | 0.50 | 2.14 | .03 |
| Tough–Tender | 0.51 | 0.56 | 0.54 | 0.64 | 0.72 | 0.53 | 0.65 | 1.80 | 0.37 | .94 |
| *J–P Facet Scales* | | | | | | | | | | |
| Systematic–Casual | 0.59 | –0.01 | 0.06 | –0.48 | –0.97 | –1.21 | –1.95 | –1.30 | 7.65 | .00 |
| Planful–Open-Ended | 0.70 | –0.42 | 0.02 | 0.14 | –0.02 | –0.59 | –0.75 | –0.80 | 1.46 | .17 |
| Early Starting–Pressure-Prompted | –0.54 | –1.02 | –1.20 | –1.55 | –2.19 | –2.17 | –2.78 | –3.20 | 6.89 | .00 |
| Scheduled–Spontaneous | –0.09 | –1.09 | –0.94 | –1.46 | –1.36 | –1.51 | –1.49 | –2.40 | 2.32 | .02 |
| Methodical–Emergent | –0.28 | –0.67 | –0.93 | –1.17 | –1.03 | –1.05 | –1.01 | –1.40 | 0.81 | .60 |

*Source:* National sample.

## Table 6.4 Correlations of Step II™ Facet Scales with One Another

| Step II™ Facet Scale | Step II™ Facet Scale | | | | | | | | | | | | | | | | | | | |
|---|---|---|---|---|---|---|---|---|---|---|---|---|---|---|---|---|---|---|---|---|
| | 1 | 2 | 3 | 4 | 5 | 6 | 7 | 8 | 9 | 10 | 11 | 12 | 13 | 14 | 15 | 16 | 17 | 18 | 19 | 20 |
| 1 Initiating–Receiving | 1.000 | | | | | | | | | | | | | | | | | | | |
| 2 Expressive–Contained | .636 | 1.000 | | | | | | | | | | | | | | | | | | |
| 3 Gregarious–Intimate | .549 | .491 | 1.000 | | | | | | | | | | | | | | | | | |
| 4 Active–Reflective | .649 | .555 | .545 | 1.000 | | | | | | | | | | | | | | | | |
| 5 Enthusiastic–Quiet | .583 | .614 | .524 | .594 | 1.000 | | | | | | | | | | | | | | | |
| 6 Concrete–Abstract | –.112 | –.146 | .009 | –.035 | –.165 | 1.000 | | | | | | | | | | | | | | |
| 7 Realistic–Imaginative | –.054 | –.144 | .018 | –.038 | –.227 | .680 | 1.000 | | | | | | | | | | | | | |
| 8 Practical–Conceptual | –.063 | –.111 | .049 | .038 | –.132 | .647 | .644 | 1.000 | | | | | | | | | | | | |
| 9 Experiential–Theoretical | –.119 | –.132 | –.020 | –.060 | –.175 | .703 | .614 | .572 | 1.000 | | | | | | | | | | | |
| 10 Traditional–Original | –.109 | –.097 | .012 | –.054 | –.204 | .625 | .604 | .580 | .594 | 1.000 | | | | | | | | | | |
| 11 Logical–Empathetic | –.061 | –.194 | –.010 | –.124 | –.122 | .128 | .121 | .025 | –.043 | –.101 | 1.000 | | | | | | | | | |
| 12 Reasonable–Compassionate | –.046 | –.178 | –.023 | –.083 | –.069 | .114 | .081 | .018 | –.052 | –.135 | .757 | 1.000 | | | | | | | | |
| 13 Questioning–Accommodating | .056 | –.010 | –.125 | –.002 | .082 | –.217 | –.147 | –.143 | –.239 | –.329 | .265 | .307 | 1.000 | | | | | | | |
| 14 Critical–Accepting | –.126 | –.169 | –.151 | –.056 | –.105 | .145 | .178 | .164 | .067 | –.033 | .462 | .501 | .246 | 1.000 | | | | | | |
| 15 Tough–Tender | –.010 | –.165 | –.062 | –.095 | –.044 | .176 | .178 | .107 | .037 | –.060 | .686 | .747 | .318 | .550 | 1.000 | | | | | |
| 16 Systematic–Casual | –.045 | –.063 | –.064 | –.217 | –.195 | .303 | .312 | .154 | .185 | .248 | .331 | .290 | –.022 | .064 | .324 | 1.000 | | | | |
| 17 Planful–Open-Ended | .107 | .188 | .102 | .041 | .046 | .093 | .086 | .016 | .076 | .179 | –.008 | –.040 | –.107 | –.036 | –.025 | .502 | 1.000 | | | |
| 18 Early Starting–Pressure-Prompted | .019 | .066 | –.022 | –.033 | –.096 | .219 | .214 | .105 | .183 | .235 | –.039 | –.097 | –.157 | –.096 | .050 | .385 | .415 | 1.000 | | |
| 19 Scheduled–Spontaneous | .092 | .123 | .065 | .010 | –.041 | .149 | .207 | .078 | .137 | .305 | .019 | –.062 | –.142 | –.049 | –.004 | .532 | .707 | .449 | 1.000 | |
| 20 Methodical–Emergent | .036 | –.005 | –.030 | –.019 | .017 | .021 | .038 | –.028 | .014 | .028 | .080 | .024 | .009 | –.096 | .043 | .353 | .468 | .346 | .425 | 1.000 |

*Source:* National sample.

*Psychological Inventory* scales suggest that there is little similarity between these two scales. Correlations among S–N and J–P facet scales reflect a similar correlation in the overall S–N and J–P dichotomies, as described in the *MBTI® Manual* (Myers et al., 1998)—in other words, the S poles of the S–N facet scales are correlated to some extent with the J poles of the J–P facet scales.

## Correlations of Step II™ Facet Scales with Step I™ Scales

Correlations between Step II facet scales and the continuous scores (theta) of Form M of the MBTI personality inventory are shown in table 6.5. The E–I facet scales correlate at .69–.88 with the E–I continuous scores of Form M; the S–N facet scales at .76–.87 with the S–N continuous scores; the T–F facet scales at .29–.90 with the T–F continuous scores; and the J–P facet scales at .51–.86 with the J–P continuous scores. The scale that shows the lowest correlation with its associated Form M continuous score is T–F Questioning–Accommodating at .29. This scale is also lowest on internal consistency and test-retest reliabilities.

In addition, the table shows correlations of Step II facet scales with Form M continuous scores associated with their own dichotomies, such as E–I scales with E–I continuous scores, that are substantially larger than correlations of Step II facet scales with continuous scores of the three other dichotomies. The magnitude of the difference between these correlations is compelling evidence for the theoretical hierarchical structure of the Step II facet scales in relation to the Step I scales.

Step II facet scales that correlate at less than .70 with their corresponding continuous scores remind us that the four dichotomies of the MBTI instrument are multifaceted constructs. While all the facets of a bipolar dichotomy are related to a core concept, they are not synonymous with it. Yet the scales are also sufficiently different from one another to emerge upon statistical analysis as separate facets.

With the exception of five scales, the correlation of revised Step II facet scales with Form M continuous scores within each dichotomy exceeds the correlation of the original Step II facet scales with Form G continuous scores within the same dichotomy, in many cases by a substantial amount. For instance, many increases are in the .12–.20 range, with a maximum increase of .25. For the five scales that show the opposite pattern, the average decrease is .05.

**Table 6.5 Correlations of Step II™ Facet Scales with MBTI® Form M Preference Scales**

| | Form M Preference Scale | | | |
|---|---|---|---|---|
| **Step II™ Facet Scale** | E–I | S–N | T–F | J–P |
| *E–I Facet Scales* | | | | |
| Initiating–Receiving | **.876** | –.114 | –.075 | .047 |
| Expressive–Contained | **.811** | –.158 | –.203 | .105 |
| Gregarious–Intimate | **.686** | –.004 | –.034 | .011 |
| Active–Reflective | **.761** | –.063 | –.114 | –.045 |
| Enthusiastic–Quiet | **.774** | –.234 | –.120 | –.063 |
| *S–N Facet Scales* | | | | |
| Concrete–Abstract | –.139 | **.872** | .176 | .194 |
| Realistic–Imaginative | –.132 | **.846** | .174 | .198 |
| Practical–Conceptual | –.098 | **.761** | .086 | .079 |
| Experiential–Theoretical | –.147 | **.841** | .021 | .133 |
| Traditional–Original | –.147 | **.759** | –.060 | .263 |
| *T–F Facet Scales* | | | | |
| Logical–Empathetic | –.128 | .050 | **.893** | .100 |
| Reasonable–Compassionate | –.107 | .017 | **.898** | .045 |
| Questioning–Accommodating | .020 | –.247 | **.292** | –.094 |
| Critical–Accepting | –.175 | .119 | **.552** | –.004 |
| Tough–Tender | –.090 | .124 | **.858** | .072 |
| *J–P Facet Scales* | | | | |
| Systematic–Casual | –.150 | .302 | .364 | **.715** |
| Planful–Open-Ended | .120 | .123 | –.018 | **.863** |
| Early Starting–Pressure-Prompted | –.044 | .257 | –.075 | **.507** |
| Scheduled–Spontaneous | .039 | .209 | .026 | **.856** |
| Methodical–Emergent | –.002 | .013 | .054 | **.598** |

*Note:* Correlations based on balanced type samples, $N = 450$; bold indicates correlations of Step I preference scales with the facet scales in that block.
*Source:* National sample.

## Apparent Inconsistencies Between Step I™ and Step II™ Results

The correlations presented above and in table 6.5 show that any given preference scale and the facet scales within that preference block are not synonymous. Thus, it is possible to observe apparent inconsistencies between Step I and Step II results. For the purposes of this discussion, an inconsistent result occurs when a person scores toward one pole on a preference scale and also scores toward the opposite pole on the *majority* of the facet scales within that preference block. Thus, in the original version of the Step II instrument, for example, a person could indicate an overall preference for Thinking on the Step I results (as measured by Form G items and weights) and yet have three, four, or, in very rare cases, even five facet scales point toward the Feeling poles on the T–F facet scales. The frequency of such inconsistencies ranged from 6% for the S–N block up to 10.9% on the T–F block. Results like this were possible because the items used for Step II facet scales did not overlap completely with the items used to score Form G Step I preference scales. Furthermore, even when the same items were used on both a preference scale and a facet scale in that block, their weights were different.

Inconsistencies of this kind are still possible with the revised Step II instrument. However, their occurrence has been reduced by 25%–65%. Results for the revised Step II tool are shown in table 6.6. The total occurrence of inconsistencies for revised Step II facet scales ranges from 4.2% on the S–N scales to 7% on the T–F scales. In other words, it is an in-frequent occurrence. No one in the national sample had all five Step II facet scales opposite his or her Form M preferences.

Such discrepancies are caused by variations in the items that make up the two sets of scales (the Step I and Step II tools) and by the different weights used to score them. Table 6.7 shows the item overlap between the two sets of scales. Clearly, the T–F preference block is the one in which the highest frequency of discrepancies occurs, primarily because of the absence of Form M items on the Questioning–Accommodating scale and the presence of only one Form M item on the Critical–Accepting scale. Furthermore, the two Form M items that are not scored on any facet scale are both T–F items. When Form M was created, an effort was made to include at least one item from each of the original Step II facet scales on the appropriate preference scale. At that time, it was possible to include only one item from the Questioning–Accommodating scale on the T–F preference scale. When revising the Step II instrument, however, the makeup of the Questioning–Accommodating scale was changed slightly in order to improve the scale's meaning and reliability. In doing so, the slight item overlap with the T–F scale from Form M was lost.

**Table 6.6 Apparent Inconsistencies Between Revised Step II™ Facet Scales and Step I™ Preferences**

| Dichotomy | Number of Step II™ Facet Scales Opposite the Step I™ Preference | | |
|---|---|---|---|
| | Three | Four | Five |
| E–I | 4.7% | 0.8% | 0.0% |
| S–N | 3.8% | 0.4% | 0.0% |
| T–F | 6.2% | 0.8% | 0.0% |
| J–P | 5.9% | 0.7% | 0.0% |

*Note:* A scale was considered to be toward the pole opposite the overall preference if the score on that scale was greater than 0 in the opposite direction.

*Source:* National sample.

**Table 6.7 Overlap Between Ste Scale Items and Form**

| Step II™ Facet Scale | Total Number of Items on Facet Scale | Form M Items on Facet Scale |
|---|---|---|
| *E–I Facet Scales* | | |
| Initiating–Receiving | 8 | 6 |
| Expressive–Contained | 8 | 5 |
| Gregarious–Intimate | 6 | 4 |
| Active–Reflective | 6 | 2 |
| Enthusiastic–Quiet | 7 | 4 |
| *S–N Facet Scales* | | |
| Concrete–Abstract | 9 | 7 |
| Realistic–Imaginative | 7 | 6 |
| Practical–Conceptual | 6 | 3 |
| Experiential–Theoretical | 6 | 6 |
| Traditional–Original | 9 | 4 |
| *T–F Facet Scales* | | |
| Logical–Empathetic | 8 | 7 |
| Reasonable–Compassionate | 9 | 8 |
| Questioning–Accommodating | 5 | 0 |
| Critical–Accepting | 6 | 1 |
| Tough–Tender | 9 | 6 |
| *J–P Facet Scales* | | |
| Systematic–Casual | 7 | 6 |
| Planful–Open-Ended | 6 | 6 |
| Early Starting–Pressure-Prompted | 6 | 1 |
| Scheduled–Spontaneous | 9 | 5 |
| Methodical–Emergent | 5 | 4 |
| T–F items not on any facet scale | 2 | 2 |
| **Total** | **144** | **93** |

*Source:* National sample.

In addition to the lack of item overlap between Step I and Step II scales, different weights are used to score those items. Even if an item occurs on both a preference scale and a facet scale within that block, it will have a different weight depending on which scale is being scored.

Both sets of scales use IRT as a scoring method. To assign a weight to an item, however, IRT must work from a criterion or keyed direction. There are different criteria for the whole (the overall preference) and for the part (a facet). An item may be weighted more heavily when it is used to determine a facet than when it determines an overall preference, or vice versa. In other words, the item provides different amounts of information depending on its purpose. Some facet scales, such as Questioning–Accommodating and Early Starting–Pressure-Prompted, tap preferences for very specific behaviors. Items that are most useful in determining a preference for that specific behavior may not provide as much information when scored for a general preference.

Although the above discussion explains, from a psychometric perspective, why the majority of facet scales in a given preference block can point toward the pole opposite the one indicated by the overall preference scale, it does not explain the meaning of these results for the individual. Meaning can only come from interactive interpretation. Thus, the use of the qualifier *apparent* in the heading for this section. Apparently inconsistent results may have profound meaning for the individual and offer great insight into particular areas of confusion. This possibility and others are discussed in chapter 5 along with case examples. A case example is also found in chapter 9.

## Comparison of Original and Revised Scales

It is vital that users accustomed to interpreting the original Step II instrument understand the relationship between the original and revised scales. Interpretations and explanations may have to be adjusted when working with some of these scales. As an aid to understanding, correlations of the original and revised Step II facet scales are shown in table 6.8. Counselors should take note of the scales that have somewhat lower correlations with the original scales and then review the scale descriptions in chapter 3 before discussing them with clients. Researchers who are making or testing hypotheses relating these scales to other variables should attend to the lower correlations, review the scale descriptions, and adjust their predictions if appropriate. The coefficients show there is a high degree of overlap between the original and revised scales. Although the correlations are in the medium or high range, the scales that changed the most upon revision were Scheduled–Spontaneous, Critical–Accepting, Gregarious–Intimate, and Experiential–Theoretical.

Another relevant comparison between the original and revised scales requires examination of which of the sixteen types have the highest mean scores on each facet scale of the original and the revised Step II tool. This comparison is shown in table 6.9. The numbers in parentheses in the "Original" column indicate the rank of that type with the revised scales. For example, using the original

**Table 6.8 Correlation Between Original and Revised Scales**

| Step II™ Facet Scale | *r* |
|---|---|
| *E–I Facet Scales* | |
| Initiating–Receiving | .89 |
| Expressive–Contained | .93 |
| Gregarious–Intimate | .68 |
| Active–Reflective | .76 |
| Enthusiastic–Quiet | .90 |
| *S–N Facet Scales* | |
| Concrete–Abstract | .84 |
| Realistic–Imaginative | .93 |
| Practical–Conceptual | .77 |
| Experiential–Theoretical | .70 |
| Traditional–Original | .87 |
| *T–F Facet Scales* | |
| Logical–Empathetic | .95 |
| Reasonable–Compassionate | .81 |
| Questioning–Accommodating | .81 |
| Critical–Accepting | .67 |
| Tough–Tender | .79 |
| *J–P Facet Scales* | |
| Systematic–Casual | .91 |
| Planful–Open-Ended | .90 |
| Early Starting–Pressure-Prompted | .95 |
| Scheduled–Spontaneous | .57 |
| Methodical–Emergent | .79 |

*Source:* National sample.

scales, ENFPs were ranked second below ENTJs on Initiating. However, with the new scales, they are ranked third (3) behind ENTJs and ENFJs. These rankings are provided because they show that for most cases in which the top two types are not identical across the original and revised scales, the type that is first or second with the original scales is often ranked third or fourth with the new scales.

This similarity in ranking suggests that, with a few exceptions, the relationship between the facet scales and the sixteen types inherent in the original version of the Step II instrument has not been altered much. For thirteen of the poles for which a different type is ranked first or second on the revised Step II tool, a dominant type with one auxiliary function has been replaced by the same dominant type with the opposite auxiliary function. The greatest change for any of the facets is found in Practical–Conceptual. An examination of the items on the original and revised scales suggests that the meaning of the scale

**Table 6.9 Two Types with the Most Extreme Facet Scale Scores for the Original and the Revised Step II™ Instrument**

| E–I Facet Scale Poles | Original | Revised | T–F Facet Scale Poles | Original | Revised |
|---|---|---|---|---|---|
| Initiating | ENTJ<br>ENFP (3) | ENTJ<br>ENFJ | Logical | INTJ<br>ISTJ (5) | INTJ<br>ENTP |
| Receiving | ISTP<br>ISFJ | ISTP<br>ISFJ | Empathetic | ENFP (3)<br>INFP | ENFJ<br>INFP |
| Expressive | ENFJ<br>ENFP | ENFJ<br>ENFP | Reasonable | INTP (6)<br>INTJ (5) | ENTP<br>ENTJ |
| Contained | ISTP (6)<br>ISTJ (3) | INTP<br>INTJ | Compassionate | ENFP (5)<br>INFP (8) | ENFJ<br>ISFP |
| Gregarious | ESTJ<br>ESTP | ESTJ<br>ESTP | Questioning | ENTJ (3)<br>ENTP | INTP<br>ENTP |
| Intimate | INFJ (7)<br>INFP (3) | INTP<br>INTJ | Accommodating | ISFJ<br>ISFP (3) | ESFJ<br>ISFJ |
| Active | ESFP (5)<br>ESFJ (3) | ESTP<br>ENFP | Critical | ISTP (3)<br>ISTJ | ESTP<br>ISTJ |
| Reflective | INTJ<br>INTP | INTJ<br>INTP | Accepting | ENFJ<br>ENFP | ENFJ<br>ENFP |
| Enthusiastic | ENTP (4)<br>ENFP | ENFP<br>ENFJ | Tough | ISTJ<br>INTJ | INTJ<br>ISTJ |
| Quiet | ISFJ (4)<br>ISTJ | ISTJ<br>INTJ | Tender | ESFJ (7)<br>INFP | ENFJ<br>INFP |

| S–N Facet Scale Poles | Original | Revised | J–P Facet Scale Poles | Original | Revised |
|---|---|---|---|---|---|
| Concrete | ISTJ<br>ESTJ | ISTJ<br>ESTJ | Systematic | ISTJ<br>ESTJ (3) | INTJ<br>ISTJ |
| Abstract | INFP (3)<br>ENFP | ENFP<br>ENTP | Casual | ENFP<br>INFP | ENFP<br>INFP |
| Realistic | ISTJ<br>ISFJ (4) | ISTJ<br>ESTJ | Planful | ESTJ (5)<br>ESFJ (3) | ENTJ<br>INFJ |
| Imaginative | INFP (3)<br>ENFP | ENFP<br>ENTP | Open-Ended | ISTP (6)<br>INTP | INTP<br>INFP |
| Practical | ESFP (8)<br>ESTP (3) | ISTJ<br>ESTJ | Early Starting | ISFJ (3)<br>ESFJ | ESFJ<br>ESTJ |
| Conceptual | INFP (8)<br>INTJ (4) | ENTJ<br>ENTP | Pressure-Prompted | ENTP<br>ENFP (3) | INTP<br>ENTP |
| Experiential | ISFJ (3)<br>ESFP (6) | ISTJ<br>ESTJ | Scheduled | ISTJ<br>ISFJ (6) | ISTJ<br>ESTJ |
| Theoretical | INTJ (4)<br>INTP (6) | ENTJ<br>ENTP | Spontaneous | ENTP<br>INTP | INTP<br>ENTP |
| Traditional | ISFJ<br>ESFJ | ISFJ<br>ESFJ | Methodical | ENTJ<br>INFJ (4) | ENTJ<br>INTJ |
| Original | ENTP<br>ENFP (3) | ENTP<br>INTP | Emergent | ESTP<br>ISTP (6) | INTP<br>ESTP |

*Source:* National sample.

has been broadened a bit so that Practical (formerly Pragmatic) now includes an interest in making things, and Conceptual (formerly Inferential) now includes creating and innovating.

## Conclusion

The new Step II instrument meets all the goals established for the revision. The new scales are similar enough to the original scales to enable an easy transition for users. At the same time, the revised Step II tool contains the following structural and psychometric improvements:

- It uses the same twenty facet scales in the same order as the original form.
- It retains, with a few variations, the meaning of the scales as described in Mitchell et al. (1997).
- It is composed of 144 items, an increase of only 13 over the original.
- It uses the same scoring methods for the Step I dichotomies (i.e., it is based on the items and scoring found on Form M).
- It is consistent with type theory in that the distributions of the twenty facet scales are typically bipolar.
- It uses the same item selection and scoring methods (item response theory) for the scales as were used in the Step I assessment.
- It bases item selection and scoring decisions on a sample balanced for type that was randomly drawn from a national random sample.
- It evidences greatly improved scale reliabilities (see chapter 7).
- It includes new validity data (see chapter 8).

# Reliability 7

CHAPTER OVERVIEW



The reliability of a scale is an estimate of how consistently its component set of items yields the same results across the set of items or over time. The terms *reliability* and *consistency* are synonymous. When items are designed to measure some human aspect, we cannot assume they will yield consistent responses from everyone. For example, an item may be worded in so confusing or vague a manner that it elicits a different response from the same person under different circumstances, depending on mood, time of day, physical environment, or preceding activities. All these factors, and others that are not relevant to what the item is attempting to measure, can be considered noise and contribute to the unreliability of the scale.

## Two Kinds of Reliability

There are two kinds of reliability to consider in measuring a construct:

- How consistently does the set of items measure the construct?
- How consistent are the responses to the items over time?

## Internal Consistency Reliability

The first kind of reliability, appropriately called *internal consistency reliability,* is concerned with how consistently people respond to a set of items that purportedly measure the same construct. Words often have slightly different meanings for different people, particularly if those people are different types. We cannot be sure, therefore, that two questions, both designed to measure the same construct, will be answered in the same way even by the same person, given factors such as testing conditions or mood that can affect a response.

The strategy applied in constructing a scale, therefore, is to use more than one item to tap the construct. Each item may attempt to approach the construct from a slightly different angle. The richer and more complex the construct, the more varied the items must be. And the more items there are, the better chance there is to achieve consistency in responses because there will be less chance that one "different" response will point the results in another direction. If consistency is the goal, all the items should attempt to measure the same underlying construct and therefore elicit the same response. In terms of the *Myers-Briggs Type Indicator* (MBTI) personality inventory, all the items of a scale with high internal consistency would address some aspect of a person's preference for, say, Extraversion or Introversion.

## Test-Retest Reliability

A second kind of reliability concerns the consistency of responses over time. This is also referred to as *stability,* or *test-retest reliability*. The question here is, If the items are administered to the same person at two different times, will the person receive the same results both times? Because we believe that type is fairly constant and preferences are not unduly influenced by day-to-day events, we would expect a person's preferences to remain fairly stable over periods of a few weeks or months. Therefore, the interval between administrations of the instrument is an important factor to consider when evaluating test-retest reliabilities. If the interval is too short, respondents' memories of the items and their previous answers may influence their subsequent responses, artificially inflating the correlations between the two administrations. On the other hand, if the retest interval is too long, and if the qualities being measured are prone to vary over time, then real changes in the measured quality may be confused with estimates of an instrument's reliability. Many personality researchers believe that personality is fairly stable in adulthood, particularly from the mid-twenties on.

## Measurement of the Two Kinds of Reliability

Both kinds of reliability can be estimated in a given group by using correlations. For internal consistency reliability, the response to each item is correlated with the response to every other item on the scale. A high correlation coefficient indicates that people in the group tend to answer each item in the same way. For test-retest reliability, scores from two different administrations are correlated. A high test-retest coefficient indicates that the group's answers are consistent over that time period. In addition to using correlations, the test-retest results of a type instrument can also be subjected to categorical analysis by examining the percentage of people scoring in the same categories over time.

# Internal Consistency of Step II™ Facet Scales

The internal consistency of the revised Step II facet scales was estimated in three samples using coefficient alpha (an average of all item-to-item correlations): the national sample and two samples that participated in the test-retest study discussed in the next section, a sample of adults[1] and a sample of college students.[2] The adult sample consisted of 137 members of a Methodist church congregation. The mean age was 46.1 years with a range of 18–76; three people in the sample were 65 years of age or older. The sample was predominantly Caucasian and consisted of 40% men and 60% women. The college sample comprised 162 students enrolled in undergraduate psychology courses. The mean age was 19.6 years; 40% were men and 60% women. The distribution of ethnic identity in the sample was Caucasian, 86%; African American, 4.3%; Asian/Pacific Islander, 4.3%; and Latino, 1.9%. Each student who participated in the study was awarded one extra credit point for the course.

The alpha reliability coefficients of the Step II continuous scores are shown in table 7.1. The alphas range from .52 for the Practical–Conceptual scale in the student sample to .87 for the Initiating–Receiving scale in the adult sample. The median alphas in the three samples are .77 in both the national sample and the adult sample and .75 in the college sample. These reliabilities demonstrate a significant improvement over the reliabilities of the original Step II facet scales, which ranged from .36 to .75, with a median of .58. As expected, on the basis of the theory and reliabilities of Form M preference scales, reliabilities of the Step II facet scales among college students are lower than those of the adults. Younger people have had neither the time nor life experience necessary to form stable preferences on all facets.

In summary, the internal consistency reliabilities of the revised Step II facet scales are quite good, especially given the number of items on the scales, and are a considerable improvement over those of the original scales.

**Table 7.1 Internal Consistency Reliability of Step II™ Facet Scales**

| Step II™ Facet Scale | No. of Items | National Sample (*N* = 1,378) | Adults (*N* = 137) | College Students (*N* = 162) |
|---|---|---|---|---|
| *E–I Facet Scales* | | | | |
| Initiating–Receiving | 8 | .85 | .87 | .83 |
| Expressive–Contained | 8 | .79 | .81 | .80 |
| Gregarious–Intimate | 6 | .60 | .65 | .63 |
| Active–Reflective | 6 | .59 | .71 | .65 |
| Enthusiastic–Quiet | 7 | .72 | .77 | .75 |
| *S–N Facet Scales* | | | | |
| Concrete–Abstract | 9 | .81 | .77 | .76 |
| Realistic–Imaginative | 7 | .79 | .77 | .77 |
| Practical–Conceptual | 6 | .67 | .62 | .52 |
| Experiential–Theoretical | 6 | .83 | .79 | .74 |
| Traditional–Original | 9 | .76 | .79 | .66 |
| *T–F Facet Scales* | | | | |
| Logical–Empathetic | 8 | .80 | .83 | .77 |
| Reasonable–Compassionate | 9 | .77 | .77 | .73 |
| Questioning–Accommodating | 5 | .57 | .54 | .53 |
| Critical–Accepting | 6 | .60 | .59 | .59 |
| Tough–Tender | 9 | .81 | .76 | .77 |
| *J–P Facet Scales* | | | | |
| Systematic–Casual | 7 | .74 | .81 | .74 |
| Planful–Open-Ended | 6 | .82 | .79 | .80 |
| Early Starting–Pressure-Prompted | 6 | .70 | .77 | .75 |
| Scheduled–Spontaneous | 9 | .82 | .86 | .83 |
| Methodical–Emergent | 5 | .71 | .66 | .71 |
| **Median** | | **.77** | **.77** | **.75** |

*Source:* Adult data were collected by Cook Research, Edina, Minnesota; college data were collected by Lisa Larson, Ph.D.

## Test-Retest Reliability of Step II™ Continuous Scores

The adults and college students in the samples described above completed Form Q twice, with an interval of 30 days between administrations. Results from these two samples will provide an estimate of the stability of the Step II facet scales in both a developing and a more mature sample. It is expected, for the reasons stated above regarding the internal consistency reliability analysis, that the stability of the scores in the college student sample will be lower than those in the adult sample.

Table 7.2 shows the test-retest coefficients for the Step II continuous scores from these two samples. The stability coefficients for the adult sample range from .56 for Questioning–Accommodating to .90 for Initiating–Receiving. The stability of the Step II facet scales in the college student sample ranges from .55 for Methodical–Emergent to .78 for Initiating–Receiving. The median coefficients are .77 for the adults and .65 for the college students.

In both samples, the E–I scales show the greatest stability over the 30-day interval, with mean coefficients of .83 and .71 in the adult and college samples, respectively. The scales with the lowest stability for the adult sample are the T–F scales ($M = .68$), due primarily to the low coefficient for Questioning–Accommodating. Without this scale, the mean 30-day test-retest reliability of the T–F scales is .72. The scales with the lowest stability for the college students are the J–P scales ($M = .59$).

**Table 7.2 Test-Retest Reliability of Step II™ Continuous Scores in Two Samples**

| Step II™ Facet Scale | Adults 30 Days (*N* = 137) | College Students 30 Days (*N* = 162) |
|---|---|---|
| *E–I Facet Scales* | | |
| Initiating–Receiving | .90 | .78 |
| Expressive–Contained | .83 | .68 |
| Gregarious–Intimate | .74 | .69 |
| Active–Reflective | .86 | .71 |
| Enthusiastic–Quiet | .80 | .70 |
| *S–N Facet Scales* | | |
| Concrete–Abstract | .75 | .74 |
| Realistic–Imaginative | .78 | .73 |
| Practical–Conceptual | .69 | .56 |
| Experiential–Theoretical | .74 | .66 |
| Traditional–Original | .74 | .59 |
| *T–F Facet Scales* | | |
| Logical–Empathetic | .79 | .77 |
| Reasonable–Compassionate | .74 | .71 |
| Questioning–Accommodating | .56 | .56 |
| Critical–Accepting | .64 | .62 |
| Tough–Tender | .69 | .64 |
| *J–P Facet Scales* | | |
| Systematic–Casual | .78 | .61 |
| Planful–Open-Ended | .83 | .60 |
| Early Starting–Pressure-Prompted | .80 | .61 |
| Scheduled–Spontaneous | .83 | .60 |
| Methodical–Emergent | .69 | .55 |
| **Median** | **.77** | **.65** |

*Source:* Adult data were collected by Cook Research, Edina, Minnesota; college data were collected by Lisa Larson, Ph.D.

The only previous study of the stability of Step II continuous scales was conducted by D. A. Johnson, who retested 74 adults who had participated in career development workshops (Johnson, 1992a). He used Form J of the MBTI instrument, which is scored using the *Type Differentiation Indicator* (TDI; Saunders, 1987) and includes the twenty Step II facet scales. The interval between administrations was 30 months. The test-retest coefficients ranged from .36 for Tough–Tender to .78 for Early Starting–Pressure-Prompted. It is interesting to note that the three scales with the lowest stability over time were from the Thinking–Feeling block. Perhaps this reflects the fact that people in career development workshops are calling on the judging function to make decisions about the future. The median test-retest correlation across the twenty scales was .66. Considering the time interval, the stability of the scales appears quite good. Although caution is advised in using these results to estimate the long-term test-retest reliability of the revised Step II facet scales (due to the differences between the scales used by Johnson and the present ones), it is hypothesized that given the higher internal consistency, the more precise scoring, and the longer scales, the test-retest reliability of the revised scales over a similar period should be comparable to or even higher than that reported by Johnson.

## Test-Retest Reliability of Step II™ Interpretive Categories

Although the test-retest coefficients of Step II continuous scores are of interest, the primary unit of interpretation for Step II facet scales is categories (see chapter 5). The most important piece of information for understanding an individual's result on a given scale is whether he or she scored toward one of the facet poles or in the midzone. It follows, therefore, that test-retest statistics designed to estimate the likelihood that a person will remain in the same category are important.

As discussed in chapter 5, there are three interpretive categories for each facet scale:

- Scores of 2 through 5 toward the left pole of the scale
- Midzone, which consists of scores of 1 or 0
- Scores of 2 through 5 toward the right pole of the facet scale

Thus, three events are of interest in determining the stability of the Step II facet scales: whether the person's score remains in the same category (left pole, right pole, or midzone) upon retest; whether the person's score moves from one of the poles toward the midzone or from the midzone toward one of the poles; or whether the person's score crosses from one pole to the opposite pole. Obviously, if the scales are to have adequate stability for interpretive purposes, the frequency of the first event (remaining in the same category) should be high and the frequency of the third event (crossing over from one pole to its opposite) should be low. The frequency of movement into or out of the midzone should fall between these two.

Table 7.3 shows the frequency of these three events in the adult sample over the 30-day interval. Those whose scores stayed in the same category upon retest display frequencies that range from 84% for Planful–Open-Ended to 57% for Questioning–Accommodating. The scale on which movement was greatest from one pole to the other was Methodical–Emergent, although only 9% of the sample crossed poles on this scale. Overall, the order of frequencies of the three possible events is as expected. The median of those remaining in the same category upon retest is 73.2%, those moving

**Table 7.3 Categorical Test-Retest Frequencies for the Adult Sample**

| | Adults | | | College Students | | |
|---|---|---|---|---|---|---|
| **Step II™ Facet Scale** | % Remaining in Same Category | % Moving to/from Midzone | % Moving to Opposite Pole | % Remaining in Same Category | % Moving to/from Midzone | % Moving to Opposite Pole |
| *E–I Facet Scales* | | | | | | |
| Initiating–Receiving | 82 | 17 | 1 | 72 | 23 | 5 |
| Expressive–Contained | 76 | 22 | 2 | 65 | 28 | 6 |
| Gregarious–Intimate | 66 | 31 | 3 | 67 | 29 | 4 |
| Active–Reflective | 79 | 17 | 4 | 70 | 26 | 4 |
| Enthusiastic–Quiet | 71 | 25 | 4 | 72 | 21 | 6 |
| *S–N Facet Scales* | | | | | | |
| Concrete–Abstract | 76 | 21 | 3 | 68 | 29 | 3 |
| Realistic–Imaginative | 71 | 26 | 3 | 69 | 27 | 4 |
| Practical–Conceptual | 66 | 30 | 4 | 64 | 31 | 6 |
| Experiential–Theoretical | 79 | 16 | 5 | 67 | 28 | 4 |
| Traditional–Original | 66 | 26 | 7 | 62 | 31 | 7 |
| *T–F Facet Scales* | | | | | | |
| Logical–Empathetic | 76 | 21 | 4 | 72 | 25 | 3 |
| Reasonable–Compassionate | 63 | 35 | 2 | 64 | 35 | 1 |
| Questioning–Accommodating | 57 | 38 | 6 | 50 | 38 | 11 |
| Critical–Accepting | 72 | 23 | 5 | 60 | 31 | 9 |
| Tough–Tender | 70 | 28 | 2 | 62 | 34 | 4 |
| *J–P Facet Scales* | | | | | | |
| Systematic–Casual | 74 | 24 | 2 | 60 | 36 | 4 |
| Planful–Open-Ended | 84 | 9 | 7 | 70 | 13 | 16 |
| Early Starting–Pressure-Prompted | 75 | 23 | 2 | 65 | 25 | 11 |
| Scheduled–Spontaneous | 74 | 24 | 1 | 59 | 34 | 7 |
| Methodical–Emergent | 68 | 23 | 9 | 59 | 27 | 14 |
| **Median** | **73.2** | **23.2** | **3.3** | **65.1** | **28.6** | **5.3** |

*Source:* Adult data were collected by Cook Research, Edina, Minnesota; college data were collected by Lisa Larson, Ph.D.

to or from the midzone represent 23.2%, and those moving from one pole to its opposite make up 3.3%.

Test-retest frequencies for the college student categories are also shown in table 7.3. The frequencies of those staying in the same category range from 72% for Initiating–Receiving, Enthusiastic–Quiet, and Logical–Empathetic to 50% for Questioning–Accommodating. The two scales showing the greatest degree of movement from one pole to the other were from the J–P dichotomy: Planful–Open-Ended (16%) and Methodical–Emergent (14%). It is interesting to note that Planful–Open-Ended is also one of the scales with the highest percentage of students who stayed in the same category. Thus, for this scale, not many students changed categories, but when they did, they tended to move to the other pole rather than to or from the midzone. The results for both these J–P scales can perhaps be interpreted as attempts by college students to determine how much order and structure they want or need. These two scales represent specific behaviors in the J–P domain for which many college students may not yet have determined a preference, perhaps because, until their college years, their environments did not require them to adopt the behaviors associated with the J poles of these facets.

On a similar theme, it is interesting to note that, among the ten scales with the lowest relative stability in the college sample, four are T–F scales and four are J–P scales. These are the two preference domains in which one would expect to find less stability in younger samples—the T–F domain because the mature judgment that flows from a clear preference is still being formed, and the J–P domain because the newly independent status of college students requires them to learn new judging behaviors while at the same time offering expanded opportunities for a spontaneous lifestyle.

Ordering of the possible events was the same for college students and adults, with many more students staying in the same category than moving from one pole to the other. The median frequency of college students who remained in the same category is 65.1%, those who moved to or from the midzone make up 28.6%, and those moving from one pole to its opposite on a given scale compose the remaining 5.3%. While the stability of the scales is quite high over this time period for college students, the frequencies are, as expected, lower than those of the adults.

## Interpretation of Reliability Estimates

When interpreting the conventional estimates of reliability discussed above, it is important to bear in mind that these are group-level statistics. The formulas used to compute the correlation coefficients in each case require the group mean and standard deviation. For this reason, it is somewhat of a misnomer to designate the "reliability" of an instrument or scale as if the estimate were some internal property of the instrument itself. Instead, users should ask about the reliability of the scales when used with a particular population.

When this question is asked, it becomes clear that the characteristics of the population or particular group of interest are crucial in understanding the results of a reliability analysis. The reliability of a scale or instrument can only be as good as the consistency or stability of the quality being measured. The characteristics of the population essentially determine a limit for reliability. For some populations, it is even possible that the reliability of a certain variable might be too high! Unexpectedly high reliabilities from some samples suggest that the scale consists of many items with slight variations in wording. While such a scale may be useful in some contexts, its validity is also limited to the narrow construct. For example, if extraversion were narrowly defined as simply frequency of socializing, it might be possible to devise a test with ten very similar items that ask about this narrow set of behaviors. While this scale might have high reliability, its validity would be limited to this one aspect of extraversion.

The same logic can be applied to test-retest estimates. For some scales—for example, those specifically designed to measure change—or with some groups that are thought to experience change on a particular characteristic over time (such as college students on rebelliousness), high reliabilities might indicate a problem for the scale. Users of the MBTI Step II instrument should therefore evaluate the reliabilities reported in this chapter and those reported later in the literature relative to the group or groups that take the instrument. This sensitivity of test-retest to the sample was observed with the college students discussed above, when the Step II facet scales with the least stability were those in the T–F and J–P dichotomies, as had been expected.

Another factor to consider when interpreting reliability estimates is that, with all other things being equal, longer scales (meaning those with more items) will generally have higher reliabilities than shorter scales. Fortunately, it is possible to determine the effect of scale length by applying the Spearman-Brown prophecy formula.

If we assume that each of the MBTI Step I preference scales has an internal consistency reliability of .90 (a slightly conservative assumption; see Myers et al., 1998) and a length of 23 items (the average length of the four Step I scales), then the Spearman-Brown formula predicts the reliability of a scale composed of 7 items (the average length of the revised Step II facet scales) will be .73. The average reliability of the Step II facet scales is .74, which indicates that, given their length (approximately one-third that of the overall preference scales), the Step II facet scales are comparably consistent. Also, although some single Step II facet scales may be below the predicted .73 value, these scales occur in facet blocks containing other facet scales that are above the predicted value. It would be more problematic for interpretation if the few scales with relatively lower reliabilities all occurred in the same facet block.

Finally, it is important to put reliability in context. Reliability is just one criterion in determining the usefulness of a scale. It is possible to develop a scale by using internal consistency reliability as the sole criterion for selecting items and for evaluating the overall quality of the scale. Long scales with very slight changes of wording across items are likely to yield high internal consistency coefficients. So while it is possible to build redundancy, and thus consistency, into a scale, it may not prove useful to practitioners or their clients. Applying a variety of criteria, such as those discussed in the validity chapter (chapter 8) and the construction chapter (chapter 6) of this manual, is likely to yield a scale that is richer and more meaningful.

## The Polarity Index

Using group-level statistics to estimate reliability provides no information about an individual client. The statistics apply only to the mythical average or typical client from a particular group of participants. In individual counseling, however, it is important to know whether the scores on the respondent's profile are consistent. Because we often want to help the client interpret a Step II profile based on one administration, we need ways of determining consistency on an individual level.

For example, it would be helpful to know whether a respondent expressed a clear preference on each of the facet scales. If the individual's answers to the items on a given scale are consistent with one another, then the resulting score should indicate a clear preference toward one or the other of the facet poles. The score would therefore fall close to the 5 on either side. If the client's answers to the items on a facet scale instead favor one pole about half the time and the opposite pole the other half, then the score will show this lack of a clear preference by being close to the 0 point. Overall, then, we can tell something about the clarity of preferences on facet scales by looking at the scoring profile and noting whether a person's scores are mostly close to the 0 point on the scales or instead are distributed near the poles (toward 5). Many scores near the 0 point and few near the poles implies less clarity on the facet scales. Many scores near the poles and few scores near the 0 point implies greater clarity. But such eyeball assessments may themselves be inconsistent.

Saunders (1989) developed the polarity index to make the assessment of individual consistency more rigorous. The polarity index is designed to describe how consistently a person has scored toward the poles of the facet scales for the profile as a whole. By providing information about an individual profile, the polarity index gives us data that traditional reliability statistics are unable to supply: the consistency of one person's responses on a single administration of the Step II assessment.

## Computing the Polarity Index

The polarity index is computed with the following formula:

$$\text{Polarity} = 20 \times \sqrt{(\Sigma x_i^2) \div 20}$$

where $x_i$ is the score on the facet scale. To compute the polarity index, first square the score on each facet scale and then sum these across all the scales. Divide this sum by 20 (the number of scales) and take the square root of the resulting quotient. Once you have the square root, multiply it by 20 to get the polarity index. Multiplying by 20 simply gives the polarity index a range of 0–100, which makes it easier to interpret.

## Meaning of the Polarity Index

If, for whatever reason, a person has responded inconsistently to the entire set of items, the facet scale scores will cluster around the 0 point on each scale. On the other hand, someone who has responded very consistently will have scale scores clustered at the poles. Someone whose scores are 0 on all the Step II facet scales will have a polarity index of 0, while another whose scores are *all* at the poles will have an index of 100. An index of 100 is obtained when a person's scale scores are all 5 in one direction, all 5 in the other direction, or a mixture of 5s in either direction, with no score falling in between these extremes.

It is important to note this last point. Despite the fact that the polarity index is summed over all the scales, it does not measure the consistency with which a person's scale scores are all at the *same* pole within each separate MBTI dichotomy. For example, a person may possibly have a score of 5 on each of the S–N facet scales, but at opposite poles on succeeding scales—a 5 toward Concrete, Imaginative, Practical, Theoretical, and Traditional and a similar pattern of 5 on all facet scales within the other three dichotomies. This person would then have a polarity index of 100, because all the responses to the items *on each scale* were at the poles. However, within each overall dichotomy, the scale scores would obviously be switching back and forth from one preference pole to the other. Thus, the polarity index does not tell us anything about such alternations between poles within the four Step I dichotomies. Alternations of this nature would instead be identified by out-of-preference scores, which are described in chapter 5.

## The Polarity Index and the National Sample

Table 7.4 displays information about the polarity index for each type in the national sample. The mean polarity index in the national sample was 64.16 (*SD* = 9.85), which indicates that 95% of people have polarity indexes between 44 and 84. The mean polarity index by type ranged from 59.03 for ISFPs to 68.38 for ISTJs. It is interesting to note that with just a few exceptions, those with a preference for Judging have a higher polarity index (*M* = 66.10) than those with a preference for Perceiving (*M* = 61.95). The exceptions are the dominant extraverted Intuitive types (ENFP and ENTP), who tend to respond more consistently to the scales than do the other Perceiving types, and, at the other end, the INFJs, whose polarity index (*M* = 60.74) is about two-thirds of a standard deviation lower than that of other

**Table 7.4 Mean Polarity Index Ranked by Type**

| Form M Type | *N* | *M* | *SD* |
|---|---|---|---|
| ISTJ | 183 | 68.38 | 10.31 |
| ENTJ | 29 | 68.28 | 8.05 |
| ENFP | 105 | 67.33 | 9.71 |
| ESTJ | 97 | 67.14 | 9.26 |
| ENTP | 25 | 66.60 | 8.94 |
| ENFJ | 38 | 65.97 | 7.44 |
| INTJ | 19 | 65.37 | 8.14 |
| ESFJ | 143 | 65.30 | 8.33 |
| ISFJ | 191 | 64.70 | 9.59 |
| INFP | 88 | 63.66 | 9.54 |
| INTP | 43 | 62.09 | 11.91 |
| ESTP | 54 | 61.85 | 9.80 |
| INFJ | 34 | 60.74 | 9.78 |
| ISTP | 73 | 60.51 | 9.32 |
| ESFP | 108 | 59.25 | 8.08 |
| ISFP | 148 | 59.03 | 8.99 |
| **Total** | **1,378** | **64.16** | **9.85** |

*Source:* National sample.

Judging types. Random responding can produce polarities as high as 30.

The overall difference on the polarity index between men ($M$ = 64.40) and women ($M$ = 63.91) is negligible. However, among men there are significant differences between those who prefer Feeling ($M$ = 61.49) and those who prefer Thinking ($M$ = 65.78). The men who prefer Thinking, which may be considered a culturally sanctioned preference, are more likely to respond more consistently to the Step II facet scales.

The polarity index shows significant differences between whites ($M$ = 64.84) and blacks ($M$ = 57.60). There are two hypotheses regarding this difference: that being a minority group member in a dominant culture may result in less clarity about preferences on the behaviors and attitudes measured by Step II facet scales, or that members of minority groups are less consistent in *reporting* their preferences, perhaps out of caution about revealing those preferences to a dominant culture. These differences should not be overinterpreted, however, given the relatively small number of blacks in the national sample ($N$ = 67, or about 5% of the sample).

The polarity index varies by educational level, as shown in table 7.5 and illustrated graphically in figure 7.1. Consistency on the Step II facet scales is seen to increase with education. Perhaps education offers people more opportunities to learn about themselves and experience challenges and new environments that promote clarity of preference on the Step II facet scales.

The relationship of the polarity index to age is shown in table 7.6 and illustrated graphically in figure 7.2. The groups with the lowest mean polarity index are the two at the ends of the age distribution, in the 18–24 and 85–93 categories; these are also the groups with the smallest sample sizes. There is an interesting pattern observable in the graph. Type theory would predict the finding that the youngest age group will have a relatively lower polarity index, since preferences on constructs measured by at least some of the Step II facet scales are still being formed. There is a slight increase at the next age level, perhaps indicating that some preferences have crystallized, followed then by a slight decrease as people move into midlife. The mean polarity index thereafter remains steady across the decades up to the oldest group, where-

**Table 7.5 Mean Polarity Index by Educational Level**

| Education | *N* | *M* | *SD* |
|---|---|---|---|
| Less than high school graduate | 98 | 59.77 | 8.77 |
| High school graduate | 444 | 63.27 | 9.61 |
| Technical school/other | 33 | 62.03 | 9.16 |
| Some college | 344 | 63.91 | 9.97 |
| College graduate | 312 | 66.11 | 9.29 |
| Graduate school or more | 133 | 67.28 | 10.81 |

*Source:* National sample.

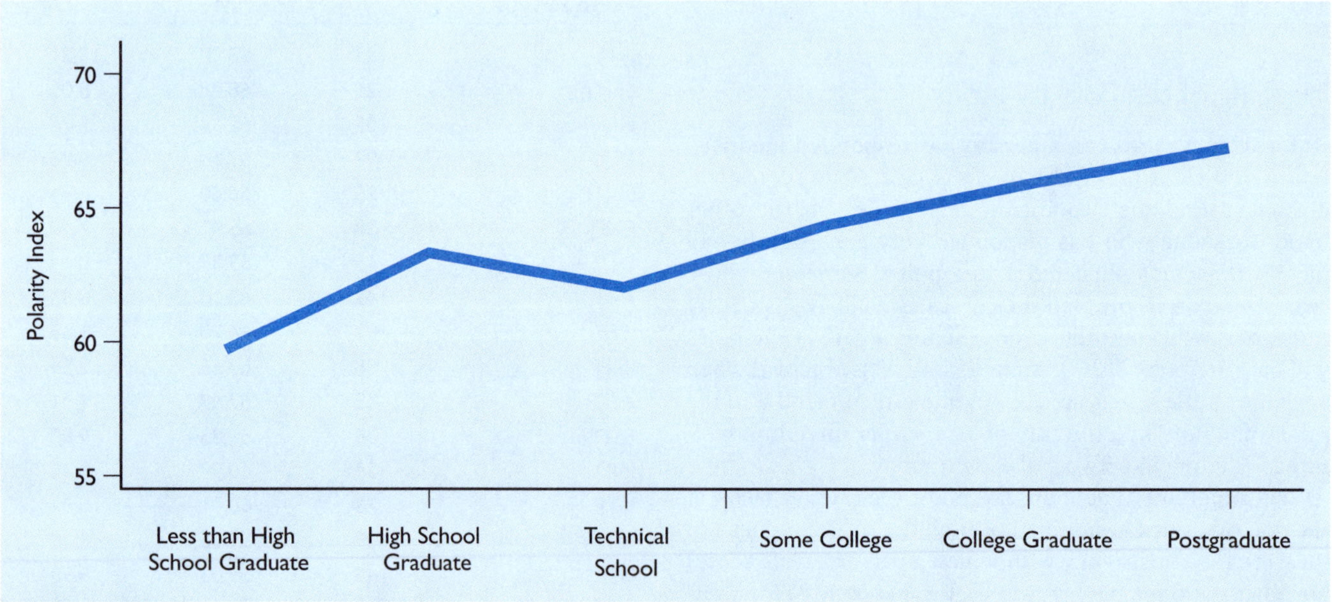


Figure 7.1 Mean Polarity Index by Educational Level

*Source:* National sample.

**Table 7.6 Means and Standard Deviations of Polarity Index by Age Group**

| Age Group | *N* | *M* | *SD* |
|---|---|---|---|
| 18–24 | 76 | 62.36 | 9.43 |
| 25–34 | 202 | 65.13 | 9.77 |
| 35–44 | 291 | 63.41 | 10.19 |
| 45–54 | 280 | 64.63 | 10.10 |
| 55–64 | 194 | 64.66 | 9.36 |
| 65–74 | 208 | 64.38 | 9.67 |
| 75–84 | 83 | 64.33 | 9.45 |
| 85–93 | 10 | 58.60 | 11.77 |
| **Total** | **1,344** | **64.22** | **9.85** |

*Source:* National sample.

upon it drops quite a bit. Is the lower polarity index in this oldest group due to transcending opposites, or is it another period of challenge, comparable to adolescence and midlife, during which reevaluation takes place? Much larger samples of older people will be needed to answer this question. It should also be noted that interpretation of this pattern relies on fairly small mean differences between age groups.

The polarity index was also examined using the Level (v.3) scale of the *California Psychological Inventory* (CPI) instrument (Gough & Bradley, 1996). The Level scale is designed to measure seven "levels of realization, or competence, or ego integration," with Level 7 representing self-reports of self-actualization. The mean polarity index by level is shown in table 7.7. There is an interesting drop in the polarity index in moving from CPI Level 1 to Level 2, and then another from Level 6 to Level 7. Overall, however, the polarity index is seen to increase somewhat with level of realization as measured by this CPI scale. People who feel higher levels of efficacy and realization tend to respond more consistently toward the poles of the Step II facet scales.

Considering the age, education, and level data together suggests that although there are some slight variations with age that are interpretable via type theory, the more noticeable changes occur when some additional factor is at work, such as, perhaps, acquiring additional education or experience that leads to greater self-realization. A discussion of how to interpret the polarity index with individual clients may be found in chapter 5.

## Conclusion

The reliability data presented in this chapter confirm that one of the goals of the Step II revision—increased reliability of the facet scales—has been realized. The median internal consistency reliability of the scales improved from .58 to .77 in adult samples. The internal consistency reliabilities of the scales in the college sample are also high but, as expected, lower than those of the adults. These coefficients are greater than or comparable to those of facet

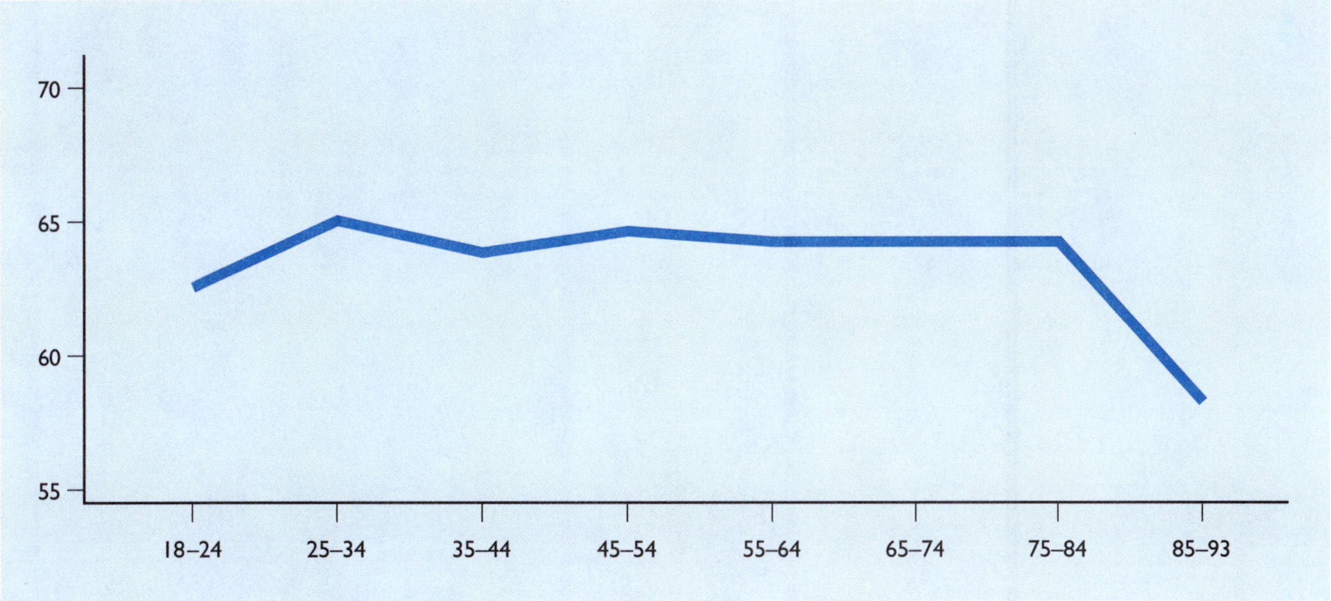


Figure 7.2 Mean Polarity Index by Age Group

Source: National sample.

**Table 7.7 Means and Standard Deviations of Polarity Index by CPI™ Level**

| Level | *N* | *M* | *SD* |
|---|---|---|---|
| 1 | 21 | 61.05 | 9.15 |
| 2 | 29 | 58.83 | 9.44 |
| 3 | 89 | 63.92 | 10.05 |
| 4 | 186 | 63.30 | 9.95 |
| 5 | 153 | 66.57 | 9.64 |
| 6 | 70 | 67.66 | 9.41 |
| 7 | 36 | 64.36 | 9.54 |

*Source:* National sample.

scales for other major personality instruments. The test-retest coefficients on the facet scale continuous scores are also respectable. Of special interest are the categorical test-retest results. The number of adults and college students who move from one pole to the opposite pole was only 3.3% and 5.3%, respectively, demonstrating the high stability of the category placements over this time interval. However, additional studies are needed over longer time periods.

The data on the polarity index shows differences by type, age, gender, educational level, and level of realization as measured by the CPI v.3 scale. These data suggest that clarity of preference across the facet scales, as measured by the polarity index, proceeds in a manner consistent with psychological type theory and that the index can serve as a useful summary of overall facet clarity.

# Validity 8

CHAPTER OVERVIEW



This chapter presents evidence regarding the validity of the Step II facet scales. The structural validity and the reliability of the scales have already been discussed in chapters 6 and 7, respectively. Here, a number of other approaches to validity will be presented, including confirmatory factor analysis of the final Step II items, examination of Step II facet scales in relation to demographic variables, correlation of Step II facet scales with the scales of other instruments, and use of the scales to explicitly test certain hypotheses derived from type theory.

This chapter includes validity studies employing both original and revised Step II facet scales. Given that the correlations between the original and revised scales ranged from .57 to .95, with a mean of .82, and that in most cases there is considerable item overlap, it is reasonable to assume validity results will generalize across versions. A number of the studies reported below used the *Myers-Briggs Type Indicator* (MBTI) Form J or Form K Expanded Analysis Report (EAR; Saunders, 1989). (Form J is used to score the *Type Differentiation Indicator* [TDI; Saunders, 1987].) Both the TDI and the EAR contain the same twenty scales and the same items for all scales. For reasons of simplicity and continuity, both are referred to here and elsewhere in this manual as the *original* Step II facet scales. Also, in the interests of more easily interpreting validity evidence, the new or revised names of the Step II facet scales have been used throughout the discussion, regardless of the version employed in the original study.

Because the Step II reports contain the individual's type (Step I results) and interpret the scales in relation to overall type, the validity of the Step I scales is also relevant for evaluating Step II results. However, since the *MBTI® Manual* (Myers et al., 1998) contains an extensive discussion of the reliability and validity of the four preference scales (E–I, S–N, T–F, and J–P), readers are referred to that publication.

## Confirmatory Factor Analysis

The intercorrelations among Step II facet scales and the correlations of Step II facet scales with Form M continuous scores (discussed in chapter 6) show strong evidence for the construct validity of the Step II facet scales. Of the 190 intercorrelations among the twenty scales, there were only two instances of a scale from one facet block correlating with a scale from another facet block at a level higher than its correlation with the others in its block, and only four scales correlated across facet blocks at magnitudes similar to correlations with scales within their own blocks. Furthermore, examination of the relationship between the Step II facet scales and the four Form M dichotomies confirmed that each of the Step II facet scales within a preference block correlated significantly higher with the Form M preference than with any of the other three preferences. These are impressive results, especially considering that some across-block correlations, both within scales and between scales and preferences, are to be expected. When people engage the world in any way, they must utilize all preferences and many facets of those preferences as well. Aspects of type that are exercised together will develop together. With repeated use, preferences and facets of preferences develop patterns of relationship that appear as correlations.

Nevertheless, rather than relying on visual examination of sets of correlations to determine structural validity, it is possible to be more precise in determining whether scales have been placed properly. A confirmatory factor analysis (CFA) was used to explicitly test the relationship of the twenty Step II facet scales to the four preference scales measured by Form M. The CFA was conducted via LISREL (Jöreskog & Sörbom, 1993), using unweighted least-squares estimates of thetas derived from item response theory (IRT) scoring of the twenty facet scales. The analysis tested the placement of five Step II facet scales within each preference block within the correct domain, confirming that they represented a facet of the specified MBTI dichotomy and not a facet of another dichotomy.

Originally, the chi-square statistic was used to indicate model fit. However, since chi-square is dependent on sample size, alternative indexes have been developed, and the trend is to report multiple fit indexes, as each reflects a different aspect of the fit. In 1989, D. Jöreskog and K. Sörbom developed the *Goodness of Fit Index* (GFI) and the *Adjusted GFI* (AGFI), which allows for degrees of freedom (cf. Tanaka & Huba, 1985). These indexes do not depend explicitly on sample size, and they measure the better fit of the model compared to no model at all. Both indexes are constructed to range between 0 and 1, with higher values indicating a better fit. The recommended cutoff value for the GFI is .90 and for the AGFI .80 (Anderson & Gerbing, 1984). The GFI for the twenty facet scales and the four preference scales is .94, with .92 for the AGFI.

Another index, the *Normed Fit Index* (NFI), was developed by Bentler and Bonett (1980) and Tucker and Lewis (1973) to provide information about the degree of fit of the model compared to a null model, that is, one in which all the correlations were 0. A value between .85 and .90 indicates a minimally acceptable model; between .90 and .95, acceptable; and above .95, good. The NFI for the facet scale model was .95. Finally, the Root Mean Square Error of Approximation was .08 for this model, indicating that model misspecification and measurement error were unlikely. (Additional details about the CFA will be forthcoming in a separate publication.)

These indexes demonstrate that the model provides an excellent fit with the data. This is not to say, however, that other models might not provide as good or even better a fit. Alternative models would have to be specified and explicitly tested against the current model.

## Correlations with Other Instruments

Correlating the scores of a new scale with those of other instruments is a common method of examining its validity. In addition to MBTI Form Q, half the national sample also completed the *California Psychological Inventory* (CPI) instrument (Gough & Bradley, 1996), and the other half were administered the *Adjective Check List* (ACL; Gough & Heilbrun, 1983). Correlations of the Step II scales with three other instruments—the *Fundamental Interpersonal Relations Orientation–Behavior* (FIRO-B) inventory, the *Eysenck Personality Questionnaire* (EPQ), and the *Rotter Locus of Control Scale*—are available in the literature.

There are a number of validity questions that apply to correlations of both the CPI and the ACL with the Step II facet scales.

- First, do the Step II facet scales within a facet block generally correlate (or not) with CPI and ACL scales in a manner predicted by theory?
- Next, do certain facet scales within a preference dichotomy correlate higher (or lower, depending on the scale) with a CPI or ACL scale than do other facet scales within that dichotomy? This question deals more narrowly with the individual facet scales.

- Finally, do certain facet scales within a preference dichotomy correlate in the *opposite* direction from the other facet scales within that preference dichotomy? What do these crossover patterns suggest about the validity of the facet scales?

## California Psychological Inventory™ Instrument

Correlations of the Step II scales with the CPI scales are shown in table 8.1. Since there are 640 correlations in this table, coefficients with $r \geq .20$, indicating the more important relationships, are in bold type. To better understand the relationships described below, the reader may refer to the brief definitions of CPI scales presented in table C.1, on page 181.

To answer the first question (that is, to examine the correlations between the two instrument at the level of overall patterns), the CPI scales are discussed by "sector" as defined by their location on the CPI profile.

**Interpersonal Scales** The first sector is made up of the seven CPI folk scales described as measures of poise, self-assurance, and interpersonal proclivities. These scales are Dominance, Capacity for Status, Sociability, Social Presence, Self-acceptance, Independence, and Empathy.

With the exception of three correlations for Gregarious–Intimate, which were close to but did not reach the .20 cutoff, all the Step II E–I and S–N facet scales are correlated with these CPI scales in the direction of the E and the N poles. There are also a number of correlations with the T–F Step II facet scales in the direction of the T poles, particularly for the CPI scales Independence and Dominance. For example, people with a high score on Independence, who are seen as self-sufficient, resourceful, and persistent, are also Logical, Reasonable, Questioning, and Tough.

**Normative Orientation and Values Scales** The next set of CPI scales, described as measures of normative orientation and values, are Responsibility, Socialization, Self-control, Good Impression, Communality, Well-being, and Tolerance.

There are fewer significant correlations here, compared to the first set of CPI scales. Responsibility and Tolerance are associated with Abstract, Conceptual, and Theoretical. The direction of the correlation with Responsibility may seem problematical, since the word as it is commonly understood has been described as a characteristic of SJ types in particular. However, while high scores on the CPI Responsibility scale are associated with self-discipline and reliability, they also describe actions undertaken in an "informed, enlightened way that permits departures from convention when appropriate" (Gough & Bradley, 1996, p. 103). Furthermore, high scores on Responsibility suggest "awareness of ongoing political and social phenomena" and valuing of "intellectual and cognitive matters" (p. 104). This expanded definition helps elucidate the relationship of Responsibility to the N pole of these S–N facet scales, while the more commonly understood meaning of the word, which is also an element in the definition, explains why Responsibility correlates toward the J poles of all the J–P facet scales (although no coefficients are above .20, probably due to the breadth of the Responsibility scale).

On the Good Impression scale, people who seek to create a favorable image and are viewed by others as somewhat formal and conventional are Traditional, Accepting, Systematic, Planful, and Scheduled. Those who score high on CPI Self-control score toward Quiet, Realistic, Traditional, Accommodating, Accepting, and Scheduled on Step II facet scales.

It is also worth noting those CPI scales that do not correlate with Step II facet scales. There are no high correlations with CPI Socialization, which describes people who are conscientious and easily accept and conform to normative rules, although Systematic and Scheduled come close to the cutoff. It seems that people at all poles of the Step II facet scales are equally socialized or not socialized. There are also no correlations (with one exception) of Communality or Well-being with Step II facet scales. Thus, a person's sense of belonging and satisfaction with his or her physical and mental health seem to be unrelated to the pole of any facet scale.

**Cognitive and Intellectual Functioning Scales** The next set of CPI scales is described as measures of cognitive and intellectual functioning. They include Achievement via Conformance, Achievement via Independence, and Intellectual Efficiency. The latter two scales, which respectively describe people who enjoy work settings that encourage freedom and individual initiative and who are insightful, correlate significantly with all the Step II S–N scales in the direction of the N pole.

**Role and Personal Style Scales** The next set of CPI scales are measures of role and personal style. They include Psychological-mindedness, Flexibility, and Femininity/Masculinity. Psychological-mindedness and Flexibility correlate significantly with all the Step II S–N scales in the direction of the N poles. In addition, Psychological-mindedness also correlates with Logical and Questioning, Flexibility correlates with all the J–P scales in the direction of the P pole, and Femininity/Masculinity—on which high scorers are described as sympathetic, sensitive, and warm—correlates with all the T–F facet scales in the direction of the F pole.

**Vector Scales** This set of CPI scales contains the structural or vector scales (v.1, v.2, and v.3). The v.1 scale is basically an Extraversion–Introversion scale, although it is not necessarily derived from Jungian definitions, and correlates with all the E–I, S–N, and T–F scales (with the exception of Logical–Empathetic) in the direction of the I, S, and F poles

**Table 8.1 Correlations of Step II™ Facet Scales with the Scales and Indexes of the *California Psychological Inventory*™ (CPI™) Instrument**

| | CPI™ Scale | | | | | | | | | | | | | |
|---|---|---|---|---|---|---|---|---|---|---|---|---|---|---|
| **Step II™ Facet Scale** | DO | CS | SY | SP | SA | IN | EM | RE | SO | SC | GI | CM | WB | TO |
| *E–I Facet Scales* | | | | | | | | | | | | | | |
| Initiating–Receiving | **–.51** | **–.51** | **–.67** | **–.47** | **–.56** | **–.45** | **–.44** | –.15 | –.10 | .03 | –.12 | –.06 | **–.22** | –.13 |
| Expressive–Contained | **–.37** | **–.39** | **–.54** | **–.37** | **–.40** | **–.33** | **–.34** | **–.21** | –.16 | .01 | –.10 | –.09 | –.16 | –.15 |
| Gregarious–Intimate | **–.25** | –.17 | **–.38** | **–.21** | **–.26** | –.19 | –.15 | –.08 | –.13 | .03 | –.08 | .09 | –.09 | –.05 |
| Active–Reflective | **–.37** | **–.27** | **–.54** | **–.42** | **–.45** | **–.28** | **–.25** | .02 | –.04 | **.21** | .08 | .05 | –.08 | .01 |
| Enthusiastic–Quiet | **–.42** | **–.38** | **–.54** | **–.51** | **–.49** | **–.31** | **–.39** | .05 | .06 | **.34** | .17 | –.02 | .01 | .02 |
| *S–N Facet Scales* | | | | | | | | | | | | | | |
| Concrete–Abstract | **.32** | **.42** | **.29** | **.35** | **.30** | **.33** | **.47** | **.21** | –.02 | –.15 | –.07 | .14 | .06 | **.21** |
| Realistic–Imaginative | **.28** | **.37** | **.22** | **.35** | **.29** | **.27** | **.44** | .11 | -.11 | **–.23** | –.18 | .13 | .02 | **.20** |
| Practical–Conceptual | **.26** | **.41** | **.22** | **.29** | **.29** | **.24** | **.40** | **.22** | –.01 | –.10 | –.07 | .18 | .10 | **.24** |
| Experiential–Theoretical | **.37** | **.45** | **.32** | **.36** | **.35** | **.36** | **.41** | **.21** | .00 | –.14 | –.05 | .10 | .10 | **.24** |
| Traditional–Original | **.36** | **.40** | **.26** | **.38** | **.35** | **.35** | **.41** | .05 | –.12 | **–.31** | **–.23** | .13 | .02 | .08 |
| *T–F Facet Scales* | | | | | | | | | | | | | | |
| Logical–Empathetic | –.19 | –.14 | –.04 | –.14 | –.12 | **–.24** | –.05 | –.01 | .02 | .11 | .07 | .00 | –.14 | –.03 |
| Reasonable–Compassionate | **–.24** | –.15 | –.08 | –.18 | –.19 | –.26 | –.04 | .08 | .08 | .19 | .16 | –.05 | –.09 | .10 |
| Questioning–Accommodating | **–.33** | **–.26** | **–.20** | **–.24** | **–.28** | **–.35** | **–.28** | –.01 | .11 | **.22** | .19 | .01 | .01 | .05 |
| Critical–Accepting | –.15 | –.02 | .05 | –.07 | –.05 | –.12 | .01 | .15 | .11 | **.24** | **.21** | .05 | .07 | **.22** |
| Tough–Tender | **–.24** | –.14 | –.08 | –.12 | –.18 | **–.25** | –.05 | .10 | .13 | .16 | .12 | .01 | –.02 | .14 |
| *J–P Facet Scales* | | | | | | | | | | | | | | |
| Systematic–Casual | .06 | .03 | .03 | .14 | .09 | .01 | .13 | –.13 | –.19 | –.19 | **–.26** | –.07 | –.14 | –.04 |
| Planful–Open-Ended | .00 | –.10 | –.13 | .03 | –.04 | .04 | .01 | –.14 | –.13 | –.14 | **–.22** | .00 | –.07 | –.08 |
| Early Starting–Pressure-Prompted | .15 | .12 | .10 | **.22** | .17 | .13 | .21 | –.04 | .00 | **–.20** | –.18 | –.06 | –.04 | –.02 |
| Scheduled–Spontaneous | .03 | –.05 | –.05 | .10 | .03 | .02 | –.01 | –.19 | –.18 | **–.23** | **–.28** | .03 | –.14 | –.13 |
| Methodical–Emergent | –.13 | –.10 | –.13 | –.01 | –.10 | –.04 | –.03 | –.16 | –.11 | –.13 | **–.20** | –.08 | –.09 | .01 |

*Note:* Bold indicates coefficients with $r \geq .20$. See table C.1, on page 181, meaning of CPI scales.
*Source:* National sample.

and with Early Starting. The v.2 scale is designed to assess a continuum that moves between a rule-questioning perspective at one pole and a rule-favoring perspective at the other. This scale correlates only with the Judging pole of the J–P scales (with the exception of Early Starting–Pressure-Prompted, on which it just misses the cutoff). The v.3 scale is a measure of self-realization. It correlates only with Abstract, Conceptual, and Theoretical.

**Special Scales** The CPI instrument also contains a number of special scales that were developed for research purposes but have not yet achieved the status of full scales. These include Managerial Potential, Work Orientation, Creative Temperament, Leadership, and Amicability.

Those high on Managerial Potential score toward Initiating and Expressive and toward the N pole on all the S–N Step II facet scales. Creative Temperament is associated with Initiating, Expressive, Enthusiastic, Questioning, and all the S–N and J–P Step II facet scales in the N and P directions. Those with high scores on Leadership score high on all the E–I and S–N Step II facet scales in the direction of E and N and also toward Methodical. Amicability is related to Traditional, Accommodating, Accepting, and Scheduled. This general pattern of correlations between CPI scales in one sector and Step II facet scales within facet blocks clearly demonstrates that the Step II facet scales are measuring their intended constructs.

**Differential Correlations Within Facet Blocks** The second question—whether certain facet scales within a preference dichotomy correlate higher (or lower, depending on the scale) with a CPI scale than do other facet scales within that dichotomy—involves correlations between CPI scales and individual facet scales that were higher or lower than the other facet scales within their blocks. Scales are not

**Table 8.1 Correlations of Step II™ Facet Scales with the Scales and Indexes of the *California Psychological Inventory*™ (CPI™) Instrument** *continued*

| | CPI™ Scale | | | | | | | | | | | | | | | |
|---|---|---|---|---|---|---|---|---|---|---|---|---|---|---|---|---|
| **Step II™ Facet Scale** | AC | AI | IE | PY | FX | FM | V1 | V2 | V3 | MP | WO | CT | LP | AMI | LEO | NAR |
| *E–I Facet Scales* | | | | | | | | | | | | | | | | |
| Initiating–Receiving | –.19 | **–.20** | **–.36** | **–.20** | –.09 | .08 | **.36** | –.14 | –.13 | **–.32** | **–.21** | **–.27** | **–.52** | –.09 | **–.30** | –.10 |
| Expressive–Contained | –.19 | –.18 | **–.26** | –.15 | –.10 | –.01 | **.31** | –.18 | –.14 | **–.27** | **–.22** | **–.21** | **–.38** | –.14 | **–.31** | –.05 |
| Gregarious–Intimate | –.10 | .04 | –.08 | –.04 | –.01 | .07 | **.22** | –.10 | –.04 | –.15 | –.08 | –.08 | **–.24** | –.11 | –.18 | –.03 |
| Active–Reflective | .00 | .00 | –.12 | –.05 | –.07 | .13 | **.40** | –.05 | .00 | –.15 | –.01 | –.17 | **–.30** | –.02 | **–.23** | **–.28** |
| Enthusiastic–Quiet | .01 | –.12 | –.19 | –.06 | –.20 | .08 | **.51** | .05 | .02 | –.11 | .02 | **–.32** | **–.29** | .13 | –.13 | **–.32** |
| *S–N Facet Scales* | | | | | | | | | | | | | | | | |
| Concrete–Abstract | .09 | **.48** | **.35** | **.37** | **.42** | .01 | **–.31** | –.10 | **.25** | **.25** | .08 | **.50** | **.28** | –.07 | .01 | .16 |
| Realistic–Imaginative | –.01 | **.39** | **.33** | **.28** | **.36** | .03 | **–.34** | –.17 | .17 | **.22** | .04 | **.51** | **.21** | –.11 | –.04 | .19 |
| Practical–Conceptual | .12 | **.48** | **.35** | **.36** | **.32** | .15 | **–.23** | –.03 | **.23** | **.28** | .13 | **.43** | **.26** | –.05 | –.05 | .08 |
| Experiential–Theoretical | .14 | **.50** | **.38** | **.37** | **.39** | –.07 | **–.31** | –.04 | **.24** | **.32** | .11 | **.52** | **.35** | –.04 | .01 | .12 |
| Traditional–Original | –.05 | **.36** | **.31** | **.34** | **.35** | –.13 | **–.41** | –.16 | .13 | .18 | –.02 | **.48** | **.26** | **–.22** | –.06 | **.34** |
| *T–F Facet Scales* | | | | | | | | | | | | | | | | |
| Logical–Empathetic | –.05 | –.12 | –.15 | **–.21** | .03 | **.38** | .16 | –.02 | –.07 | –.16 | –.08 | –.13 | –.15 | .06 | .08 | –.17 |
| Reasonable–Compassionate | .01 | –.05 | –.15 | –.19 | .14 | **.43** | .21 | –.02 | .04 | –.12 | –.01 | –.07 | –.16 | .15 | .01 | **–.29** |
| Questioning–Accommodating | .04 | **–.20** | **–.26** | **–.22** | –.15 | **.25** | **.32** | .07 | –.01 | –.13 | .05 | **–.26** | –.19 | **.23** | –.02 | **–.33** |
| Critical–Accepting | .08 | .10 | .00 | –.01 | .14 | **.38** | **.23** | .03 | .15 | .06 | .12 | .01 | .00 | **.24** | .05 | **–.37** |
| Tough–Tender | .01 | .03 | –.12 | –.13 | .16 | **.46** | **.23** | –.06 | .10 | –.07 | .03 | .00 | –.15 | .16 | –.08 | **–.26** |
| *J–P Facet Scales* | | | | | | | | | | | | | | | | |
| Systematic–Casual | **–.28** | .03 | –.03 | .02 | **.38** | .04 | –.12 | **–.35** | –.02 | –.10 | –.15 | **.28** | –.10 | –.17 | –.08 | .15 |
| Planful–Open-Ended | **–.32** | –.04 | –.06 | .00 | **.27** | –.14 | –.02 | **–.35** | –.07 | –.12 | –.11 | **.21** | –.16 | –.12 | –.07 | .17 |
| Early Starting–Pressure-Prompted | –.15 | .09 | .04 | .13 | **.26** | –.18 | **–.22** | –.19 | .04 | .03 | –.07 | **.34** | .02 | –.09 | –.08 | **.20** |
| Scheduled–Spontaneous | **–.34** | –.02 | –.06 | –.03 | **.27** | –.07 | –.09 | **–.36** | –.08 | –.14 | –.17 | **.25** | –.16 | **–.22** | –.13 | **.22** |
| Methodical–Emergent | **–.28** | –.06 | –.11 | –.06 | **.27** | –.11 | .04 | **–.36** | .00 | –.11 | –.11 | .19 | **–.21** | –.06 | –.14 | .05 |

mentioned here if they are part of a general pattern that was already discussed above.

Within the E–I facet block, Initiating and Expressive both correlate higher with Intellectual Efficiency (which contains components of ambition, expression of ideas, and initiative in addition to intellectual functioning), Managerial Potential, Work Orientation, and Creative Temperament than do the other three E–I facet scales (with the one exception noted below). Initiating correlates higher with Well-being (–.22), and Expressive correlates higher with Responsibility (–.21), perhaps due to the fact that one aspect of the Responsibility scale is "a participative temperament." Reflective and Quiet correlate higher with Self-control, while their opposites, Active and Enthusiastic, correlate higher with Narcissism than do the other three E–I facet scales. Enthusiastic correlates higher with Flexibility (–.20) and Creative Temperament (–.32).

For the S–N block, only the Traditional–Original scale offers correlations that are not discussed above. The correlation of this scale with CPI Tolerance is low (.08), whereas the correlations of the other S–N facet scales with Tolerance range from .20 to .24. Also, the Traditional pole correlates at higher levels with Amicability (–.22) and the Original pole with Narcissism (.34) than do the other S–N facet scales.

Within the T–F facet block, Questioning correlates higher with Sociability (–.20), Empathy (–.28), and Creative Temperament (–.26) than do the other T–F scales. In addition, Accepting correlates higher with Tolerance (.22) and lower with Leadership Potential (.00).

Within the J–P facet block, the only scale that exhibits a different level of correlations compared to the other scales in that block is Early Starting–Pressure-Prompted. Compared to the other J–P facet scales, Pressure-Prompted correlates higher with Social Presence (.22) and Empathy (.21) and lower with Leadership Potential (.02), while Early Starting correlates higher with v.1 (–.22).

**Opposite Correlations Within Facet Blocks** There are also a number of crossover correlations within a facet block—

that is, the sign of the coefficient for one or more scales in a block is opposite those of the other scales. This analysis considers some correlations of less than .20 because the sign of the coefficient is of primary interest; however, those close to 0 are not analyzed, regardless of sign.

Quiet correlates positively with Good Impression (.17), while the correlations of the other scales in the E–I facet block point toward the E poles (except for Active–Reflective, which is .08). Correlations with Achievement via Independence are toward the T poles of Questioning–Accommodating (–.20) and Logical–Empathetic (–.12) but toward the F pole of Critical–Accepting (.10). Questioning–Accommodating also correlates (–.15) with Flexibility, while all the other correlations with Flexibility point toward the F poles. Accommodating people will tend to agree with and approve of others, but that is not the same as being flexible. On the other hand, healthy questioning assumes different viewpoints from the start and attempts to uncover the differences. This in turn may lead to a change of opinion and thus to a demonstration of flexibility. ("Undeveloped" questioning, which is adversarial in nature, is not the same.) Correlations with Dominance and with Self-acceptance show opposite signs for two J–P scales: respectively, .15 and .17 with Early Starting–Pressure-Prompted and –.13 and –.10 with Methodical–Emergent.

**CPI™ Correlations in a Sample of Managers** In another study, the CPI instrument was correlated with a modified version of the original Step II facet scales using a large database of 4,042 participants at leadership programs at the Center for Creative Leadership® (CCL®; Fleenor & Van Velsor, 1995). It was necessary to use a modified version of the scales because CCL participants were administered Form F of the MBTI personality inventory, which does not contain all the necessary items for scoring the original Step II facet scales. To make these modified scales comparable to the full Step II facet scales, item weights were recomputed to keep scale scores in the 0–10 range. Correlations between the modified and full original Step II facet scales ranged from .87 to 1.0. For sixteen of the twenty original scales, these correlations were > .95. In only two cases were the correlations < .90, with the lowest being .87. Additional tests were conducted as a check on internal consistency and to verify that the factor structure was the same for the reduced scales and the originals. The alphas for the reduced scales dropped only slightly, mostly due to fewer items in the scales, and the factor structure remained the same. All of these checks verified that correlations of the reduced scales with the CPI scales could be extrapolated to the original Step II facet scales.

The CCL sample was 69% male and 90% Caucasian, with a mean age of 41. Of the respondents, 88% had at least four years of college and 96% occupied middle-management positions or higher. The CPI Dominance scale was correlated with the E poles of all five of the Step II E–I facet scales. Other CPI scales correlating with the E poles of all five E–I scales were Capacity for Status, Socialization, Social Presence, and Self-acceptance. CPI Empathy correlated with the E poles of four E–I scales. These same CPI scales also correlated with the N poles of several S–N scales. In addition, the CPI scales Achievement via Independence, Intellectual Efficiency, Psychological-mindedness, Independence, Empathy, and Flexibility correlated with the N poles of all five S–N scales. CPI Flexibility correlated positively with the P poles of all five J–P scales, while Achievement via Conformance correlated with the J poles of four J–P scales.

Among the CPI structural scales, v.1 was positively correlated with the I poles of all five E–I scales, and v.2 with the J poles of all five J–P scales. Finally, v.3 was positively correlated with the N poles of all five S–N scales.

The correlations of the Step II facet scales in two samples, one a national representative sample and one a very large sample of managers, verify that the scales are indeed valid measures of the facets.

## Adjective Check List

The *Adjective Check List* (Gough & Heilbrun, 1983) was administered to about half the national sample, and both the scale and the adjectives themselves were correlated with the Step II facet scales.

**ACL Scales** The same three questions that applied to the interpretation of CPI scales are also relevant to ACL scales. These questions apply to general patterns, a facet scale that is more highly correlated with an ACL scale than with the other facet scales in its block, and a facet scale that correlates opposite to other facet scales in its block. The correlations of the ACL scales and the Step II facet scales are shown in table 8.2. Because there are 720 coefficients presented in this table, the discussion below will focus on those for which $r \geq .20$. To better understand the relationships described below, the reader may refer to the brief definitions of all ACL scales presented in table C.2, on page 182.

**Overall Pattern of Correlations** All the E–I facet scales are positively related to Affiliation, Dominance, Exhibition, Heterosexuality, Personal Adjustment, Self-confidence, and Low Origence/Low Intellectance (for which two of the E–I scales are just below the .20 cutoff) in the E direction and with Self-control in the I direction. All the S–N facet scales correlate with Change, Creative Personality, Number of Favorable Items Checked, Ideal Self, and High Origence/High Intellectance in the direction of the N poles, and three are associated with Low Origence/High Intellectance. All T–F facet scales correlate with Abasement, Deference, and Nurturance in the F direction and with Dominance in the T direction. The J–P Step II facet scales all correlate with Order in the J direction. Thus, we see evidence that the Step II facet scales within a preference dichotomy do indeed generally correlate with ACL scales as would be predicted by theory.

**Table 8.2 Correlations of Step II™ Facet Scales with *Adjective Check List* (ACL) Scales**

| | ACL Scale | | | | | | | | | | | |
|---|---|---|---|---|---|---|---|---|---|---|---|---|
| **Step II™ Facet Scale** | Abasement | Adapt. Child | Achv. | Adult | Affiliation | Aggression | Autonomy | Chnge | Communality | Crit. Parent | Creatv. Pers. | Couns. Read. |
| *E–I Facet Scales* | | | | | | | | | | | | |
| Initiating–Receiving | **.24** | **.24** | **–.24** | –.15 | **–.24** | –.19 | –.15 | –.17 | –.02 | –.05 | **–.20** | .09 |
| Expressive–Contained | .10 | .13 | –.14 | –.06 | **–.21** | –.12 | –.03 | –.16 | –.10 | –.01 | –.10 | .04 |
| Gregarious–Intimate | .12 | .18 | –.15 | –.10 | **–.22** | –.02 | –.01 | –.16 | –.11 | .03 | –.12 | .18 |
| Active–Reflective | .10 | .15 | –.16 | –.04 | **–.26** | –.08 | –.04 | –.18 | –.02 | .02 | –.15 | .16 |
| Enthusiastic–Quiet | **.33** | .19 | **–.24** | .01 | **–.25** | –.30 | **–.23** | **–.28** | –.01 | –.13 | **–.20** | .07 |
| *S–N Facet Scales* | | | | | | | | | | | | |
| Concrete–Abstract | –.04 | –.16 | **.21** | .09 | .17 | .00 | .14 | **.35** | .13 | .08 | **.41** | .05 |
| Realistic–Imaginative | –.04 | –.11 | .17 | –.01 | .18 | .03 | .14 | **.44** | .17 | .08 | **.41** | –.06 |
| Practical–Conceptual | .02 | –.18 | **.20** | .15 | .20 | –.07 | .05 | **.22** | .17 | .05 | **.39** | .09 |
| Experiential–Theoretical | –.15 | **–.20** | **.25** | .11 | .16 | .07 | **.22** | **.40** | .12 | .16 | **.48** | –.02 |
| Traditional–Original | **–.23** | **–.23** | **.33** | .18 | .15 | .10 | **.32** | **.40** | .03 | .18 | **.52** | –.14 |
| *T–F Facet Scales* | | | | | | | | | | | | |
| Logical–Empathetic | **.29** | .16 | –.14 | **–.22** | .19 | –.16 | –.16 | .00 | .13 | –.16 | –.13 | **.27** |
| Reasonable–Compassionate | **.35** | **.20** | –.21 | **–.26** | .16 | –.19 | **–.25** | –.04 | .09 | **–.24** | **–.20** | **.26** |
| Questioning–Accommodating | **.30** | .07 | **–.22** | –.02 | –.04 | **–.35** | **–.41** | **–.30** | .03 | **–.35** | **–.30** | .14 |
| Critical–Accepting | **.26** | .02 | –.10 | .00 | .11 | **–.27** | **–.26** | –.02 | .18 | **–.23** | –.04 | **.26** |
| Tough–Tender | **.39** | .16 | –.18 | –.14 | .19 | **–.25** | **–.26** | .00 | **.20** | **–.27** | –.07 | .15 |
| *J–P Facet Scales* | | | | | | | | | | | | |
| Systematic–Casual | –.07 | .14 | –.16 | **–.28** | –.03 | .04 | .11 | .39 | –.08 | –.15 | .10 | –.09 |
| Planful–Open-Ended | –.09 | .03 | –.09 | –.10 | –.09 | –.01 | .08 | .18 | –.09 | –.01 | .03 | –.08 |
| Early Starting–Pressure-Prompted | –.06 | .08 | –.11 | **–.21** | –.05 | .09 | .09 | **.20** | –.03 | .01 | .10 | –.06 |
| Scheduled–Spontaneous | –.10 | .04 | –.18 | –.14 | –.11 | –.01 | .08 | **.24** | –.10 | –.13 | .08 | –.10 |
| Methodical–Emergent | –.04 | .11 | –.19 | **–.22** | –.13 | .06 | .06 | .17 | –.06 | –.10 | –.12 | –.02 |

*Note:* Bold indicates coefficients with r ≥ .20. See table C.2, on page 182, for meaning of ACL scales.

*Source:* National sample.

*continues*

### Differential Correlations Within Facet Blocks

Evidence to address this question comes primarily from five examples.

First, the ACL Autonomy scale (to act independently of others or of social values and expectations) correlates with the Original pole of the Traditional–Original scale at $r = .32$. The other four S–N facet scales correlate at .05–.22 with this ACL scale. Second, while all the S–N scales correlate with Creative Personality, the Step II facet scale with the largest correlation is the Original pole of the Traditional–Original scale, at $r = .52$. Third, the ACL Change scale correlates with only one of the T–F scales. The correlation is $r = -.30$ for the Questioning pole of the Questioning–Accommodating facet scale and about 0 for the four other T–F scales. Fourth, the Accommodating pole of the Questioning–Accommodating scale correlates at $r = .35$ with ACL Self-control, while the other T–F scales have correlations that range from about 0 to .12. Fifth, Low Origence/High Intellectance is more related to the J poles of Systematic–Casual and Methodical–Emergent than to the other J–P facet scales.

These examples suggest that the differential correlations of facet scales within a dichotomy also support the validity of the Step II facet scales.

### Opposite Correlations Within Facet Blocks

There are two examples of fairly low crossover correlations, which provide evidence regarding the question of opposite correlations within facet blocks.

**Table 8.2 Correlations of Step II™ Facet Scales with *Adjective Check List* (ACL) Scales** *continued*

| | ACL Scale | | | | | | | | | | | |
|---|---|---|---|---|---|---|---|---|---|---|---|---|
| **Step II™ Facet Scale** | Deference | Dominance | Endurance | Exhibition | # Fav. Chckd. | Free Child | Fem. Att. | Hetero. | Intraception | Ideal Self | Masc. Att. | Mil. Leader. |
| *E–I Facet Scales* | | | | | | | | | | | | |
| Initiating–Receiving | .17 | **–.37** | –.14 | **–.49** | –.19 | **–.48** | –.10 | **–.30** | –.10 | **–.20** | –.15 | –.11 |
| Expressive–Contained | .05 | **–.22** | –.05 | **–.41** | –.15 | **–.41** | –.12 | **–.27** | –.10 | –.09 | .00 | –.08 |
| Gregarious–Intimate | .04 | **–.26** | –.08 | **–.35** | –.16 | **–.37** | –.08 | **–.32** | –.10 | –.17 | –.07 | –.10 |
| Active–Reflective | .06 | **–.24** | –.04 | **–.41** | –.18 | **–.40** | –.12 | **–.41** | –.09 | –.15 | –.11 | –.04 |
| Enthusiastic–Quiet | .24 | **–.42** | –.03 | **–.57** | –.18 | **–.56** | –.14 | **–.40** | –.05 | –.12 | **–.22** | –.07 |
| *S–N Facet Scales* | | | | | | | | | | | | |
| Concrete–Abstract | –.16 | .13 | .08 | .08 | **.23** | **.26** | .14 | .15 | **.20** | **.29** | .12 | .13 |
| Realistic–Imaginative | –.16 | .08 | .00 | .13 | **.21** | **.30** | .16 | .14 | .14 | **.27** | .10 | .10 |
| Practical–Conceptual | –.06 | .05 | .15 | .01 | **.27** | .18 | **.21** | .14 | **.31** | **.31** | .06 | **.21** |
| Experiential–Theoretical | **–.23** | .17 | .08 | .18 | **.24** | **.29** | .09 | .12 | **.22** | **.32** | **.20** | .12 |
| Traditional–Original | **–.34** | **.29** | .17 | **.22** | **.23** | **.35** | .09 | .13 | **.21** | **.37** | **.26** | **.22** |
| *T–F Facet Scales* | | | | | | | | | | | | |
| Logical–Empathetic | **.21** | **–.23** | –.12 | –.06 | .09 | .01 | **.29** | **.25** | .06 | –.16 | –.15 | –.15 |
| Reasonable–Compassionate | **.29** | **–.27** | –.18 | –.10 | .05 | –.06 | **.27** | **.20** | .02 | –.17 | **–.20** | –.17 |
| Questioning–Accommodating | **.40** | **–.29** | –.11 | **–.29** | –.09 | **–.26** | .02 | –.11 | –.03 | –.14 | **–.29** | –.04 |
| Critical–Accepting | **.25** | **–.23** | –.05 | –.12 | .08 | –.01 | **.22** | .04 | .12 | .00 | **–.25** | –.03 |
| Tough–Tender | **.32** | **–.29** | –.16 | –.09 | .12 | –.02 | **.29** | **.22** | .11 | –.08 | **–.22** | –.10 |
| *J–P Facet Scales* | | | | | | | | | | | | |
| Systematic–Casual | –.16 | –.03 | **–.37** | .15 | –.11 | **.22** | –.09 | .10 | –.15 | –.06 | –.05 | **–.26** |
| Planful–Open-Ended | –.13 | –.04 | –.19 | –.06 | –.09 | –.01 | –.11 | –.07 | –.05 | –.03 | .06 | –.07 |
| Early Starting–Pressure-Prompted | –.14 | –.04 | –.24 | .08 | –.06 | .13 | –.05 | .03 | –.09 | .01 | .02 | –.14 |
| Scheduled–Spontaneous | –.14 | –.08 | **–.30** | –.03 | –.12 | .07 | –.17 | –.10 | –.12 | –.02 | –.01 | –.15 |
| Methodical–Emergent | –.10 | –.08 | **–.32** | .00 | –.17 | .00 | –.17 | –.13 | –.18 | –.17 | –.08 | –.16 |

ACL Succorance (to solicit sympathy, affection, or emotional support from others) correlates with the Expressive pole of the Expressive–Contained facet at $r = -.13$, while all the other E–I facet scales correlate slightly toward the Introverted poles on the E–I scales. The ACL Creative Personality scale, which is defined as having the desire to do and think differently from the norm along with a talent for originality, correlates at –.12 with Methodical–Emergent—that is, in the direction of Methodical—but correlates positively with the P poles of the other J–P scales, with $r = .03$–.10.

While an association between Creative Personality and Methodical may seem counter to the intention of the Methodical scale, an explanation may reside in the method of development for the ACL scale. Criterion groups for the Creative Personality scale consisted of mathematicians and architects who had been nominated as creative by expert judges; engineering and psychology students rated as creative were also included (Gough & Heilbrun, 1983). In other words, group members had already demonstrated creativity, not simply by formulating ideas but by their output. This kind of accomplishment may have involved the behaviors measured by the Methodical scale. An alternative hypothesis, given the number of correlations and the size of this one, is that the correlation occurred by chance.

**Table 8.2 Correlations of Step II™ Facet Scales with *Adjective Check List* (ACL) Scales** *continued*

| | ACL Scale | | | | | | | | | | | |
|---|---|---|---|---|---|---|---|---|---|---|---|---|
| **Step II™ Facet Scale** | Nurtur. Parent | Nurtur-ance | Order | Personal Adjust. | Self-conf. | Self-control | Succor-ance | # Unfav. Chckd. | High Orig/ Low Intell. | High Orig./ High Intell. | Low Orig./ Low Intell. | Low Orig./ High Intell. |
| *E–I Facet Scales* | | | | | | | | | | | | |
| Initiating–Receiving | **–.27** | **–.21** | –.11 | **–.22** | **–.40** | **.33** | .09 | .08 | –.06 | .05 | **–.21** | –.06 |
| Expressive–Contained | **–.21** | **–.27** | –.04 | **–.23** | **–.26** | **.29** | –.13 | .07 | .00 | .08 | **–.22** | .00 |
| Gregarious–Intimate | **–.27** | **–.23** | –.04 | **–.30** | **–.31** | **.25** | .05 | .13 | –.11 | .06 | –.18 | –.05 |
| Active–Reflective | **–.26** | **–.27** | .02 | **–.26** | **–.33** | **.29** | .02 | .08 | –.19 | .03 | **–.28** | –.03 |
| Enthusiastic–Quiet | –.18 | **–.20** | .02 | **–.21** | **–.40** | **.48** | .07 | .00 | –.16 | –.01 | –.19 | –.04 |
| *S–N Facet Scales* | | | | | | | | | | | | |
| Concrete–Abstract | –.01 | .05 | .04 | .16 | .19 | –.17 | –.03 | .00 | .15 | **.27** | .06 | .17 |
| Realistic–Imaginative | –.06 | .04 | –.03 | .12 | **.21** | **–.21** | .01 | .03 | .14 | **.29** | .08 | .12 |
| Practical–Conceptual | .01 | .09 | .14 | **.20** | .18 | –.01 | –.02 | .00 | .14 | **.24** | .12 | **.23** |
| Experiential–Theoretical | –.05 | –.05 | .07 | .12 | **.26** | **–.24** | –.06 | .09 | .16 | **.32** | .04 | **.20** |
| Traditional–Original | –.03 | –.02 | .12 | .13 | **.31** | **–.24** | –.18 | .03 | .16 | **.34** | .02 | **.24** |
| *T–F Facet Scales* | | | | | | | | | | | | |
| Logical–Empathetic | .08 | **.32** | –.14 | .10 | –.10 | –.02 | **.34** | .07 | .09 | .02 | **.25** | –.04 |
| Reasonable–Compassionate | .13 | **.33** | –.19 | .11 | –.15 | .00 | **.39** | .05 | .07 | –.07 | **.24** | –.11 |
| Questioning–Accommodating | .13 | **.21** | –.10 | .06 | –.23 | **.35** | .15 | –.14 | –.15 | **–.29** | .06 | –.13 |
| Critical–Accepting | .11 | **.25** | –.08 | .15 | –.09 | .12 | **.22** | –.06 | –.07 | –.03 | .17 | .00 |
| Tough–Tender | .15 | **.36** | –.13 | .15 | –.10 | .02 | **.40** | –.01 | .04 | –.03 | **.28** | –.05 |
| *J–P Facet Scales* | | | | | | | | | | | | |
| Systematic–Casual | –.14 | –.02 | **–.43** | –.09 | –.04 | **–.27** | –.06 | –.04 | .08 | .06 | –.05 | **–.21** |
| Planful–Open-Ended | –.13 | –.13 | **–.20** | –.08 | –.09 | –.04 | **–.22** | –.02 | .01 | .11 | –.11 | –.06 |
| Early Starting–Pressure-Prompted | –.16 | –.10 | **–.25** | –.12 | –.04 | –.16 | –.09 | .04 | .09 | .12 | –.09 | –.09 |
| Scheduled–Spontaneous | –.14 | –.11 | **–.31** | –.11 | –.07 | –.10 | **–.27** | –.10 | .01 | .06 | –.12 | –.14 |
| Methodical–Emergent | –.13 | –.12 | **–.35** | –.13 | –.11 | –.11 | –.08 | –.02 | –.07 | –.04 | –.12 | **–.22** |

## ACL Adjectives

The Step II facet scales were also correlated with the 300 adjectives that make up the *Adjective Check List*. An additional 13 adjectives were also included to round out the possible descriptive terms. All 313 adjectives were used for self-descriptions by participants in the national sample. The adjectives and the coefficient associated with each facet scale are shown in table 8.3.

In general, an adjective was listed in the table if the correlation coefficient was ≥ .20. However, for a few facet scales, so few adjectives met this criterion that additional adjectives (indicated by an asterisk) were necessary to round out the description, although this was not possible for all facet scales. On the other hand, other scales had so many adjectives associated with them that only the top twenty appear in the table; the remainder with coefficients ≥ .20 were listed in parentheses.

The table yields a number of interesting results. Overall, the pattern of correlations clearly supports the intention and description of the facet scales. Adjectives that correlate with the scales in one facet block generally are not associated with scales from another facet block. This is compelling evidence that the facet scales are effective in describing unique aspects of people.

**Table 8.3 Correlations of Step II™ Facet Scales with Adjectives from the *Adjective Check List***

| E–I Scales | | | | S–N Scales | | | |
|---|---|---|---|---|---|---|---|
| **Initiating** | | **Receiving** | | **Concrete** | | **Abstract** | |
| sociable | .510 | shy | .437 | interests narrow* | .196 | imaginative | .456 |
| talkative | .487 | quiet | .397 | fussy* | .150 | artistic | .332 |
| outgoing | .460 | silent | .393 | | | introspective | .305 |
| cheerful | .327 | reserved | .277 | | | zany | .288 |
| confident | .287 | withdrawn | .211 | | | insightful | .285 |
| friendly | .261 | timid | .207 | | | initiative | .283 |
| outspoken | .238 | | | | | curious | .279 |
| assertive | .229 | | | | | intelligent | .277 |
| aggressive | .227 | | | | | idealistic | .274 |
| enthusiastic | .213 | | | | | unconventional | .266 |
| organized | .206 | | | | | individualistic | .264 |
| energetic | .202 | | | | | original | .264 |
| | | | | | | inventive | .264 |
| | | | | | | enterprising | .254 |
| | | | | | | clever | .239 |
| | | | | | | interests wide | .237 |
| | | | | | | resourceful | .236 |
| | | | | | | emotional | .231 |
| | | | | | | reflective | .216 |
| | | | | | | rebellious | .215 (+6) |
| **Expressive** | | **Contained** | | **Realistic** | | **Imaginative** | |
| talkative | .408 | silent | .440 | conservative* | .176 | imaginative | .424 |
| sociable | .390 | quiet | .381 | stern* | .173 | introspective | .330 |
| outgoing | .366 | reserved | .324 | interests narrow* | .163 | curious | .312 |
| cheerful | .311 | shy | .260 | | | dreamy | .295 |
| affectionate | .277 | complicated | .246 | | | artistic | .293 |
| friendly | .248 | aloof | .211 | | | optimistic | .289 |
| warm | .242 | irritable | .209 | | | original | .287 |
| sympathetic | .213 | cold | .204 | | | unconventional | .277 |
| trusting | .208 | withdrawn | .203 | | | ingenious | .277 |
| jolly | .200 | | | | | humorous | .260 |
| | | | | | | enthusiastic | .256 |
| | | | | | | insightful | .255 |
| | | | | | | intelligent | .255 |
| | | | | | | zany | .251 |
| | | | | | | interests wide | .251 |
| | | | | | | adaptable | .247 |
| | | | | | | spontaneous | .246 |
| | | | | | | inventive | .243 |
| | | | | | | complicated | .237 |
| | | | | | | sharp-witted | .231 **(+7)** |
| **Gregarious** | | **Intimate** | | **Practical** | | **Conceptual** | |
| sociable | .398 | silent | .268 | conservative* | .174 | imaginative | .511 |
| outgoing | .349 | shy | .256 | | | intelligent | .381 |
| active | .240 | quiet | .253 | | | introspective | .373 |
| friendly | .232 | cynical | .240 | | | curious | .363 |
| cheerful | .222 | withdrawn | .222 | | | artistic | .326 |
| outspoken | .215 | reserved | .211 | | | insightful | .316 |
| loud | .211 | wary | .208 | | | optimistic | .304 |
| spontaneous | .209 | complicated | .200 | | | reflective | .303 |
| confident | .201 | | | | | original | .299 |
| | | | | | | inventive | .280 |
| | | | | | | idealistic | .275 |

*Notes:* In general, an adjective was listed in the table if the correlation coefficient was ≥ .20; an asterisk (*) indicates an adjective with a correlation coefficient of ≤ .20. Bold number in parentheses is number of adjectives with coefficients of ≥ .20 that were not listed for reasons of space.

*Source:* National sample.

**Table 8.3 Correlations of Step II™ Facet Scales with Adjectives from the *Adjective Check List*** *continued*

| E–I Scales | | | | S–N Scales | | | |
|---|---|---|---|---|---|---|---|
| **Gregarious** | | **Intimate** | | **Practical** | | **Conceptual** | |
| | | | | | | ingenious | .270 |
| | | | | | | sophisticated | .257 |
| | | | | | | resourceful | .254 |
| | | | | | | unconventional | .238 |
| | | | | | | sharp-witted | .229 |
| | | | | | | progressive | .226 |
| | | | | | | complicated | .226 |
| | | | | | | praising | .219 |
| | | | | | | alert | .208 **(+4)** |
| **Active** | | **Reflective** | | **Experiential** | | **Theoretical** | |
| sociable | .483 | moody | .308 | conventional* | .155 | imaginative | .397 |
| outgoing | .458 | reserved | .287 | interests narrow* | .175 | intelligent | .342 |
| talkative | .384 | tense | .278 | conservative* | .175 | insightful | .341 |
| jolly | .326 | silent | .265 | | | unconventional | .337 |
| friendly | .273 | quiet | .265 | | | introspective | .322 |
| wise | .261 | shy | .224 | | | curious | .309 |
| loud | .260 | aloof | .208 | | | original | .299 |
| cheerful | .253 | inhibited | .208 | | | idealistic | .293 |
| active | .207 | interests narrow | .204 | | | inventive | .289 |
| spontaneous | .204 | | | | | initiative | .288 |
| confident | .203 | | | | | zany | .286 |
| affectionate | .202 | | | | | freewheeling | .280 |
| pleasure-seeking | .202 | | | | | artistic | .275 |
| whiny | .201 | | | | | interests wide | .263 |
| charming | .200 | | | | | complicated | .261 |
| | | | | | | clever | .261 |
| | | | | | | enterprising | .257 |
| | | | | | | industrious | .252 |
| | | | | | | sophisticated | .248 |
| | | | | | | rebellious | .246 **(+10)** |
| **Enthusiastic** | | **Quiet** | | **Traditional** | | **Original** | |
| bold | .270 | quiet | .450 | conservative | .205 | imaginative | .419 |
| jolly | .256 | silent | .319 | conventional* | .185 | original | .406 |
| enthusiastic | .256 | shy | .314 | | | unconventional | .376 |
| uninhibited | .251 | reserved | .313 | | | inventive | .351 |
| powerful | .246 | withdrawn | .255 | | | individualistic | .338 |
| robust | .244 | unfriendly | .211 | | | zany | .333 |
| outspoken | .240 | discreet* | .176 | | | ingenious | .322 |
| charming | .237 | serious* | .175 | | | daring | .322 |
| excitable | .229 | | | | | curious | .315 |
| assertive | .229 | | | | | resourceful | .302 |
| alert | .224 | | | | | initiative | .300 |
| competitive | .216 | | | | | enterprising | .294 |
| warm | .213 | | | | | freewheeling | .291 |
| trusting | .209 | | | | | introspective | .289 |
| affectionate | .206 | | | | | assertive | .265 |
| | | | | | | insightful | .264 |
| | | | | | | bold | .254 |
| | | | | | | rebellious | .253 |
| | | | | | | progressive | .253 |
| | | | | | | intelligent | .250 **(+14)** |

*continues*

**Table 8.3 Correlations of Step II™ Facet Scales with Adjectives from the *Adjective Check List*** *continued*

| T–F Scales | | | | J–P Scales | | | |
|---|---|---|---|---|---|---|---|
| **Logical** | | **Empathetic** | | **Systematic** | | **Casual** | |
| ambitious | .232 | emotional | .453 | methodical | .377 | disorderly | .350 |
| unconventional* | .195 | affectionate | .331 | organized | .310 | spontaneous | .325 |
| masculine* | .189 | softhearted | .325 | deliberate | .213 | freewheeling | .273 |
| unemotional* | .171 | warm | .322 | steady | .209 | easygoing | .217 |
| shrewd* | .170 | sympathetic | .312 | stable | .207 | immature | .206 |
| foresighted* | .161 | sentimental | .291 | complaining | .204 | noisy | .206 |
| unexcitable* | .149 | feminine | .278 | conservative | .201 | | |
| | | kind | .276 | | | | |
| | | submissive | .266 | | | | |
| | | shy | .254 | | | | |
| | | trusting | .242 | | | | |
| | | superstitious | .237 | | | | |
| | | dreamy | .229 | | | | |
| | | obliging | .223 | | | | |
| | | generous | .222 | | | | |
| | | awkward | .205 | | | | |
| | | thankless | .204 | | | | |
| | | compliant | .202 | | | | |
| | | artistic | .200 | | | | |

| **Reasonable** | | **Compassionate** | | **Planful** | | **Open-Ended** | |
|---|---|---|---|---|---|---|---|
| unconventional | .285 | emotional | .350 | organized | .344 | quiet | .234 |
| ambitious | .260 | affectionate | .345 | sociable | .271 | freewheeling | .223 |
| foresighted | .226 | warm | .341 | talkative | .212 | masculine | .216 |
| masculine | .217 | kind | .326 | warm | .209 | daring* | .196 |
| ingenious | .207 | feminine | .314 | affectionate | .201 | | |
| deliberate | .201 | softhearted | .309 | | | | |
| assertive* | .197 | sympathetic | .294 | | | | |
| aloof* | .197 | sentimental | .280 | | | | |
| shrewd* | .192 | excitable | .271 | | | | |
| demanding* | .192 | forgiving | .227 | | | | |
| | | shy | .220 | | | | |
| | | nervous | .219 | | | | |
| | | anxious | .218 | | | | |
| | | generous | .216 | | | | |
| | | talkative | .212 | | | | |
| | | pleasant | .206 | | | | |
| | | whiny | .203 | | | | |
| | | peaceable | .203 | | | | |

| **Questioning** | | **Accommodating** | | **Early Starting** | | **Pressure-Prompted** | |
|---|---|---|---|---|---|---|---|
| sarcastic | .295 | peaceable* | .182 | organized | .289 | disorderly | .293 |
| daring | .291 | cooperative* | .180 | cautious* | .194 | sarcastic | .251 |
| dominant | .285 | softhearted* | .174 | steady* | .169 | leisurely | .205 |
| freewheeling | .281 | easygoing* | .174 | active* | .168 | rebellious* | .181 |
| unconventional | .277 | dull* | .173 | | | | |
| cynical | .270 | patient* | .166 | | | | |
| initiative | .257 | mild* | .166 | | | | |
| shrewd | .252 | obliging* | .162 | | | | |
| demanding | .249 | gentle* | .160 | | | | |
| introspective | .240 | generous* | .157 | | | | |
| individualistic | .235 | pleasant* | .156 | | | | |
| sly | .233 | | | | | | |
| sharp-witted | .233 | | | | | | |
| tough | .229 | | | | | | |

**Table 8.3 Correlations of Step II™ Facet Scales with Adjectives from the *Adjective Check List*** *continued*

| T–F Scales | | | | J–P Scales | | | |
|---|---|---|---|---|---|---|---|
| **Questioning** | | **Accommodating** | | **Early Starting** | | **Pressure-Prompted** | |
| wary | .228 | | | | | | |
| frank | .222 | | | | | | |
| stern | .222 | | | | | | |
| blustery | .221 | | | | | | |
| assertive | .218 | | | | | | |
| good-looking | .217 **(+3)** | | | | | | |
| **Critical** | | **Accepting** | | **Scheduled** | | **Spontaneous** | |
| frank | .251 | feminine | .269 | organized | .328 | disorderly | .234 |
| fault-finding | .229 | affectionate | .267 | complaining | .265 | freewheeling | .213 |
| aggressive | .227 | forgiving | .255 | serious | .241 | leisurely | .204 |
| vindictive | .218 | peaceable | .249 | warm | .235 | masculine* | .177 |
| stern | .212 | merciful | .226 | talkative | .222 | adventurous* | .155 |
| unemotional | .208 | sympathetic | .223 | considerate | .217 | spontaneous* | .152 |
| masculine | .202 | mannerly | .208 | affectionate | .207 | easygoing* | .152 |
| assertive* | .196 | cheerful | .208 | praising | .206 | | |
| quarrelsome* | .185 | trusting | .207 | | | | |
| | | conscientious | .203 | | | | |
| **Tough** | | **Tender** | | **Methodical** | | **Emergent** | |
| tough | .259 | affectionate | .374 | insightful | .248 | disorderly* | .143 |
| demanding | .249 | sympathetic | .308 | organized | .244 | aggressive* | .135 |
| aggressive | .231 | warm | .302 | reflective | .224 | changeable* | .130 |
| ambitious | .214 | emotional | .298 | responsible | .204 | | |
| unemotional* | .196 | peaceable | .293 | methodical* | .196 | | |
| dominant* | .195 | kind | .291 | | | | |
| competitive* | .192 | softhearted | .288 | | | | |
| strong* | .191 | sentimental | .271 | | | | |
| | | contented | .269 | | | | |
| | | submissive | .233 | | | | |
| | | feminine | .215 | | | | |
| | | merciful | .215 | | | | |
| | | trusting | .212 | | | | |
| | | pleasant | .210 | | | | |
| | | generous | .209 | | | | |
| | | cheerful | .204 | | | | |
| | | nervous | .202 | | | | |
| | | obliging | .201 | | | | |
| | | praising | .200 | | | | |

There are, however, a few curious results that do not fit the overall pattern. For example, it is not clear why people who score toward Planful would see themselves as sociable, talkative, warm, and affectionate as well as organized. At the other pole of that same scale, Open-Ended people chose the unexpected *quiet* as part of their self-descriptions. There are a number of possible explanations for these findings. For one, given the large number of correlations calculated, some of the results are doubtless due to chance. For another, the coefficients reflect the underlying distribution of dichotomous preferences in the sample (a high frequency of FJs). And last, these adjectives may reveal heretofore undiscovered meanings of these scales. These hypotheses may be fruitful avenues of exploration for further research.

The results in the table also illustrate that, for most facet scales, there are both similarities *and* differences in adjectives associated with the scales within a block. The similarities reflect the scales' function as facets of larger constructs. The scale intercorrelations discussed in chapter 6 demonstrate the relationships that exist both among the scales within a facet block and with the overarching preference dichotomy of which they are a part. Differences in the adjectives associated with the scales within a block demonstrate that the facets have unique components as well. They therefore fulfill their purpose of describing individual differences.

Another observation to be drawn from the table concerns the criterion measure, the *Adjective Check List,* rather than the facet scales themselves. For whatever reason, the ACL clearly does not include many adjectival descriptors that are applicable to the facets of Sensing, which accounts for the very low number of adjectives associated with the S–N facet scales. This result illustrates the need to consider the properties of the criterion measure when conducting research on the Step II tool. As discussed below, Harker and Reynierse (1999) recognized this problem with the ACL and augmented the Sensing adjectives, to good effect.

## Fundamental Interpersonal Relations Orientation–Behavior™ (FIRO-B®) Inventory

Fleenor and Van Velsor (1995) correlated the modified original Step II facet scales (see section above for a description of the modifications) with the *Fundamental Interpersonal Relations Orientation–Behavior* (FIRO-B) inventory in a sample of 7,949 CCL program participants. This sample was 69% male, of whom 86% had at least four years of college and 93% were in middle-management positions or higher. The correlations are shown in table 8.4.

Almost all the E–I facet scales correlated with Expressed Inclusion and Wanted Inclusion in the direction of the E poles; the exception was Expressive with Wanted Inclusion. Similarly, the E–I facet scales, except for Gregarious–Intimate, correlated with Expressed and Wanted Affection in the direction of the E poles. The Gregarious–Intimate exception is understandable, as people who score toward Intimate are equally interested in expressing or receiving affection, just with fewer people. Since the FIRO-B scales explicitly ask for both frequency and selectivity of the behavior, it is not surprising that the correlation with Gregarious–Intimate is in the Gregarious direction but somewhat lower than the correlation with the other facets, particularly for Wanted Affection. Within the T–F dichotomy, Logical–Empathetic, Reasonable–Compassionate, and Tough–Tender all correlate in the direction of the F poles with Expressed Affection and Wanted Affection. Two T–F facet scales correlate with Expressed Control, with people who score toward Questioning and Tough exhibiting higher scores. There were no significant correlations with any S–N or J–P facet scales.

This pattern of correlations is congruent with the intended meaning of the scores of the two instruments and with the theories that underlie each. Given that the FIRO-B instrument is a measure of *interpersonal* needs, correlations are to be expected between FIRO-B scores (particularly those measuring Inclusion and Affection) and Step II facet scales belonging to the E–I and T–F dichotomies. Likewise, there would be no reason to believe that scales measuring interpersonal needs would correlate with personality scales designed to measure modes of perception (S–N) or styles of living in the outer world (J–P), and indeed there are no significant correlations among these dichotomies.

Some might question why the Judging poles of the J–P facet scales are not more highly correlated with the Expressed Control scale of the FIRO-B instrument. However, the constructs measured by the two instruments are only superficially related. While those with a preference toward the Judging poles of the facet scales and those scoring high on Expressed Control may both like structure and consistency, there are more differences than similarities. The FIRO-B scale as a measure of interpersonal need focuses on control of other people; the Judging poles of the facet scales are instead concerned with preferences such as desire for a schedule, long-range plans, and a methodical approach to a project.

## Eysenck Personality Questionnaire

Poling and Johnson (1991) combined items from three instruments and factor-analyzed the entire set. The instruments were the MBTI *Type Differentiation Indicator* (TDI), which contains the original Step II facet scales, the *Eysenck Personality Questionnaire* (EPQ), and the *Rotter Locus of Control Scale.* The sample consisted of 296 students from an urban liberal arts university. Analysis yielded five factors; four corresponded to the MBTI preference scales (E–I, S–N, T–F, and J–P), and the fifth, which they labeled a neuroticism factor, correlated with loadings from the EPQ Neuroticism scale and certain MBTI Form J items that are scored on the Comfort–Discomfort scales of the TDI.

These same authors correlated the EPQ scales with the TDI scales in a sample of 573 undergraduates (Poling & Johnson, 1995). Correlations with a significance that reached $p < .001$ are shown in table 8.5. If we overlook the unfortunate names of the EPQ scales and understand the meaning

**Table 8.4 Correlations of Step II™ Facet Scales with the Scales of the *Fundamental Interpersonal Relations Orientation–Behavior*™ (FIRO-B®) Inventory**

| | FIRO-B® Scale | | | | | |
|---|---|---|---|---|---|---|
| **Step II™ Facet Scale** | Expressed Inclusion | Wanted Inclusion | Expressed Control | Wanted Control | Expressed Affection | Wanted Affection |
| *E–I Facet Scales* | | | | | | |
| Initiating–Receiving | **–.41** | **–.24** | –.17 | .07 | **–.35** | **–.20** |
| Expressive–Contained | **–.34** | –.19 | –.08 | –.01 | **–.42** | **–.26** |
| Gregarious–Intimate | **–.31** | **–.24** | –.09 | –.01 | –.18 | –.15 |
| Active–Reflective | **–.37** | **–.26** | –.06 | .01 | **–.26** | **–.22** |
| Enthusiastic–Quiet | **–.37** | **–.27** | –.14 | .02 | **–.34** | **–.22** |
| *S–N Facet Scales* | | | | | | |
| Concrete–Abstract | .04 | .05 | .00 | –.01 | .08 | .02 |
| Realistic–Imaginative | .09 | .13 | .09 | –.01 | .10 | .08 |
| Practical–Conceptual | –.02 | .00 | .01 | –.03 | .03 | –.04 |
| Experiential–Theoretical | .01 | .03 | .05 | –.02 | .02 | –.01 |
| Traditional–Original | .03 | .04 | .10 | –.09 | .06 | .00 |
| *T–F Facet Scales* | | | | | | |
| Logical–Empathetic | .14 | .12 | –.12 | .08 | **.26** | **.23** |
| Reasonable–Compassionate | .13 | .11 | –.13 | .10 | **.22** | **.20** |
| Questioning–Accommodating | .00 | .02 | **–.20** | .13 | .03 | .10 |
| Critical–Accepting | .13 | .05 | –.13 | .09 | .18 | .17 |
| Tough–Tender | .11 | .11 | **–.20** | .14 | **.21** | **.22** |
| *J–P Facet Scales* | | | | | | |
| Systematic–Casual | .05 | .06 | –.12 | .05 | .12 | .09 |
| Planful–Open-Ended | –.06 | –.02 | –.04 | .00 | –.02 | –.02 |
| Early Starting–Pressure-Prompted | .02 | .05 | .07 | –.03 | .01 | .01 |
| Scheduled–Spontaneous | .02 | .03 | .08 | –.07 | .02 | .00 |
| Methodical–Emergent | –.08 | –.02 | –.01 | .00 | –.07 | –.01 |

*Notes:* N = 7,949 managers from programs at the Center for Creative Leadership. MBTI scales are based on a reduced-item version of MBTI Step II scoring. Negative correlations are in the direction of the left pole of the facet scale; positive correlations are in the direction of the right pole; bold indicates correlation coefficient of ≥.20.

*Source:* Adapted from Fleenor and Van Velsor (1995). Used with permission.

of the scores, we can see that the coefficients in general support the validity of Step II facet scales.

Psychoticism is a measure of adaptivity, "particularly social values, mores, and institutions" (Poling & Johnson, 1995, p. 102). People with high scores tend to disregard social expectations and therefore are seen by others as impulsive and tough-minded. Thus, correlations with Critical and Tough and with four of the five J–P facets in the Perceiving direction make sense.

High levels of Neuroticism are associated with anxiety, tension, or worry. There are only three significant correlations here—all low—in the direction of Receiving, Intimate, and Experiential. Correlation with the E–I poles is to be expected, given the association of Introversion with anxiety in Eysenck's theory. The largest correlations by far are those between Eysenck's Extraversion and the five E–I facets of the Step II instrument, as would be predicted.

The Lie scale is an index-of-response set that indicates a bias toward answering the questions in a socially desirable manner. This scale correlates primarily with the five J–P facet scales in the direction of the Judging poles, which again should be no surprise, given type theory.

## Correlations with Behavioral Descriptors

Five studies have correlated Step II facet scale scores with independent observer ratings. These studies are reported below.

**Table 8.5 Correlations of Step II™ Facet Scales with the Scales of the *Eysenck Personality Questionnaire***

| | Eysenck Scale | | | |
|---|---|---|---|---|
| **Step II™ Facet Scale** | Psychoticism | Neuroticism | Extraversion | Lie |
| *E–I Facet Scales* | | | | |
| Initiating–Receiving | | .15 | -.69 | |
| Expressive–Contained | | | -.39 | |
| Gregarious–Intimate | | .16 | –.40 | |
| Active–Reflective | | | –.52 | |
| Enthusiastic–Quiet | | | –.59 | |
| *S–N Facet Scales* | | | | |
| Concrete–Abstract | | | | |
| Realistic–Imaginative | | | | –.17 |
| Practical–Conceptual | | | –.14 | |
| Experiential–Theoretical | | –.14 | | |
| Traditional–Original | | | | |
| *T–F Facet Scales* | | | | |
| Logical–Empathetic | –.14 | | | |
| Reasonable–Compassionate | | | | |
| Questioning–Accommodating | | | –.18 | |
| Critical–Accepting | –.28 | | | |
| Tough–Tender | –.23 | | | |
| *J–P Facet Scales* | | | | |
| Systematic–Casual | | | .18 | –.14 |
| Planful–Open-Ended | .25 | | | –.15 |
| Early Starting–Pressure-Prompted | .29 | | .22 | –.20 |
| Scheduled–Spontaneous | .25 | | .15 | –.20 |
| Methodical–Emergent | .24 | | | –.18 |

*Notes:* Coefficients shown if $p < .001$. See text for a discussion of the meaning of the unfortunately named EPQ scales.

*Source:* Adapted from Poling and Johnson, 1995. Used with permission.

Harker and Reynierse (1999) developed a 276-item rating questionnaire consisting of adjectives and descriptive phrases, including phrases used by Saunders (1989) as descriptors for the twenty Step II facet scales. Although the questionnaire made use of these descriptors, the authors also point out that "many items were descriptive of behaviors and traits not immediately or directly related to the subscales" (p. 14). According to the authors, including such descriptors is advantageous because when they are shown to be related to Step II facet scales, they expand our understanding of those scales. The downside is that nonsignificant results do not necessarily suggest lack of validity for those scales.

The subjects were 641 individuals who completed either Form K or Form J of the MBTI personality inventory; 37.4% of this sample were men and 62.6% were women. Each subject selected one individual who knew him or her well to complete the rating questionnaire with the subject in mind. The rater sample consisted of 53% spouses and 47% nonspouses (either another family member, a coworker, or a friend). Stepwise regression was performed for each item in the rating scale across the twenty Step II facet scales. Because of the size of the tables reported in the article, only a portion of the results is summarized here.

Table 8.6 shows the top three descriptors for each pole of the Step II facet scales, ranked by size of the beta coefficient. In some cases, when the coefficients were identical, more than three descriptors are listed. Both poles of the Initiating–Receiving facet, as well as the Empathetic pole of the Logical–Empathetic facet, had many significant descriptors associated with them. These two facet scales were also highly correlated with their respective Step I preference scales. Only three of the poles had no statistically significant descriptors associated with them: Gregarious, Practical, and Tough (although see following discussion of Van Velsor & Fleenor [1997] for descriptors for these scales in a sample of managers).

On the other hand, the table shows an impressive match between observer ratings and reported subject preferences for the majority of the poles of the Step II facet scales. In many instances, the adjective used to describe the subject is the

**Table 8.6 Summary of Adjectival Descriptions by Others for Each Facet Scale**

| E–I Facet Scales | | S–N Facet Scales | | T–F Facet Scales | | J–P Facet Scales | |
|---|---|---|---|---|---|---|---|
| **Initiating** | **Receiving** | **Concrete** | **Abstract** | **Logical** | **Empathetic** | **Systematic** | **Casual** |
| Assertively outgoing<br>Good mixer<br>Gregarious<br>Social facilitator<br>Talkative | Quiet<br>Reserved<br>Shy | Concrete<br>Conservative<br>Factual<br>Literal | Abstract<br>Uncomfortable with routines<br>Nervy | Analytical<br>Logical<br>Objective | Feeling<br>Emotional<br>Sentimental | Methodical<br>Meticulous<br>Precise | Impulsive<br>Changeable<br>Easygoing |
| **Expressive** | **Contained** | **Realistic** | **Imaginative** | **Reasonable** | **Compassionate** | **Planful** | **Open-Ended** |
| Expresses feelings easily<br>Easy to know<br>Engaging | Emotions are internalized<br>Hard to know<br>Confiding in others is difficult | Cautious<br>Traditional<br>Protective | Wide interests | Enjoys pressure<br>Opinionated<br>Values cleverness | Likes harmony<br>Empathetic<br>Devout | Scheduled<br>Plans ahead<br>Responsible | Casual<br>Spontaneous |
| **Gregarious** | **Intimate** | **Practical** | **Conceptual** | **Questioning** | **Accommodating** | **Early Starting** | **Pressure-Prompted** |
| (None) | Prefers one-on-one | (None) | Likes to read and write<br>Enjoys role of scholar<br>Idealistic | Outspoken<br>Assertive<br>Demanding | Mild<br>Meek<br>Serene | Efficient<br>Exact<br>Dependable | Disorderly<br>Informal<br>Enjoys pressure |
| **Active** | **Reflective** | **Experiential** | **Theoretical** | **Critical** | **Accepting** | **Scheduled** | **Spontaneous** |
| Enjoys being with others<br>Fun loving<br>Easy to know | Enjoys solitude<br>Likes to read and write | Prefers easy practicality<br>Likes things settled | Visionary<br>Inquisitive<br>Theoretical | Critical<br>Skeptical | Accepting<br>Approving<br>Appreciative<br>Considerate | Structured<br>Structure oriented<br>Likes tested routines | Uncomfortable with routines<br>Ad hoc approach<br>Likes diversity |
| **Enthusiastic** | **Quiet** | **Traditional** | **Original** | **Tough** | **Tender** | **Methodical** | **Emergent** |
| Flirtatious<br>Amusing<br>Gregarious | Unexcitable<br>Patient<br>Quiet | Conformist<br>Likes tried methods<br>Moderate | Unconventional<br>Imaginative<br>Idea oriented | (None) | Hesitant | Orderly<br>Organized<br>Perfectionist | Procrastinates<br>Forgetful<br>Careless |

*Source:* Descriptions by others adapted from Harker and Reynierse, 1999. Used with permission.

same as the scale name (e.g., *concrete* was the best descriptor for the Concrete pole and *abstract* for the Abstract pole). In other cases, the significant descriptors are descriptors of the poles (*good mixer* and *social facilitator* for the Initiating pole). In rare cases, the adjectives seem not to match the meaning of the pole (for examples, see Realistic and Reasonable). Perhaps there were few descriptors available that captured the intent of the poles. Or the preferences manifested by these poles may not be apparent to outside observers as are some of the behaviors associated with other poles.

The authors of the questionnaire conclude: "It is apparent that many of the EAR subscales have unique descriptive capabilities for differentiating particular people. At the same time, they represent a range of effectiveness in which some subscales are clearly better predictors and contribute more than the others" (Harker & Reynierse, 1999, p. 14). Obviously, the range will depend to some degree on the sample of both individuals and raters and the available descriptors.

Reynierse and Harker (1999) used the same sample, questionnaire, raters, and analysis to examine ratings by independent observers for those with "extreme" scores on the subscales, defined as scores of 0, 1 or 9, 10. They also limited the descriptors tested to those 160 (out of 276 on the entire questionnaire) that approximated the titles of the scales or the text used to describe the scales as they appeared in the original EAR manual (Saunders, 1989). The names of the subscales used as descriptors were slightly more accurate, and the text definitions from the manual slightly less so, than they were in the study that used people with the entire range of scores.

According to the authors of this study, "Although the intended meanings for many subscales were confirmed, the extent to which subscales matched their EAR Manual definitions varied widely" (Reynierse & Harker, 1999, p. 20). For the purpose of establishing the validity of the scales, confirming their meaning through independent observers is more important than corroborating every adjective used in the original EAR manual, especially as the manual preceded extensive experience with the scales and interpretive material was subsequently published (Kummerow & Quenk, 1992a). According to Reynierse and Harker, their results cast doubt on the importance of interpreting out-of-pattern scales (now called *out-of-preference scores*), although it is difficult to see how this is so since they did not test this hypothesis. They note some overlap in the descriptors for subscales within any preference and conclude that "Clearly, each preference has primacy over individual subscales" (1999, p. 26). The observation is to be expected, and the conclusion is consistent with the suggested interpretation of Step II facet scales.

Van Velsor and Fleenor (1997) also report on the relationship between self-ratings and other ratings and the modified Step II facet scales. The rating instrument reported in this study was *Benchmarks*®, a feedback instrument that solicits ratings from self, subordinates, superiors, and peers on 22 managerial scales. These scales are divided into two sections: Managerial Skills and Perspectives (16 scales, 106 items) and Potential Flaws (6 scales, 26 items). The *Benchmarks* ratings were correlated with the modified original Step II facet scales in a sample of 1,134 CCL participants. The significant relationships between self- and superior ratings and the Step II facet scales are shown in table 8.7.

For self-ratings, Doing Whatever It Takes and Decisiveness were positively related to Initiating and Expressive. Being a Quick Study was related to Conceptual, and Difficulty Confronting Problem Employees with Casual. Building/Mending Relationships was positively related to Expressive, and Compassion/Sensitivity was correlated positively with Expressive, Accepting, Tender, Empathetic, and Compassionate. Putting People at Ease was positively related to Gregarious, Initiating, Expressive, Accepting, Tender, Empathetic, and Compassionate. Acting with Flexibility correlated positively with Expressive, and Lack of Follow-through was positively correlated with Pressure-Prompted, Open-Ended, and Emergent.

For superior ratings, using $N > .20$, Compassion/Sensitivity was positively related to Accepting, with Putting People at Ease positively related to Expressive, Accepting, and Empathetic. A number of TDI Comfort–Discomfort scales were also correlated with self- and superior ratings. None of the Step II facet scales correlated at above .20 with ratings from peers or subordinates. According to Van Velsor and Fleenor (1997), reviews of studies "do show evidence of the added value of the TDI subscales in the study of leadership skills" (p. 157).

Fleenor and Van Velsor (1995) also examined the relationship between the modified original Step II facet scales and ratings by independent observers of trainee participation ($N = 225$) in two group exercises, one of which was competitive and the other cooperative in nature. The authors report that most behavioral assessment ratings tend to have low correlations with self-report instruments and the Step II facet scales were no exception. Nevertheless, several of the scales did correlate at > .20 with observer ratings. In the competitive exercise, Activity Level, Led Discussion, and Task Orientation were positively related to Initiating and Expressive, while Problem Analysis and Verbal Effectiveness were also positively correlated with the Expressive pole. None of the Step II facet scales correlated at > .20 with observer ratings in the cooperative exercise.

Johnson and Golden (1994) studied the relationship between the 27 TDI scales and the *Survey of Management Practices* (SMP; Clark Wilson Group). The SMP is a 360-degree feedback instrument with scales measuring organizational skills and climate variables. A total of 208 managers from companies in the health care, grocery distribution, construction engineering, and pharmaceutical industries completed the TDI. These managers were rated on the SMP by 1,766 supervisors, subordinates, and peers, whose ratings were combined and correlated with TDI scales. Ten Step II facet scales (and one TDI Comfort–Discomfort scale) showed significant patterns of correlations with SMP scales, ranging from .05 to .22: Enthusiastic–Quiet, Initiating–Receiving, Expressive–Contained, Concrete–Abstract, Realistic–

**Table 8.7 Correlations of Step II™ Facet Scales with Self- and Superior Ratings from *Benchmarks*®**

| Step II™ Facet Scale* | Self-Ratings** | Superior Ratings |
|---|---|---|
| **Initiating**–Receiving | Doing whatever it takes<br>Decisiveness<br>Putting people at ease | |
| **Expressive**–Contained | Doing whatever it takes<br>Decisiveness<br>Putting people at ease<br>Building and mending relationships<br>Compassion and sensitivity<br>Acting with flexibility | Decisiveness (–.15)<br>Putting people at ease (–.22)<br>Doing whatever it takes (–.18)<br>Difficulty confronting problem employees (–.17) |
| **Gregarious**–Intimate | | Putting people at ease (–.16) |
| Practical–**Conceptual** | Being a quick study | Being a quick study (.19) |
| Logical–**Empathetic** | Compassion and sensitivity<br>Putting people at ease | Compassion and sensitivity (.18))<br>Putting people at ease (.20) |
| Reasonable–**Compassionate** | Compassion and sensitivity<br>Putting people at ease | Compassion and sensitivity (.17)<br>Putting people at ease (.18) |
| Critical–**Accepting** | Compassion and sensitivity<br>Putting people at ease | Compassion and sensitivity (.21)<br>Putting people at ease (.22)<br>Building and mending relationships (.16) |
| Tough–**Tender** | Compassion and sensitivity<br>Putting people at ease | Compassion and sensitivity (.17)<br>Putting people at ease (.16) |
| Systematic–**Casual** | Difficulty confronting problem employees | |
| Planful–**Open-Ended** | Lack of follow-through | |
| Early Starting–**Pressure-Prompted** | Lack of follow-through | |
| Methodical–**Emergent** | Lack of follow-through | |

*Pole correlated shown in bold.

**Coefficients not provided.

*Source:* Adapted from Van Velsor and Fleenor, 1997. Used with permission.

Imaginative, Critical–Accepting, Tough–Tender, Questioning–Accommodating, Logical–Empathetic, and Methodical–Emergent. The significant correlations, although they appear low, are in the range typically obtained from composite ratings by others. Step II facet scales from all four MBTI dichotomies were represented, but in no instance were *all* five scales within a dichotomy significantly correlated to any SMP scale, which suggests that the characteristics represented by Step II facet scales make an important contribution to understanding management behavior. Those correlations of $r > .15$ are shown in table 8.8.

## Additional Variance Explained by the Step II™ Facet Scales

The survey administered to the national sample contained 33 questions designed to elicit self-descriptions of attitudes and behaviors in the domains of work, health, stress and coping, relationships, and values. To determine whether the Step II facet scales add to our understanding of these variables, a series of hierarchical regressions were

**Table 8.8 Correlations of Step II™ Facet Scales with Composite Ratings of Others from *Survey of Management Practices* (SMP)**

| Step II™ Facet Scale | SMP Scale | Step II™ Pole |
|---|---|---|
| Initiating–Receiving | Upward communication (–.18) | Initiating |
| | Feedback (–.16) | Initiating |
| | Recognizing good performance (–.21) | Initiating |
| | Team building (–.17) | Initiating |
| | Interest in growth of subordinates (–.20) | Initiating |
| Logical–Empathetic | Upward communication (.16) | Empathetic |
| | Goal pressure (–.21) | Logical |
| | Delegation (permissiveness) (.16) | Empathetic |
| | Approachability (.19) | Empathetic |
| | Team building (.16) | Empathetic |
| Questioning–Accommodating | Goal pressure (–.19) | Questioning |
| Critical–Accepting | Upward communication (.16) | Accepting |
| | Goal pressure (–.17) | Critical |
| | Recognizing good performance (.15) | Accepting |
| | Approachability (.15) | Accepting |
| | Team building (.15) | Accepting |
| | Interest in growth of subordinates (.17) | Accepting |
| Tough–Tender | Goal pressure (–.22) | Tough |
| | Approachability (.16) | Tender |

*Source:* Adapted from Van Velsor and Fleenor, 1997. Used with permission.

performed, with the survey questions as the dependent variables.

As the first step in the analysis, the four Step I preference clarity index (pci) scores were entered as the independent variables. In the second step, the scores of the twenty Step II facet scales were entered. The $R^2$, which is the variance in the dependent variable that can be attributed to the set of independent variables, was then compared across the two steps. Since the second regression equation contains both Step I and Step II scores, this analysis allows an examination of how much *additional* variance is explained by the facet scales, holding constant the variance explained by the Step I scales. We know from table 6.5, on page 104, that the correlations between facet scales and their associated preference scales range from .292 to .898. This raises the question of how much *additional* explanatory power resides in the Step II facet scales. The hierarchical regression analysis can help answer this question.

The facet scales contributed additional explained variance for all the dependent variables tested. Relevant statistics for only those variables showing significant $R^2$ change are presented in table 8.9. For example, in predicting whether people would like to work in an organization that has clear structures for assigning responsibility, we see in the $R^2$ column that the four dichotomies account for about 6% of the variance in this variable. When scores from the twenty facet scales are added to the regression equation, the amount of variance accounted for increases by about 10%, a difference significant at $p < .001$. For those who are unfamiliar with interpreting $R^2$, these magnitudes may appear fairly small. However, as Cohen points out, a variable (or in this case, a set of variables) that accounts for 9% of the variance in a dependent variable is said to have a medium-effect size (Cohen 1988; Cohen & Cohen, 1983). He observes that, in the behavioral sciences, $R^2$ is rarely larger than .25, which is defined as a large-effect size. The combination of Step I scales and Step II facet scales accounted for a variance in this particular variable of 16%, about midway between medium- and large-effect size.

Table 8.9 clearly shows that, overall, the Step II facet scales increase the amount of variance explained in a dependent variable over and above that explained by the four Step I preferences. This conclusion raises another question: How can the individual scales within a facet block aid in understanding the dependent variables? The answer is not as simple as examining the regression coefficients of each of the facet scales in the regression analyses described above. The correlations among facet scales within preference blocks create a condition among the independent variables called *multicollinearity*

**Table 8.9 Contribution of Step I™ Scales and Step II™ Facet Scales to the Prediction of Various Dependent Variables**

| Dependent Variable | Independent Variables in Equation | R | $R^2$ | $R^2$ Change | Sig. of Change |
|---|---|---|---|---|---|
| *Preferred Organizational Environment* | | | | | |
| Clear structures | 4 dichotomies | .235 | .055 | | |
| | 4 dichotomies + 20 facets | .397 | .158 | .103 | .000 |
| Everyone must toe the line | 4 dichotomies | .164 | .027 | | |
| | 4 dichotomies + 20 facets | .366 | .134 | .107 | .000 |
| Variety of tasks | 4 dichotomies | .119 | .014 | | |
| | 4 dichotomies + 20 facets | .318 | .101 | .087 | .006 |
| Part of a team | 4 dichotomies | .225 | .051 | | |
| | 4 dichotomies + 20 facets | .354 | .125 | .075 | .022 |
| *Organizational Behaviors* | | | | | |
| Punctuality | 4 dichotomies | .165 | .027 | | |
| | 4 dichotomies + 20 facets | .399 | .160 | .132 | .000 |
| Finish the job | 4 dichotomies | .187 | .035 | | |
| | 4 dichotomies + 20 facets | .344 | .118 | .083 | .014 |
| Self-control at work | 4 dichotomies | .157 | .025 | | |
| | 4 dichotomies + 20 facets | .315 | .099 | .074 | .044 |
| *Health* | | | | | |
| Smoking | 4 dichotomies | .083 | .007 | | |
| | 4 dichotomies + 20 facets | .321 | .103 | .096 | .002 |
| Hypertension | 4 dichotomies | .089 | .008 | | |
| | 4 dichotomies + 20 facets | .302 | .091 | .084 | .012 |
| Heart problems | 4 dichotomies | .123 | .015 | | |
| | 4 dichotomies + 20 facets | .310 | .096 | .081 | .016 |
| *Coping with Stress* | | | | | |
| Upset/angry and show it | 4 dichotomies | .125 | .016 | | |
| | 4 dichotomies + 20 facets | .355 | .126 | .110 | .000 |
| Optimism | 4 dichotomies | .252 | .064 | | |
| | 4 dichotomies + 20 facets | .396 | .157 | .093 | .001 |
| Talk to someone close | 4 dichotomies | .223 | .050 | | |
| | 4 dichotomies + 20 facets | .349 | .122 | .072 | .024 |
| Avoid stressful situations | 4 dichotomies | .185 | .034 | | |
| | 4 dichotomies + 20 facets | .321 | .103 | .069 | .043 |
| Rely on religious beliefs | 4 dichotomies | .244 | .060 | | |
| | 4 dichotomies + 20 facets | .356 | .127 | .067 | .043 |

*Source:* National sample.

*continues*

**Table 8.9 Contribution of Step I™ Scales and Step II™ Facet Scales to the Prediction of Various Dependent Variables** *continued*

| Dependent Variable | Independent Variables in Equation | R | $R^2$ | $R^2$ Change | Sig. of Change |
|---|---|---|---|---|---|
| *Values* | | | | | |
| Religion/spirituality | 4 dichotomies | .281 | .079 | | |
| | 4 dichotomies + 20 facets | .467 | .218 | .140 | .000 |
| Intellectual stimulation | 4 dichotomies | .413 | .171 | | |
| | 4 dichotomies + 20 facets | .511 | .261 | .090 | .000 |
| Power | 4 dichotomies | .251 | .063 | | |
| | 4 dichotomies + 20 facets | .444 | .197 | .134 | .000 |
| Prestige/status | 4 dichotomies | .247 | .061 | | |
| | 4 dichotomies + 20 facets | .422 | .178 | .117 | .000 |
| Excitement | 4 dichotomies | .221 | .049 | | |
| | 4 dichotomies + 20 facets | .439 | .193 | .144 | .000 |
| Education/learning | 4 dichotomies | .257 | .066 | | |
| | 4 dichotomies + 20 facets | .382 | .146 | .079 | .009 |
| Health | 4 dichotomies | .221 | .049 | | |
| | 4 dichotomies + 20 facets | .351 | .123 | .074 | .022 |
| Recreation | 4 dichotomies | .162 | .026 | | |
| | 4 dichotomies + 20 facets | .320 | .102 | .076 | .023 |
| Achievement/accomplishment | 4 dichotomies | .247 | .061 | | |
| | 4 dichotomies + 20 facets | .361 | .130 | .070 | .035 |
| Relationships/friendships | 4 dichotomies | .402 | .161 | | |
| | 4 dichotomies + 20 facets | .471 | .222 | .061 | .043 |

(Cohen & Cohen, 1983), and this makes simple interpretation of the regression coefficients problematic.

Furthermore, the purpose of this discussion is not to establish prediction equations for specific dependent variables but rather to examine the differential meaning and usefulness of the facet scales, which calls for a different analysis. This analysis is based on another question from the national survey, which inquired about degrees of satisfaction with different aspects of work. Respondents were offered a four-point response scale from "very satisfied" to "very dissatisfied." Because the distribution of responses was so skewed toward satisfaction, the two satisfaction categories were collapsed, as were the two dissatisfaction categories. The two combined categories were then used as independent variables in an analysis of variance (ANOVA), a type of statistical analysis.

The contributions of these analyses are twofold. They are relevant to the question raised here about the differential utility of Step II facet scales compared to the overall preference scales, and, since they deal with job satisfaction, they are also pertinent to the discussion in chapter 9 involving the use of the Step II facets in career counseling. (Results for the Step II facet scales discussed below are therefore found in table 9.1, on p. 161.) For the purpose of comparing Step I preference scales to Step II facet scales, the significance criterion for the Step I scales was set at .05, while for the Step II scales it was .01. These criteria were determined by the number of scales in each set and by the desire to examine overall patterns rather than test specific hypotheses.

For some of the job satisfaction questions, the results were significant for both the Step I preference scale *and* all five facet scales within that preference block. For example, for satisfaction with job security, the overall E–I preference was significant ($p < .001$), with Extraverts being more satisfied, and all five of the E–I facet scales were also significant (all $p < .01$), with those scoring toward the Extraverted poles being more satisfied. Likewise, for the question on satisfaction with coworkers, there were significant differences for the overall E–I preference ($p < .001$) and the T–F preference ($p < .001$), with the satisfied group having mean scores toward Extraversion and Feeling. Furthermore, four of the five E–I facet scales and all five of the T–F facet scales showed the same pattern as the overall preferences. Only Enthusiastic–Quiet did not fit the pattern, reaching significance at $p < .02$.

For other aspects of work satisfaction, however, Step I results were different from Step II results. With some variables, the Step I preference was significant, but only selected Step II scales showed significant differences between those who were satisfied and those who were not. For example, when asked about satisfaction with day-to-day tasks, the differences between the satisfied and dissatisfied were significant for three of the Step I preferences. For the E–I preference, the mean of the group satisfied with day-to-day tasks was toward Extraversion ($p < .04$). Of the E–I facet scales, however, only the Expressive–Contained scale showed significant differences ($p < .005$). Both groups had means toward Sensing in the S–N preference, reflecting the distribution of types in the national sample, but those who were satisfied with day-to-day tasks had a mean score significantly more toward Sensing ($p < .04$). For the S–N facet scales, only Traditional–Original showed a significant difference ($p < .006$) toward the Sensing pole, or Traditional. There was also a significant difference for the J–P preference ($p < .03$), with the dissatisfied group having a mean score toward Perceiving and the satisfied group a mean score toward Judging. Of the J–P facet scales, only Scheduled–Spontaneous showed a significant difference ($p < .005$); both the satisfied and dissatisfied groups had mean scores toward Judging, but those who were satisfied with day-to-day tasks scored significantly closer to the Judging pole.

Another kind of difference between the two sets of scales was also observed. In some instances, the Step I preference scale was not significant, but one or more of the facets within the block were. For example, respondents were asked to gauge their satisfaction with the amount of responsibility they had at work. There were no significant differences between the satisfied and dissatisfied groups for any of the four Step I preferences. However, there were significant differences for the facets of Traditional–Original and Questioning–Accommodating in the direction of the Traditional and Accommodating poles.

The analyses reported in this section confirm that Step II facet scales furnish additional explanatory power beyond that of Step I preference scales. Regression analysis showed that the twenty facet scales as a set contribute significant additional variance to the explanation of 25 separate variables across five different life domains—organizational environment, organizational behavior, coping, health, and values. The analysis of variance demonstrated that individual facet scales supply meaningful information about differences between people who were satisfied or dissatisfied with eleven different aspects of their work. These results augmented information elicited by the Step I scales. In some cases, when a Step I preference showed a significant difference on a work aspect, four or five of the facet scales within that preference block also showed the same pattern of significance. In other cases, only one or two facet scales showed significant differences. For other aspects of work, the Step I preference did not reveal a significant difference, while one or two facet scales within that preference block did show significant differences.

The fact that Step II scales, both as a whole set and individually, add to the understanding of this broad set of variables illustrates their potential usefulness in a wide variety of settings. In addition, individual facet scales within a preference block provide unique information that is not captured by the Step I preference, demonstrating that the facet scales are performing their function and contributing to the understanding of individual differences within type.

The studies reported above in this section compared the differential contributions of Step I and Step II scales. Research studies have also been conducted with the Step II scales alone that suggest their relevance for use in particular applications.

## Studies Providing Evidence for Applications of Step II™ Results

A number of questions submitted to participants in the national sample permitted analyses that provide evidence for how Step II results may be used. These included questions about attitudes toward features of the organizational environment and aspects of work satisfaction. Additional studies using the original scales were available in the literature on topics such as management and leadership, coping, learning, and couples satisfaction.

### Attitudes Toward Organizational Environment Features

Participants in the national sample were presented with eleven features of organizations and asked to indicate whether they would "like," "dislike," or be "indifferent" to each one. The correlations are presented in table 8.10. Because the response scale for these questions consisted of only three options, the correlations are probably smaller than those that would have been obtained with a broader response scale. For this reason, correlations of $\geq .15$ are considered meaningful.

Within the E–I facet block, Expressive, Gregarious, and Active are related to enjoyment of teamwork. Those with scores toward Initiating, Expressive, and Enthusiastic like to work in organizations that employ people from different backgrounds, and Enthusiastic is related to liking a variety of tasks.

The scales in the S–N block are related to many of the organizational variables. The S poles of all the S–N facet scales are related to liking an organization that offers employee loyalty, provides lifetime job security, does everything "by the book,"

## Table 8.10 Correlations of Step II™ Facet Scales with Attitudes Toward Organizational Environments

| | Attitudes Toward Organizational Environments | | | | | | | | | | |
|---|---|---|---|---|---|---|---|---|---|---|---|
| Step II™ Facet Scale | Clear structures and respon-sibilities | Indepen-dence and individual achievement | Employee loyalty and lifetime job security | Everything done by the book | Teamwork | Opportuni-ties to work in other countries | Simplify jobs | Employees from different backgrounds | Variety of tasks | Everyone must toe the line | Advance-ment and high pay, but less job security |
| *E–I Facet Scales* | | | | | | | | | | | |
| Initiating–Receiving | .08 | .02 | .01 | .02 | –.10 | –.09 | .06 | **–.15** | –.06 | .04 | –.03 |
| Expressive–Contained | .06 | –.02 | .03 | .05 | **–.13** | –.02 | .09 | **–.16** | –.03 | .03 | .07 |
| Gregarious–Intimate | .00 | .02 | –.05 | –.02 | **–.17** | .05 | –.06 | –.02 | –.01 | –.05 | –.02 |
| Active–Reflective | –.02 | .06 | –.06 | –.05 | **–.19** | –.02 | –.01 | –.06 | –.04 | –.03 | –.02 |
| Enthusiastic–Quiet | –.01 | –.02 | .00 | .00 | –.10 | –.08 | .05 | **–.15** | **–.16** | –.07 | .00 |
| *S–N Facet Scales* | | | | | | | | | | | |
| Concrete–Abstract | –.14 | .09 | **–.19** | **–.24** | –.05 | **.21** | **–.25** | .14 | .13 | –.14 | .08 |
| Realistic–Imaginative | –.09 | .08 | **–.16** | **–.25** | –.13 | **.22** | **–.24** | .12 | .12 | –.12 | .02 |
| Practical–Conceptual | –.07 | .06 | **–.16** | **–.15** | –.09 | **.24** | **–.20** | .09 | .04 | –.10 | .07 |
| Experiential–Theoretical | –.12 | .09 | **–.20** | **–.24** | –.05 | **.21** | **–.22** | .11 | .07 | **–.17** | .08 |
| Traditional–Original | **–.19** | .12 | **–.20** | **–.24** | –.14 | **.21** | **–.24** | .09 | .09 | **–.15** | **.16** |
| *T–F Facet Scales* | | | | | | | | | | | |
| Logical–Empathetic | .10 | –.08 | .09 | –.02 | .08 | –.06 | .09 | .13 | .03 | .06 | **–.23** |
| Reasonable–Compassionate | .12 | –.10 | .11 | .02 | .13 | –.11 | .14 | .13 | –.04 | .01 | **–.29** |
| Questioning–Accommodating | .06 | –.07 | .09 | .14 | **.15** | **–.16** | **.16** | .04 | –.12 | .04 | **–.16** |
| Critical–Accepting | .03 | –.04 | .00 | .00 | .09 | –.04 | .08 | .10 | –.03 | –.02 | –.11 |
| Tough–Tender | .12 | –.08 | .06 | –.05 | .10 | –.12 | .10 | .09 | –.07 | –.08 | **–.20** |
| *J–P Facet Scales* | | | | | | | | | | | |
| Systematic–Casual | **–.17** | –.02 | –.01 | –.12 | –.06 | –.04 | –.03 | .02 | .03 | –.09 | –.07 |
| Planful–Open-Ended | –.08 | –.06 | .01 | –.05 | –.09 | .03 | .01 | –.06 | .02 | –.08 | .06 |
| Early Starting–Pressure-Prompted | **–.17** | .02 | –.10 | –.11 | –.13 | .08 | –.13 | –.07 | .02 | –.03 | .13 |
| Scheduled–Spontaneous | **–.18** | .00 | –.02 | –.12 | **–.15** | .00 | –.05 | –.10 | .02 | –.14 | .05 |
| Methodical–Emergent | –.07 | –.06 | –.01 | –.11 | –.07 | –.03 | .00 | –.08 | .04 | –.12 | .06 |

*Note:* Bold indicates correlations at ≥.15.

*Source:* National sample.

and simplifies jobs. The N poles of all the S–N facet scales are associated with liking opportunities to work in other countries. In addition to the above, those with scores toward Traditional appreciate clear structures and responsibilities and an environment in which everyone follows the rules (shared by those with scores toward Experiential), while their opposites at the Original pole prefer, in addition to the characteristics discussed above, opportunities for advancement and high pay, even when job security is limited.

Within the T–F facets—with the exception of Critical–Accepting, which is in the same direction but did not reach the cutoff—all the T poles are related to liking advancement and high pay, even at the expense of job security. In addition, those scoring toward Questioning like opportunities to work in other countries, and their opposites at the Accommodating pole prefer teamwork and simplification of jobs.

In the J–P block, Systematic–Casual, Early Starting–Pressure-Prompted, and Scheduled–Spontaneous are related to liking clear structures and responsibilities, all in the direction of the J poles of these scales. Those scoring toward Scheduled like to work as part of a team. Overall, the direction of the correlations reported above supports the validity of the facet scales.

## Work Satisfaction

Participants in the national sample were also asked to rate various aspects of work satisfaction using a four-point scale that ranged from "very satisfied" to "very dissatisfied." Correlations with Step II facet scales showed that scores on the Initiating–Receiving scale were related, in the direction of Initiating, to the following aspects of job satisfaction at $r \geq .15$: job stability, security, opportunities for learning, opportunities to contribute to society, type of work, day-to-day tasks, coworkers, and future work opportunities.

All the E–I scales correlated with satisfaction with job stability in the direction of the E pole. In addition, Gregarious was related to satisfaction with job security, opportunities for learning, and coworkers; Enthusiastic was related to satisfaction with supervisors and employers. Scores toward Theoretical were related to satisfaction with future work opportunities. People scoring toward Compassionate and Accepting were satisfied with coworkers. Scores toward Scheduled were associated with satisfaction with salary.

Researchers on job satisfaction and the dichotomous preferences (Myers et al., 1998) found a relationship between Extraversion and Judging and global measures of work satisfaction. Analysis of the facet scales suggests that the relationship with Extraversion may be attributable primarily to the Initiating–Receiving facet, which is the one most highly correlated with the E–I preference dichotomy. This analysis did not replicate the finding on Judging and job satisfaction at the level of the facet scales. Perhaps job satisfaction is a complex phenomenon that is a function of type dynamics (e.g., most people who report being very satisfied with various aspects of their jobs are Extraverted Judging types) and not an isolated function of individual facet scales.

## Leadership and Management

Johnson (1992b) compared those who had been promoted to division-level managers in the wholesale grocery industry to fellow employees who had not been promoted. The findings were also cross-validated by comparing the top achievers to a control group in a competing firm. In both analyses, the results for the two groups of managers were almost identical, showing that 64% of the managers were identified as top achievers. The top achievers had higher mean scores on all five S–N scales compared to others from the same company and from the competing company. In addition, the top achievers scored significantly higher on Questioning and Spontaneous and also had significantly higher polarity indexes, indicating greater clarity of preferences across the Step II facet scales. The cross-validation study replicated the above results and also revealed higher scores on Reasonable for the top achievers.

In these analyses, the results regarding the S–N scales do not add significantly to data that could have been obtained with the Step I instrument. However, results for the Questioning–Accommodating scale from the T–F dichotomy and the Scheduled–Spontaneous scale from the J–P dichotomy demonstrate the unique contribution of the Step II facet scales. The finding that higher scores on Spontaneous are related to high achievement is particularly interesting, given that 73% of the achievers demonstrated an overall preference for Judging. Johnson cites other literature that supports the finding that top achievers are more spontaneous. He speculates that those who score toward the Spontaneous pole on this Step II scale may become dissatisfied with routine jobs and are thus motivated to seek new assignments and promotion.

## Coping

Hammer (1993) investigated the contribution of the original Step II facet scales to prediction of coping resources in a sample of 225 chronic pain patients. The measure used was the *Coping Resources Inventory* (CRI; Hammer & Marting, 1988), a 60-item instrument comprising five scales (cognitive, emotional, social, spiritual/philosophical, and physical) designed to measure a person's resources for handling stress. The CRI scales have proved to be significant predictors of physical and psychological symptoms for adolescents (Zeidner & Hammer, 1990), of reactions to the highly stressful situations of war (Zeidner & Hammer, 1992), and of responses to unemployment (Wanberg, 1992). For this study, however, only the CRI total resource score was used as the dependent variable in a regression analysis.

In the sample of chronic pain patients, six of the original Step II facet scales were significant in predicting total resources, as evidenced by beta weights with significance levels at $p < .01$. The signs of the coefficients indicated that the following poles were associated with higher resources: Initiating, Expressive, Active, Realistic, Accepting, and Systematic. All four preference domains are represented by these six Step II facet scales.

The results for the three E–I scales suggest that people who initiate social contact, express their thoughts and feelings, and participate in group activities tend to have more resources than those at the opposite poles of these scales. Interestingly, previous research has demonstrated that Extraverts in general are inclined to greater coping resources than are Introverts (Hammer, 1991), but the results for the Step II facet scales reveal that not all the Extraversion facet poles are equally useful. Scores toward Gregarious and Enthusiastic do not seem to contribute to greater resources.

Within the S–N dichotomy, scores toward Realistic suggest that people who pride themselves on their common sense (Kummerow & Quenk, 1992a) tend to have greater resources. This, along with their efficiency and practicality, may help them cope more successfully than people who do not have these characteristics.

Within the Thinking–Feeling dichotomy, the tolerance of those who score toward Accepting, and their tendency to look for win-win solutions to problems, may be why they have higher resources. And among the Judging–Perceiving facet scales, those who score toward Systematic have higher resources, perhaps because they use structure and planning to avoid stress in the first place.

A hierarchical regression was then run to determine the unique contribution of the Step II facet scales: first, the four Step I scales were entered as independent variables, then the twenty Step II facet scales were added, and finally, subsequent changes in $R^2$ were noted. The Step I scales accounted for 34% of the variance in coping resources, while the Step I scales and Step II facet scales together accounted for 41% of the variance. Thus, the Step II facet scales represent a significant increase in explained variance—in other words, they provide more information for the purpose of predicting coping resources than do the four Step I scales alone.

Holland and VanBenshoten (1991) also investigated the relationship of the original Step II facet scales to coping, using two tools—the *COPE Inventory* and the *Ways of Coping*—with 202 people in a wide variety of settings.

The COPE instrument was used as a measure of dispositional coping. The four Step I scales accounted for 46% of the variance in the COPE scores; adding the Step II facet scales raised this figure to 92%.

Four Step II facet scales, one from each of the four dichotomies, proved to be significant predictors: Expressive–Contained, Traditional–Original, Logical–Empathetic, and Systematic–Casual. The Expressive pole was related to Emotional and Instrumental Social Support, Venting, and Interpretation; the Contained pole was associated with higher scores on Mental Disengagement. The Traditional pole correlated with Denial, Mental Disengagement, Behavioral Disengagement, and Use of Alcohol, while the Original pole was related to Active Coping, Planning, and Interpretation. The Logical pole was associated with Planning, while the Empathetic pole correlated with Emotional and Instrumental Social Support, Venting, and Interpretation. The Systematic pole was associated with Active Coping, Planning, Suppression, and Mental Disengagement, with Casual related to Use of Alcohol.

The *Ways of Coping* instrument was designed to measure situational coping. With this instrument, the four Step I scales accounted for 43% of the variance, which increased to 87% with the addition of the Step II facet scales. The contributing Step II facet scales were not identified.

## Adult Success with Learning a Foreign Language

Ehrman (1994) used the TDI to study nearly 800 adults from the Foreign Service, U.S. Information Agency, Department of Defense, and other federal agencies who were undergoing intensive foreign language training. For the purposes of post-training analysis, students were grouped into three proficiency levels (high, medium, and low) for each of three outcome variables (speaking, reading, and faculty rankings). Those with high proficiency in speaking scored significantly higher on Questioning; students with a medium level of proficiency on speaking had higher mean scores on Accepting; low proficiency on speaking was related to high scores on Concrete, Realistic, and Practical. Students graded as having high proficiency on reading scored significantly higher on Critical, Tough, Questioning, and Logical. Those ranked lowest by the faculty had high scores on Realistic and Practical. No Step II facet scales differentiated students ranked high by the faculty.

Ehrman also reports more than 100 significant correlations of Step II facet scales with measures such as language aptitude, proficiency, anxiety, learning strategies, verbal risk, and a host of other variables. Although too numerous to report here, the overall pattern is compelling evidence for the differential relationship of Step II facet scales with other measures and for relationships that are distinct from those found for the four MBTI dichotomies.

Ehrman also found that a higher polarity index for the twenty Step II facet scales (i.e., scores more consistently toward the poles of the scales) was related to lower anxiety about training outcomes. She suggests that the pattern of correlations for the separate scales could aid language teachers in developing strategies and programs for individualizing training at different stages of learning.

## Attraction and Satisfaction of Couples

Marioles, Strickert, and Hammer (1996) studied the attraction and satisfaction of 426 marital and premarital couples using the 27 TDI scales. The *Dyadic Adjustment Scale* (DAS) was used as the measure of couple satisfaction. Although the authors used the DAS to construct various measures of agreement and difference between the partners, the only variable to yield significant results was the sum of each partner's score on the instrument.

The data were analyzed using canonical correlation analysis, which begins with two sets of variables, often from two different instruments. The procedure identifies two clusters of items (or scales), called *canonical variates,* from each of the two instruments, which maximizes the correlation between those variates. The canonical correlation is therefore computed between the two variates rather than between two single variables or scales.

For the sample of married couples, two EAR scales, Enthusiastic–Quiet and Expressive–Contained, loaded on the MBTI canonical variate. When combined with three scales from the TDI Comfort–Discomfort dimension that also loaded on this variate, all five scales accounted for 58% of the variance in the DAS canonical variate. Partners who scored toward Enthusiastic and Expressive were more likely to have greater combined satisfaction scores on the DAS. When samples for the marital and premarital couples were combined, the EAR scales Expressive–Contained, Questioning–Accommodating, and Planful–Open-Ended loaded on the canonical variate, along with two other scales from the TDI Comfort–Discomfort dimension, accounting for 44% of the variance in combined satisfaction.

The authors suggest that differences in the clustered variables in the two analyses seem to reflect variations in stages of relationship, with premarital couples more likely to take part in questioning, accommodating, and planning than were the married couples. These differences would not have been apparent with consideration of only the Step I type letter preferences of the couples.

## Use of the Step II™ Facet Scales to Test Type Theory

In all the studies described so far in this chapter, the Step II facet scales have been used either as variables in correlational analyses or as independent variables. In the latter type of study, differences in Step II facet scales are used to predict or explain the variance in another variable or set of variables. Mitchell (1991) reversed this procedure and used the TDI scales as dependent variables to test explicit hypotheses about type theory. Using type theory, the author identified three groups of types defined by the dominant and auxiliary forms of the four functions, attitudes in which the dominant and auxiliary forms of the functions are used, and attitudes in which functions are used among Extraverts and Introverts. He looked for mean differences on the TDI scales in each group, using gender as another grouping variable and controlling for age. Since we are concerned here with Step II facet scales, only those results are reported.

For the first group, the dominant and auxiliary forms of the four functions, he found measurable differences on at least one TDI scale between types having dominant and auxiliary forms of all four functions: males whose dominant function was Thinking (ISTP, INTP, ESTJ, ENTJ) scored more toward the Tough pole of Tough–Tender than did males for whom Thinking was auxiliary (ISTJ, INTJ, ESTP, ENTP); females whose dominant function was Intuition (INFJ, INTJ, ENFP, ENTP) scored more toward the Abstract pole of Concrete–Abstract and more toward the Enthusiastic pole of Enthusiastic–Quiet than did females with Intuition as their auxiliary function (INFP, INTP, ENFJ, ENTJ).

For the second analysis, in which grouping was by attitudes using dominant and auxiliary forms of the functions, he found significant differences for every function. For example, among males who are dominant Thinking types and females who are dominant Feeling types, the males who extravert their Thinking (ESTJ, ENTJ) and the females who extravert their Feeling (ESFJ, ENFJ) score more toward Questioning than do the males who introvert their dominant Thinking (ISTP, INTP) or the females who introvert their dominant Feeling (ISFP, INFP). In other words, extraverting a dominant judging function seems to be related to adopting a questioning stance when faced with differences of opinion.

The third analysis examined differences in how Extraverts and Introverts use the same function, that is, the types who introvert a function would appear more introverted in their use of it than those who extravert the same function. For this analysis, Mitchell found that predictions for the Thinking and Feeling functions were confirmed; however, for the Sensing and Intuition functions, three of the four significant findings were opposite to type predictions.

This was an important study, notable for both its novel approach to testing type theory and its significant confirmations of that theory. While these analyses were conducted to test specific hypotheses derived from type theory, rather than to provide evidence of the validity of the Step II facet scales, the results are also relevant to the purposes of this chapter. As stated throughout this manual, the Step II facet scales are to be interpreted within the context of the person's whole type. Mitchell's findings suggest that patterns of Step II facet scales may indeed reflect type dynamics and perhaps aid clients in clarifying their best-fit type.

Mitchell (1993) conducted a number of additional tests of type theory that also provide indirect evidence for the validity of the TDI scales. First, he compared a sample of 110 subjects with hypertension to a convenience control sample and found that when the two groups were compared on the basis of deviations from the norms for their own type, the hypertension patients differed from the control group on ten scales (unfortunately, the scales were not specified).

Second, he compared older and younger samples (with age 43 as the cutoff), using the same deviation scores, and found that they differed significantly on 20 of the 27 TDI scales.

Third, Mitchell tested for the existence of regression discontinuities by comparing opposite types on the TDI scales. He gives two examples of his findings for this analysis. For ISTJs and ENFPs, he found regression discontinuities on Concrete–Abstract, Logical–Empathetic, and Early Starting–Pressure-Prompted. For ISTPs and ENTJs, the discontinuities were on Enthusiastic–Quiet, Concrete–Abstract, Critical–Accepting, and Early Starting–Pressure-Prompted.

Fourth, using a balanced sample of $N = 110$ of each type, he compared upper and lower boundaries on the TDI scales for each of the 32 pairs of types that differed by only one preference—for example, ENFJs were compared to ENTJs. The boundaries were defined as above (or below) the scores of 95% of the people of that type. Boundaries for the two types were not considered different unless they varied by 2 or more scale points. Every pair of similar types except the INTJ/ENTJ pair exhibited differences on one or more facets belonging to their shared preferences. No comparisons were made on the scales of opposite preferences, since the types would obviously be different on those facets.

Although these studies were not conducted to address the validity of the Step II facet scales, and the details are therefore sketchy when utilized for that purpose, the findings do shed light on the usefulness of the scales in discriminating between people of different and similar types and between those with hypertension and a control group.

## Conclusion

The data presented in this chapter provide evidence in support of the validity of the twenty Step II facet scales. Confirmatory factor analysis showed that the relationship of the facets to the preference dichotomies is as predicted. Correlations of the facet scales with the scales of other instruments are consistent with the intended meaning of the scales. These correlations reveal two patterns consistent with the proposed uses of the facet scales. First, the overall pattern of correlations within a facet block with external variables is as expected. Second, there are differential findings for facet scales within the same dichotomy (i.e., correlations that are higher, lower, or opposite in sign from the other scales within that block) that support the uniqueness of the facets.

There were also five studies that showed meaningful correlations between the facet scales and behavioral descriptors. A number of studies also demonstrated the usefulness of the facet scales in understanding attitudes toward organizational environments, job satisfaction, leadership and management behaviors, coping, learning a foreign language, and understanding the satisfaction of couples. The practical implications of these studies are discussed in greater detail in the following chapters.

The facet scales were also shown to explain additional variance—that is, variance beyond that explained by the four Step I dichotomies—in variables that cover the domains of organizational behaviors, preferred organizational environments, health, coping, and values. Finally, the facet scales were used as dependent variables in a number of explicit tests of type theory whose results supported not only the theory but also the use of the facet scales in understanding individual differences within type.

PART

# Uses of the Step II™ Instrument

# IV

Applications for the Step I instrument are also appropriate for the Step II instrument, so there is a good deal of overlap between their basic philosophies and approaches. The two chapters in part IV therefore focus on issues specific to using the Step II tool, although always with the reminder that it must be solidly grounded within Step I understanding.

Chapter 9, "Using the Step II™ Instrument in a Counseling Environment," covers administration and interpretation issues relevant to individual, couples, and career counseling. Supporting research is provided in these areas.

Chapter 10, "Using the Step II™ Instrument in an Organizational Environment," gives recommendations for ensuring confidentiality and a beneficial mind-set, which encourage candid responses to the questionnaire. Facet scales are identified that are particularly important for communication, decision making, dealing with change, conflict management, team behavior, and leadership. The chapter includes relevant research on a number of organizational variables in these important areas.

# Using the Step II™ Instrument in a Counseling Environment

9

CHAPTER OVERVIEW



The Step II instrument can be used in any setting that is appropriate for the Step I instrument. In personal counseling and psychotherapy, it highlights the multifaceted nature of type constructs in a way that can be enlightening and affirming to individuals, couples, and career counseling clients. The goal of this chapter is to provide professionals with basic information relevant to using the Step II tool in these three areas of counseling. The information contained in the preceding chapters, especially chapter 5, provides the basis for these uses of the Step II tool. In addition, research relevant to each of these areas is included. Most of this research was based on data collected concurrently from members of the national sample that was used to create the Step II revision (see appendix B for a description of that sample).

## Using the Step II™ Instrument in Individual Counseling and Psychotherapy

Counselors and psychotherapists have an advantage over many other type practitioners because they tend to see clients for extended periods of time. They can thus more readily follow the recommendations in chapter 5 regarding the optimal time span between interpretations of Step I and Step II results. In addition, they are aided by the ongoing nature of their relationships with clients. Information from both tools can be used to advantage over the entire course of counseling and psychotherapy. Ideally, type should become integral to the counseling process. Applying the Step II tool with clients over time also provides an excellent opportunity to increase a professional's depth of knowledge and understanding of typology.

Given the reality of the limited number of sessions allowed for clients in many outpatient settings, however, the ideal does not always prevail. Counselors and psychotherapists who wish to introduce a client to type must decide whether adding the Step II assessment is the best use of the limited time available for a particular client. This will, of course, depend on presenting problems, client interest, whether Step II results might help clarify any doubts about Step I results, and other individual variables.

## Special Administration and Interpretation Issues

A counselor or psychotherapist who is not sure whether the Step II instrument will be helpful for a particular client might consider the following procedure:

- Administer Form Q rather than Form M.
- Use template scoring to assess the client's probable type.
- Interpret Step I results.
- Decide whether to interpret Step II results.
- Have Form Q computer scored to produce a profile or report.
- Interpret Step II results at an appropriate time during the course of therapy.

**Timing of Step II™ Interpretation** Unless there are serious constraints on the number of sessions available, it is usually a good idea to wait several sessions before introducing the *Myers-Briggs Type Indicator* (MBTI) personality inventory. The professional thus remains open to the client's distinctive presentation of himself or herself. Premature awareness of a client's type may increase the risk of interpreting his or her words and actions primarily through the filter of type. Important issues that are either peripheral to type or outside a type perspective may be overlooked.

**Using the Step II™ Tool with Seriously Disturbed Clients** Clinicians must use their judgment with regard to administering any psychological instrument to clients who suffer from the more severe psychological disorders, such as major depression, obsessive-compulsive disorder, borderline personality, and psychotic disorders. This caution is true for both the Step I and Step II instruments. However, using type with a seriously disturbed individual offers the advantage of addressing healthy aspects of the client's personality and functioning, which can be an effective way of validating the client, encouraging hope, and increasing motivation to deal with pressing psychological problems. Psychological type also provides a positive or neutral language in which to effectively discuss client problems and make difficulties appear more manageable and subject to modification (see Quenk, 2000a, for further discussion of these and similar issues in using the Step I instrument in clinical settings).

If interpreting Step II results is deemed appropriate for such clients, the usual verification and interpretation procedures can be used, bearing in mind that some clients may have difficulty verifying both their type and their facet placements. It is advisable to minimize the importance of precise verification in such cases and to focus instead on the reasons for administering the Step II assessment. If verification difficulties appear likely and may prove counterproductive, it is best not to interpret Step II results or even administer the Step I assessment. For example, clients with obsessive-compulsive disorder may react to the forced-choice format of the questions with distress when they are unable to make choices.

## Integrating the Step II™ Instrument into Counseling Settings

After deciding to proceed with a Step II interpretation, the therapist should follow standard verification and interpretation procedures. When Step II interpretation is complete, the profile or the report typically remains with the client. The therapist will want to keep the Interpreter's Summary (the last page of the profile and of the report) for easy reference. The Interpreter's Summary contains the client's Step I type, facet scale results, polarity index, average range of scores for the client's type, and information about omissions. When the therapist judges the results to be relevant, the client can be asked to bring the profile or report to subsequent sessions. The counselor can weave appropriate examples into the discussion, using information from the Step I instrument and previous therapy sessions to address presenting issues when possible. Client and therapist can then make helpful connections to relevant aspects of the client's personality functioning.

For example, James, a 35-year-old ENTP, sought help in dealing with the breakup of a year-long relationship. Apparently, one of the reasons for the breakup was his persistent dissatisfaction with the level of intimacy, which led his girlfriend to end the relationship. James wanted to share everything personal about himself, but his girlfriend was often distant and withholding. She accused him of being intrusive and clinging. He had never been in love before, and his previous relationships had been fairly superficial. He was having a very hard time accepting the breakup and believed there must be something wrong with him. Apart from this one relationship, he was not particularly interested in sharing his feelings and knowing about the feelings of others.

On the Step II assessment, James was out-of-preference in being Intimate on the E–I facet block and Tender on the T–F block. The therapist pointed out that Intimate Extraverts tend to place a very high value on sharing feelings in intimate relationships and can be quite dissatisfied when they are unable to do this. Further, Intimate Extraverts are sometimes seen by their partners as extremely intense and demanding of intimacy. James was quite sure his girlfriend was an Introvert. If she was in-preference on the Expressive–Contained facet (i.e., Contained), she might well react negatively to James' insistence that she share her deepest thoughts and feelings with him. James related his preference for the Tender pole of the Tough–Tender facet to his "embarrassing" tendency to back down on some of his decisions when another person's feelings were obviously hurt. He was asked to read the statements in his Step II report about Intimate Extraverts and Tender Thinking types. It reassured him to know that the facet patterns he showed were shared by others and were a normal expression of his personality. Therapy was then able to focus productively on James' reported difficulties with relationships and his previous desire to keep them brief and superficial.

Tammy, a nineteen-year-old college student, came to the school counseling center quite distressed because she felt she had made bad choices about her academic program. She was having trouble with friendships and intimate relationships and was so distracted that she was unable to plan her time effectively. She had tentatively verified her Step I type as ESFJ, with some doubts about her preferences on T–F and J–P. Her Step II results showed clear preferences for all the Extraverted poles of the E–I facets and all the Sensing poles of the S–N facets, a midzone pattern on T–F (no clear preferences), and clear preferences for Casual (out-of-preference), Planful (in-preference), Pressure-Prompted (out-of-preference), Scheduled (in-preference), and Methodical (in-preference) on J–P.

With this young woman, counseling focused on her process of making decisions and accomplishing tasks, with particular attention paid to whether her difficulties were habitual or of recent origin. She described her problems in these areas as noticeable in high school but currently more extreme. As Tammy discussed the T–F and J–P facets in detail with her counselor, she began to recognize that the pressures and tensions she experienced in these dichotomies were likely connected to a number of familial and educational influences. She had a strong need to please everyone around her and conform to their expectations.

It was easier and more productive to begin by discussing the Step II facets separately rather than address her underlying preferences for T or F and J or P. The narrower content of the facets stimulated relevant examples and enabled Tammy to identify her natural tendencies. Over the course of counseling, Tammy realized that her best-fit preference was for Perceiving rather than Judging, and that ESFP rather than ESFJ was therefore her natural type. She reread the type description for ESFP and realized that she had been ignoring some of her most important needs and sources of enjoyment. Her increasing comfort with herself allowed her to trust her own judgment and gave her new confidence in her ability to accomplish tasks in an enjoyable and effective way.

Therapists who are experienced with the Step II instrument will find many opportunities to refer to type and the facets during counseling and psychotherapy. The most effective way to use type knowledge is to have it available as an integral part of the therapy process. As type-relevant issues arise in the course of therapy, both client and therapist can make useful connections and explore avenues of development using the positive or neutral language of typology and the supporting details of the Step II facets.

## Research Relevant to Individual Counseling

Dealing with stress is an issue that often brings people to counseling. Participants in the national sample were asked to indicate their "typical level of stress" on a five-point scale ("very low," "low," "moderate," "high," and "very high"). The two high and the two low categories were combined and, along with "moderate," were subjected to an analysis of variance (ANOVA) on the twenty facet scales and a separate ANOVA on the four overall preference scales.

Analysis of the preferences showed that Introverts report significantly higher levels of stress ($p < 0.001$) than do Extraverts. However, from analysis of the facet scales, we see that, of the E–I scales, only Expressive–Contained and Gregarious–Intimate showed significant differences across the three stress categories. Furthermore, a facet scale from the T–F preference block, Critical–Accepting, also revealed significant differences. The results for these three facet scales are displayed in figure 9.1. In each case, there is an ordering from low to high stress along the facet scale. These results suggest that counselors should be alert for profiles exhibiting scores toward Contained and Intimate and toward the midzone on Critical, which may indicate clients who are experiencing high levels of stress. The findings show that Step II scales can be used to form hypotheses about which clients may be sensitive to stressors and which scales may be the focus of interventions.

Another hypothesis was that out-of-preference scores might be related to stress. Given the findings above, the following question was asked: Were Introverts who were out-of-preference on any of the E–I facet scales more likely to have higher levels of stress than Introverts whose

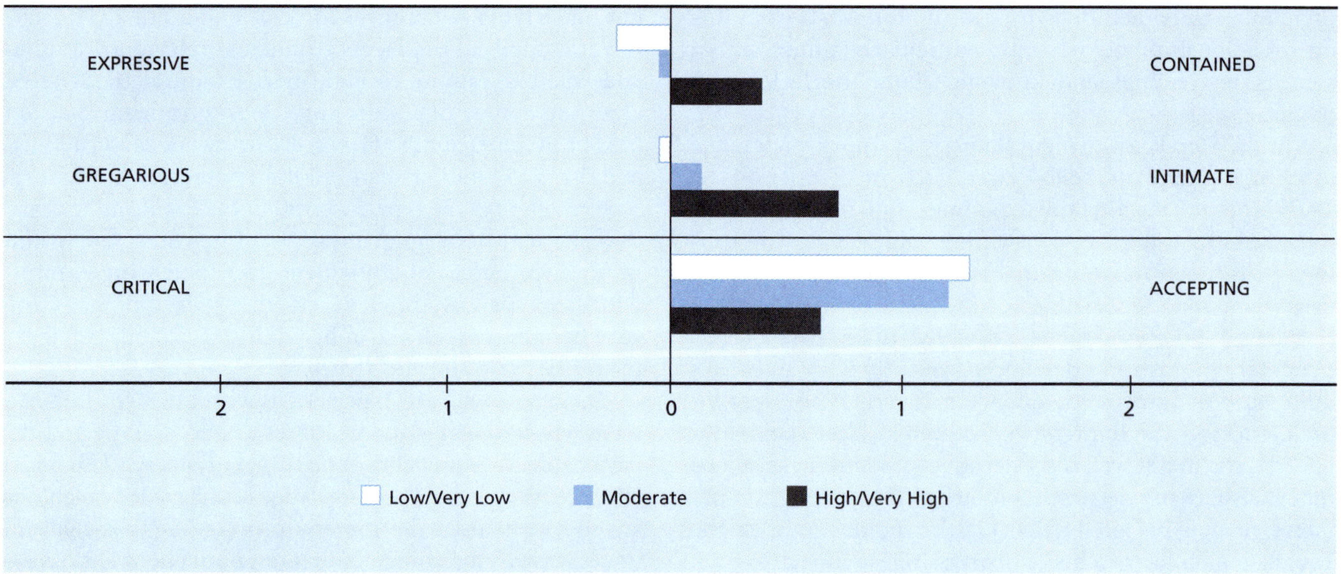


**Figure 9.1** Typical Level of Stress in Relation to Three Facet Scales
*Source:* National sample.

scores were in-preference? The answer was no. Regardless of whether the scores were in-preference or out-of-preference, a preference for Introversion was the determining factor. In performing this analysis, however, it appeared that being in-preference or out-of-preference on an E–I facet scale did make a difference for Extraverts. Quiet Extraverts had significantly lower levels of stress compared to those who were in-preference or in the midzone on the Enthusiastic–Quiet scale.

Physical problems also surface as issues in individual counseling, either as symptoms of stress or as topics in their own right. The national survey asked whether people had ever experienced hypertension, heart problems, insomnia, or chronic pain. Response options for the first two conditions were "yes" or "no"; responses for the latter two used a four-point scale of "never," "rarely," "occasionally," and "frequently." For the purposes of analysis, the first two and last two response categories were combined. ANOVAs were used to analyze the twenty facet scales, and $p < 0.01$ was used as the cutoff.

Of the national sample, 28% reported experiencing hypertension (the term was not defined on the survey). Compared to those who answered "no," these people had means toward Reflective ($p < 0.001$), Quiet ($p < 0.01$), and Realistic ($p < 0.01$).

Regarding heart problems, 15% of the national sample responded in the affirmative. All the S–N facet scales showed significant differences ($p < 0.01$), with those who experienced such problems scoring more toward the S pole of these scales. In addition, those reporting heart problems scored more toward Systematic and Early Starting (both $p < 0.01$). A pattern on the Gregarious–Intimate scale, although it did not satisfy the significance criteria, was nonetheless interesting. Those reporting heart problems had a mean toward Gregarious ($p < 0.03$), while the trend for the other E–I facets was toward the I poles. Further analysis revealed these people were *not* Introverts scoring out-of-preference on this scale, but rather Extraverts scoring in-preference. This may illustrate a situation in which whole-type analysis possibly provides more insight than examination of the facet scales.

In the national sample, 38% of the respondents reported frequent or occasional insomnia. There were no differences on any of the S–N or J–P facet scales. The results for the E–I and T–F facet scales are shown in figure 9.2. Those who reported insomnia score significantly closer to the poles of Contained, Intimate, Reflective, Empathetic, Accommodating, and Tender.

When asked about chronic pain, 33% of the sample reported frequent or occasional occurrences. Facet scale scores for these people were significantly closer to the poles of Empathetic, Compassionate, Accepting, and Tender.

The survey of the national sample contained two other questions about health-related behaviors that might be addressed in counseling. Participants were asked how frequently they drank alcohol or smoked.

Those who reported drinking frequently or occasionally had means significantly closer to the E poles for four of the E–I facet scales (the exception was Gregarious, at $p < .03$) and toward the N poles of all five S–N facet scales. In addi-

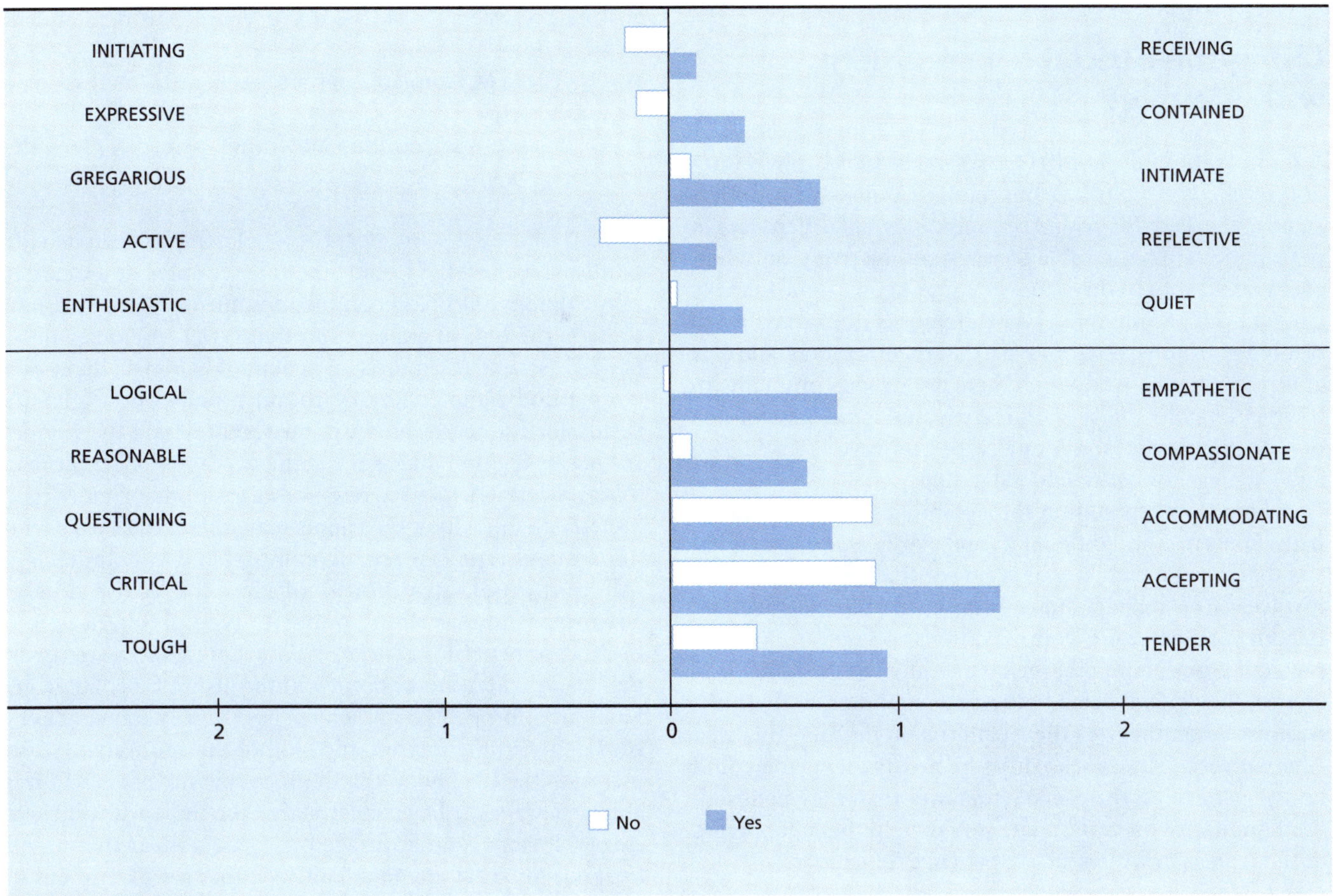


Figure 9.2 Insomnia in Relation to E–I and T–F Facets

*Source:* National sample.

tion, on the T–F facet scales, those who reported drinking frequently or occasionally scored toward Reasonable and Questioning; on the J–P facet scales they scored toward Casual, Pressure-Prompted, and Spontaneous. Given the large number of Step II scales involved in the analysis of drinking behavior, it was hypothesized that the Step I preferences may suffice to explain this behavior. Indeed, all four preferences showed significant differences ($p < 0.01$) in the direction of E, N, T, and P, and when analyzed by type, ENTP reported the highest incidence of drinking behavior.

There were fewer scales involved in differentiating smoking behavior. Those who said they smoked more frequently scored toward Original, Questioning, Open-Ended, and Spontaneous. This would not have been predicted by the preferences alone, as only the J–P scales showed significance at $p < 0.02$. The results suggest that Step II facet scales can be very useful in forming hypotheses about behaviors that may play a part in physical symptoms and health-related behaviors. A further possibility is that these same scales not only can be used as indicators but also may suggest interventions.

Relationship problems are another issue that frequently motivates people to seek counseling. Relationships with spouses are discussed below in the section on using the Step II instrument with couples. Here, we focus on satisfaction with relationships with friends and family members (defined as parents and siblings). Participants in the national sample were asked to rate their satisfaction with each relationship on a four-point scale. The response categories were collapsed into "satisfied" and "dissatisfied," and the two questions were submitted to ANOVA on the twenty-facet scales. Those who were more satisfied with their friendships had mean scores significantly toward the E poles on four of the five E–I facet scales (with the exception of Enthusiastic–Quiet) and toward Accommodating within the T–F facet block. Those who were more satisfied with their family relationships had mean scores significantly toward Initiating, Gregarious, Active, Accommodating, and Accepting.

## Using the Step II™ Instrument with Couples

Administration of the MBTI assessment tool is often integral to effective couples counseling. Couples who understand and accept the reality of similarities and differences in personality are better able to work productively on whatever issues brought them to seek help. At times, the insights gained from awareness of type differences can be central to resolving troublesome and persistent misunderstandings and resentments. And when there are serious problems in the relationship and/or with the psychological state of one or both members of the couple, type can serve as a bridge to and language for better understanding.

A Step II interpretation for a couple can further illuminate similarities and differences and clarify type characteristics that may be puzzling or seem contradictory. This often involves facets that are out-of-preference or in the midzone. If both members of a couple verify the same underlying preference but doubt that the other *really* has the same preference, they may reach a better understanding of their differences when they see their patterns on the Step II facets. Alternatively, couples who differ markedly in type may find that they have more areas of similarity than they believed; their similarity on certain facets may help them cooperate in those areas in which they experience difficulties.

### Special Administration and Interpretation Issues

Working with couples usually involves fewer sessions compared to individual counseling and psychotherapy, so external time constraints may be less of an issue. Nevertheless, circumstances will determine whether a Step II interpretation will be beneficial. If the therapist is in doubt about the advisability of adding the Step II intrument, it may be productive, as with individuals, to use Form Q and decide later whether to score it using Step II scoring. Information garnered during the Step I interpretation will probably enable an informed decision about interpreting Step II results.

A standard procedure when using the MBTI instrument with couples is to ask the partners to answer the assessment twice—the first time for themselves, the second time (at least a day later) answering the way they think the partner would answer (for further information about this procedure, see Myers et al., 1998, chapter 10). With the Step II instrument, the following modifications are recommended:

- Ask both partners to answer Form Q for themselves.
- Ask them to answer Form M (preferably the template-scorable version because it is less costly) the way they think the partner would answer.
- Determine both clients' Step I type preferences by using Form M templates to score Form Q.
- Interpret Step I results for the couple, using standard procedures.
- Use Form M templates to score each partner's responses for the other.
- Discuss self-perceptions and other perceptions as described below.

**Timing of Step II™ Interpretation** Therapists can usually administer the MBTI instrument to couples at an earlier point than would be recommended for individuals. First, there is the typical expectation that fewer sessions will be needed. Second, the potential benefit of helping a distressed couple find some common ground usually outweighs the counselor's concerns about prematurely typing the couple. In fact, it is often an asset for the therapist to tentatively assess a couple's likely types—or at least one or more type preferences on which the clients may differ. Therapists who understand type can readily comprehend and appreciate different typological points of view. There are several advantages to describing opposite type preferences in a positive or neutral way *before* administering the assessment, especially when this is done without using type language. Such an approach promotes rapport and increases client confidence in the interest and skill of the counselor. It also increases the likelihood that both couple members will feel affirmed and can allay concerns that the therapist will "take sides." It can also discourage one person's fear that it will turn out to be "all my fault" or hope that it will turn out to be "all his or her fault."

Depending on what is standard for the counselor, Form Q (and Form M, for responding as the partner would respond) can be given to the couple after a few sessions, or even at the end of the first session, if it seems appropriate. It is best to explain that Step I results may be interpreted very soon, and Step II results at a later time. An explanation of the Step I and Step II assessments and why they are being administered should be made to couple members at the same time, and extra care should be taken to ensure that both partners achieve the same understanding of purpose and procedure.

**When *Not* to Use the Step II™ Tool with Couples** Neither the Step I nor Step II assessment should be administered if it appears likely that either or both members of a couple will add type to their armament of blame and accusation. If such a reaction seems likely, it is best to delay a decision about giving the assessment and may be wise to avoid the procedure altogether.

Even after the Step I assessment has been given via Form Q, the counselor may decide that interpreting Step II results would not be helpful to a particular couple for a number of reasons. For instance, one or both partners may show disinterest in the Step I results and/or may consider them irrelevant. Alternatively, partners may regard type differences as verification of their incompatibility, despite the therapist's explanations to the contrary, because one or both partners have entered counseling mainly to receive confirmation from a "professional." In such cases, the prognosis is quite poor, and the therapist may decide to apply type knowledge to help the couple terminate the relationship. Sometimes the therapist discovers that the couple is in greater distress or the partners are contending with more pressing individual problems than was first recognized, which could make the Step II interpretation both beside the point and distracting. On the other hand, the initial Step I interpretation may make such a dramatic difference in a couple's relationship that introducing Step II results could be disruptive instead of enhancing. If this is true, it would be a good idea to postpone a Step II interpretation, perhaps indefinitely.

## Integrating Step II™ Results into the Counseling Process

Couples usually find great value in understanding their typological similarities and differences through a Step I interpretation. As counseling progresses, both therapist and clients are likely to find that many areas of the couple's relationship are influenced by their types. Inevitably, however, as time goes by, some of the insights provided by type can take the form of unhelpful stereotypes.

Applying type dynamics can often help diminish a stereotypical understanding of type. For example, an ENTJ woman says (with some heat) to her INFP husband, "You're the Feeling type! How come you didn't tell me how you felt about it?" At this point, it can be helpful to explain or remind the couple that introverted Feeling types are naturally reticent about sharing their feelings because their dominant function is introverted.

Another kind of stereotyping that is common with couples involves one partner assuming that the other partner has *all* of the qualities associated with a preference, especially if the couple are different on that dichotomy. In a couple who differ on T–F, for example, one partner might attribute *all* of the opposite T–F items to the other when filling out the MBTI instrument "the way their partner would answer it." Similarly, an Introvert might answer all E–I items for her Extraverted husband as favoring Extraversion; or a Perceiving husband might answer for his wife by showing her to be solidly committed to a Judging approach. Typically, the partner being described is actually more varied in his or her responses to the questions on the dichotomies involved. For this reason, it is fairly common for couple members to misunderstand the nuances of their partners' expression of their type. Step II results can be invaluable in providing concrete "evidence" that tempers a one-sided notion of each other.

Earl, an INTP, and Janice, an ESFJ, experienced this situation. Both had verified their reported types as accurate for them, but Janice complained that Earl frequently nagged her to spend more time with him, while Earl complained that Janice talked more to her friends than she did to him and hardly ever revealed her deepest feelings. They both agreed that these characteristics did not fit well with their type descriptions.

Figure 9.3 shows the patterns on the E–I facets for Earl and Janice. Earl appears as an Expressive INTP, and Janice as a Contained ESFJ! Earl's desire for the intimacy of sharing feelings with his wife was unfulfilled because, as a Contained Extravert, she tended to keep her deepest thoughts and feelings to herself, despite being a dominant extraverted Feeling type. Her distinctive expression of her type did not include readily revealing her inner self.

Earl was able to recognize that Janice did not share herself with her friends in this way either. Although she talked with them often, her end of the phone conversations (which he often overheard) was rarely of a deeply personal nature. Earl acknowledged that his expressiveness as an INTP was focused primarily on his relationship with his wife and that it was very important to him. Her reluctance to open up to him made him feel unloved and undesirable.

Therapy for this couple was significantly enhanced by examining the origins and adaptive value of their out-of-preference E–I characteristics. They were able to recognize that these particular characteristics were persisting in ways that were no longer adaptive. Sharing their hopes and fears regarding intimacy brought them closer together and greatly improved their mutual understanding and comfort with their relationship.

## Research Relevant to Couples Counseling

As discussed in chapter 8, Marioles et al. (1996) analyzed a sample of married couples and found that when both partners scored toward Enthusiastic and Expressive, those couples were more likely to have greater combined satisfaction as measured by the sum of each partner's satisfaction score on the *Dyadic Adjustment Scale*. When marital and premarital samples were combined, the poles of the Step II scales associated with combined satisfaction were Expressive, Accommodating, and Planful.

Marital satisfaction was also examined in the national sample, although by individual rather than by couple. Participants were asked how satisfied they were with their "marriage/intimate relationship" and were given a four-point response scale. For purposes of analysis, "very satisfied" and "somewhat satisfied" were combined and compared to those who were "very dissatisfied" or "somewhat dissatisfied." ANOVAs were run on all twenty facet scales, and $p < 0.01$ was used as the criterion for significance. Selected results are shown in figure 9.4.

Of the E–I facet scales, all but Enthusiastic–Quiet show significant differences. On the Gregarious–Intimate scale, both groups score toward Intimate, but those who are dissatisfied score significantly more in that direction. There are no significant differences among the S–N facet scales. Among the T–F facet scales, only Questioning–Accommodating shows a mean difference, with those scoring more toward

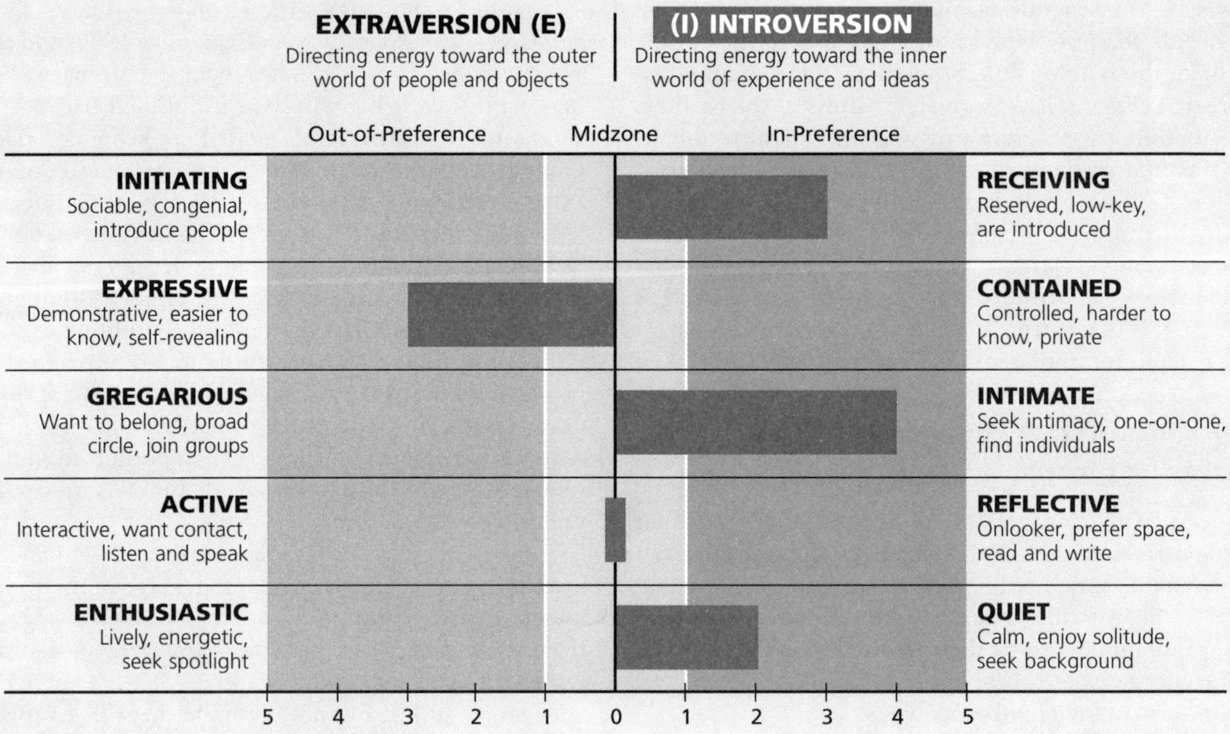


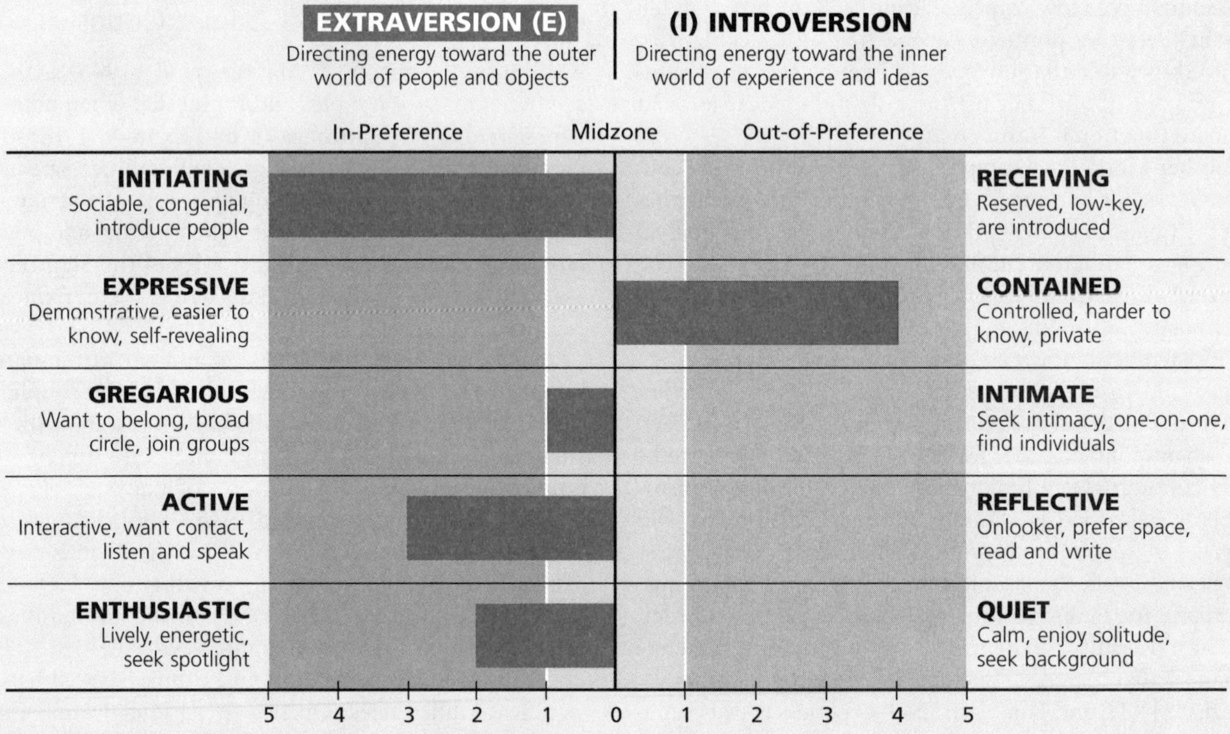


Figure 9.3 E–I Profiles for Earl (Top Figure) and Janice (Bottom Figure)

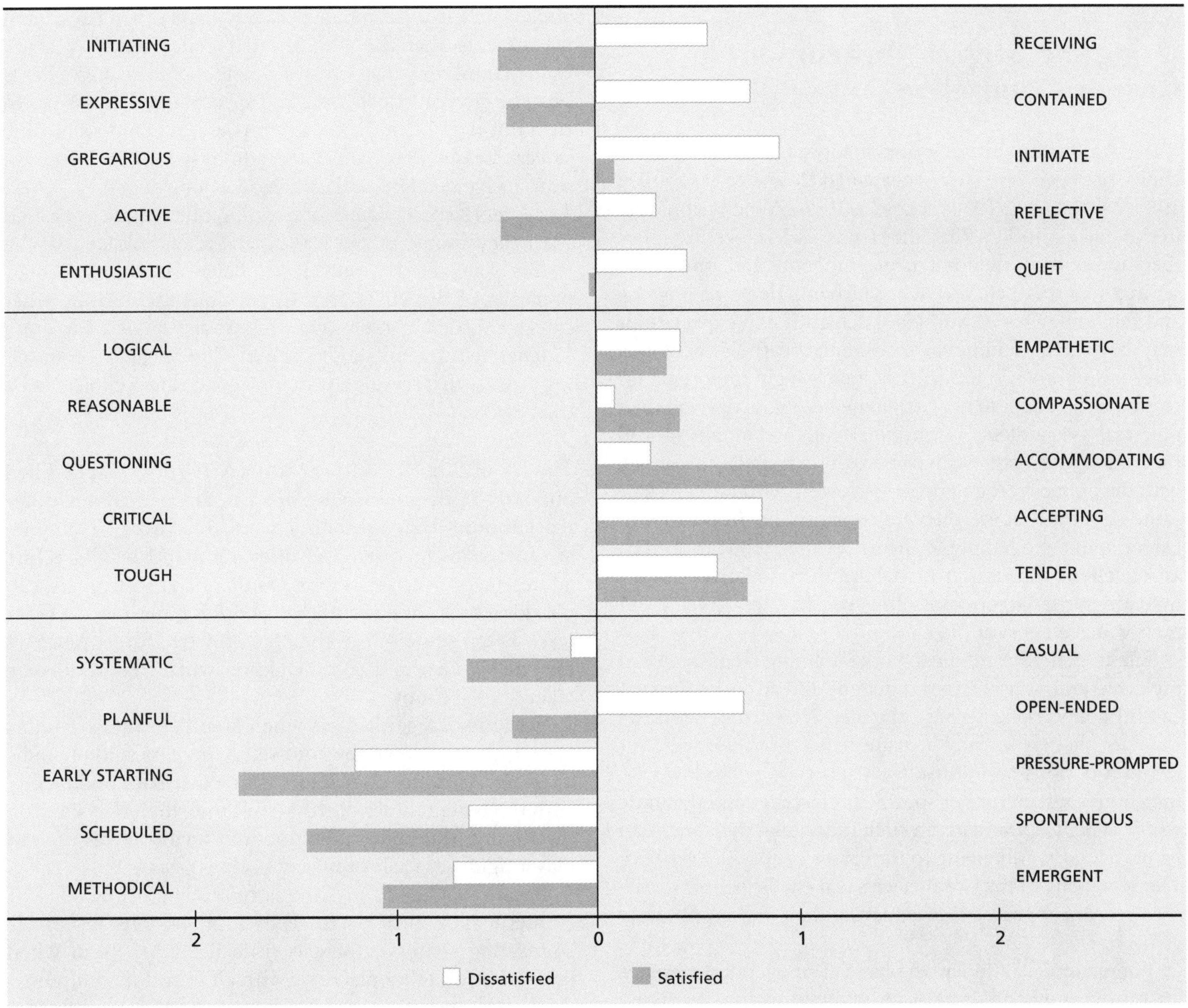


Figure 9.4 Satisfaction with Marriage/Intimate Relationships

*Source:* National sample.

Accommodating reporting more satisfaction. The overall T–F preference was not significant. Three J–P facet scales showed significant differences. On Planful–Open-Ended, those scoring toward Planful were more satisfied than those scoring toward Open-Ended. Both satisfied and dissatisfied people scored toward Early Starting (as is characteristic of the sample overall), but satisfied people scored significantly more toward Early Starting than did those who were Pressure-Prompted. Both satisfied and dissatisfied people scored toward Scheduled, but those who were satisfied scored significantly more toward Scheduled than did those who were dissatisfied.

Participants were also asked how many times they had been married and were offered choices of "0," "1," "2," or "3 or more." All the S–N facet scales showed significant differences, with those who had been married more often having mean scores toward the S poles of these scales. Stated conversely, those who had never married scored more toward the N poles of these scales. Although none of the T–F scales met the significance criterion, an interesting pattern was observed on the Critical–Accepting scale ($p < 0.02$). Those who had never married or had been married once or twice scored more toward Accepting, while those who had been married three or more times scored more toward Critical. Four of the five J–P facet scales showed significant differences. Those who had never married scored toward the Casual, Pressure-Prompted, and Spontaneous poles. The Planful–Open-Ended scale showed a different pattern, with those who had never married and those who had been married more than three times scoring more toward the Open-Ended pole, and those who had been married once or twice scoring toward Planful.

## Using the Step II™ Instrument in Career Counseling

The relationship between psychological type and career choice has been very well documented (Myers & McCaulley, 1985; Myers et al., 1998; Hammer, 1996). When people are free to make career choices, they tend to select jobs that allow them to use their preferred mental functions and attitudes in settings that they believe will be satisfying. However, ongoing and rapid changes in workplace demands and expectations may be placing additional constraints on the selection of careers and work settings. It is increasingly important for employees to adapt to new requirements and to develop their potential—regardless of their initial skills and interests—and the field of career counseling has expanded rapidly, in keeping with the public's recognition of its growing need for help. The same criteria that are relevant to using the Step I tool in career counseling apply to the use of the Step II tool. (For an excellent discussion of the application of the Step I instrument in career counseling, see chapter 12 by Kummerow in Myers et al., 1998.)

Life in general, and most work situations, require use of preferred and nonpreferred functions and attitudes for successful adaptation. Because the Step II instrument shows how people may already be using aspects of their less preferred functions and attitudes, it serves as a window into the complex structure of specific preferences and dynamic whole type. Capitalizing on such individual dynamics can be particularly enhancing to the career counseling process. The specificity of the twenty facets can enable people to further develop approaches to achieving their important career goals.

For example, a trainer who has a clear overall preference for Introversion and is midzone on the Initiating–Receiving facet can use the extraverted qualities associated with Initiating when he engages in the people-oriented activities required of him. Similar developmental opportunities may occur for the other facets, regardless of whether they are midzone or out-of-preference aspects of an individual's personality. Even someone who quite clearly operates in an Emergent fashion can temporarily adopt the style described for a Methodical person if a particular situation is best served by a methodical approach.

### Special Administration and Interpretation Issues

If the Step instrument is an appropriate tool for a client, administering Form Q is likely to be the most efficient procedure for obtaining both Step I and Step II information. Relevant general recommendations provided in chapter 5 apply here as well.

It is important that clients understand clearly the purposes and characteristics of the MBTI personality inventory and are able to differentiate between it and other assessment instruments that are administered concurrently. Because career counseling may involve a battery of measures, clients must be given adequate time and specific instructions not to rush through the measurement process. When possible, the career assessment battery can be administered over a few sessions to avoid fatigue and confusion among measures.

Clients seeking career counseling often want to be told what they should do, so it is crucial to emphasize that the results of any measure must never dictate a career path. Interpretation of the MBTI Step II instrument as well as other career counseling tools (e.g., the *Strong Interest Inventory* [*Strong*] instrument) should be part of an integrated counseling process that reveals a plan for a good career choice, not a career label.

**Timing of Step II™ Interpretation** Form Q can be filled out early in the counseling process, along with any other instruments that are being used. However, it may be advantageous to verify and interpret Step I results before addressing other assessments, as the MBTI instrument can provide a broad and useful framework for interpreting other tests. Later, some of the client's distinctive career qualities may make sense and become clearer when facet results are taken into account.

Of course, regardless of when Step II results are interpreted, their value in the counseling process is likely to be ongoing. As career counselors gain experience and facility with the potentialities of the Step II tool, their decisions on the timing of the interpretation and review of results can play a significant role in the counseling process.

Because career counseling is typically a brief endeavor (sometimes as little as three or four sessions in college counseling centers), there is little flexibility as to when interpretation takes place. As with all forms of counseling, the better the counselor's knowledge of the client before type information is provided, the more accurate the interpretation will be. Career counseling that involves workplace interventions may provide more flexibility and has the advantage of an ongoing relationship between the counselor or human resources professional and the client.

**When *Not* to Use the Step II™ Tool for Career Counseling** If the Step I tool is deemed inappropriate, the Step II tool will be inappropriate as well. Career counselors are sometimes faced with clients whose expectations and needs lie outside a career counseling context. Some individuals would be best served by referrals for personal therapy so that they may benefit from career counseling at a later time.

For example, a 40-year-old woman came for counseling because a physical injury had forced her to give up her current career as a gymnastics instructor. She was highly motivated to explore her ongoing interests in public relations or perhaps obtain training as a medical technician. The client had taken the MBTI Step I assessment some years before and had some questions about the results. She was therefore eager to take the Step II assessment as part of the counseling procedure.

Unknown to the career counselor, however, this client was in treatment for a moderately severe anxiety disorder. While reviewing the Step I assessment, the client became very upset about a discrepancy between her previous and current results, insisting that she had to know her "correct" preference on S–N in order to choose a career. It was then that she informed the career counselor of her ongoing treatment for debilitating anxiety. It became increasingly clear during the feedback session that this client would not be able to benefit from further exploration of her personality preferences, especially in the detail provided by the Step II tool. The career counselor therefore suggested that the client confer with her personal therapist for advice about whether and when career counseling might be beneficial

As a general rule, the Step II assessment should not be administered if there is a chance that the information will be used to make assumptions about occupational performance. Although people of each type have clear preferences for a given set of work behaviors, it is never appropriate to assume that individuals have not developed or cannot acquire the skills necessary to perform the less preferred behaviors of their indicated type. Further, there is no evidence to suggest that types who predominate in a particular occupation perform better than less frequent types.

## Integrating the Step II™ Instrument into the Counseling Process

Once Step II results have been verified and interpreted, the counselor should have the Interpreter's Summary (the last page of the profile and of the report) available for subsequent counseling sessions. This page contains a summary of the client's Step I type, facet scale results, polarity index, average range of scores for the client's type, and information about omissions. If the Interpretive Report is available (recommended for most career counseling situations), that, too, should be at hand throughout the counseling process. It is likely that some of the client's out-of-preference and midzone results may enhance the value of other test results, such as those from the *Strong* instrument. Many career counselors attest to the value of combining MBTI Step I information with results from the *Strong* assessment. A number of resources are available for this endeavor, for example, Davis and Handschin, 1998; Grutter and Hammer, 1995; and Hammer and Kummerow, 1996. When both *Strong* and MBTI Step I results have been interpreted for the client, Step II information can provide valuable insights into job and workplace needs and preferences.

For example, Jane, a 39-year-old woman, had been working as an office manager for fifteen years. She expressed a long-standing desire to become an author and illustrator of children's books. Because such a switch would be a major change for her, she sought career counseling to help her decide whether she would be happy in a new situation. Her *Strong* results indicated a high interest in the Artistic, Social, and Conventional general occupational themes. Several years earlier, she had received feedback on Step I results in which she indicated a preference for ISFJ. She believed this was her true type and that the *Strong* instrument was accurately identifying her career interest areas. However, she wondered whether she would really be happy spending all her time doing unstructured and creative tasks.

With the Step II assessment, she again reported ISFJ as her type, but her preference for S over N was slight. In discussing S–N, Jane was certain that she favored Sensing. Her MBTI Step II results helped her understand how she could be satisfied in an artistic career: On both Realistic–Imaginative and Traditional–Original, she indicated two clear out-of-preference results toward the Imaginative (4) and Original (4) poles. In discussions, she recognized that she had been exercising these preferences throughout her career as an office manager, always finding new ways of doing office tasks and enjoying the challenge of coming up with alternative procedures.

Jane revealed two other concerns about her proposed career change—presenting her work to others and the need to persevere with her artistic tasks. Although she clearly favored the Introversion poles of four of the five E–I facets, her out-of-preference result on Enthusiastic–Quiet (Enthusiastic 5) was reassuring to her. She stated that talking to a group has never been a problem for her if she has passionate feelings about the subject. In fact, everyone in the office building knew of her desire to write and illustrate children's books! In terms of her ability to remain focused on her artistic endeavors, Jane's out-of-preference result on the J–P Planful–Open-Ended facet (Open-Ended 3) was revealing. The description of Open-Ended as tending toward being present-focused, going with the flow, and liking flexible plans represented a group of behaviors she had learned in response to the demands of her current job. Her more natural tendency was to plan and set goals. When Jane was encouraged to think about how her learned Open-Ended behaviors would be of benefit in her proposed new career, she came up with a list of ways in which these behaviors fit her conception of a writer and illustrator. She could depend on her other J preferences to help keep her on track.

Jane's experience illustrates how the Step II instrument can provide clarity and meaningful explanations for the individual differences that affect career choice. The Step II interpretation helped Jane realize she already had qualities that would be of value in her proposed new career. Jane had previously received Step I feedback, and this points out the dangers of stereotyping a type or a dichotomy, since she believed that her preference for S somehow meant she would not be creative.[1] Career counselors must always remain open to individual expressions of type in their clients, and Step II results help facilitate an understanding of the differences. Jane's profile also highlights the importance of the interaction between client and interpreter when using the Step I and Step

II tools. A cursory appraisal of her S–N preference clarity index on Step I might lead to the judgment that Jane was unsure whether she preferred Sensing or Intuition. In discussions, Jane indicated that Sensing was definitely her preference. And her prevailing assumptions about what it took to be creative would not have been revealed and clarified without sensitive interactions with her Step II interpreter.

Step II facet results were also enlightening for Joan, an ESFJ who had been a career navy officer with command responsibility. She retired early and decided to resume her education. Joan completed Form Q as part of a career workshop and reported two out-of-preference results. She was a Theoretical Sensing type, which conformed to her interest in earning a doctoral degree in human resources or organization development. Her other out-of-preference result was a score toward Pressure-Prompted. She wondered if this was a temporary reaction to being out of the navy, where all her time had been structured for her. When she described her career move, she said she was changing her life, not just her career.

## Research Relevant to Career Counseling

Participants in the national sample were asked three global questions about work satisfaction with a four-point response scale ranging from "very satisfied" to "very dissatisfied." Because the distribution of responses was so skewed toward satisfaction on all three questions, the two satisfaction categories were collapsed, as were the two dissatisfaction categories. The two resulting categories were then used as independent variables in ANOVAs with $p <$ .01 established as the cutoff for significance. The results are shown in table 9.1.

Previous research, mentioned in chapter 8, had suggested that global measures of satisfaction with work tend to be associated with a preference for Extraversion and Judging, and the results of the national survey generally confirmed this finding. However, when the individual facet scales were examined for each question, it was found that there was no occurrence when all five E–I facet scales were significant for any one of the questions. Each question yielded a different pattern, with some overlap and some unique scales. The means of the E–I facet scales for those satisfied and dissatisfied with their type of work are graphed in figure 9.5.

The Initiating–Receiving ($p < 0.006$) and Active–Reflective ($p < 0.009$) scales showed the greatest differences, with the satisfied group scoring toward the E poles on these scales. Although they did not reach the cutoff probability value, the Expressive–Contained ($p < 0.04$) and Gregarious–Intimate ($p < 0.05$) scales also showed significant differences, in the direction of the E pole for Expressive–Contained for those who were satisfied. And although both satisfied and dissatisfied people scored toward the Intimate pole, those who were dissatisfied more clearly favored that pole. There were no significant differences on Enthusiastic–Quiet. The results suggest that career counselors should pay particular attention to the Initiating–Receiving and Active–Reflective scales and the role they may play in job satisfaction. There were no Step II scales from the J–P facet block showing significant differences between the satisfied and the dissatisfied, which may mean that a whole-type analysis is necessary to explain the significant results for the overall J–P preference reported in other research.

Participants were also asked to gauge their levels of satisfaction with specific aspects of their work. The same four-point response format was offered, and, as described above, responses were collapsed into two categories and subjected to ANOVA. Poles associated with the satisfied group for facets showing significant differences between the satisfied and the dissatisfied are shown in table 9.1. To mention one example, the differences between those who

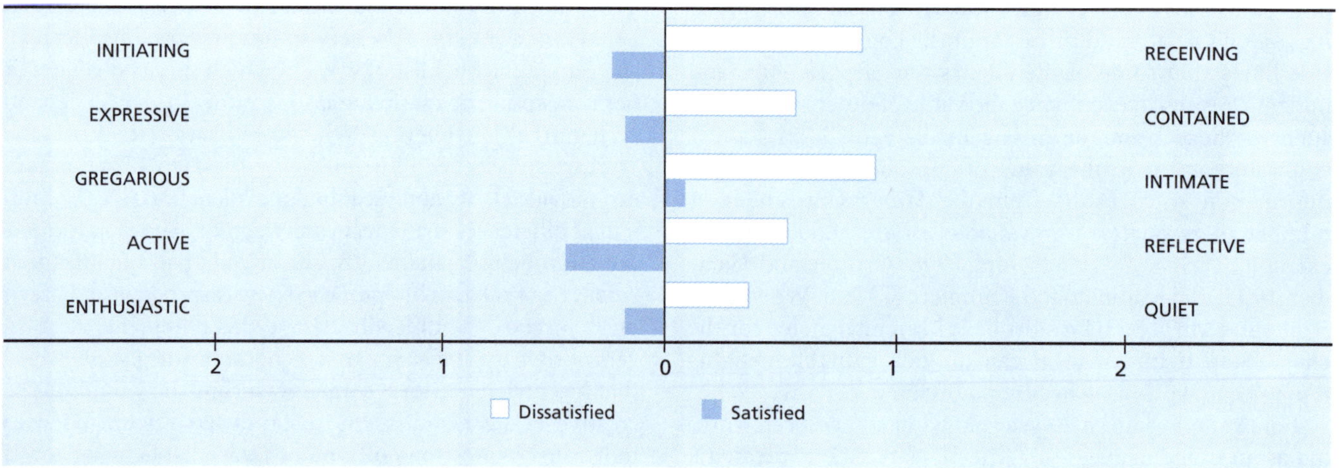


Figure 9.5 Satisfaction with Kind of Work

*Source:* National sample.

## Table 9.1 Poles of Step II™ Facet Scales Related to Global and Specific Job Satisfaction

**Global Aspects**

| *Satisfaction with:* | *Step II Pole with Mean for Satisfied Group* |
|---|---|
| Kind of work | Initiating<br>Active |
| Company/organization | Expressive |
| Future work opportunities | Receiving<br>Expressive<br>Gregarious<br>Active |

**Specific Aspects**

| *Satisfaction with:* | *Step II Pole with Mean for Satisfied Group* |
|---|---|
| Day-to-day tasks | Expressive<br>Traditional<br>Spontaneous[a] |
| Job security | Initiating<br>Expressive<br>Gregarious[b]<br>Active<br>Enthusiastic |
| Coworkers | Initiating<br>Expressive<br>Gregarious[a]<br>Active<br>Empathetic<br>Compassionate<br>Accommodating<br>Accepting<br>Tender |
| Opportunity for learning | Initiating<br>Active |
| Opportunity for promotion | Expressive |
| Opportunity for accomplishments | Initiating<br>Expressive<br>Gregarious[b]<br>Active<br>Accepting[c] |

**Specific Aspects**

| *Satisfaction with:* | *Step II Pole with Mean for Satisfied Group* |
|---|---|
| Responsibility | Traditional<br>Accommodating |
| Predictability and stability of job | Initiating<br>Expressive<br>Gregarious[a]<br>Active<br>Accepting[c] |
| Salary | Expressive<br>Gregarious[b]<br>Active<br>Concrete<br>Realistic[c]<br>Practical[c]<br>Traditional[c]<br>Accommodating[c]<br>Systematic<br>Planned<br>Scheduled[c] |
| Stress level | Initiating<br>Expressive<br>Active |
| Working conditions (hours, vacations, benefits, etc). | Planful |

*Notes:* Poles are listed for the Satisfied group if $p < .01$ for the scale; no note mark for the pole indicates that the Satisfied group's mean was on this side of the 0 point and the Dissatisfied group's mean was on the opposite side of the 0 point.
[a]All means on opposite side of 0; Satisfied group mean significantly more toward indicated pole.
[b]Satisfied group mean near 0; Dissatisfied group mean toward opposite pole.
[c]All means on this side of 0; Satisfied group mean significantly more toward indicated pole.

*Source:* National sample.

Figure 9.6 Satisfaction with Day-to-Day Tasks
*Source:* National sample.

were satisfied and those who were dissatisfied with their day-to-day tasks were significant for three of the Step II facets. Satisfied respondents had means toward Expressive, Traditional, and Scheduled. These are shown in figure 9.6. Overall, the results in table 9.1 suggest that different facets are involved in satisfaction with different aspects of work. It is possible that identifying these scales with individual clients may suggest interventions designed to improve satisfaction.

## Correlations between the Step II™ Facets and the *Strong Interest Inventory®* Instrument

During a portion of the test-retest data collection, a sample of 77 male and 13 female college students was also administered the *Strong* instrument. The correlations between the Step II facet scales and the Holland-based General Occupational Themes (GOTs) are shown in table 9.2. It must be kept in mind that due to the small number of females in the sample, the correlations are more reflective of relationships between facets and GOTs for males.

As seen in table 9.2, the higher scores on the Realistic dimension have a positive relationship with the facet of Enthusiastic–Quiet and a negative relationship with four of the five T–F facet scales. Given that individuals who score high (very interested) on the Realistic scale tend to prefer more solitary work environments and to be in occupations that emphasize logical decision making (engineer, electrician, auto mechanic), these relationships are consistent.

All five T–F facets are related to the *Strong* Investigative scale (high Investigative is toward the T orientation). The correlation toward Pressure-Prompted on the Early Starting–Pressure-Prompted facet also makes sense: Investigative individuals are typically seen as nonconforming and following their own processes and interests.

The Artistic scale of the *Strong* instrument is positively related to the Practical–Conceptual and Realistic–Imaginative facets. It was modestly negatively related to the J–P facet of Systematic–Casual. The relationship with the N poles of the two S–N scales is consistent with descriptions of Artistic; the relationship with Systematic makes sense in light of the technical artists represented in this college sample.

The Traditional–Original facet was negatively related to the *Strong* Social theme. The occupations associated with high interests on this dimension may be more consistent with S preferences (schoolteacher, human resources professional).

With the exception of Questioning–Accommodating, four T–F facets were negatively related to the Enterprising theme (i.e., correlated with T facets). This theme correlates positively with Early Starting–Pressure-Prompted. Enterprising individuals often take a logical approach to their successes and failures and respond to the moment. For example, many successful salespeople think of sales rejection as a logical reaction rather than a personal rebuff.

The Conventional theme on the *Strong* instrument tends to indicate individuals who enjoy consistent, fact-based procedures and logically constructed environments. The negative relationship with two S–N and two T–F facets is consistent with the practical and logical occupations found for individuals with conventional interests (e.g., accounting and quality control).

In evaluating these results, it is important to recognize the small size of the sample, which was mostly male in composition and contained a large number of engineering students. These characteristics alone would tend to move the facets toward the S and T poles. It is possible that other relationships may emerge when different populations are studied.

**Table 9.2 Correlations of Step II™ Facet Scales with *Strong Interest Inventory*® Themes**

| | *Strong* Theme | | | | | |
|---|---|---|---|---|---|---|
| **Step II™ Facet Scale** | Realistic | Investigative | Artistic | Social | Enterprising | Conventional |
| *E–I Facet Scales* | | | | | | |
| Initiating–Receiving | –.002 | –.011 | –.015 | –.175 | .027 | .124 |
| Expressive–Contained | .083 | .134 | .009 | –.118 | –.038 | .460 |
| Gregarious–Intimate | .020 | .061 | –.044 | –.053 | –.121 | .120 |
| Active-Reflective | .060 | –.041 | –.041 | –.196 | .009 | .094 |
| Enthusiastic–Quiet | .231 | .083 | –.031 | –.151 | .050 | .193 |
| *S–N Facet Scales* | | | | | | |
| Concrete–Abstract | .029 | –.058 | .123 | –.006 | .064 | –.167 |
| Realistic–Imaginative | .147 | –.096 | .266 | –.113 | –.164 | –.219 |
| Practical–Conceptual | .010 | .043 | .312 | –.090 | –.103 | –.170 |
| Experiential–Theoretical | .045 | –.118 | .114 | –.042 | .071 | –.093 |
| Traditional–Original | –.014 | .046 | –.040 | –.263 | –.131 | –.261 |
| *T–F Facet Scales* | | | | | | |
| Logical-Empathetic | –.369 | –.414 | .020 | –.100 | –.438 | –.377 |
| Reasonable–Compassionate | –.337 | –.374 | .029 | .150 | –.232 | –.227 |
| Questioning–Accommodating | –.217 | –.220 | –.105 | .039 | –.147 | –.007 |
| Critical–Accepting | –.226 | –.262 | .068 | .211 | –.290 | –.137 |
| Tough–Tender | –.287 | –.302 | –.020 | .172 | –.235 | –.098 |
| *J–P Facet Scales* | | | | | | |
| Systematic–Casual | –.084 | –.125 | –.227 | –.082 | –.020 | –.188 |
| Planful–Open-Ended | –.036 | .019 | –.217 | –.106 | –.016 | –.058 |
| Early Starting–Pressure-Prompted | .204 | .240 | .013 | .022 | .378 | .169 |
| Scheduled–Spontaneous | .046 | –.093 | –.176 | –.159 | .167 | –.034 |
| Methodical–Emergent | –.001 | .045 | –.059 | –.109 | .022 | –.113 |

*Note:* Correlations of .219–.270 are significant at < .05; those that are .28 or higher are significant at < .01.

*Source:* National sample.

## Conclusion

Using the Step II instrument for personal counseling and psychotherapy with individuals and couples builds on Jung's lifelong focus on individuality and Myers' goal of making the complexity of that individuality accessible and useful in people's lives. The information in this chapter gives counselors and therapists a solid basis on which to understand and apply the rich explanatory system provided by the Step II tool. This is also true in the increasingly important area of career counseling. Professionals in this field are encouraged to become familiar with issues that are relevant to personal counseling; the motivations and needs of clients seeking career counseling often overlap with personal issues, confusing the counseling process. The research information provided can broaden the perspective of counselors in both of these arenas and sensitize practitioners to the motivations and needs of their clients.

# Using the Step II™ Instrument in an Organizational Environment

# 10

CHAPTER OVERVIEW



Organizational uses of the Step II instrument have increased dramatically since it became available in its revised form in 1996. In such areas as, for example, training, team building, executive coaching, and conflict resolution, it can often clarify some of the interactions that remain puzzling after Step I results have been received. Step II facet scale differences may prove enlightening to team members of the same type who "should" see eye-to-eye typologically. Increased understanding can encourage people to capitalize on within-type differences rather than focus on resentment and divisions within the team. Managers may find new ways to provide constructive criticism and validate the people they supervise, and coaches may be able to suggest alternative ways of working and accomplishing goals that take advantage of their clients' out-of-preference or midzone results.

This chapter covers guidelines for using the Step II assessment in organizational settings, discusses relevant administration and interpretation issues, and offers details about the tool in the areas of communication, decision making, dealing with change and transition, conflict management, team building, and leadership development. The chapter also includes pertinent research evidence from the national sample that was used to develop the revised Step II assessment (see appendix B for a description of the national sample). The goal of this chapter is to provide practitioners who work in organizational settings with a solid base from which to expand their use of Step I type applications by including the rich and varied information provided by the Step II tool.[1]

Recommendations and guidelines that apply to using the Step I tool in organizations typically apply to Step II applications as well. Except as noted, such material is not repeated in this chapter. It is therefore strongly recommended that readers familiarize themselves with the material in chapter 13 of the *MBTI® Manual* (Myers et al., 1998). Using the Step II tool effectively in organizations requires solid understanding of Step I applications.

## Special Administration and Interpretation Issues

All the information and recommendations provided in chapter 4 ("Administering the Step II™ Instrument") and chapter 5 ("Interpreting and Verifying the Step II™ Instrument") are generally relevant in organizational settings. Readers of this chapter are encouraged to review the material in the above-mentioned chapters as they plan applications of the Step II tool.

### Ensuring Confidentiality and Voluntary Participation in the Step II™ Assessment

Confidentiality and voluntary participation are even more critical in organizational and work situations than in other settings. The freedom to respond to questions candidly can also be more problematic, because an employee's career advancement and job security may be a perceived issue. Just as for the Step I tool, explicit and subtle pressures to conform to a particular model of acceptable organizational behavior can influence Step II responses.

**Recommendations** It is therefore advisable to take extra pains to communicate the legitimacy of all types and all aspects of type. Remind people of the following:

- Having a preference is not the same as having a particular skill or ability. We are all free and able to develop the skills necessary to perform work tasks, if we so choose.
- Knowing our own preferences and those of others is valuable because it promotes understanding of natural styles of communicating, handling conflict, contributing to a team, being a leader, and many other endeavors that are part of organizational life.

### Minimizing Inappropriate Mind-sets and Encouraging Candid Responses

Perhaps the most important issue in administering and interpreting both the Step I and Step II assessments in a work setting is the respondent's frame of mind. Although the following example focuses on the Step I tool, it is instructive.

Mike's reported and verified type was ISFP shortly after completing engineering school. His first job was in aeronautical engineering. Two years after starting work, Mike took the *Myers-Briggs Type Indicator* (MBTI) personality inventory when he was in personal counseling. His reported and verified type was again ISFP. Several years later, Mike took the assessment as part of a management training course. He reported ISTJ as his type. Over the next six years, he took the assessment twice for work purposes, both times reporting ISTJ even more clearly than before. "I guess I must really be an ISTJ," he told a friend from engineering school. Mike's friend, who had also verified ISFP as his type just after engineering school, had been working since that time at a high-tech electronics company. He told Mike the same thing had happened to him. He'd taken the assessment twice at work, and both times his results reported his type as ISTJ. However, the friends later attended a workshop on type dynamics together, and they both recognized that ISFP was indeed their best-fit type. They offered many examples in support of their conclusions and identified similar areas of discomfort when they felt they had to behave like ISTJs at work.

Another example of situational pressure was revealed during an MBTI feedback session that took place on the third day of an intensive manager-training assessment session. Prior to the arrival of the MBTI professional, management trainees filled out the self-scorable form of the assessment and scored it immediately. They were given no information or instructions other than what appears in the MBTI booklet. As mentioned in chapter 5, this is not a recommended procedure for verifying MBTI type. Fortunately, these management trainees had no idea of the meaning of their results, so the interpreter was able to introduce them to type and have them assess their likely preferences before looking at their results. Standard verification procedures were used and each person was able to verify a best-fit type. However, in comparing their best-fit types to their results on the self-scorable form, half the group shifted from a reported T preference to a verified F preference, from a reported S preference to a verified N preference, and from a reported J preference to a verified P preference, while a quarter of them verified Introversion rather than Extraversion as their preference. The modal type of the group changed from ESTJ to ENFP. This was not surprising, since these trainees had been specifically chosen for their innovative practices and ability to motivate others. The people whose results had changed acknowledged that they had answered according to what they thought a good manager *should* be.

Type falsification is a common response to explicit organizational values and implicit assumptions about the qualities that are desired or required for success. Interpretation of Step II facets can help correct such falsification and encourage employees to recognize and value their own natural type preferences and those of others.

**Recommendations** Suggestions for encouraging this use of the Step II tool are discussed in a later section of this chapter. However, it is best to minimize inappropriate mind-sets and encourage candid responses before administering the Step II assessment. To do this, one or more of the following approaches are recommended.

- If possible, hold an introductory session with group members and provide them with verbal and written information about the MBTI instrument. Practitioners who employ this procedure report that such a meeting often reveals incorrect beliefs about the instrument or negative feelings about taking it. In one case, group members said they had been required to take the assessment five years before, and, afterward, type was used by their supervisor to categorize and demean the staff. By talking to the group in advance, the practitioner was able to deal effectively with their concerns and validate their feelings about the prior experience.
- If you will not be meeting with the group beforehand, be sure to send a clear letter of explanation to each person. Important areas to cover within organization contexts can be found in chapter 13 of the *MBTI® Manual* (Myers et al., 1998), on page 362. A brief description of the purposes of the Step II tool, as described in chapter 4 of this manual, can easily be incorporated into that list.
- If at all possible, have participants complete the MBTI personality inventory at home, not at work. But regardless of the location, emphasize that responses should reflect what is natural and preferred when people are free to do as they wish, not what they can do or are willing to do when they must. Answering in accord with natural preferences enables people to better recognize the ways in which they may be accommodating the demands of the workplace. Quite often, the facets of their type preferences that have become habitual and comfortable for them will be revealed as out-of-preference or midzone results on the Step II assessment.

## Timing of Step II™ Interpretation

The appropriate time to administer and interpret Step II results will vary according to its intended purposes and with the particular situation. Ideally, Step II results should be interpreted after people have an adequate understanding of the Step I tool but before their possibly limited understanding of type has led to stereotyping. In organizational contexts, stereotyping is especially likely if Step I feedback has been cursory, if other systems of understanding behavior have led to rigid and simplistic labels, and if there is little opportunity to integrate type knowledge into the daily activities of employees.

It is advisable to introduce the Step I assessment fairly early in the team formation process so that team members can capitalize on type understanding from the outset. It is usually also desirable to follow up with Step II feedback as quickly as possible. This inhibits false assumptions and judgments team members may make based on their Step I knowledge. For example, a Pressure-Prompted INTJ may initially be seen as immature or obstructive when he doesn't "act like a J," who should like starting early and working steadily on a project. Or a Contained ENFP might be judged as silently critical and "superior" before her out-of-preference facet result is known and understood.

## When *Not* to Use the Step II™ Instrument

An organization, group, or team will not benefit from taking the Step II or Step I assessment when situations such as conflicts, power struggles, and hidden agendas are ongoing and pervasive. Many consultants who use the MBTI instrument in organizations attest to the value of knowing as much as possible about their potential client groups before they introduce type. Serious conflict and persistent stress make it less likely that type will be accurately reported. (For information about the effects of chronic stress at work, see Quenk, 2000.) In addition, an organization under stress may use Step II information destructively, as can also be done with Step I results. With the Step II assessment, there are twenty potential ways of "type bashing," which can only make a bad situation worse. If it is administered before the practitioner discovers its inappropriateness for the group or organization, it is best to deal with the conflict and delay interpretation of results. Neither the Step I nor the Step II tool is a panacea for resolving all problems or curing a dysfunctional organization.

Many organizations have used Step I type for quite some time and wish to add the Step II tool to their understanding of personality. It is important that the consultant get a sense of how type is being used in the organization or group, identify possible areas of incomplete understanding, and make sure people new to the organization, work group, or team understand the Step I tool sufficiently before moving on to the Step II tool. Wide variation in Step I knowledge is not necessarily a reason to forgo use of the Step II tool. However, it is important to be sure that all the people involved are comfortable with their type understanding.

An obvious criterion for introducing the Step II instrument is the amount of time the organization is willing to commit. A practitioner should allow at least twice as much time for Step II interpretation as for Step I interpretation. In an organization with individuals at different levels of understanding and varying motivations to participate, a half day (preferably a day) is advisable. If sufficient time is not set aside, it is best to delay the application of the Step II instrument or perhaps not use it at all.

## Using the Step II™ Instrument to Enhance Organizational Applications of Type

For most people, their work lives play a critical part in their overall satisfaction and sense of self. The kind of work they do, the environment in which they do it, and the people with whom they work interact in complex ways. Together, these elements contribute to a general assessment of work satisfaction. Not surprisingly, wide variations have been observed among the types in variables such as preferred work characteristics and the value placed on specific features of their jobs. Some of these differences were presented in Myers et al. (1998), and the application of Step I type to all aspects of organizations is covered in chapter 13 of that manual. A review of research in this growing area of application can also be found in Hammer (1996). Many other publications provide both research and experiential results about the ways in which work and organizational variables are influenced by type (Hirsh, 1990; Hirsh & Kise, 1996; Hirsh & Kummerow, 1998; and Kummerow, Barger, & Kirby, 1997).

In an organizational setting, the Step II tool adds to the richness and depth of type by identifying individual differences within types. Knowing about the specific facets of type included in the Step II assessment permits people to more fully understand and appreciate their own and their colleagues' ways of doing things. This understanding can provide direction and rationale for improving communication, making better decisions, dealing most effectively with change and transition, managing conflict within the organization, and maximizing the effectiveness of teams.

Individuals and organizations benefit when employees recognize their distinctiveness within their type and are affirmed by others for their special contributions. For example, it is widely known that organizations tend to promote and value a Thinking over a Feeling approach to decision making. Reading the descriptions of the specific Thinking and Feeling facet poles in the T–F facet block (see chapter 3) is a very effective way for people with a Thinking preference to understand more thoroughly how Feeling types make decisions; Feeling types can also learn more about the decision-making criteria applied by Thinking types.

In addition, many people with an underlying preference for Thinking have one or more T–F facets that are out-of-preference or in the midzone. When evidence of individuality is verified by Thinking types, it can provide an avenue for increased understanding both of themselves and of Feeling types. People with an underlying preference for Feeling often have out-of-preference or midzone results as well. Discussing these facets openly may not only enhance understanding of how Thinking types make decisions but also help Feeling types recognize which of their out-of-preference or midzone results are comfortable and natural for them and which have been learned in order to survive in a Thinking environment.

Most important, perhaps, knowledge of the T–F facets can promote greater appreciation of the contributions to the organization of a Feeling approach. People in the organization will then be better able to evaluate when one or the other judging function is more appropriate for a particular situation or whether both approaches will yield the best results.

Organizational consultants and others who use type in organizations will find most of the information in the preceding chapters relevant for applying the Step II assessment in this area. This section highlights some of the areas in which understanding of Step II facets can enhance organizational uses of type. The first four areas discussed below correspond to the application areas for which the Step II report provides individualized facet results.

### The Step II™ Instrument and Communication

Effective communication is key to all aspects of organizational life. Type theory and the MBTI personality inventory provide critical insights into the various communication methods of the sixteen types. Implications for understanding communication differences among the types permeate a broad range of related books and articles, but only a few can be mentioned here. Styles of communication for different types are discussed in chapter 10 of the *MBTI® Manual* (Myers et al., 1998), and information specific to organizations is summarized in chapter 13 of that manual. Other insightful discussions can be found in Bridges (1992), Barger & Kirby (1997), and Hammer & Huszczo (1996).

The Step II facet scales further refine our understanding of the ways in which type qualities influence communication. Members of each type share some common ways of conveying and receiving information. And each dichotomy has an overall influence on communication styles, especially the E–I dichotomy. When we look at the Step II facets, it is not surprising that four of the five E–I facets make an obvious contribution to communication. These are Initiating–Receiving (our basic orientation to communicating with and connecting to others), Expressive–Contained (communicating our emotional state, feelings, interests, and experiences), Active–Reflective (our approach to engaging with the general environment for entertainment, socializing, and learning), and Enthusiastic–Quiet (the level and kind of energy we bring to exchanges with others). The Gregarious–Intimate facet, which involves the breadth and depth of our connections to others, appears to be less important for communication than the other four, perhaps because it focuses on the numbers of people involved rather than on stylistic factors.

Facets of the other three dichotomies are also important for communication. In the S–N facet block, Concrete–Abstract (our general perception of the world and the kinds of things to which we direct our attention) appears important. The three T–F facets specifically identified are Questioning–Accommodating (how we deal with differences of opinion), Critical–Accepting (the approach we take after initial judgment has been made), and Tough–Tender (how we carry out judgments we believe are correct). Most important for communication among the J–P facets is Methodical–Emergent (sequencing of tasks within larger projects). This facet's influence on communication may not be immediately apparent; it takes into account the tendency of Methodical people to communicate required procedures to others at the outset, whereas Emergent people are likely to wait until the need arises.

## The Step II™ Instrument and Decision Making

The processes we use for making decisions or reaching conclusions are the second of the two major constructs of type theory, the first being how we perceive or gather information. In elucidating the distinction between Thinking judgment and Feeling judgment, type theory and the MBTI assessment have made enormous advances toward understanding different decision-making approaches. It goes without saying that both the decisions themselves and the manner in which they are made are critical to successful organizational functioning. These factors, along with differences in ways of communicating, which were discussed in the preceding section, go a long way toward explaining and perhaps enhancing organizational performance by allowing practitioners and their clients increased understanding of and greater control over decision-making processes.

As with communication, the relationship of type to decision making pervades the research and application literature for the MBTI assessment. Information specific to the impact of type on organizational decision making appears in chapter 13 of the *MBTI® Manual* (Myers et al., 1998) and in several chapters in Fitzgerald and Kirby (1997). Note particularly the chapter by S. G. Clancy titled "STJs and Change: Resistance, Reaction, or Misunderstanding?" (pp. 415–38).

The perceiving functions Sensing and Intuition and the judging functions Thinking and Feeling are all involved in making decisions. It is generally agreed that the best decisions utilize these four functions in sequence: Sensing to look at the facts, Intuition to consider the possibilities, Thinking to anticipate the logical consequences, and Feeling to recognize what is important to people. The five Sensing–Intuition facets, Concrete–Abstract, Realistic–Imaginative, Practical–Conceptual, Experiential–Theoretical, and Traditional–Original, provide clear avenues to performing the first two functions. The five Thinking–Feeling facets, Logical–Empathetic, Reasonable–Compassionate, Questioning–Accommodating, Critical–Accepting, and Tough–Tender, are equally useful in completing the latter functions. Individuals, work groups, management teams, or other decision makers can proceed systematically through these ten facets to ensure that all relevant considerations have been addressed.

A combination of results on the first two T–F facets (Logical–Empathetic and Reasonable–Compassionate) has been identified as representing five distinctly different decision-making styles. As implied in the descriptions of these facets, the Logical–Empathetic facet appears to reflect our desired or "ideal" approach to decision making, while the Reasonable–Compassionate facet is associated with our actual process of making decisions. Using the poles and the midzone[2] as criteria, the five styles are as follows.

- *Logical and Reasonable:* Applies logic in both ideal and actual decision making. Among the national sample, 26.9% reported this style.
- *Empathetic and Compassionate:* Uses values as both ideal and actual way of making decisions; represented by 36.1% of the national sample.
- *Midzone:* Tries to accommodate both Thinking and Feeling in ideal and actual decision making; 28.9% of the national sample had this style. The underlying preference for either Thinking or Feeling can be important in deciding how and when to apply either of the two opposite approaches. Therefore, the Interpretive Report provides slightly different statements for those with an underlying Thinking or Feeling preference.
- *Logical and Compassionate:* Believes that applying logic is ideal but may actually make decisions by attending to Feeling values. This style accounted for just 3.2% of the national sample.
- *Empathetic and Reasonable:* Believes that considering values is the ideal way to make decisions but actually uses a logical approach based on principles of fairness and responsibilities to the group or organization. May experience tension in decisions that contrast the welfare of individuals against that of the group. This style was reported by 4.9% of the national sample.

When we look at decision-making styles for each of the sixteen types, some interesting differences emerge. Table 10.1 shows these results. Of the Thinking types, ENTPs have the highest percentage of the Logical and Reasonable style (84%), and ESTPs the lowest (54%). The percentages of Feeling types who favor both an Empathetic and a Compassionate approach run quite a bit lower than the comparable style for Thinking types. Of the Feeling types, ENFJs (66%) and ISFPs (65%) have the highest percent-

**Table 10.1 Percent of Decision-Making Styles by Type**

| Type | *N* | Logical and Reasonable | Empathetic and Compassionate | Midzone Both | Logical and Compassionate | Empathetic and Reasonable |
|---|---|---|---|---|---|---|
| **ESTJ** | 97 | 68 | 0 | 26 | 4 | 2 |
| **ENTJ** | 29 | 79 | 0 | 14 | 3 | 3 |
| **ISTP** | 73 | 64 | 1 | 27 | 0 | 7 |
| **INTP** | 43 | 70 | 0 | 28 | 0 | 2 |
| **ESFJ** | 143 | 1 | 57 | 36 | 3 | 3 |
| **ENFJ** | 38 | 0 | 66 | 26 | 0 | 8 |
| **ISFP** | 148 | 0 | 65 | 26 | 4 | 5 |
| **INFP** | 88 | 0 | 59 | 27 | 3 | 10 |
| **ESTP** | 54 | 54 | 0 | 44 | 0 | 2 |
| **ESFP** | 108 | 0 | 58 | 32 | 2 | 7 |
| **ISTJ** | 183 | 74 | 0 | 20 | 4 | 2 |
| **ISFJ** | 191 | 1 | 50 | 38 | 6 | 4 |
| **ENTP** | 25 | 84 | 0 | 4 | 8 | 4 |
| **ENFP** | 105 | 1 | 61 | 26 | 2 | 10 |
| **INTJ** | 19 | 79 | 0 | 21 | 0 | 0 |
| **INFJ** | 34 | 0 | 56 | 35 | 3 | 6 |

*Source:* National sample.

ages, while ISFJs are the lowest (50%). More ESTPs report a midzone style than other types (44%), and ENTPs infrequently report a midzone style (4%). Although it is a rare style, the two top percentages for Logical and Compassionate are two opposite types—ENTP (8%) and ISFJ (6%). It would be most interesting to discover what factors are involved in the decision making of ENTPs and ISFJs who show this pattern. The top percentages for the Empathetic and Reasonable style were INFPs and ENFPs (both 10%), the two types that extravert Intuition and introvert Feeling. This style is reported least frequently by INTJs (0%).

## The Step II™ Instrument and Dealing with Change

Dealing with changes and transitions within organizations has become a commonplace event in today's work world. The influence of type in this area is well documented (Barger & Kirby, 1995, 1997). Expanding our knowledge with the Step II tool enhances understanding of this important area. When we know the specific aspects of the dichotomies involved, we can deal more effectively with what is occurring typologically. This in turn enables employees to tolerate change, adapt to it, and contribute their skills and talents to the process.

Of the E–I facets, Expressive–Contained and Gregarious–Intimate appear to be influential. Four of the five S–N facets have an impact on dealing with change: Concrete–Abstract, Realistic–Imaginative, Experiential–Theoretical, and Traditional–Original. Of greatest importance on the T–F dichotomy is the Tough–Tender facet. The J–P facets Planful–Open-Ended and Methodical–Emergent are most influential in dealing with organizational change.

## The Step II™ Instrument and Conflict Management

Conflict within organizations has become prevalent as understaffing, reorganization and downsizing, increased competition, and resultant generalized stress have become chronic aspects of our work lives. The growing number of professional mediators and assessment instruments specific to conflict management attest to the critical need for intervention. Not all conflicts are type related; however, good information on the effects of Step I type and conflict in organizations can be found in chapter 13 of the *MBTI® Manual* (Myers et al., 1998) and in Myers, Kirby, and Myers, 1998; Hirsh and Kummerow, 1998; Pearman and Albritton, 1997; and Van Sant and Payne, 1995.

The effectiveness of type can be enhanced by understanding how specific facets contribute to the various ways in which different types respond to conflict. The E–I facet Expressive–Contained reflects whether conflict is dealt with openly and at the outset or later, after a period of individual reflection; another E–I facet, Gregarious–Intimate, identifies the number of people an individual will usually involve in dealing with conflicts. No specific S–N facets stand out in handling conflict. However, not surprisingly, nearly all the T–F facets are involved, the first two (Logical–Empathetic and Reasonable–Compassionate) as the five decision-making styles. In addition, Questioning–Accommodating and Tough–Tender are both important. Though not immediately obvious, the J–P facet Early Starting–Pressure-Prompted can be involved in conflict management. Early Starting people try to inhibit conflict by beginning projects well in advance of the deadline, while those who are Pressure-Prompted may inadvertently stimulate conflict when others have to deal with their style.

## The Step II™ Instrument and Teams

There is a good deal of literature about the Step I tool and team functioning. In addition to excellent information in Myers et al., 1998, and Hammer, 1996, see Hammer and Huszczo, 1996, and Hirsh, 1998.

It has generally been noted that the E–I dichotomy is the most differentiating in regard to team functioning. Introverts commonly feel that they are at a disadvantage on teams. Indeed, the results shown in table 10.2 in the research section of this chapter (p. 174) attest to the presence of all the E facet poles as characteristic of people who *like* to work on teams.

The introverted approach may lead others to conclude that Introverts are not team players. As a result, their talents and expertise may go unrecognized or unused in environments that favor group involvement. All the E–I facet scales identified as important for communication (the central feature of team activity) are vital for some depth of understanding among team members. When working with a team, consultants would do well to include exercises that highlight the contributions made to team functioning by people who favor each facet pole. Such exercises enable those with Introverted facet poles to recognize the assets they bring to the team and to have their contributions understood and valued by other team members. Simply grouping people according to their status at a pole or in the midzone of each E–I facet and asking them to discuss and list their group's contributions to a team can be very effective.

Facet understanding in teams may also be helpful in accounting for "missing" type perspectives—for instance, the absence of those who prefer Feeling. Using Step II data may reveal team members who are out-of-preference or, at the very least, in the midzone on one or more of the T–F facets. In some cases, openly discussing and confirming the value of all facets may enable team members to identify and use previously unacknowledged preferences, to the benefit of both themselves and the group. It is interesting to note that the data in table 10.2 that apply to working as part of a team show that all the E facet poles significantly differentiate respondents, as do one S facet pole, two N facet poles, four of the five F facet poles, one J facet pole, and two P facet poles. This variation within type dichotomies provides an excellent opportunity for understanding what attracts people to teams and how to maximize the effectiveness of each team member.

## The Step II™ Instrument and Leadership

Step II facets help identify leadership styles that might be puzzling when Step I dichotomies alone are considered. For example, the leadership style of an Expressive, Accepting, Methodical INTP may appear confusing to people who are accustomed to the more common Contained, Critical, Emergent INTPs. Similarly, leaders might gain a better understanding of employees and thus make appropriate use of individuals whose facet results could bring unique perspectives to teams or organizations.

The Step II instrument affords everyone involved in leadership development an opportunity to temper the prevalent and sometimes overwhelming opinion that the TJ approach is the best way of being a leader. The four TJ types tend to gravitate naturally to leadership roles, but other types also lead successfully, although their styles may differ markedly from that of TJs. By enabling recognition of the out-of-preference facets of a successful leader, particularly on Thinking–Feeling and Judging–Perceiving, Step II facets enable others to understand the source of a leader's distinctive approach, even when he or she is not a stereotypical leader type. For example, although ISFPs as a type are generally reluctant to take on leadership roles, an ISFP who is Expressive, Reasonable, and Methodical may well be attracted to leading others.

The Feeling and Perceiving facet poles may enhance as well as impede effective leadership. A leader whose decision-making style is Logical and Compassionate may be seen as unpredictable or guilty of favoritism when he or she ignores a stated procedure and arbitrarily chooses a close associate for a coveted assignment. By openly acknowledging the potential difficulties promoted by this style, the leader can take steps to defuse this issue, perhaps by providing acceptable explanations of such decisions to employees.

The Step II instrument also offers a rational basis for choosing preferred ways of accomplishing organizational goals in a comfortable manner. Some of the results in table 10.2 may be helpful.

There is a voluminous general literature on leadership available from booksellers and in professional journals in a number of relevant fields. Among practitioners of type as well, the area of leadership development and differing styles of leadership is receiving increasing attention. Fitzgerald and Kirby (1997) edited a book devoted to type and leadership, and one chapter in that book (Kummerow & Olson, 1997) presents the earlier version of the Step II tool in leader and manager development.

## Research on the Step II™ Instrument and Organizational Variables

Research on the contribution of the Step II tool to organizational variables sheds light on specific facets while it details instances in which whole type and type dynamics provide insight into organizational behavior. The discussion that follows highlights these results.

### Preferred Organizational Characteristics Research

This section presents available research dealing with preferred organizational characteristics. Participants in the national sample were presented with a list of organizational characteristics and asked to indicate how they would feel about working in such an organization. The response format offered three choices: "like," "indifferent," and "dislike."

**Advancement and High Pay** One of the characteristics participants were asked to consider was "Has opportunities for advancement and high pay, though job security may be limited." The Step II scales on which there were significant differences among the three categories are shown in figure 10.1. Only the Like (*N* = 148) and Dislike (*N* = 133) categories are graphed because the means for those who were indifferent were all close to 0.

Respondents who liked an organization with possibilities for advancement and high pay but limited job security were those scoring toward Original, Logical, Reasonable, and Tough. There was also a significant difference on the Questioning–Accommodating scale, due primarily to the fact that those who disliked such an organization scored toward the Accommodating pole, while those who liked such an organization were spread fairly evenly across the scale so that the mean was about 0. On the Early Starting–Pressure-Prompted scale, both groups scored toward Early Starting, congruent with the norms for this scale, but those who disliked this organizational characteristic scored significantly more toward Early Starting.

**Working as Part of a Team** Another characteristic listed on the survey was "Allows you to work as part of a team." There were significant differences on fifteen of the twenty facet scales. The means for the Like and Dislike groups are shown in figure 10.2. Only 22 people from the national sample responded "dislike" to this organizational characteristic. Despite the small percentage, the pattern of responses warrants discussion, since this is a major attribute of the modern corporation.

All five E–I facet scales showed a significant difference. Those who liked teamwork tended to have means near 0 on all the scales, indicating a large spread of scores on each scale. However, those who disliked teams had means toward the I poles of each scale.

Three of the S–N facet scales show significant differences, but for two scales, the differences are in opposite directions. On the Concrete–Abstract scale, those who liked teamwork scored less toward the S pole, or against the norms) while on the Traditional–Original scale, those who liked teams scored more toward the S, or Traditional, pole. The difference on the Experiential–Theoretical pole

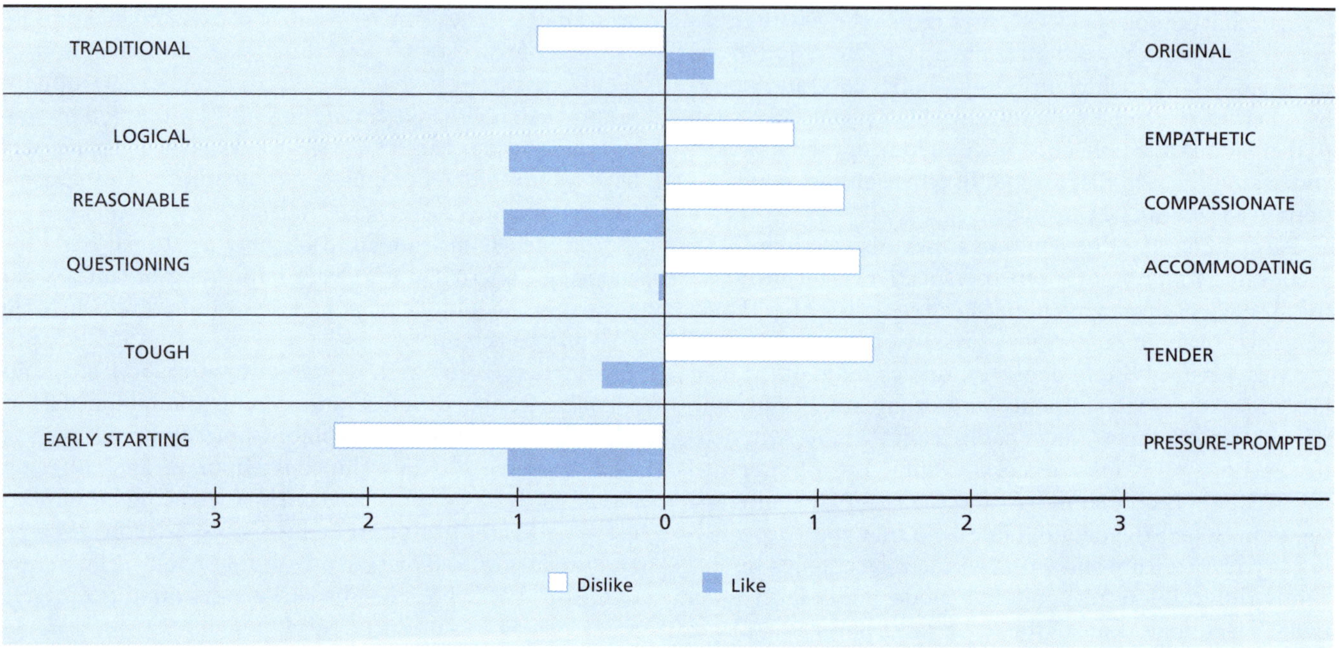


Figure 10.1 Advancement and High Pay but Limited Security

*Source:* National sample.

is also significant, but here the difference was caused by the fact that those who were indifferent toward teamwork (not shown on the graph) had a mean close to 0 on this scale, while those who liked or disliked teams had similar means.

Four T–F facet scales showed significant differences, with those who liked teams scoring toward the F poles and those who disliked teams scoring toward the T poles.

In the J–P dichotomy, three facet scales showed significant differences. On the Early Starting–Pressure-Prompted scale, those who liked teamwork scored more toward the J pole. On Scheduled–Spontaneous and Planful–Open-Ended, the significant differences were between those who were indifferent toward teams (not shown on the graph) and the other two groups. On Scheduled–Spontaneous, the Indifferent group scored much closer to 0, while on the Planful–Open-Ended scale, this group scored toward the Pressure-Prompted pole, as opposed to the Like and Dislike groups, who both scored toward the J pole.

Table 10.2 shows the remaining organizational characteristics and the poles of the Step II scales on which there were significant differences between the Like, Indifferent, and Dislike groups. For some of these characteristics, few people said "dislike," suggesting that a response scale with more differentiated options should have been used. For these scales, the differences between the groups may be exaggerated (i.e., the standard error of the mean is much higher when comparing means for small groups with those of larger ones) and should be interpreted with caution. To enable easy identification of these scales, the number of people saying "dislike" is included in the second column of the table.

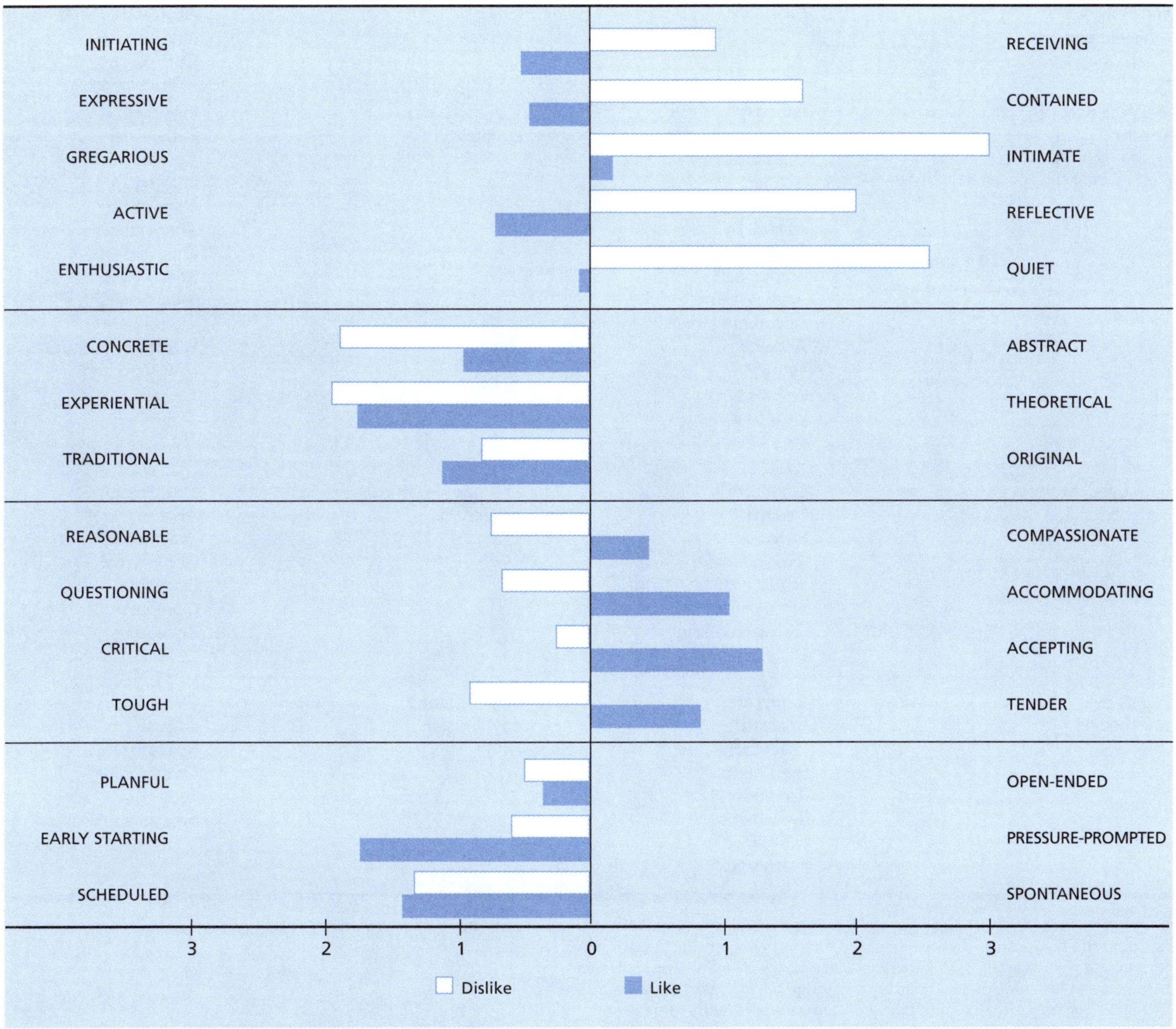


**Figure 10.2** Allows You to Work as Part of a Team

*Source:* National sample.

**Table 10.2 Poles of Significant Step II™ Facet Scales for Those Who Like This Organizational Characteristic**

| Organizational Characteristic | *N*[e] (Dislike) | Pole of Step II™ Scale for Like Group | Organizational Characteristic | *N* (Dislike) | Pole of Step II™ Scale for Like Group |
|---|---|---|---|---|---|
| Clear structures and lines of responsibility | 27 | Concrete<br>Realistic[a]<br>Experiential[b]<br>Traditional<br>Systematic<br>Planful<br>Early Starting<br>Scheduled<br>Methodical[b] | Does everything by the book | 504 | Concrete[b]<br>Realistic[b]<br>Practical[b]<br>Experiential[b]<br>Traditional[b]<br>Accommodating[b]<br>Systematic<br>Planful<br>Early Starting[b]<br>Scheduled[b]<br>Methodical[b] |
| Independence and individual achievement | 31 | Imaginative[c]<br>Original[c] | Has variety of tasks | 13 | Enthusiastic<br>Abstract[c]<br>Imaginative[c]<br>Original[c] |
| Work as part of a team | 22 | Initiating[d]<br>Expressive[d]<br>Gregarious[b]<br>Active[d]<br>Enthusiastic[d]<br>Abstract[b]<br>Theoretical[a]<br>Traditional[b]<br>Compassionate<br>Accommodating<br>Accepting<br>Tender<br>Open-Ended[a]<br>Early Starting[b]<br>Spontaneous[a] | Work in more than one country | 317 | Initiating<br>Enthusiastic<br>Abstract[b]<br>Imaginative[b]<br>Conceptual[b]<br>Theoretical[b]<br>Original[b]<br>Reasonable<br>Questioning[c]<br>Open-Ended<br>Pressure-Prompted[c]<br>Spontaneous[b] |
| Employee loyalty and job for life | 34 | Concrete[b]<br>Realistic[b]<br>Practical[b]<br>Experiential[b]<br>Traditional[b]<br>Empathetic<br>Compassionate<br>Early Starting[b] | Employs people of many different backgrounds | 35 | Enthusiastic<br>Abstract[c]<br>Imaginative[c]<br>Conceptual[c]<br>Empathetic<br>Compassionate<br>Accepting[b]<br>Tender[b] |
| Makes everyone toe the line | 458 | Concrete[b]<br>Realistic[b]<br>Practical[b]<br>Experiential[b]<br>Traditional[b]<br>Systematic[b]<br>Scheduled[b]<br>Methodical[b] | Advancement and high pay, limited job security | 406 | Original<br>Logical<br>Reasonable<br>Questioning[d]<br>Tough<br>Pressure-Prompted[b] |

*Notes:* Poles listed for the Like group if $p < .01$ for the scale; no note mark with poles indicates that the mean of the Like group was in the direction of this pole and the mean of the Dislike group was on the other side of the 0 point.
[a]Indifferent group significantly different from other two in direction indicated.
[b]All means on this side of 0; Like group mean significantly more toward indicated pole.
[c]All means on opposite side of 0; Like group mean significantly more toward indicated pole.
[d]Like group mean near 0; Dislike group mean toward opposite pole.
[e]*N* (Dislike) refers to the number of people who answered "dislike"; provided as a caution to not overinterpret findings based on small sample sizes.
*Source*: National sample.

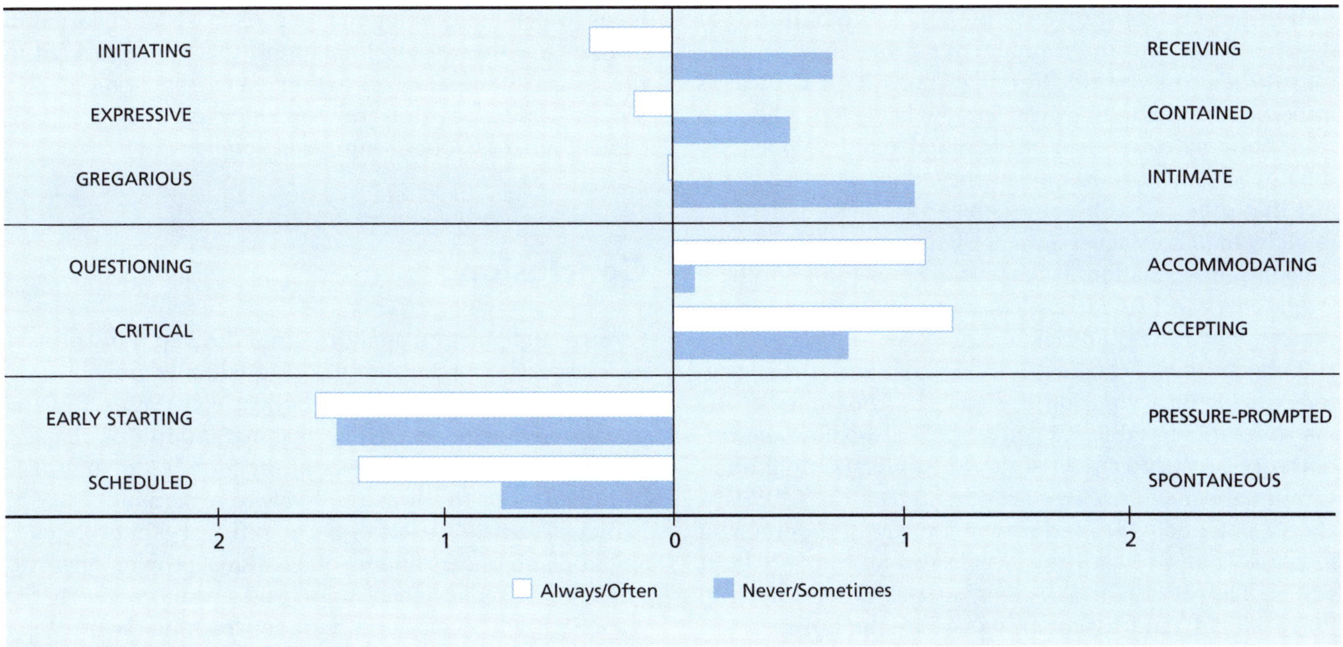


Figure 10.3 Support My Manager's Decisions
*Source:* National sample.

Of most interest are those characteristics for which significant differences exist on only a subset of the five scales within any facet, for it is with these characteristics that the unique and additional explanatory power of the Step II scales comes into play. For example, people who like an organization that emphasizes the independence and achievement of individual employees score more toward Imaginative and Original than do those in the Indifferent or Dislike groups. On the other hand, liking an organization that emphasizes employee loyalty and lifetime job security is related to scoring more toward the S pole of all the S–N facet scales. Of special interest, however, is the fact that two of the T–F facet scales also show significant differences. Those who like this kind of organization score toward Empathetic and Compassionate.

## Organizational Behavior Research

This section presents available research dealing with organizational behavior.

### Support Decisions of Manager

A question on the national survey asked how often the respondent supported the decisions of his or her supervisor or manager. The response format used a four-point scale: "almost always," "often," "sometimes," and "almost never." However, for the purpose of graphing the results and because the number of people answering "almost never" was low ($N = 15$), respondents were categorized into two groups: almost always/often ($N = 754$) and sometimes/almost never ($N = 191$). Figure 10.3 shows the Step II facet scales on which these two groups differed significantly.

Those who scored toward Receiving, Contained, and Intimate were less likely to support their managers' decisions. Within the T–F block, both supportive and nonsupportive groups scored toward Accommodating and Accepting, but nonsupportive people significantly less so. In the J–P block, the significant differences on the Early Starting–Pressure-Prompted scale were between those who said "almost never" ($M = -0.27$) and those who said "almost always" ($M = -1.92$), a very large mean difference. The graph does not reflect this, however, due to the dampening effect of the middle two categories that were combined with these scale anchors. A profile showing this pattern of scales should provide many hypotheses about specific behaviors that may affect the respondent's advancement within an organization.

### Additional Research on the Step II™ Instrument and Behavior in Organizations

Additional evidence for the relationship of the Step II scales to behavior in organizations can be seen in tables 8.7 and 8.8, on pages 137 and 138. These tables show the relationship between the facet scales and the scales of two different 360-degree rating scales. Step II scales are meaningfully related to self, superior, and composite ratings (composite ratings combine superior, peer, and subordinate ratings). Thirteen of the twenty Step II scales show such relationships, and in no instance are all five scales within any facet block related to the ratings, which supports the differential effectiveness of the facet scales in describing organizational behavior. The relationships shown in these two tables could also be used as the focus of leadership development efforts with individual clients. For example, an organization that requires leaders to build productive teams may perceive those who score toward Receiving, Logical, or Critical as underperforming in this area. Specific behaviors related to team building could then be identified and developed. Or those who score toward Empathetic could be alerted to the fact that other leaders with scores toward this pole were rated by their colleagues as in need of improved delegating skills. An examination of the relationships found in these two tables can provide a plethora of hypotheses for the professional leadership coach.

Correlations of the Step II facet scales with the special indexes of the *California Psychological Inventory* (CPI) instrument (see table 8.1, on p. 122) also show the importance of various facet scales for understanding organizational behavior. Those scoring high on the CPI Managerial Potential (MP) index scored toward Initiating and Expressive and toward the N poles on all the S–N facet scales. Those with high scores on the CPI Leadership Potential (LP) index scored high on all the E–I and S–N facet scales in the direction of E and N and also toward the Methodical pole of the Methodical–Emergent scale. Because different Step II scales are related to managerial and leadership behaviors, these findings may also help focus leadership development efforts. Also, as reported in chapter 8, Johnson (1992b) found that top achievers in the grocery industry had higher mean scores on all five S–N scales. In addition, the top achievers scored significantly higher on Questioning and Spontaneous.

## Conclusion

Creative and practical applications of the Step II instrument to all aspects of organizational life are limited only by considerations such as time and budget constraints and the practitioner's experience and imagination. In this chapter, we have suggested some uses of the Step II tool and have identified facets that are most likely to make a difference in particular areas. As users of the Step II tool gain experience and in-depth understanding of individual profiles, opportunities for effective intervention and enhancement in the workplace will become ever more apparent. Just as the Step I tool adds immensely to organizational effectiveness, so the application of the Step II tool can augment this knowledge and lead to increased satisfaction and productivity for all involved.

# Comparison of the MBTI® Step II™ Expanded Interpretive Report (1996) and the MBTI® Expanded Analysis Report

# A

The MBTI® Expanded Analysis Report (EAR; Saunders, 1989) was the first version of the Step II instrument. The EAR was renamed the MBTI® Step II Expanded Interpretive Report (EIR) in 1996, and changes were made in some subscale names as well as in the order in which subscales appear within each dichotomy. Some subscale names were changed to improve grammatical consistency, and others to better reflect the content of items included in the subscales. The ordering of some of the subscales was changed to better reflect the "contribution" of the subscale to its underlying dichotomy, to approximate the "order" in which components would typically be used by an individual, or, in some cases, for both reasons. In the 1996 Step II assessment, the subscale that appeared either conceptually or empirically to best represent the underlying dichotomy was placed first.

The subscale descriptions that were included in *MBTI® Step II™: A Description of the Subscales* were written as part of an ongoing revision process. As the result of analyses concluded prior to the revision described in this manual, three of the subscales were renamed to reflect their content more accurately. The name of one pole of a fourth subscale was changed for the same reason. It should be noted that the order of presentation introduced in 1996 is retained in the current revision. However, the names of several facet scale poles were modified. Table A.1 shows the names and order that were introduced in 1996 compared to those on the EAR.

In addition to these content changes, two Step II profiles replaced the single profile provided as the EAR. Three descriptive words or phrases beneath each pole of the subscales were also provided on the two-page client profile. The words or phrases identified the general meaning of the pole. The last page of the report repeated the subscale scores without the three descriptive words and included preference clarity indexes, type-specific norms, and the polarity index. Underlying age/gender norms, which were shown on the EAR profile, were dropped in 1996. Practitioner experience indicated that underlying norms were not sufficiently useful to warrant their retention. Furthermore, such norms shifted the focus from a typological system to a trait-based system that is inappropriate for the MBTI personality inventory.

**Table A.1 Name and Order of Step II™ EIR Subscales Compared to EAR Subscales**

| E–I Subscales | | | |
|---|---|---|---|
| *New Order* | *New Subscale Name* | *Old Order* | *Original Subscale Name* |
| 1 | Initiating–Receiving | 3 | Initiator–Receptor |
| 2 | Expressive–Contained | 4 | Expressive–Contained |
| 3 | Gregarious–Intimate | 1 | Gregarious–Intimate |
| 4 | Participative–Reflective | 5 | Auditory–Visual |
| 5 | Enthusiastic–Quiet | 2 | Enthusiastic–Quiet |
| **S–N Subscales** | | | |
| *New Order* | *New Subscale Name* | *Old Order* | *Original Subscale Name* |
| 1 | Concrete–Abstract | 1 | Concrete–Abstract |
| 2 | Realistic–Imaginative | 2 | Realistic–Imaginative |
| 3 | Practical–Inferential | 3 | Pragmatic–Intellectual |
| 4 | Experiential–Theoretical | 4 | Experiential–Theoretical |
| 5 | Traditional–Original | 5 | Traditional–Original |
| **T–F Subscales** | | | |
| *New Order* | *New Subscale Name* | *Old Order* | *Original Subscale Name* |
| 1 | Logical–Empathetic | 4 | Logical–Affective |
| 2 | Reasonable–Compassionate | 5 | Reasonable–Compassionate |
| 3 | Questioning–Accommodating | 3 | Questioning–Accommodating |
| 4 | Critical–Accepting | 1 | Critical–Accepting |
| 5 | Tough–Tender | 2 | Tough–Tender |
| **J–P Subscales** | | | |
| *New Order* | *New Subscale Name* | *Old Order* | *Original Subscale Name* |
| 1 | Systematic–Casual | 3 | Systematic–Casual |
| 2 | Planful–Open-Ended | 4 | Planful–Open-Ended |
| 3 | Early Starting–Pressure-Prompted | 1 | Stress Avoider–Polyactive |
| 4 | Scheduled–Spontaneous | 2 | Scheduled–Spontaneous |
| 5 | Methodical–Emergent | 5 | Methodical–Emergent |

# B Sources and Descriptions of Samples for the Revision

**Table B.1 Samples by Age and Gender**

| | | Age | | Gender | |
|---|---|---|---|---|---|
| **Sample** | *N* | *M* | *SD* | Female | Male |
| National Sample | 1,378 | 49 | 16 | 57% | 43% |
| Test-Retest | | | | | |
| Adult | 137 | 46 | 10 | 60% | 40% |
| College | 162 | 19 | 1 | 45% | 55% |

**Table B.2 Samples by Ethnicity**

| | Ethnicity | | | | |
|---|---|---|---|---|---|
| **Sample** | Caucasian | African American | Other | Refused | Missing |
| National Sample | 1,186 | 67 | 54 | 7 | 64 |
| Test-Retest | | | | | |
| Adult | 135 | 1 | | 1 | |
| College | 85 | 10 | | | 67 |

# C California Psychological Inventory™ and Adjective Check List Scale Descriptions

**Table C.1 Brief Descriptions of *California Psychological Inventory*™ (CPI™) Scales**

| Scale | | Brief Description |
|---|---|---|
| Do | Dominance | Confident, assertive, dominant, task-oriented |
| Cs | Capacity for Status | Ambitious, wants to be a success, independent |
| Sy | Sociability | Sociable, likes to be with people, friendly |
| Sp | Social Presence | Self-assured; spontaneous; a good talker; not easily embarrassed |
| Sa | Self-acceptance | Has good opinion of self; sees self as talented, personally attractive |
| In | Independence | Self-sufficient, resourceful, detached |
| Em | Empathy | Comfortable with self and well accepted by others; understands the feelings of others |
| Re | Responsibility | Responsible, reasonable, takes duties seriously |
| So | Socialization | Comfortably accepts ordinary rules and regulations, finds it easy to conform |
| Sc | Self-control | Tries to control emotions and temper; takes pride in being self-disciplined |
| Gi | Good Impression | Wants to make a good impression; tries to do what will please others |
| Cm | Communality | Fits in easily, sees self as a quite average person |
| Wb | Well-being | Feels in good physical and emotional health; optimistic about the future |
| To | Tolerance | Is tolerant of others' beliefs and values, even when different from or counter to own beliefs |
| Ac | Achievement via Conformance | Has strong drive to do well; likes to work in settings where tasks conformance and expectations are clearly defined |
| Ai | Achievement via Independence | Has strong drive to do well, likes working in settings that encourage freedom and individual initiative |
| Ie | Intellectual Efficiency | Efficient in use of intellectual abilities, keeps on task where others might give up; insightful, resourceful |
| Py | Psychological-mindedness | Insightful, perceptive, understands others' feelings but not necessarily supportive, nurturant |
| Fx | Flexibility | Flexible, likes change and variety; easily bored by routine, everyday experience; may be impatient; clever, imaginative |
| F/M | Femininity/Masculinity | Among males seen as high-strung, sensitive, esthetically reactive; females seen as sympathetic, warm, modest, dependent |
| V1 | Internality | Desires involvement, participation, and extraversion |
| V2 | Norm Favoring | Favors rules, responsibility, conscientiousness |
| V3 | Ego Integration | Has achieved self-realization, psychological competence, ego integration |
| Mp | Managerial Potential | Seeks managerial positions and has potential for good performance in those roles |
| Wo | Work Orientation | Has a strong, selfless, disciplined will to work |
| Ct | Creative Temperament | Is rated highly by observers as being creative |
| Lp | Leadership Potential | Has the potential to achieve leadership positions |
| Ami | Amicability | Is seen by others as cooperative, friendly, good-natured, etc. |
| Nar | Narcissism | Focuses on own exaggerated self-esteem, devaluation of others |

*Source:* Gough and Bradley, 1996. Used with permission.

## Table C.2 Brief Descriptions of *Adjective Check List* (ACL) Scales

| Need Scales<br>*(Assessing psychological needs or wants)* | |
|---|---|
| Achievement:<br>Ach | To strive to be outstanding in pursuits of socially recognized significance |
| Dominance:<br>Dom | To seek and maintain a role as leader in groups, or to be influential and controlling in individual relationships |
| Endurance:<br>End | To persist in any task undertaken |
| Order:<br>Ord | To place special emphasis on neatness, organization, and planning in one's activities |
| Intraception:<br>Int | To engage in attempts to understand one's own behavior or the behavior of others |
| Nurturance:<br>Nur | To engage in behaviors that provide material or emotional benefits to others |
| Affiliation:<br>Aff | To seek and maintain numerous personal friendships |
| Heterosexuality:<br>Het | To seek the company of and derive emotional satisfaction from interactions with opposite-sex peers |
| Exhibition:<br>Exh | To behave in such a way as to elicit the immediate attention of others |
| Autonomy:<br>Aut | To act independently of others or of social values and expectations |
| Aggression:<br>Agg | To engage in behaviors that attack or hurt others |
| Change:<br>Cha | To seek novelty of experience and to avoid routine |
| Succorance:<br>Suc | To solicit sympathy, affection, or emotional support from others |
| Abasement:<br>Aba | To express feelings of inferiority through self-criticism, guilt, or social impotence |
| Deference:<br>Def | To seek and maintain subordinate roles in relationships with others |

| Topical Scales<br>*(Assessing a diverse set of attributes, potentialities, and role characteristics)* | |
|---|---|
| Counseling Readiness Scale:<br>Crs | Readiness to accept counseling or professional advice in regard to personal problems, psychological difficulties and the like |
| Self-control:<br>S-Cn | The extent to which self-control is imposed and valued |
| Self-confidence:<br>S-Cfd | Self-confidence, poise, and self-assurance |
| Personal Adjustment:<br>P-Adj | Good adjustment in the sense of the ability to cope with situational and interpersonal demands, and a feeling of efficacy |

*Source:* Heilbrun and Bradley, 1983. Used with permission.

**Table C.2 Brief Descriptions of *Adjective Check List* (ACL) Scales** *continued*

| | |
|---|---|
| | **Topical Scales**<br>***(Assessing a diverse set of attributes, potentialities, and role characteristics)*** |
| Ideal Self Scale: Iss | Strong sense of personal worth; or, harmony between what one is and what one wants to be |
| Creative Personality Scale: Cps | The desire to do and think differently from the norm, and a talent for originality |
| Military Leadership Scale: Mls | Steadiness, self-discipline, and good judgment of the kind required in positions of military (or related) leadership |
| Masculine attributes scale: Mas | Role-qualities such as ambition, assertiveness, and initiative associated with everyday notions of masculinity |
| Feminine attributes scale: Fem | Role-qualities such as helpfulness, sympathy, and affection associated with everyday notions of femininity |
| | **Transactional Analysis Scales**<br>***(Assessing components of ego-functioning)*** |
| Critical Parent scale: CP | Attitudes of evaluation, severity, and skepticism associated with the concept of a "critical parent" |
| Nurturing Parent scale: NP | Attitudes of support, stability, and acceptance associated with the concept of a "nurturing parent" |
| Adult scale: A | Attitudes of independence, objectivity, and industriousness associated with the concept of "mature adult" |
| Free Child scale: FC | Attitudes of playfulness, impulsivity, and self-centeredness associated with the concept of a "free" or very expressive child |
| Adapted Child scale: AC | Attitudes of deference, conformity, and self-discipline associated with the concept of an "adapted" or very dutiful child |
| | **Origence–Intellectence Scales**<br>***(Assessing the balance between preferences for affective-emotional and rational-realistic modes of functioning)*** |
| High Origence, Low Intellectence: A-1 | Feelings and emotion (high origence) valued more highly than detachment and rationality (low intellectence). High scores suggest informality, vitality, and playfulness. |
| High Origence, High Intellectence: A-2 | High value placed on both affect (origence) and rationality (intellectence). High scores suggest versatility,unconventionality, and individuality. |
| Low Origence, Low Intellectence: A-3 | No particular value placed on either origence or intellectence. High scores suggest contentment, conventionality, and optimism. |
| Low Origence, High Intellectence: A-4 | Rationality and analysis (intellectence) valued more highly than feelings and emotion (origence). High scores suggest logicality, industriousness, and cognitive clarity. |

# Means, Standard Deviations, and Average Ranges of Scores for the Sixteen Types

# D

The information in this appendix is arrayed for ease of use by practitioners. For each of the sixteen types, the following information is provided:

- The number of people of the type in the national sample
- The average (mean) score for each facet scale
- The standard deviation for each facet scale
- The range of scores that vary from –1 to +1 standard deviations from the mean score

The order in which the types are presented is designed to approximate the familiar type table, with IJ types (the top row of the type table) listed first, followed by the IP types (the second row of the type table), then the EP types (the third row) and the EJ types (the last row).

The sample sizes for some types are quite small. However, the types represented here were the result of a randomly drawn national sample designed to approximate the U.S. population of adults who are eighteen years of age or older (see appendix B). Although larger sample sizes were available for the earlier (1996) version of the Step II instrument, those data were based on samples of convenience and were not representative samples.

Mean scores that are to the left of the 0 center point are designated with a minus sign (–) (i.e., scores on the E, S, T, and J side) in order to distinguish them from scores to the right of the 0 center point (i.e., scores on the I, N, F, and P side). When subtracting or adding the standard deviation to the mean resulted in a score greater than 5 or less than –5, the result was recorded as a 5 or –5, respectively, since these scores designate the endpoints of each scale. It was possible for such calculated hypothetical scores to fall beyond the endpoints of the scales because in most cases the facet scale scores do not assume a normal distribution. Furthermore, the distribution of scores for each type, which is the focus of the tables below, also does not assume a normal distribution. Some types are more likely to score toward the endpoints of the scales than are other types. (See chapter 6 for a discussion of scale score distributions.)

## Table D.1 Means, Standard Deviations, and Average Ranges of Scores for the IJ Types

| | ISTJ (N = 183) | | | ISFJ (N = 191) | | | INFJ (N = 34) | | | INTJ (N = 19) | | |
|---|---|---|---|---|---|---|---|---|---|---|---|---|
| **Step II™ Facet Scale** | *M* | *SD* | Range | *M* | *SD* | Range | *M* | *SD* | Range | *M* | *SD* | Range |
| *E–I Facet Scales* | | | | | | | | | | | | |
| Initiating–Receiving | 2.4 | 2.3 | 0.1 – 4.7 | 2.5 | 2.1 | 0.4 – 4.6 | 2.2 | 2.2 | 0.0 – 4.4 | 0.9 | 3.0 | –2.1 – 3.9 |
| Expressive–Contained | 2.1 | 2.2 | –0.1 – 4.3 | 1.3 | 2.4 | –1.1 – 3.7 | 1.4 | 2.1 | –0.7 – 3.5 | 2.3 | 1.2 | 1.1 – 3.5 |
| Gregarious–Intimate | 1.8 | 2.5 | –0.7 – 4.3 | 1.7 | 2.5 | –0.8 – 4.2 | 1.7 | 2.4 | –0.7 – 4.1 | 2.3 | 1.9 | 0.4 – 4.2 |
| Active–Reflective | 1.6 | 2.3 | –0.7 – 3.9 | 1.4 | 2.2 | –0.8 – 3.6 | 1.2 | 2.4 | –1.2 – 3.6 | 2.3 | 2.0 | 0.3 – 4.3 |
| Enthusiastic–Quiet | 2.7 | 2.0 | 0.7 – 4.7 | 2.2 | 2.5 | –0.3 – 4.7 | 0.8 | 3.0 | –2.2 – 3.8 | 2.6 | 1.6 | 1.0 – 4.2 |
| *S–N Facet Scales* | | | | | | | | | | | | |
| Concrete–Abstract | –3.0 | 1.8 | –4.8 – –1.2 | –2.2 | 1.9 | –4.1 – –0.3 | 1.9 | 2.2 | –0.3 – 4.1 | 1.9 | 2.6 | –0.7 – 4.5 |
| Realistic–Imaginative | –3.1 | 1.9 | –5.0 – –1.2 | –2.4 | 2.3 | –4.7 – –0.1 | 2.1 | 1.8 | 0.3 – 3.9 | 1.7 | 2.5 | –0.8 – 4.2 |
| Practical–Conceptual | –2.4 | 2.3 | –4.7 – –0.1 | –1.8 | 2.5 | –4.3 – 0.7 | 2.4 | 1.9 | 0.5 – 4.3 | 2.3 | 1.7 | 0.6 – 4.0 |
| Experiential–Theoretical | –3.6 | 2.0 | –5.0 – –1.6 | –3.4 | 1.9 | –5.0 – –1.5 | 1.1 | 2.3 | –1.2 – 3.4 | 2.6 | 2.7 | –0.1 – 5.0 |
| Traditional–Original | –2.4 | 2.1 | –4.5 – –0.3 | –2.7 | 2.1 | –4.8 – –0.6 | 0.3 | 2.2 | –1.9 – 2.5 | 1.4 | 2.7 | –1.3 – 4.1 |
| *T–F Facet Scales* | | | | | | | | | | | | |
| Logical–Empathetic | –2.7 | 1.8 | –4.5 – –0.9 | 1.4 | 2.2 | –0.8– 3.6 | 1.8 | 2.2 | –0.4 – 4.0 | –2.8 | 1.7 | –4.5 – –1.1 |
| Reasonable–Compassionate | –2.6 | 2.0 | –4.6 – –0.6 | 1.9 | 1.8 | 0.1– 3.7 | 1.9 | 1.7 | 0.2 – 3.6 | –2.5 | 2.1 | –4.6 – –0.4 |
| Questioning–Accommodating | 0.3 | 3.0 | –2.7 – 3.3 | 1.9 | 2.7 | –0.8– 4.6 | 1.5 | 2.6 | –1.1 – 4.1 | –1.0 | 2.4 | –3.4 – 1.4 |
| Critical–Accepting | –1.0 | 3.1 | –4.1 – 2.1 | 2.1 | 2.8 | –0.7– 4.9 | 2.4 | 3.1 | –.7 – 5.0 | –0.1 | 3.5 | –3.6 – 3.4 |
| Tough–Tender | –2.3 | 2.1 | –4.4 – –0.2 | 2.3 | 2.3 | 0.0– 4.6 | 2.7 | 2.4 | 0.3 – 5.0 | –2.8 | 1.6 | –4.4 – –1.2 |
| *J–P Facet Scales* | | | | | | | | | | | | |
| Systematic–Casual | –3.3 | 2.0 | –5.0 – –1.3 | –2.0 | 2.2 | –4.2 – 0.2 | –0.2 | 2.0 | –2.2 – 1.8 | –3.5 | 2.0 | –5.0 – –1.5 |
| Planful–Open-Ended | –2.9 | 2.7 | –5.0 – –0.2 | –2.8 | 2.6 | –5.0 – –0.2 | –3.2 | 2.2 | –5.0 – –1.0 | –1.4 | 3.9 | –5.0 – 2.5 |
| Early Starting–Pressure-Prompted | –2.7 | 2.7 | –4.7 – 0.0 | –2.9 | 2.6 | –5.0 – –0.3 | –2.7 | 2.3 | –5.0 – –0.4 | –1.6 | 2.7 | –4.3 – 1.1 |
| Scheduled–Spontaneous | –3.9 | 1.8 | –5.0 – –2.1 | –3.3 | 2.1 | –5.0 – –1.2 | –2.7 | 2.5 | –5.0 – –0.2 | –3.2 | 2.2 | –5.0 – –1.0 |
| Methodical–Emergent | –2.6 | 2.7 | –5.0 – 0.1 | –2.3 | 2.7 | –5.0 – 0.4 | –2.9 | 2.7 | –5.0 – –0.2 | –3.2 | 2.1 | –5.0 – –1.1 |

*Source:* National sample.

**Table D.2 Means, Standard Deviations, and Average Ranges of Scores for the IP Types**

| | ISTP (*N* = 73) | | | ISFP (*N* = 148) | | | INFP (*N* = 88) | | | INTP (*N* = 43) | | |
|---|---|---|---|---|---|---|---|---|---|---|---|---|
| **Step II™ Facet Scale** | *M* | *SD* | Range | *M* | *SD* | Range | *M* | *SD* | Range | *M* | *SD* | Range |
| *E–I Facet Scales* | | | | | | | | | | | | |
| Initiating–Receiving | 2.6 | 2.0 | 0.6 – 4.6 | 2.2 | 2.3 | –0.1 – 4.5 | 2.2 | 2.5 | –0.3 – 4.7 | 2.0 | 2.4 | –0.4 – 4.4 |
| Expressive–Contained | 1.8 | 2.5 | –0.7 – 4.3 | 1.9 | 1.9 | 0.0 – 3.8 | 1.8 | 2.4 | –0.6 – 4.2 | 2.6 | 2.1 | 0.5 – 4.7 |
| Gregarious–Intimate | 1.4 | 2.4 | –1.0 – 3.8 | 1.9 | 2.5 | –0.6 – 4.4 | 2.0 | 2.4 | –0.4 – 4.4 | 2.5 | 2.1 | 0.4 – 4.6 |
| Active–Reflective | 1.1 | 2.3 | –1.2 – 3.4 | 1.5 | 2.2 | –0.7 – 3.7 | 1.3 | 2.4 | –1.1 – 3.7 | 1.7 | 2.0 | –0.3 – 3.7 |
| Enthusiastic–Quiet | 2.2 | 2.5 | –0.3 – 4.7 | 1.8 | 2.6 | –0.8 – 4.4 | 1.0 | 2.8 | –1.8 – 3.8 | 1.2 | 2.5 | –1.3 – 3.7 |
| *S–N Facet Scales* | | | | | | | | | | | | |
| Concrete–Abstract | –2.0 | 2.2 | –4.2 – 0.2 | –1.4 | 2.0 | –3.4 – 0.6 | 2.9 | 2.1 | 0.8 – 5.0 | 2.2 | 2.2 | 0.0 – 4.4 |
| Realistic–Imaginative | –2.9 | 1.9 | –4.8 – –1.0 | –2.1 | 2.1 | –4.2 – 0.0 | 2.4 | 2.0 | 0.4 – 4.4 | 2.1 | 2.5 | –0.4 – 4.6 |
| Practical–Conceptual | –1.7 | 2.5 | –4.2 – 0.8 | –2.0 | 2.0 | –4.0 – 0.0 | 1.7 | 2.1 | –0.4 – 3.8 | 2.2 | 2.0 | 0.2 – 4.2 |
| Experiential–Theoretical | –2.9 | 2.4 | –5.0 – –0.5 | –2.6 | 2.3 | –4.9 – –0.3 | 2.1 | 3.0 | –0.9 – 5.0 | 2.1 | 2.5 | –0.4 – 4.6 |
| Traditional–Original | –1.5 | 2.4 | –3.9 – 0.9 | –1.9 | 2.2 | –4.1 – 0.3 | 1.7 | 2.4 | –0.7 – 4.1 | 2.5 | 2.6 | –0.1 – 5.0 |
| *T–F Facet Scales* | | | | | | | | | | | | |
| Logical–Empathetic | –2.1 | 2.1 | –4.2 – 0.0 | 2.0 | 1.8 | 0.2 – 3.8 | 2.8 | 2.0 | 0.8 – 4.8 | –2.8 | 1.7 | –4.5 – –1.1 |
| Reasonable–Compassionate | –2.6 | 1.8 | –4.4 – –0.8 | 2.2 | 1.8 | 0.4 – 4.0 | 1.8 | 2.0 | –0.2 – 3.8 | –2.5 | 1.9 | –4.4 – –0.6 |
| Questioning–Accommodating | 0.6 | 3.2 | –2.6 – 3.8 | 1.8 | 2.8 | –1.0 – 4.6 | 0.2 | 3.0 | –2.8 – 3.2 | –1.6 | 2.5 | –4.1 – 0.9 |
| Critical–Accepting | –1.0 | 2.8 | –3.8 – 1.8 | 1.6 | 1.6 | 0.0 – 3.2 | 2.5 | 2.7 | –0.2 – 5.0 | –0.6 | 3.0 | –3.6 – 2.4 |
| Tough–Tender | –2.0 | 2.0 | –4.0 – 0.0 | 2.1 | 2.4 | –0.3 – 4.5 | 2.7 | 2.2 | 0.5 – 4.9 | –1.9 | 2.2 | –4.1 – 0.3 |
| *J–P Facet Scales* | | | | | | | | | | | | |
| Systematic–Casual | 0.2 | 2.5 | –2.3 – 2.7 | 1.0 | 2.2 | –1.2 – 3.2 | 2.9 | 1.8 | 1.1 – 4.7 | 0.5 | 2.6 | –2.1 – 3.1 |
| Planful–Open-Ended | 3.0 | 2.4 | 0.6 – 5.0 | 2.9 | 2.4 | 0.5 – 5.0 | 3.3 | 2.3 | 1.0 – 5.0 | 3.8 | 1.7 | 2.1 – 5.0 |
| Early Starting–Pressure-Prompted | –0.5 | 3.0 | –3.5 – 2.5 | –1.5 | 2.7 | –4.2 – 1.2 | 0.0 | 3.1 | –3.1 – 3.1 | 0.7 | 3.0 | –2.3 – 3.7 |
| Scheduled–Spontaneous | 1.0 | 2.2 | –1.2 – 3.2 | 1.2 | 1.6 | –0.4 – 2.8 | 1.8 | 1.8 | 0.0 – 3.6 | 2.1 | 2.0 | 0.1 – 4.1 |
| Methodical–Emergent | 0.6 | 3.1 | –2.5 – 3.7 | 1.0 | 3.0 | –2.0 – 4.0 | 1.0 | 3.4 | –2.4 – 4.4 | 1.7 | 3.2 | –1.5 – 4.9 |

*Source:* National sample.

## Table D.3 Means, Standard Deviations, and Average Ranges of Scores for the EP Types

| | ESTP (N = 54) | | | ESFP (N = 108) | | | ENFP (N = 105) | | | ENTP (N = 25) | | |
|---|---|---|---|---|---|---|---|---|---|---|---|---|
| **Step II™ Facet Scale** | *M* | *SD* | Range | *M* | *SD* | Range | *M* | *SD* | Range | *M* | *SD* | Range |
| *E–I Facet Scales* | | | | | | | | | | | | |
| Initiating–Receiving | −3.0 | 2.2 | −5.0 – −0.8 | −3.2 | 1.8 | −5.0 – −1.4 | −3.4 | 1.9 | −5.0 – −1.5 | −2.9 | 2.1 | −5.0 – −0.8 |
| Expressive–Contained | −1.4 | 2.6 | −4.0 – 1.2 | −2.2 | 2.1 | −4.3 – −0.1 | −2.9 | 2.1 | −5.0 – −0.8 | −2.0 | 2.4 | −4.4 – 0.4 |
| Gregarious–Intimate | −2.1 | 2.1 | −4.2 – 0.0 | −1.3 | 2.6 | −3.9 – 1.3 | −1.8 | 2.4 | −4.2 – 0.6 | −1.5 | 2.1 | −3.6 – 0.6 |
| Active–Reflective | −2.8 | 2.1 | −4.9 – −0.7 | −2.1 | 2.2 | −4.3 – 0.1 | −2.7 | 2.5 | −5.0 – −0.2 | −2.3 | 2.2 | −4.5 – −0.1 |
| Enthusiastic–Quiet | −2.2 | 2.2 | −4.4 – 0.0 | −2.1 | 2.3 | −4.4 – 0.2 | −3.2 | 1.9 | −5.0 – −1.3 | −2.8 | 2.7 | −5.0 – −0.1 |
| *S–N Facet Scales* | | | | | | | | | | | | |
| Concrete–Abstract | −2.1 | 1.8 | −3.9 – −0.3 | −1.3 | 1.8 | −3.1 – .5 | 3.0 | 1.8 | 1.2 – 4.8 | 3.0 | 2.2 | 0.8 – 5.0 |
| Realistic–Imaginative | −2.3 | 2.0 | −4.3 – −0.3 | −1.4 | 2.6 | −4.0 – 1.2 | 3.1 | 1.7 | 1.4 – 4.8 | 2.6 | 2.2 | 0.4 – 4.8 |
| Practical–Conceptual | −2.0 | 2.8 | −4.8 – 0.8 | −1.5 | 2.5 | −4.0 – 1.0 | 1.9 | 2.3 | −0.4 – 4.2 | 2.5 | 1.8 | 0.7 – 4.3 |
| Experiential–Theoretical | −2.4 | 2.5 | −4.9 – 0.1 | −2.7 | 2.3 | −5.0 – −0.4 | 2.8 | 2.5 | 0.3 – 5.0 | 3.0 | 2.5 | 0.5 – 5.0 |
| Traditional–Original | −1.4 | 2.0 | −3.8 – 1.0 | −1.7 | 2.5 | −4.2 – 0.8 | 2.3 | 2.0 | 0.3 – 4.3 | 3.2 | 1.8 | 1.4 – 5.0 |
| *T–F Facet Scales* | | | | | | | | | | | | |
| Logical–Empathetic | −2.0 | 2.2 | −4.2 – 0.2 | 2.3 | 1.9 | 0.4 – 4.2 | 2.6 | 2.1 | 0.5 – 4.7 | −3.4 | 1.5 | −4.9 – −1.9 |
| Reasonable–Compassionate | −2.0 | 2.0 | −4.0 – 0.0 | 2.0 | 1.9 | 0.1 – 3.9 | 1.9 | 2.0 | −0.1 – 3.9 | −2.9 | 1.8 | −4.7 – −1.1 |
| Questioning–Accommodating | −0.5 | 3.0 | −3.5 – 2.5 | 1.2 | 2.9 | −1.7 – 4.1 | 0.1 | 2.7 | −2.6 – 2.8 | −1.4 | 3.0 | −4.4 – 1.6 |
| Critical–Accepting | −1.1 | 3.0 | −4.1 – 1.9 | 2.2 | 2.6 | −0.4 – 4.8 | 2.6 | 2.7 | −0.1 – 5.0 | −0.1 | 3.0 | −3.1 – 2.9 |
| Tough–Tender | −2.2 | 2.0 | −4.2 – −0.2 | 1.9 | 2.3 | −0.4 – 4.2 | 2.4 | 2.2 | 0.2 – 4.6 | −1.1 | 2.5 | −3.6 – 1.4 |
| *J–P Facet Scales* | | | | | | | | | | | | |
| Systematic–Casual | 0.6 | 2.7 | −2.1 – 3.3 | 1.1 | 2.4 | −1.3 – 3.5 | 3.3 | 2.0 | 1.3 – 5.0 | 1.8 | 3.0 | −1.2 – 4.8 |
| Planful–Open-Ended | 3.1 | 2.5 | 0.6 – 5.0 | 2.5 | 2.6 | −0.1 – 5.0 | 3.2 | 2.5 | 0.7 – 5.0 | 3.3 | 2.7 | 0.6 – 5.0 |
| Early Starting–Pressure-Prompted | 0.0 | 3.3 | −3.3 – 3.3 | −0.7 | 2.7 | −3.4 – 2.0 | 0.7 | 3.0 | −2.3 – 3.7 | 0.7 | 3.1 | −2.4 – 3.8 |
| Scheduled–Spontaneous | 1.1 | 2.0 | −0.9 – 3.1 | 1.1 | 1.6 | −0.5 – 2.7 | 1.7 | 2.1 | −0.4 – 3.8 | 2.0 | 1.9 | 0.1 – 3.9 |
| Methodical–Emergent | 1.6 | 2.9 | −1.3 – 4.5 | 0.4 | 3.0 | −2.6 – 3.4 | 1.1 | 3.3 | −2.2 – 4.4 | 0.5 | 3.6 | −3.1 – 4.1 |

*Source:* National sample.

## Table D.4 Means, Standard Deviations, and Average Ranges of Scores for the EJ Types

| | ESTJ (*N* = 97) | | | ESFJ (*N* = 143) | | | ENFJ (*N* = 38) | | | ENTJ (*N* = 29) | | |
|---|---|---|---|---|---|---|---|---|---|---|---|---|
| **Step II™ Facet Scale** | *M* | *SD* | Range | *M* | *SD* | Range | *M* | *SD* | Range | *M* | *SD* | Range |
| *E–I Facet Scales* | | | | | | | | | | | | |
| Initiating–Receiving | −3.4 | 1.6 | −5.0. – −1.8 | −3.1 | 1.8 | −4.9 – −1.3 | −3.4 | 1.6 | −5.0 – −1.8 | −3.6 | 1.7 | −5.0 – −1.9 |
| Expressive–Contained | −1.8 | 2.5 | −4.3 – 0.7 | −2.6 | 2.0 | −4.6 – −0.6 | −3.2 | 1.9 | −5.0 – −1.3 | −2.9 | 2.4 | −5.0 – −0.5 |
| Gregarious–Intimate | −2.1 | 2.4 | −4.5 – 0.3 | −2.0 | 2.0 | −4.0 – 0.0 | −1.2 | 2.7 | −3.9 – 1.5 | −1.3 | 2.9 | −4.2 – 1.6 |
| Active–Reflective | −1.6 | 2.4 | −4.0 – 0.8 | −2.4 | 2.1 | −4.5 – −0.3 | −2.1 | 2.4 | −4.5 – 0.3 | −2.1 | 2.1 | −4.2 – 0.0 |
| Enthusiastic–Quiet | −1.9 | 2.3 | −4.2 – 0.4 | −1.8 | 2.5 | −4.3 – 0.7 | −3.1 | 2.0 | −5.0 – −1.1 | −2.9 | 2.1 | −5.0 – −0.8 |
| *S–N Facet Scales* | | | | | | | | | | | | |
| Concrete–Abstract | −2.5 | 2.0 | −4.5– −0.5 | −2.0 | 2.0 | −4.0 – 0.0 | 2.4 | 1.9 | 0.5 – 4.3 | 2.5 | 2.0 | 0.5 – 4.5 |
| Realistic–Imaginative | −2.9 | 1.8 | −4.7– −1.1 | −2.0 | 2.3 | −4.3 – 0.3 | 2.3 | 1.8 | 0.5 – 4.1 | 1.6 | 2.6 | −1.0 – 4.2 |
| Practical–Conceptual | −2.4 | 2.3 | −4.7– −0.1 | −1.7 | 2.2 | −3.9 – 0.5 | 2.1 | 1.8 | 0.3 – 3.9 | 2.6 | 1.9 | 0.7 – 4.5 |
| Experiential–Theoretical | −3.4 | 2.0 | −5.0– −1.4 | −3.2 | 2.0 | −5.0 – −1.2 | 1.7 | 3.0 | −1.3 – 4.7 | 3.7 | 1.8 | 1.9 – 5.0 |
| Traditional–Original | −2.0 | 2.0 | −4.0– 0.0 | −2.5 | 2.0 | −4.5 – −0.5 | 1.1 | 1.8 | −0.7 – 2.9 | 1.4 | 2.1 | −0.7 – 3.5 |
| *T–F Facet Scales* | | | | | | | | | | | | |
| Logical–Empathetic | −2.6 | 1.7 | −4.3 – −0.9 | 1.7 | 2.0 | −0.3 – 3.7 | 3.1 | 1.8 | 1.3 – 4.9 | −2.9 | 1.7 | −4.6 – −1.2 |
| Reasonable–Compassionate | −2.4 | 1.9 | −4.3 – −0.5 | 2.0 | 1.8 | 0.2 – 3.8 | 2.4 | 2.1 | 0.3 – 4.5 | −2.8 | 1.8 | −4.6 – −1.0 |
| Questioning–Accommodating | 0.6 | 3.1 | −2.5 – 3.7 | 2.2 | 2.4 | −0.2 – 4.6 | 0.6 | 2.4 | −1.8 – 3.0 | −1.0 | 2.6 | −3.6 – 1.6 |
| Critical–Accepting | −0.4 | 3.1 | −3.5 – 2.7 | 2.4 | 2.8 | −0.4 – 5.0 | 3.1 | 2.3 | 0.8 – 5.0 | 0.3 | 3.3 | −3.0 – 3.6 |
| Tough–Tender | −1.9 | 2.2 | −4.1 – 0.3 | 2.2 | 2.3 | −0.1 – 4.5 | 2.8 | 2.0 | 0.8 – 4.8 | −1.9 | 2.2 | −4.1 – 0.3 |
| *J–P Facet Scales* | | | | | | | | | | | | |
| Systematic–Casual | −3.0 | 2.1 | −5.0 – −0.9 | −1.6 | 2.1 | −3.7 – 0.5 | −0.6 | 2.6 | −3.2 – 2.0 | −2.9 | 2.2 | −5.0 – −0.7 |
| Planful–Open-Ended | −3.1 | 2.5 | −5.0 – −0.6 | −3.1 | 2.6 | −5.0 – −0.5 | −3.1 | 2.6 | −5.0 – −0.5 | −3.2 | 2.4 | −5.0 – −0.8 |
| Early Starting–Pressure-Prompted | −2.9 | 2.3 | −5.0 – −0.6 | −3.1 | 2.4 | −5.0 – −0.7 | −2.5 | 2.3 | −4.8 – −0.2 | −1.7 | 3.1 | −4.8 – 1.4 |
| Scheduled–Spontaneous | −3.8 | 1.9 | −5.0 – −1.9 | −3.6 | 1.9 | −5.0 – −1.7 | −3.3 | 2.1 | −5.0 – −1.2 | −3.4 | 2.2 | −5.0 – −1.2 |
| Methodical–Emergent | −2.9 | 2.6 | −5.0 – −0.3 | −2.4 | 2.7 | −5.0 – 0.3 | −2.8 | 2.6 | −5.0 – −0.2 | −3.3 | 2.5 | −5.0 – −0.8 |

*Source:* National sample.

# Notes

## Chapter 1

1. Saunders' original subscales were described in *The Type Differentiation Indicator Manual* (1987) and *Manual: MBTI® Expanded Analysis Report* (1989). Interested readers can find relevant details in those sources.
2. Readers may note the similarity between Conceptual and Theoretical as facet pole names. In fact, the content of Practical–Conceptual and Experiential–Theoretical is substantially different. In distinguishing between the meanings of *conceptual* and *theoretical*, it may be helpful to think of *conceptual* as referring to the unit of thought, while *theoretical* focuses on relating various ideas into an overall pattern or theory.

## Chapter 2

1. A caveat in this regard is the moderate correlation between the S–N and J–P scales of the MBTI instrument. For information about the rationale and issues involved, see Myers et al., 1998.

## Chapter 3

1. Both the Logical–Empathetic and the Reasonable–Compassionate facets address the issue of preferring the Thinking or Feeling approach to decision making. However, there is a good deal of evidence to suggest that Logical–Empathetic reflects an intended or "ideal" decision-making style, while Reasonable–Compassionate reflects a person's actual way of making decisions. The combination of scores on these first two facets of the T–F block were used to create five different "problem-solving styles": Logical and Reasonable, Empathetic and Compassionate, Logical and Compassionate, Empathetic and Reasonable, and midzone on both, with either a T underlying preference or an F underlying preference. These styles and their occurrence in the national sample are described in chapter 10, on page 169.

## Chapter 5

1. The 1996 Expanded Interpretive Report applied different score criteria to determine in-preference, out-of-preference, and midzone results on two subscales: Critical–Accepting and Tough–Tender. These subscales were strongly skewed toward the Feeling poles, even among people with an underlying preference for Thinking, and an adjustment was therefore deemed appropriate. For example, a score of 8 was the cutoff for a Thinking type to be considered out-of-preference on Critical–Accepting and Tough–Tender, instead of the 7 required for the other eighteen subscales. No such adjustments were judged necessary in this revision, even for facet scales with clearly skewed distributions. This decision acknowledges the social pressures exerted on certain facets and the value of the information provided by respondents' actual, unadjusted responses to the items in those facets.
2. This is due to the difference in the set of statements for in-preference and out-of-preference results. The statements are based on self-reports of people who have verified their facet scale results.
3. Possible evidence is provided by respondents with midzone patterns who obtain preference clarity indexes in the "clear" category, suggesting that their preference for one pole of the dichotomy is consistently elicited in a manner that is not a function of the dichotomy's five facets.

## Chapter 7

1. Data collected by Cook Research of Edina, Minnesota.
2. Data collected by Lisa Larson, Ph.D.

## Chapter 9

1. The prevalent belief is that creativity is associated with Intuition rather than Sensing. A footnote in chapter 3 of the *MBTI® Manual* (Myers et al., 1998) offers a perspective on this important issue and is reproduced here with permission:

> Intellectual tradition and various research approaches have associated *creativity* with an intuitive preference. When creativity is defined as the creation of something new that has not existed before, one can appropriately describe Sensing perception as "creative" as well. The *process* whereby Sensing perception develops something new may be the step-by-step, methodical, and detailed procedure characteristic of *introverted* Sensing, or the *extraverted Sensing* process of creating something new by adapting and combining whatever elements are available in the current situation. The Sensing process is in contrast to the flashes of insight that we associate with intuition. However, the *product* created through either introverted to extraverted Sensing may be a new one that has not existed

before. A likely example of introverted Sensing creativity may be Thomas Edison's invention of electricity, which reportedly resulted from a long series of trial-and-error efforts to find an effective conductor. (p. 387)

## Chapter 10

1. There will be a forthcoming publication devoted to Step II applications, facilitation, and training.
2. When scores are at one or the other pole on one facet and in the midzone on the other, accurate identification of the respondent's decision-making style may be difficult. The Step II report uses a set of criteria for such cases. Practitioners should make sure that such "ambiguous" profiles are adequately verified by clients.

# Glossary of Terms

**alpha.** A measure of internal consistency of items in a facet scale. Statistically speaking, it is the aveveage correlation among the items on a scale.

**analysis of variance (ANOVA).** Statistical analysis used to determine the effects of one or more categorical independent variables on the variance of a continuous dependent variable. The analysis indicates which independent variables have a significant effect on the dependent variable and also identifies any statistical interactions among the independent variables that may affect the dependent variable.

**ANOVA.** *See* **analysis of variance.**

**a posteriori.** A probability that has been revised based on prior information; a probability that is conditioned upon a prior event or prior knowledge.

**asymptote.** A straight line that is approached by a given curve as one of the variables defining the curve approaches infinity; the theoretical upper or lower limit of such a curve. A curve is asymptotic if it approaches such a limit.

**attitude.** In Jungian theory, introversion and extraversion are two bipolar attitudes related to the direction in which psychic energy flows: inward for introversion and outward for extraversion. The *Myers-Briggs Type Indicator* (MBTI) personality inventory also uses *attitude* to refer to selection of the judging preference (T or F) or perceiving preference (S or N) as a means of dealing with the outer world. The term *orientation* is used interchangeably with *attitude*.

**attitude of the function.** This refers to whether a function (S, N, T, or F) is used in the extraverted or introverted attitude. If a function is used in the extraverted attitude, the psychic energy of that function flows outward. If it is used in the introverted attitude, the psychic energy of the function flows inward.

**auxiliary function.** In Jungian theory, this is the function (S, N, T, or F) that is second in importance. With respect to the dominant function, it provides a balance between introversion and extraversion and between the judging and perceiving functions. If the dominant function is a judging function used in the extraverted attitude, then the auxiliary function will be a perceiving function used in the introverted attitude.

**average.** The value obtained by adding together the scores of each individual in a sample or group and then dividing the sum by the number of individuals. In type research, many different averages may be computed, depending on the combination of type preferences or the whole type under consideration.

**bipolar.** In type theory, there are four basic dichotomies that make up the MBTI typology. Each dichotomy is bipolar, meaning that it describes psychologically opposite characteristics and that there is a threshold near the middle of the distribution of scores on either side of which people are *qualitatively* different.

**categorical response.** A response in which a person indicates his or her choice among different kinds of things, such as activities, word pairs, or beliefs. In choosing among different kinds of things, the person is indicating only which of the alternatives is preferred, *not* how strongly it is preferred.

**characteristic.** A distinctive feature, attribute, or part of a person that can be measured or studied as distinct from the whole person. In type theory, each preference consists of many characteristics, some of which are measured by the Step II facets.

**chi-square test.** A statistical test used to determine the degree of independence or relationship between nominal and categorical variables. The test involves a comparison of the observed and the expected frequencies in each category and determines the probability that the differences between them occurred by chance.

**classical test theory (CTT).** A model used to construct, score, and evaluate instruments designed to measure individual differences. Classical test theory assumes every individual has a hypothetical but unobservable true score on a given variable, but this true score is estimated through an observed score on a measuring instrument. Because the observed score is only an estimate of the hypothetical true score, CTT uses methods for determining the reliability of observed scores and includes estimates of an item's difficulty and ability to discriminate.

**Comfort–Discomfort scales.** Seven scales for which scores are obtained with the *Type Differentiation Indicator* (TDI) but not with the Step II tool. Although the comfort scales are somewhat correlated to type preferences, they do not measure the characteristics we normally ascribe to the eight MBTI preferences.

**concept.** A generalized, abstract idea that refers to attributes that are held in common by many specific instances or examples of something. The concept of extraversion, for example, is an abstract idea that includes the characteristics shared by certain people (extraverts). The concept of extraversion does not include the unique personal qualities that make each extravert different from every other extravert.

**construct.** A concept that has been modified by experts in a field to make it more useful as part of a theory, to give it a more precise meaning than it has in everyday usage, or to increase its ability to explain a subject of interest in the field.

**continuous scores.** On Form M and Form Q, the continuous scores are theta scores from the item response theory (IRT) scoring program. On Form M, theta is used to estimate the preference clarity index. Continuous scores are applied in research; interpreting them to clients is not recommended.

**correlation.** In statistics, the situation in which the values of two variables tend to change simultaneously.

**data.** In research, data are measurements or observations that have been collected by systematic methods, often for the purpose of answering questions or testing hypotheses in a scientific field. When data are collected using systematic rules, subsequent investigators can collect their own data and perform the original study again to confirm whether the same results can be produced and verified.

**dependent variable.** In a research study or statistical analysis, the dependent variable is the one that is acted upon (influenced by) the other variables. Whether a given variable is considered independent or dependent may vary according to the study design or analysis.

**dichotomy.** In MBTI usage, the four sets of preferences: E–I, S–N, T–F, and J–P. Unlike the traits in other personality instruments, the four MBTI dichotomies are bipolar. That is, they describe psychologically opposite characteristics and have a threshold, which is near the middle of the range of scores, that separates people who prefer different *kinds* of psychic attitudes or functions.

**dominant function.** The function (S, N, T, or F) that is assumed to be first developed, most preferred, most differentiated, most easily used, and most consciously accessible. It is used in the attitude described by the first letter of a person's type.

**EAR.** *See* **Expanded Analysis Report.**

**empirical.** Based on systematic measurement, observation, or experiment.

**Expanded Analysis Report (EAR).** The Expanded Analysis Report was the name given to the original version of the MBTI instrument that generated a person's type and profile on twenty subscales. It allowed a fuller description of how a person might express his or her four-letter type. The EAR has been replaced by the Step II instrument.

**facet.** A single aspect or quality contained in a much broader concept that includes many facets. Each MBTI dichotomy contains interrelated facets, five of which have been identified and are measured by the Step II scoring system.

**facet scale.** One of the twenty scales of the Step II instrument; each scale contains two opposite poles. *See* **subscale.**

**factor.** A group of correlated items, as identified in factor analysis. Because items that correlate tend to measure the same thing, researchers often give the factor a name that reflects the common property measured by the factor's items.

**factor analysis.** A statistical procedure that analyzes the correlations among a pool of items in order to find items that tend to correlate more highly with one another than with the other items in the pool. When analyzing a large pool of items, it is common to find several such "clusters" of items. By looking at the content of the items that cluster together, a researcher can make inferences about the characteristic measured by that item cluster. There are two primary kinds of factor analysis, *exploratory* and *confirmatory*. *Exploratory factor analysis* is conducted when the researcher has little theory or prior evidence to suggest how many factors may be present in the data set. *Confirmatory factor analysis* is more rigorous and is conducted to test a specific hypothesis about how many factors are present and which items form those factors.

**fit index.** One of many indexes used in *confirmatory factor analysis* (*see* **factor analysis**) to quantify the degree of fit between a hypothesized model and the actual data.

**forced-choice.** A format for test items in which each item presents several alternative choices from which the respondent may choose only one.

**Form J.** A form of the MBTI assessment tool containing 290 items that are scored to yield the *Type Differentiation Indicator* (TDI). The TDI profile contains scores on 27 subscales, 7 of which describe characteristics that expand our understanding of how type may be expressed but that are not descriptive of bipolar type preferences.

**Form K.** The form of the MBTI instrument that preceded Form Q. It contains 131 items that were scored to yield the Step II™ Profile.

**function.** One of the two basic psychic processes of perceiving (Sensing or Intuition), or one of the two basic psychic processes of making judgments (Thinking or Feeling). In MBTI theory, each of these four processes is also called a preference.

**independent variable.** A variable that, in the limited context of a particular research study or statistical analysis, is thought to affect and produce changes in other variables. An independent variable is separate from and not influenced by other variables.

**inferior function.** The most unconscious form or level in the hierarchy of four functions described by Jung, the other three being the dominant function, auxiliary function, and tertiary function. Often refers to the function that takes this form for an individual, as in "her inferior function is extraverted Sensing."

**in-preference score.** Facet score that lies beyond the midzone of 0 or 1 in the direction of either pole and is on the same side of the midzone as the underlying preference—that is, to the right for I, N, F, or P and to the left for E,S,T, or J.

**instrument.** A tool for making measurements. In psychology, an instrument is often a set of printed items that presents the individual with a series of possible responses. The individual's choices are recorded according to a set of rules or instructions. In some cases, a score may then be obtained from an additional set of rules or instructions that explains how to summarize the responses in a way that reflects personality type (for example, the MBTI personality inventory), ability (achievement tests), or skill (aptitude tests).

**internal consistency.** The degree to which the items included in a scale or instrument tend to measure the same content.

**item.** A single question or statement requiring a response that constitutes part of an instrument. Collected responses are then used to obtain a score that represents a measurement of a characteristic of the individual.

**item characteristic curve (ICC).** In item response theory, a curve describing a test item. It shows the rate at which an item would hypothetically be endorsed by people who have varying levels of the characteristic in question. The rate of item endorsement varies from 0% to 100% and is plotted on the vertical axis. The horizontal axis shows levels of the psychological characteristic.

**item response theory (IRT).** An approach to measurement that is concerned with modeling the relationship between item responses and the underlying characteristic assessed by the scale or test the item is designed to measure. IRT can be used to select items for a test and/or to score the items.

**kurtosis.** The degree to which a distribution of scores is peaked or flat. A normal curve has a kurtosis of 0.

**LISREL.** A statistical software package used to model and test the causal relationships among a system of variables. It allows for the simultaneous evaluation of both the measurement and the causal components in a set of variables.

**measurement.** In its most general sense, this means assigning numbers to observations according to rules. In psychology, observations can be noted by a researcher or may be an individual's responses to items on a questionnaire. When we use rules to assign numbers to our observations (as in the case of aptitude or skill tests), we try to design the rules so that the numbers depict amounts of characteristics. In the case of the MBTI instrument, the numbers are not used to quantify amounts but rather to determine which of several preferences best describe the individual.

**midpoint.** On most scales, the midpoint is the numerical center of the scale. For the bipolar scales of the MBTI Step I instrument, the psychological midpoint is the point that separates people showing one preference from people showing the opposite preference. This is not necessarily the numerical center of the scale.

**midzone.** The small number of items on the Step II facet scales makes it impossible to determine the psychological midpoint of the facets with much precision. Therefore, a midzone range on each facet scale is defined numerically as 0 to 1 on both sides of 0. This midzone is used as the basis for out-of-preference scores. A person whose facet scale score lies *on the other side of the midzone* from the pole of his or her overall preference is said to be out-of-preference on that facet.

**midzone pattern.** A pattern of responses to *all* the facet scales in a particular preference block (rather than on just one facet). A person with a midzone pattern has scores in the midzone on four or more facet scales in a block and also has no score of 4 or 5 on the remaining facet scale in that block. A midzone pattern suggests that the person has not reported a clear preference for either pole on most of the facet scales in a given preference block.

**multifaceted.** Having many facets or aspects. In psychological theory, this term describes a construct of many integrated characteristics that together constitute a complex psychological process or phenomenon. Multifaceted constructs can create problems for traditional measurement procedures because they include many different facets rather than just one single, clearly defined idea.

**norm.** The average score for a large number of people (who are often assumed to represent the population at large) on the various parts or scales of a psychological instrument. Average scores or norms may also be reported for particular categories of people, such as those classified by age, sex, or ethnicity.

**orientation.** *See* **attitude.**

**out-of-preference score.** A facet scale score that is on the opposite side of the midzone from the underlying Step I preference on that dichotomy.

**personality.** The totality of relatively enduring qualities and characteristics that compose the psychic identity we recognize as uniquely associated with a given person.

**polarity index.** An index calculated to assess the consistency with which a person exhibits clear preferences across all the Step II facet scales. See chapter 7, page 115, for the actual formula.

**pole.** Either end of a given MBTI preference scale, or either end of a Step II facet scale. The MBTI scales and most of the Step II facet scales are largely bipolar.

**preference.** One pole of each of the four fundamental dichotomies or bipolarities that are used to describe the sixteen MBTI types. The four preferences are Extraversion or Introversion, Sensing or Intuition, Thinking or Feeling, and Judging or Perceiving.

**preference clarity index (pci).** A ratio showing how consistently a person answered the question on the scale of interest compared to the maximum possible score on that scale. The pci is the basic result of scoring the MBTI instrument. It consists of a letter to denote the direction of the preference and a number to indicate the clarity or consistency with which the person has indicated that preference. The pci is derived by dividing the theta score by the maximum theta possible for that preference on that scale (using the national sample as the base population), multiplying by 30, and rounding up to the nearest integer. Thus, all preference clarity indexes are standardized from 1 to 30.

**profile.** A graphical display of a person's scores on an instrument. The MBTI® Step II™ Profile displays the scores on all twenty Step II facet scales.

**psychological midpoint.** The threshold on a bipolar continuum that separates the poles of the continuum. It marks the point to either side of which lie characteristics that are not just quantitatively but categorically and qualitatively different. People whose scores lie on one side of the psychological midpoint do not just have more or less of some characteristic than do people on the other side; in type theory, people on either side of the psychological midpoints of the bipolar dichotomies are believed to behave differently because they prefer to exercise quite different kinds of psychic processes.

**psychometric.** Having to do with the design and construction of tests to measure psychological variables.

**qualitative.** Refers to differences in characteristics or qualities of people rather than to differences in the amount of some particular characteristic. For example, one person may prefer to use Sensing to perceive the world, while another may prefer Intuition. The difference between a preference for Sensing and a preference for Intuition is not a matter of degree; it is a difference in the *kind* of perception preferred.

**quantitative.** Refers to differences in amounts or quantities of characteristics. For example, one person may be much more self-confident than another. The difference between such people is quantitative in the sense that one person has more self-confidence than the other.

**regression.** A statistical analysis used to determine the effects of one or more categorical or continuous independent variables on the variance of one or more continuous dependent variables. The analysis indicates which independent variables have a significant effect on the variance of the dependent variable and can also identify any statistical interactions among the independent variables that may affect the dependent variable.

**reliability.** In psychometrics, this refers to the consistency or repeatability of an instrument. For example, if we measure the same person at different times and get the same results, we can then say our instrument is reliable. There are different kinds of reliability. Coefficient alpha, for example, tells us about the consistency among the items contained in an instrument.

**scale.** A series of items to which a person indicates his or her response. The responses are then scored according to rules that normally produce one number representing the respondent's score on the scale. Because the items contained in the scale measure pretty much the same thing, the scale is often given a name that reflects the shared content of the items. Scales generally contain about twenty or more items and have reliabilities that range from .80 through .99.

**skewness.** The degree to which a distribution of scores is asymmetrical. A normal distribution, which is symmetrical around the mean, has a skewness of 0. The skewness index ranges from –1 to +1.

**Spearman-Brown formula.** A formula for estimating the reliability of a long form by using the known reliabilities of a form with fewer items.

**standard deviation.** A statistical measure describing the degree to which the scores from a sample either bunch up close to or are scattered widely around the mean for the sample.

**step function.** A hypothetical item characteristic curve in the shape of a step; no one to the left of the midpoint endorses the item in the keyed direction, and all people to the right of the midpoint endorse the item in the keyed direction.

**Step II instrument.** The name for the revision of the Expanded Analysis Report.

**subscale.** Similar to a scale, except that it generally contains fewer items (less than twenty) and has a lower reliability, often less than .80. The "scales" of the Step II istrument are, technically speaking, subscales. In this revision, the term *facet scale* has largely replaced the term *subscale*. However, for readability, *scale* is often used as a synonym for the Step II facet scales.

**TDI.** *See* ***Type Differentiation Indicator.***

**tertiary function.** In type theory, the function that is the bipolar opposite to the auxiliary function. Thus, if the auxiliary function is Sensing, the tertiary function will be Intuition, and vice versa. If the auxiliary function is Feeling, the tertiary function will be Thinking, and vice versa.

**theta.** In the terminology of item response theory, test scores on a psychological characteristic that are roughly equivalent to the "true scores" of classical test theory. Theta scores correspond directly to MBTI continuous scores that were calculated using the prediction ratio method developed by Isabel Myers. Theta scores can be dichotomized by identifying a cutoff point or midpoint that separates individuals into two groups, associated with the poles of a dichotomy.

**theory.** A statement about the relationships among abstract, interrelated concepts and constructs. These statements help us explain, understand, or predict some aspect of the world that can be studied using scientific methods. Theories are stated in the abstract so they can be applied to many different concrete examples or situations.

**trait.** In the field of personality, a single personality characteristic that is present in varying degrees in all people. When personality is described in terms of traits, we assume everyone has the same characteristics. In this view, the only differences between people are due to how much they have of each of the traits that describe human personality.

**type.** In the field of personality, a unique combination of mental attitudes and perceiving and judging preferences that is more than the sum of its parts. These combinations of attitudes and preferences are called types and can be used to classify and describe the personalities of individuals. The MBTI typology has sixteen types, each described in terms of qualitative rather than quantitative differences.

***Type Differentiation Indicator* (TDI).** A profile scored from Form J of the MBTI instrument. In addition to the twenty facet scales of the Step II instrument, it includes seven Comfort–Discomfort scales that do not belong to any of the four preference domains of the MBTI typology. Unlike the Step II tool, which is a level-B instrument, the TDI is a level-C instrument.

**type theory.** A theory, based on Jung's work and elaborated by Isabel Myers and Katherine Briggs, that describes personality in terms of four bipolar dichotomies. In all possible combinations, these bipolar dichotomies describe sixteen different personality types.

**typology.** A systematic way of classifying types based on characteristics that are shared in various ways by the types.

**validity.** The degree to which an instrument measures what it is intended to measure. In psychometrics, there are different kinds of validity, each requiring a different kind of evidence.

**variable.** A characteristic or property that manifests itself in different ways (qualitative variation) or in different amounts (quantitative variation). Sex is a variable that manifests itself in two variations: male and female. Dominance is a psychological trait that manifests itself in graduated amounts ranging from none to small to large.

# References


Anderson, J. C., & and D. W. Gerbing. (1984). "The effect of sampling error on convergence, improper solutions, and goodness-of-fit indexes for maximum likelihood confirmatory factor analysis." *Psychometrika, 49,* 155–73.

Barger, N. J., & L. K. Kirby. (1995). *The Challenge of Change in Organizations: Helping Employees Thrive in the New Frontier.* Boston: Davies-Black Publishing.

———. (1997). *MBTI® Type and Change.* Mountain View, CA: CPP, Inc.

Bentler, P. M., & D. G. Bonett. (1980). "Significance tests and goodness of fit in the analysis of covariance structures." *Psychological Bulletin, 88,* 588–606.

Bridges, W. (1992). *Managing Transitions.* Reading, MA: Addison-Wesley.

Carver, C. S. (1989). "How should multifaceted personality constructs be tested? Issues illustrated by self-monitoring, attributional style, and hardiness." *Journal of Personality and Social Psychology, 56,* 577–85.

Cohen, J. (1988). *Statistical Power Analysis for the Behavioral Sciences* (2nd ed.). Hillsdale, NJ: Lawrence Erlbaum Associates.

Cohen, J., & P. Cohen. (1983). *Applied Multiple Regression/ Correlation Analysis for the Behavioral Sciences* (2nd ed.). Hillsdale, NJ: Lawrence Erlbaum Associates.

Davis, S., & B. Handschin. (1998). *Reinventing Yourself: Life Planning After 50 Using the* Strong *and the MBTI®.* Mountain View, CA: CPP, Inc.

Drasgow, F., & C. L. Hulin. (1990). "Item response theory." In M. D. Dunnette and L. M. Hough (eds.), *Handbook of Industrial and Organizational Psychology*, Volume 1 (2nd ed.), pp. 577–636. Boston: Davies-Black Publishing.

Ehrman, M. E. (1994). "The *Type Differentiation Indicator* and adult foreign language development." *Journal of Psychological Type* 30, 10–29.

Fitzgerald, C., & L. K. Kirby. (1997). *Developing Leaders: Research and Applications in Psychological Type and Leadership.* Boston: Davies-Black Publishing.

Fleenor, J. W., & E. Van Velsor. (1995). *The Reliability of the MBTI Expanded Analysis Report Subscales.* Greensboro, NC: Center for Creative Leadership.

Gough, H. G., & P. Bradley. (1996). *CPI™ Manual* (3rd ed.). Mountain View, CA: CPP, Inc.

Gough, H. G., & A. B. Heilbrun. (1983). *The Adjective Check List Manual.* Mountain View, CA: CPP, Inc.

Grutter, J., & A. L. Hammer. (1995). Strong and MBTI® Career Report. Mountain View, CA: CPP, Inc.

Hammer, A. L. (1991). "Type and Coping Resources." Presented at the Bay Area Association of Psychological Type, Stanford University, Stanford, CA.

———. (1993). "Coping Resources and Scores on the Type Differentiation Indicator." Panel presentation on type and health. Tenth Conference of the Association for Psychological Type, Newport Beach, CA.

——— (ed.). (1996). *MBTI® Applications: A Decade of Research on the Myers-Briggs Type Indicator®.* Mountain View, CA: CPP, Inc.

Hammer, A. L., & G. E. Huszczo. (1996). "Teams." In A. L. Hammer (ed.), *MBTI® Applications: A Decade of Research on the Myers-Briggs Type Indicator.®* Mountain View, CA: CPP, Inc.

Hammer, A. L., & J. M. Kummerow. (1996). *Strong and MBTI® Career Development Guide* (rev. ed.). Mountain View, CA: CPP, Inc.

Hammer, A. L., & S. Marting. (1988). *Manual for the* Coping Resources Inventory. Mountain View, CA: CPP, Inc.

Hammer, A. L., & W. D. Mitchell. (1996). "The distribution of MBTI® types in the U.S. by gender and ethnic group." *Journal of Psychological Type, 37,* 2–15.

Harker, J. B., & J. H. Reynierse. (1999). "Independent observer ratings and the correlates of the EAR subscales with their behavioral descriptors." *Journal of Psychological Type, 49,* 5–19.

Harvey, R. J. (1996). "Reliability and validity." In A. L. Hammer (ed.), *MBTI® Applications: A Decade of Research on the Myers-Briggs Type Indicator,®* pp. 5–29. Mountain View, CA: CPP, Inc.

Harvey, R. J., & A. L. Hammer. (1999). "Item response theory." *The Counseling Psychologist, 27*(3), 353–83.

Harvey, R. J., & L. Thomas. (1996). "Using item response theory to score the Myers-Briggs Type Indicator®: Rationale and research findings." *Journal of Psychological Type, 37,* 16–60.

Hirsh, S. K. (1990). *Using the Myers-Briggs Type Indicator® in Organizations* (2nd ed.). Mountain View, CA: CPP, Inc.

———. (1998). *Introduction to Type® and Teams.* Mountain View, CA: CPP, Inc.

Hirsh, S. K., & J. A. G. Kise. (1996). *Work It Out: Clues for Solving People Problems at Work.* Boston: Davies-Black Publishing.

Hirsh, S. K., & J. M. Kummerow. (1998). *Introduction to Type® in Organizations* (3rd ed.). Mountain View, CA: CPP, Inc.

Holland, C. L., & S. VanBenshoten. (1991). "Coping styles and the TDI." Presented at the Conference on Advanced Applications for MBTI Technology, Princeton, NJ.

Johnson, D. A. (1992a). "Test-retest reliabilities of the Myers-Briggs Type Indicator® and the Type Differentiation Indicator over a 30-month period." *Journal of Psychological Type, 24,* 54–58.

———. (1992b). "Predicting promotion to management in the wholesale grocery industry using the *Type Differentiation Indicator.*" *Journal of Psychological Type, 23,* 51–59.

Johnson, D. A., & J. P. Golden. (1994). "How psychological type influences effective leadership: The Survey of Management Practices and the *Type Differentiation Indicator* (TDI)." In Proceedings of the International Research Conference on the *Myers-Briggs Type Indicator®* and Leadership. National Institute for Leadership, University of Maryland, College Park, MD.

Jöreskog, K., & D. Sörbom. (1993). *LISREL 8: Structural Equation Modelling with the Simplis Command Language.* Hillsdale, NJ: Lawrence Erlbaum Associates.

Jung, C. G. (1971). *Psychological Types.* Trans. by H. G. Baynes, rev. by R. F. C. Hull. Volume 6 of *The Collected Works of C. G. Jung.* Princeton, NJ: Princeton University Press. (Original work published in 1921.)

Kummerow, J. M., N. J. Barger, & L. K. Kirby. (1997). *WORKTypes.* New York: Warner Books.

Kummerow, J. M., & R. D. Olson. (1997). "Using the MBTI® Step II™ with leaders and managers." In C. Fitzgerald and L. K. Kirby (eds.), *Developing Leaders: Research and Applications in Psychological Type and Leadership Development.* Boston: Davies-Black Publishing.

Kummerow, J. M., & N. L. Quenk. (1992a). *Interpretive Guide for the MBTI® Expanded Analysis Report.* Mountain View, CA: CPP, Inc.

———. (1992b). *Workbook for the MBTI® Expanded Analysis Report.* Mountain View, CA: CPP, Inc.

Marioles, N., D. P. Strickert, & A. L. Hammer. (1996). "Attraction, satisfaction, and psychological types of couples." *Journal of Psychological Type, 36,* 16–27.

McCaulley, M. H. (1997, Spring). "Isabel Myers: A double legacy." *Bulletin of Psychological Type, 20*(2), 24–25.

Mitchell, W. D. (1991). "A test of type theory using the TDI." *Journal of Psychological Type, 22,* 15–26.

———. (1993a). "Are types real?" In "Conscious Choices, Unconscious Forces." Proceedings of the 10th Biennial International Conference of the Association for Psychological Type, Newport Beach, CA.

———. (1993b). "Empirical verification of the Jungian typology." In J. Newman (chair), Theory and Research Symposium. Symposium conducted at the 10th Biennial Conference of the Association for Psychological Type, Newport Beach, CA.

Mitchell, W. D., N. L. Quenk, & J. M. Kummerow. (1997). *MBTI® Step II™: A Description of the Subscales.* Mountain View, CA: CPP, Inc.

Myers, I. B. (1995). *Gifts Differing.* Mountain View, CA: CPP, Inc.

Myers, I. B., & K. C. Briggs (1996). MBTI® Step II™ Expanded Profile. Mountain View, CA: CPP, Inc.

Myers, I. B., with L. K. Kirby & K. D. Myers. (1998). *Introduction to Type®* (6th ed.). Mountain View, CA: CPP, Inc.

Myers, I. B., & M. H. McCaulley. (1985). *MBTI® Manual: A Guide to the Development and Use of the Myers-Briggs Type Indicator.®* Mountain View, CA: CPP, Inc.

Myers, I. B., M. H. McCaulley, N. L. Quenk, & A. L. Hammer. (1998). *MBTI® Manual: A Guide to the Development and Use of the Myers-Briggs Type Indicator®.* Mountain View, CA: CPP, Inc.

Myers, K. D., & L. K. Kirby. (1994). *Introduction to Type® Dynamics and Development.* Mountain View, CA: CPP, Inc.

Pearman, R. R., & S. C. Albritton. (1997). *I'm Not Crazy, I'm Just Not You: The Real Meaning of the Sixteen Personality Types.* Boston: Davies-Black Publishing.

Poling, T. H., & J. Johnson. (1991). "Communalities among the TDI scales, locus of control, and Eysenck's dimensions of personality." Presented at the Conference on Advanced Applications for MBTI Technology, Princeton, NJ.

———. (1995). "The *Type Differentiation Indicator* and Eysenck's Dimensions of Personality." In J. Newman (ed.), *Measures of the Five Factor Model and Psychological Type: A Major Convergence of Research and Theory* (pp. 101–16). Gainesville, FL: Center for Applications of Psychological Type.

Quenk, N. L. (1993). *Beside Ourselves: Our Hidden Personality in Everyday Life.* Boston: Davies-Black Publishing.

———. (2000a). *Essentials of Myers-Briggs Type Indicator® Assessment.* New York: John Wiley & Sons.

———. (2000b). *In the Grip: Understanding Type, Stress, and the Inferior Function* (2nd ed.). Mountain View, CA: CPP, Inc.

Quenk, N. L., & J. M. Kummerow. (1996). MBTI® Step II™ Expanded Interpretive Report: Form K. Mountain View, CA: CPP, Inc.

———. (2001). MBTI® Step II™ Interpretive Report: Form Q. Mountain View, CA: CPP, Inc.

———. (2011). *MBTI® Step II™ User's Guide: Practitioner's Tool for Making the Most of Step II™ Interpretations.* Mountain View, CA: CPP, Inc.

Reynierse, J. H., & J. B. Harker. (1999). "Extreme scores and the validity of the EAR subscales." *Journal of Psychological Type, 49,* 20–26.

Saunders, D. R. (1960, April). "The contribution of communality estimation to the achievement of factorial invariance with special reference to the MMPI." *ETS Research Bulletin* 60-5. Princeton, NJ: Educational Testing Service.

———. (1987). *The Type Differentiation Indicator Manual.* Mountain View, CA: CPP, Inc.

———. (1989). *Manual: MBTI® Expanded Analysis Report.* Mountain View, CA: CPP, Inc.

Tanaka, J. S., & G. J. Huba. (1985). "A fit index for covariance structure models under arbitrary GLS estimation." *British Journal of Mathematical and Statistical Psychology, 42,* 233–39.

Toothaker, L. E. (1991). *Multiple Comparisons for Researchers.* Newbury Park, CA: Sage Publications.

Tucker, L. R., & C. Lewis. (1973). "A reliability coefficient for maximum likelihood factor analysis." *Psychometrika, 38,* 1–10.

Van Sant, S., & D. Payne. (1995). *Psychological Type in Schools: Applications for Educators.* Gainesville, FL: Center for Applications of Psychological Type.

Van Velsor, E., & J. W. Fleenor. (1997). "The MBTI® and leadership skills: Relationships between the MBTI® and four 360-degree management feedback instruments" (pp. 139–62). In C. Fitzgerald and L. K. Kirby (eds.), *Developing Leaders: Research and Applications in Psychological Type and Leadership Development.* Boston: Davies-Black Publishing.

Wanberg, C. R. (1992). "Men and women without jobs: A study of factors predictive of psychological and physical health." Unpublished doctoral dissertation, Iowa State University.

Zeidner, M., & A. L. Hammer. (1990). "Life events and coping resources as predictors of stress symptoms in adolescents." *Personality and Individual Differences, 11*(7), 693–703.

———. (1992). "Coping with missile attack: Resources, strategies and outcomes." *Journal of Personality, 60*(4), 709–746.

Zimowski, M., E. Muraki, R. J. Mislevy, & R. D. Bock. (1997). *BiLog-MG Item Maintenance Program: Logistic Item Response Model (V1.1C).* Chicago, IL: Scientific Software.

# Index